The Legal Foundations of the Single European Market

THE
LEGAL FOUNDATIONS
OF THE
SINGLE EUROPEAN MARKET

Nicholas Green

LL B, LL M, Ph.D
Barrister at Law
Inner Temple

Trevor C. Hartley

BA, LL B (Cape Town); LL M (London)
Professor of Law
London School of Economics

and

John A. Usher

LL B (Newcastle)
Professor of European Law and
Director of the Centre for European Legal Studies
University of Exeter

Editor
Trevor C. Hartley

OXFORD UNIVERSITY PRESS

Oxford University Press, Walton Street, Oxford OX2 6DP

Oxford New York
Athens Auckland Bangkok Bombay
Calcutta Cape Town Dar es Salaam Delhi
Florence Hong Kong Istanbul Karachi
Kuala Lumpur Madras Madrid Melbourne
Mexico City Nairobi Paris Singapore
Taipei Tokyo Toronto
and associated companies in
Berlin Ibadan

Oxford is a trade mark of Oxford University Press

Published in the United States by
Oxford University Press Inc., New York

British Library Cataloguing in Publication Data
Data available

Library of Congress Cataloging in Publication Data
Green, Nicholas, Ph.D.
The legal foundations of the single European market/Nicholas Green,
Trevor C. Hartley, and John A. Usher.
Includes bibliographical references and index.
1. Europe—Economic integration. 2. Europe, 1992. 3. Trade
regulation—European Economic Community countries. 4. Free choice
of employment—European Economic Community countries. 5. Freedom of
movement—European Economic Community countries. 6. Duty-free importation—Law
and legislation—European Economic Community countries. 7. Restraint of
trade—European Economic Community countries. I. Hartley, Trevor C.
II. Usher, John Anthony. III. Title.
KJE6417.G74 1991 343.4'08—dc20 [344.038] 91–79
ISBN 0–19–825631–0
ISBN 0–19–825628–0

5 7 9 10 8 6 4

Printed in Great Britain
on acid-free paper by
Biddles Ltd, Guildford and King's Lynn

Editor's Preface

In 1992 the largest single market in the world comes into existence. It will be in Europe. Like the Community itself, the single European market will be founded on law, and this book is about those aspects of Community law that provide the foundations of the single market. It does not, therefore, deal with the general (constitutional and administrative) part of Community law[1]—it assumes the reader is familiar with this—but concentrates on the topics most directly relevant to the functioning of the single market.

Anyone planning a book of this kind is faced with a choice. Either he can try to cover everything (which means a long book or a superficial level of treatment) or he can be selective. I chose to be selective. Since this is a students' textbook, I decided to cover only three topics, thus allowing sufficient space for each to be treated in reasonable depth without making the book too long. The topics I chose were free movement of goods, free movement of persons and competition law. The first two are the most obvious components of the single market; the third, though less obvious at first sight, is in fact equally vital: free competition in a free market is the principle on which the common market is based, and the founders of the Community considered it essential that the Community should have its own competition law. For the legal practitioner it is probably the most important area of Community law.

I decided to write the part on free movement of persons myself, but I needed two co-authors for the other parts. Nicholas Green, a former academic now in practice as a barrister, had just written a well-received practitioners' book on competition law:[2] he seemed the obvious choice for that part. I was grateful that he was able to accept. John Usher is one of the leading Community lawyers in academic life in England. His expertise extends to almost every area of Community law, including the free movement of goods. I was very pleased that he agreed to cover that topic.

I suggested the basic outline of each part and the general approach, which is to emphasize principles rather than details and to pay particular attention to policy. I also have the task of ensuring the overall

---

[1] This is dealt with in Hartley, *The Foundations of European Community Law* (2nd edn. 1988).

[2] Green, *Commercial Agreements and Competition Law: Practice and Procedure in the UK and EEC* (1986).

unity of the book. Beyond this, each author is responsible for his own part, though each has been read, and commented on, by me.

Our aim has been to produce a textbook suitable for law courses at universities and polytechnics in Britain (though others trying to get to grips with the subject may also find it useful). We very much welcome comments from users to tell us whether we have succeeded and how we can improve it.

We have tried to state the law as at 1 January 1991.

T.C.H.
1 January 1991

Contents

PART III

Competition Law

Citations and Tables

European Court cases are cited only to the European Court Reports (unless they have not yet been published in that series). Alternative citations may be found in the Table of Cases, which lists European Court cases both numerically and alphabetically.

Citations are not normally given in footnotes for Community legislation, since it is believed that most readers will use one of the well-known compilations of Community legislation such as Rudden and Wyatt, *Basic Community Laws* (2nd edn., 1988). Citations are, however, given in the Table of Community Legislation.

Acknowledgement

We would like to acknowledge the help we have received from our research assistant, Marie-Pierre Fiorio-Bazen. She saved us from many errors. Her assistance was made possible through a grant from the London School of Economics.

Bibliography

GENERAL WORKS

Green, *Commercial Agreements and Competition Law: Practice and Procedure in the UK and EEC* (1986).
Hartley, *The Foundations of European Community Law* (2nd edn, 1988).
——*EEC Immigration Law* (1978).
Kapteyn and VerLoren van Themaat, *Introduction to the Law of the European Communities* (2nd edn by Gormley, 1989).
Wyatt and Dashwood, *The Substantive Law of the EEC* (2nd edn, 1987).

CHAPTER 1

Forrester, 'EEC Customs Law: Rules of Origin and Preferential Duty Treatment' (1980) 5 E.L.Rev. 167 and 257.
Oliver and Yatanagas, 'The Harmonized System of Customs Classification' (1987) 7 YEL 113.
Usher, 'Uniform External Protection—EEC Customs Legislation before the European Court of Justice' (1982) 19 C.M.L.Rev. 389.
Voorst and Van Dam, 'Europe 1992: Free Movement of Goods in the Wider Context of a Changing Europe' (1988) 25 C.M.L.Rev. 693.

CHAPTER 2

Bourgeois, 'The Tokyo Round Agreements on Technical Barriers and on Government Procurement in International and EEC Perspectives' (1982) 19 C.M.L.Rev. 5.
Cremona, 'The Completion of the Internal Market and the Incomplete Commercial Policy of the European Community' (1990) 15 E.L.Rev. 283.
Denton, 'The New Commercial Policy Instrument' (1988) 8 E.L.Rev. 3.
——'The Nonmarket Economy Rules of the European Community's Anti-Dumping and Countervailing Duties Legislation' (1987) 36 ICLQ 198.
Usher, 'The Single Market and Goods Imported from Third Countries' (1986) 6 YEL 159.

CHAPTER 3

Wooldridge and Plender, 'Charges Having an Effect Equivalent to Customs Duties' (1978) 3 E.L.Rev. 101.

CHAPTER 4

Easson, *Tax Law and Policy in the EEC* (1980).

Chapter 5

Gormley, *Prohibiting Restrictions on Trade within the EEC* (1985).
Oliver, *The Free Movement of Goods in the EEC* (2nd edn, 1988).
Meij and Winter, 'Measures Having an Effect Equivalent to Quantitative Restrictions' (1976) 13 C.M.L.Rev. 79.
Quinn and McGowan, 'Could Art. 30 Impose Obligations on Individuals?' (1987) 12 E.L.Rev. 163.

CHAPTER 6

Dashwood, 'The *Cassis de Dijon* Line of Authority' in Bares *et al.* (eds), *In Memorian J. D. B. Mitchell* (1983).
Gormley, *Prohibiting Restrictions on Trade within the EEC* (1985).
Oliver, *The Free Movement of Goods in the EEC* (2nd edn, 1988).
Weatherill, 'Consumer Safety Legislation in the United Kingdom and Art. 30 EEC' (1988) 13 E.L.Rev. 87.

CHAPTER 7

Burrows 'Harmonization of Technical Standards' (1990) 53 MLR 597.
Evans, 'Economic Policy and Free Movement of Goods in EEC Law' (1983) 32 ICLQ 577.
Flynn, 'How Will Art. 100A(4) Work?' (1987) 24 C.M.L.Rev. 689.
Forwood and Clough, 'The Single European Act and Free Movement' (1986) 11 E.L.Rev. 383.
Gormley, *Prohibiting Restrictions on Trade within the EEC* (1985).
McGee and Weatherill, 'The Evolution of the Single Market—Harmonization or Liberalization' (1990) 53 MLR 578.
Oliver, *The Free Movement of Goods in the EEC* (2nd edn, 1988).

CHAPTER 8

Durand, 'European Citizenship' (1979) 4 E.L.Rev. 3.
Duyssens, 'Migrant Workers from Third Countries in the European Community' (1977) 14 C.M.L.Rev. 501.
Evans, 'Nationality Law and the Free Movement of Persons in the EEC: with Special Reference to the British Nationality Act 1981' (1982) 2 YEL 173.
——'European Citizenship' (1982) 45 MLR 497.
Hartley, 'The International Scope of the Community Provisions Concerning Free

Movement of Workers', in Jacobs (ed.), *European Law and the Individual* (1976), p. 19.
——'The Internal Personal Scope of the EEC Immigration Provisions' (1978) 3 E.L.Rev 191.
——*EEC Immigration Law* (1978), Chaps 1–3.
Oliver, 'Non-Community Nationals and the Treaty of Rome' (1985) 5 YEL 57.
Plender, 'Competence, European Community Law and Nationals of Non-Member States' (1990) 39 1 CLQ 599.
Simmonds, 'The British Nationality Act 1981 and the Definition of the Term "National" for Community Purposes' (1984) 21 C.M.L.Rev. 675.

CHAPTER 9

Hartley, *EEC Immigration Law* (1978), Chap. 4.

CHAPTER 10

Barav and Thomson, 'Deportation of EEC Nationals from the United Kingdom in the Light of the *Bouchereau* Case' (1977) 2 LIEI 1.
Barav, 'Court Recommendation to Deport and the Free Movement of Workers in EEC Law' (1981) 6 E.L.Rev. 139.
Evans, '*Ordre Public*, Public Policy and United Kingdom Immigration Law' (1978) 3 E.L.Rev. 370.
——'Entry Formalities in the European Community' (1981) 6 E.L.Rev. 3.
Hartley, *EEC Immigration Law* (1978), Chap. 5.
O'Keefe, 'Practical Difficulties in the Application of Article 48 of the EEC Treaty' (1982) 19 C.M.L.Rev. 35.

CHAPTER 11

Brita Sundberg-Weitman, *Discrimination on Grounds of Nationality* (1977).
Evans, 'Development of European Community Law Regarding the Trade Union and Related Rights of Migrant Workers' (1979) 28 ICLQ 354.
Handoll, 'Article 48(4) EEC and Non-National Access to Public Employment' (1988) 13 E.L.Rev. 223.
O'Keefe, 'Equal Rights for Migrants: The Concept of Social Advantages in Article 7(2), Regulation 1612/68' (1985) 5 YEL 93.

CHAPTER 12

Edward, 'Freedom of Movement for the Regulated Professions', in White and Smythe (eds), *Current Issues in European and International Law* (1990).
Eidenmüller, 'Deregulating the Market for Legal Services in the European Community' (1990) 53 MLR 604.

Wägenbaur, 'The Mutual Recognition of Qualifications in the EEC', in Jacobs (ed.), *European Law and the Individual* (1976).

CHAPTER 13

Lonbay, 'Education and Law: The Community Context' (1989) 14 E.L.Rev. 363.

CHAPTER 15

Scherer, *Industrial Market Structure and Economic Performance* (2nd edn., 1979).
Williamson, *Antitrust Economics* (1987).

CHAPTER 16

Whish, *Competition Law* (1989).
Korah, *An Introductory Guide to EEC Competition Law and Practice* (1990).

TABLE OF CASES
(ALPHABETICAL)

TABLE OF CASES
(NUMERICAL)

TABLE OF COMMISSION DECISIONS

TABLE OF COMMUNITY TREATIES

TABLE OF COMMUNITY REGULATIONS

Table of community regulations

TABLE OF COMMUNITY DIRECTIVES

TABLE OF UNITED KINGDOM STATUTES

OTHER EEC STATUTORY MATERIAL

Part I

Free Movement of Goods

1

The External Aspects of the Single Market: The Customs Union

Introduction

The Single European Act introduced into the EEC Treaty a new Article 8A providing for the establishment of the *internal* market by the end of 1992. The internal market is there defined as an area without internal frontiers in which, *inter alia*, the free movement of goods is ensured in accordance with the provisions of the Treaty. The EEC Treaty provisions on the free movement of goods form the first title in the part entitled 'Foundations of the Community', and it is made clear at the outset, in Article 9, that the internal free movement of goods is linked to the adoption of a common customs tariff as part of a customs union. In turn, the common customs tariff is linked to the development of a common commercial policy towards third countries in Article 3, which sets out the objectives of the Treaty.

Very simply, the concept of a customs union as exemplified in the EEC Treaty means that third country goods should receive the same customs and commercial policy treatment wherever they enter the Community (and the directly applicable instrument of the Regulation provides a mechanism capable of achieving this aim), and that within the customs union both goods produced within the Community and goods legitimately imported from third countries should be able to move from Member State to Member State without being subject to customs duties and charges equivalent thereto,[1] without being subject to quantitative restrictions or measures equivalent thereto,[2] and without being subject to discriminatory or protective internal taxation,[3] The extent to which this aim has been achieved will be considered in the following chapters.

This aim may be contrasted with that of a free-trade area, as under Article 4 of the Convention establishing the European Free Trade Association (EFTA). This does not establish a common customs tariff,

[1] Arts. 9–16. [2] Arts. 30–6. [3] Art. 95.

and only treats goods as eligible for 'area tariff treatment' (that is, free trade) if they are of 'Area origin' as there defined. However, following the accession of the United Kingdom, Ireland, and Denmark to the European Community in 1973, the EEC as a single unit entered into free-trade agreements with the remaining EFTA countries. This has developed to the point where the customs union of the EEC is the centre of a wider free-trade arrangement with the EFTA countries, using the same model transit documents,[4] and in 1990 negotiations began on the creation of a European Economic Zone involving the EEC, the EFTA states, and Liechtenstein.

Under Article 23(3) of the EEC Treaty, the common customs tariff was due to be established by the end of the original transitional period (1 January 1970), but by a Council Decision of 26 July 1966,[5] the original Member States agreed to apply a common tariff as from 1 July 1968, eighteen months before the deadline. The system established in 1968 comprised three main elements, each of which was enacted in directly applicable Regulations: goods were classified and tariffs set according to a uniform nomenclature,[6] they were valued according to uniform Community rules,[7] and their origin was determined according to Community rules.[8] The Regulation on origin is the only member of the trio to remain in force as such, but the current legislation continues to follow the same pattern.

It may be noted that the existence of the Common Customs Tariff has had some influence upon the institutional structure of the Community, insofar as the duties raised under the Common Customs Tariff are treated as being part of the Community's own resources for the purposes of the Community budget. Under the original 1970 Decision on the system of own resources,[9] a gradually increasing proportion of customs duties were appropriated to the Community over the period from 1971 to 1975, until from 1 January 1975 all customs duties were paid to the Community by the Member States subject to a refund of 10 per cent to cover the expenses of collecting the customs duties on the part of the national customs administrations. Under a system in which the same customs duties are payable wherever goods are imported into the Community, and the goods which have paid those duties are able to enter into free circulation anywhere else in the Community, it would obviously be unacceptable that those Member States which had the good fortune to have the best, or most convenient, port facilities and

---

[4] See Council Reg. 2011/89 on the simplification of formalities in trade between the EEC and EFTA countries (OJ 1989, L 200/1).

[5] JO 1966, p. 2,971.

[6] Council Reg. 950/68 (JO 1968, L 172/1).

[7] Council Reg. 803/68 (JO 1968, L 148/6).

[8] Council Reg. 802/68 (JO 1968, L 148/1).

[9] Council Dec. 70/243 (JO 1970, L 94/19).

thus attracted the major part of Community imports should themselves take the benefit of the Community system of customs duties.

In one sense, therefore, it becomes possible to talk of the Community as a single unit in world trade from the introduction of the common customs tariff. In so far as judgments of the European Court may be relevant in the matter, a detailed analysis of the relationship of the EEC to the General Agreement on Tariffs and Trade (GATT) was made in the judgment in *Italian Finance Administration* v. *SPI and SAMI*.[10] In that judgment it is stated that, while the Community took part in the so-called Dillon Round in 1960 to 1961, the General Agreement on Tariffs and Trade could only be regarded as having become an act of the Community institutions (rather than of the Member States) for the purposes of a reference for a preliminary ruling under Article 177 of the EEC Treaty as to its interpretation, from 1968. From that year, following the introduction of the Common Customs Tariff, the Community is taken by the Court to have succeeded to the rights and obligations of its Member States under GATT and under the International Customs Conventions.

On the other hand, Article 113 of the EEC Treaty required the common commercial policy to be achieved by 1970, and it was not until 1975 that the Court finally decided that the Community's competence in matters of commercial policy was in fact exclusive,[11] a judgment not easy to reconcile at first sight with the 1969 Council Decision[12] on the renewal and extension of agreements entered into by Member States as such, which purported, albeit in limited circumstances, to empower Member States to continue to negotiate their own agreements until 1972.

However, the adoption of the Single European Act in 1986 has emphasized that the achievement of the Single Internal Market of the Community may not be as clear cut as was once thought. Indeed, the early introduction of the common customs tariff was not in reality automatically reflected in the rules governing the free movement of goods inside the Community. Whilst the prohibition on discriminatory internal taxation of goods from other Member States became directly effective in 1962,[13] and customs duties as such, and quotas as such, in trade between Member States had been abolished by the time of the introduction of the common external tariff in 1968, the European Court has consistently held that the prohibition on charges equivalent to customs duties and the prohibition on measures equivalent to quantitative restrictions, only became directly effective, in other words could only be invoked by individual traders, from 1 January 1970.[14] Furthermore,

[10] Cases 267–269/81, [1983] ECR 801, p. 824.
[11] *Opinion* 1/75 [1975] ECR 1355.
[12] Dec. 69/494 (JO 1969, L 326/39).
[13] See *Lutticke* v. *Saarlouis*, Case 57/65, [1966] ECR 205.
[14] *EGAV* v. *ENCC*, Case 94/74, [1975] ECR 699 (charges equivalent to customs duties): *Donckerwolcke*, Case 41/76, [1976] ECR 1921 (measures equivalent to quantitative restrictions).

although the European Court has developed the general principle that goods lawfully sold in one Member State should in principle also be able to be marketed in another Member State, it has recognized that Member States are entitled, where there are no Community rules in the matter, to maintain in force legislation which may have the effect of restricting trade with other Member States where that legislation is intended to serve certain so-called mandatory requirements, including the protection of health and the protection of consumers.[15] It is in this context that the aims of the internal-market provisions of the Single European Act may be assessed. It may, therefore, be suggested that the declared intention of the Single European Act of achieving the completion of the internal market by the end of 1992 should not be seen as an attempt to add a new transitional period, but rather as a realization that decision-making processes had to be changed if common Community rules were to be enacted to replace those national rules which were still regarded as legitimate, and which may still restrict trade between Member States. Hence Article 100A of the EEC Treaty, introduced by the Single European Act, enables the Council to act by qualified majority in co-operation with the European Parliament where the approximation or harmonization of national legislation is required for the purpose of achieving the internal market by the end of 1992.

Common Customs Tariff

Nomenclature and Tariff

As has been mentioned above, the single external tariff was introduced eighteen months early, on 1 July 1968, and is built upon common rules on nomenclature, valuation, and origin. No doubt for practical reasons, the geographical area to which it applies is defined in detail by secondary legislation.[16] The nomenclature was in fact originally based on the 1950 Customs Co-operation Council Nomenclature Convention, to which all the Member States were parties. In the eyes of the European Court,[17] the Community replaced the Member States in their commitments arising under this Convention and was bound by those commitments, in particular the obligation to make no changes in the Chapter or Section notes in that Nomenclature in such a manner as to modify the scope of the chapters, sections, and headings laid down in

[15] *Rewe* v. *Bundesmonopolverwaltung für Branntwein*, Case 120/78, [1979] ECR 649.
[16] Originally Council Reg. 1496/68 (JO 1968, L 238/1), replaced by Reg. 2151/84 (OJ 1984, L 197/1) as amended. It is this secondary legislation, rather than any Treaty provision, which excludes Gibraltar from the scope of the Common Customs Tariff.
[17] *Nederlandse Spoorwegen* v. *Inspecteur der Invoerrechten*, Case 38/75, [1975] ECR 1439.

the Nomenclature. Although Regulation 950/68[18] was made under the EEC Treaty, it also listed the products falling under the EURATOM Treaty,[19] and, for convenience, products falling within the ECSC Treaty.[20]

The Community itself was a party to the negotiations leading to the International Convention on a Harmonized Commodity Description and Coding System, which has formed the basis of the nomenclature from 1 January 1988, following the adoption of a decision by the Council concluding the Convention on behalf of the Community in April 1987 and the enactment of Council Regulation 2658/87 on a common nomenclature and tariff.[21] The structure of the new nomenclature is in fact broadly similar to the old one, the analysis of products being largely based on a progression from raw materials to processed products, although there are changes in detail, and the codes for each classification are now entirely numerical, to aid computerized transactions.[22]

Valuation

The legislation on the valuation of goods for customs purposes shows a similar progression from the Community taking over an agreement previously binding on its Member States to the Community actively negotiating a new international agreement. In this case, the original Regulation in 1968[23] was based on the 1950 Customs Co-operation Council Valuation Convention, to which all the Member States were parties, and this was replaced in 1980 by Regulation 1224/80[24] based on the agreements reached on the implementation of Article 7 of the General Agreement on Tariffs and Trade in the context of the Tokyo Round negotiations in 1979, negotiations to which the EEC as such was party. It may be observed that the EEC Treaty contains no express

---

[18] JO 1968, L 172/1.
[19] Set by an agreement between the Member States of 22 Dec. 1958 (JO 1959, p. 408).
[20] ECSC duties are technically imposed by the Member States pursuant to Commission Recommendation 1/64 (JO 1964, p. 99), but successive Decisions of the Representatives of the Governments of the Member States of the ECSC meeting within the Council have provided that the nomenclature and conventional duties (i.e. the duties applying to imports from parties to GATT and from States benefiting from most-favoured nation treatment)—see e.g. Dec. 79/35/ECSC (OJ 1979, L 10/13). This pattern has been continued after the introduction of the new nomenclature and tariff by Dec. 87/597/ECSC (OJ 1987, L 363/67). The view that the ECSC Treaty creates something less than a full customs union for the products falling within its scope was expressed by the European Court in *Mabanaft* v. *HZA Emmerich*, Case 36/83, [1984] ECR 2497; see Usher, 'The Single Market and Goods Imported from Third Countries' (1986), YEL 159.
[21] OJ 1987, L 256/1. Consolidated amended texts are issued by the Commission.
[22] For a more detailed discussion of classification problems, see Usher, 'Uniform External Protection—EEC customs legislation before the European Court of Justice' (1982), 19 C.M.L.Rev. 389.
[23] Council Reg. 803/68 (JO 1968, L 148/6).
[24] OJ 1980, L 134/1.

authority empowering the institutions to issue rules governing the valuation of goods for customs purposes. Hence, the 1968 Regulation was enacted under Article 235 of the Treaty, which enables the Council to act where the Treaty has not provided the necessary powers. In one of the very first cases to be referred to the European Court on the question of the valuation legislation,[25] the argument was put that, since all the Member States were already parties to the 1950 Valuation Convention, there was no necessity for action by the Community under Article 235. However, the Court found that, as was stated in the recitals to the Regulation, the definition of value and the interpretative notes set out in the 1950 Convention had been embodied into the legislation of the Member States in differing ways, and also certain optional provisions of the interpretative notes were being applied differently in different Member States. The Court, therefore, held that the fact that the Member States had all signed the Customs Co-operation Council's Valuation Convention would not lead to the necessary extent to the uniform determination of the valuation for customs purposes of imported goods required for the functioning of a customs union. It therefore held the use of legislation under Article 235 to be justified.[26]

The fundamental distinction between the system of valuation derived from the 1950 Convention and that derived from the 1979 Tokyo Round agreement is that, whilst the former was based on the concept of a hypothetical normal price, in other words the price which the goods would fetch in a sale on the open market between a buyer and seller independent of each other, the Tokyo Round agreement is based on the concept of transaction value, which is defined as the price actually paid or payable for the goods when sold for export to the country of importation. Important as this change may be, the concept of the normal price was not always taken to its logical conclusion: in particular, in *Chatain*, [27] the Court refused to accept that the declaration of a price above the normal price on importation breached the Community rules. It was there alleged by the French authorities that the French subsidiary of Sandoz had declared goods supplied by its Swiss parent as having a value nearly twice the normal price when imported into France.[28] Although Advocate General Capotorti suggested that the concept of a normal price meant that an overvaluation should be reduced just as

[25] *HZA Bremerhaven* v. *Massey Ferguson*, Case 8/73, [1973] ECR 897.

[26] While this is still authority for the proposition that the Community needed its own rules on customs valuation, it may be wondered whether, following *Commission* v. *Council*, Case 165/87, [1988] ECR 5545, the requisite powers were not already contained in Art. 28 on the common customs tariff and Art. 113 on the common commercial policy.

[27] Case 65/79, [1980] ECR 1345.

[28] It was further alleged that this was done to ensure that profits were made in Switzerland rather than France (a practice commonly referred to as transfer pricing), so as to avoid the payment of French tax.

much as an undervaluation should be increased, the Court held that the essential aim of the legislation was to prevent goods being undervalued and that the adjustments permitted to the price paid or payable were all intended to avoid undervaluation. Similarly under the current system, it appears that, in circumstances where the invoice price cannot wholly be relied upon, Article 8 of Regulation 1224/80[29] only allows for additions to the price actually paid or payable.

The essential aspect of the valuation of goods for customs purposes under Community law is that goods are valued at their point of entry into the Community. This means that costs incurred within Community Territory, such as warehousing costs[30] or transport costs[31] (even if the bulk of the transport costs are within the Community), are not included in the value provided they can be distinguished from the price paid or payable. On the other hand, factors such as the cost of obtaining an import licence or an unused share of a quota are also, perhaps more surprisingly, not taken into account in the assessment of value on importation,[32] though the cost of a certificate of authenticity showing that Community quality criteria are met, will be,[32A] as will commissions payable on purchase and payments for waiting time in part.[32B]

DETERMINATION OF ORIGIN

The third basic element of the Community customs legislation concerns the determination of the origin of goods for customs purposes.[33] Here, the Community legislation is autonomous, because there was no international agreement on the matter in 1968 when the Community rules were enacted, although provisions on the matter are contained in the 1973 Kyoto Convention on the simplification and harmonization of customs procedures.[34] Again, Article 235 was invoked as authority for the enactment of this legislation, but in conjunction with the Treaty provisions regulating the common commercial policy. Recent amendments have been based on the latter provisions alone.[35]

The central provision of this Regulation is its Article 5, which states that

a product in the production of which two or more countries were concerned

---

[29] OJ 1980, L 134/1.
[30] *Enka* v. *Inspecteur der Invoerrechten*, Case 38/77, [1977] ECR 2203.
[31] See e.g. *HZA Frankfurt am Main-Ost* v. *Olivetti*, Case C–17/89 (6 June 1990).
[32] *Ospig* v. *HZA Bremen-Ost*, Case 7/83, [1984] ECR 609.
[32A] Case C–219/88 *Malt* v. *HZA Düsseldorf* (28 March 1990)
[32B] Case C–11/89 *Unifert* v. *HZA Münster* (6 June 1990)
[33] Council Reg. 802/68 (JO 1968, L 148/1).
[34] The relevant Annexes (D1 to D3) were accepted by the Community by Council Dec. 77/415 (OJ 1977, L 166/1).
[35] See e.g. Council Reg. 1769/89 on certificates of origin (OJ 1989, L 174/11).

shall be regarded as originating in the country in which the last substantial process or operation that is economically justified was performed, having been carried out in an undertaking equipped for the purpose, and resulting in the manufacture of a new product or representing an important stage of manufacture.

It may be observed that this definition does not make any reference to percentages of added value, leaving scope for interpretation of what may be regarded as a 'substantial process'. It is clear that cleaning, grinding, and packing a product does not confer origin.[36] On the other hand, it would appear from the *Yoshida* cases[37] that assembly operations which are economically justified, carried out in specially equipped premises and resulting in a new product or an important stage of manufacture, may well confer origin. Those cases involved the manufacture of slide fasteners, and it would appear that the assembly plants within the Community wove, bound, and dyed tapes, pressed metal scoops or nylon interlocking spirals, fixed the scoops or spirals to the tapes, fixed the end lugs, inserted the slider, and cut the fasteners into separate slide fasteners. What they did not do was to manufacture the actual sliders, which were imported from Japan. The Court stated that what was done led to the manufacture of a new product which, unlike the products from which it was made, was a method of joining material together which could be repeatedly done up and undone; the slider itself was only one element in this, its price was hardly decisive, and although it was a characteristic of a slide fastener it was of no use until incorporated into the whole unit. Hence the sliders were of Community origin. In the light of this, the enthusiasm of Japanese manufacturers to set up car-assembly plants within the Community may be understood.[38]

Despite the absence of any express reference to added value in the definition, it is an important element in determining whether a process is substantial, particularly where the finished product has not changed its intrinsic nature. It has thus been held that the gassing, mercerizing, dyeing, and spooling of cotton yarn, which on the evidence added 159 per cent to its value, could confer origin, even though the ultimate product was still cotton yarn.[39] On the other hand, in *Brother International* v. *HZA Giessen*,[40] it was held that an added value of less than 10 per cent was clearly not enough, and the Court referred to the Kyoto Convention as authority for the proposition that simple assembly operations, which do not require a skilled work-force or specially equipped premises, do not confer origin. In so far as it may be relevant

[36] *Überseehandel* v. *Handelskammer Hamburg*, Case 49/76, [1977] ECR 41.
[37] Cases 34/78 and 114/78, [ECR 115 and 151.
[38] It may be recalled that before United Kingdom Accession, British Leyland established a plant in Belgium to assemble Minis for exactly the same reasons. It was closed after Accession.
[39] *Cousin*, Case 162/83, [1983] ECR 1101.
[40] Case C–26/88 (13 Dec. 1989).

in this context, the provisions of the EEC anti-dumping legislation, which enable duties to be imposed on products assembled in the Community if duties would be imposed on direct importations of the finished product,[41] lay down that anti-dumping duties may only be imposed if the value of the imported elements exceeds the rest by at least 50 per cent. Putting it the other way round, the adding of 40 per cent of its value within the Community prevents a product being treated as a dumped imported product; it remains to be seen if it is enough truly to confer origin.

Much more detailed rules on origin have been incorporated into arrangements made by the Community which give preferential treatment to imports from certain non-member States, whether they be the free-trade agreements with the Members of EFTA, or the agreements with the developing countries under the Lomé Conventions, or under generalized tariff preferences. It has now clearly been held by the Court[42] that the Council does have power to adopt stricter rules on origin when granting preferential treatment to certain imports and that these more specific rules prevail over the general rules with regard to those imports to which they relate.

Charges Equivalent to Customs Duties

Just as the EEC Treaty made no express provision for the enactment of common rules on the valuation for goods for customs purposes or on the determination of the origin of goods for customs purposes, so also it contains no express prohibition on Member States imposing charges equivalent to customs duties[43] on imports from non-member States after the Common Customs Tariff entered into force. In practice, the agricultural legislation of the Community does usually expressly prohibit such charges, and such a prohibition is also contained in some of the specific trade arrangements negotiated by the Community, but there is still no general legislative prohibition on such charges. Hence, this is a matter in which the general principles have been laid down in the case-law of the European Court. The matter came before the Court in 1973 in the context of Belgian legislation imposing a charge on imports of rough diamonds from non-member States for the benefit of the Belgian social fund for diamond workers.[44] Having determined that this was a charge levied only by reason of importation, therefore equivalent in its

---

[41] Council Reg. 2423/88 (OJ 1988, L 209/1) Art. 13(10). See p. 17 below.

[42] *SR Industries* v. *Administration des Douanes*, Case 385/85, [1986] ECR.

[43] In effect, a charge other than a customs duty as such levied by reason of crossing a frontier. For a discussion of the concept in the context of internal Community trade see Chap. 3 below.

[44] *Diamantarbeiders* v. *Indiamex*, Cases 37 and 38/73, [1973] ECR 1609.

nature to a customs duty, the Court held that it was clear from the objectives of the Common Customs Tariff that Member States could not alter the level of protection defined by that tariff by means of charges supplementing the Common Customs Tariff duties. Furthermore, the Court noted that even if the charge were not protective in nature, nevertheless its very existence could hardly be reconciled with the requirements of a common commercial policy. The Court therefore concluded that Member States could not, following the establishment of the Common Customs Tariff, introduce in a unilateral manner new charges on goods imported directly from third countries or raise the level of those in existence at the time the tariff was introduced. The basic tenor of the Court's judgment appears to be that a Common Customs Tariff and a common commercial policy require uniform external protection at the external frontiers of the Community's Single Market.

However, the problems of achieving this objective by case-law in the absence of express legislation came clearly to a head in *Simmenthal* v. *Italian Finance Administration*,[45] which involved charges levied under Italian legislation in relation to the health inspection of meat imported into Italy from Uruguay. The Court here recognized that it was the Community policy of achieving a uniform external protection which prevented Member States from imposing their own charges having equivalent effect to customs duties on imports from non-member States, but it accepted that the Council and Commission could create exceptions or derogations for the prohibition on charges having equivalent effect to customs duties provided that the charges involved had a uniform effect in all Member States in trade with third countries. However, in this case the Court was faced with the difficulty that health inspections would have been required in Community internal trade and that under the relevant Community legislation, national provisions relating to imports from third countries were not to be more favourable than those governing intra-Community trade. The Court therefore found itself having to accept that a Member State must hold inspections and charge for them where such inspections would be held and could be charged for in internal Community trade. In internal Community trade, such charges are in principle permissible if they do not exceed the actual cost of carrying out the inspection, but the Court in *Land Berlin* v. *Wigei*[46] had to accept that in order to avoid reverse discrimination against Community products, the charges imposed for the inspection of products imported from non-member States could exceed those levied on inspections of Community products provided they were not manifestly disproportionate. Subsequently, the Court has expressly accepted that the lawfulness of imposing a charge for a health inspection could not be

---

[45] Case 70/77, [1978] ECR 1453.
[46] Case 30/79, [1980] ECR 151.

subject to the existence of comparable charges in all the other Member States, at least where the charge corresponded to the cost of the inspection;[47] hence, this would appear to amount to an admission that there can be different treatment of imports from non-member States depending on the Member State into which they are imported.

This particular problem might appear to have been resolved by the enactment of Council Directive 85/73[48] on the financing of health inspections and controls of fresh meat and poultry meat, which was intended to introduce common rules and criteria. However, the Directive expressly allowed Member States to exceed the level fixed under the Directive if the total fee collected by the Member State is lower than or equal to the real figure for inspection costs. In the light of this provision it may be wondered whether the Directive really added very much to the situation already reached in the case-law.

The possibility that there may still be some national charges equivalent to customs duties on direct imports from non-member States should not, however, be allowed to detract from the overall achievement of the Common Customs Tariff.

[47] *Intercontinentale Fleischhandelsgesellschaft* v. *Bavaria*, Case 1/83, [1984] ECR 349.
[48] OJ 1985, L 32/14.

2

External Trade: The Common Commercial Policy

Structure of the Common Commercial Policy

As has already been mentioned, Article 113 of the EEC Treaty required the common commercial policy, that is, its policy on trade with non-member States, to be developed by 1 January 1970, and it must be said that in 1969, two important pieces of legislation were enacted which are still in force.

The first of these is Regulation 2603/69[1] laying down common rules for exports. This sets out a basic principle of freedom to export, but its Annex lists products of which the export need not be liberalized until the Council issues common rules with regard to them. This Annex was held still to be in force in 1986 in *Bulk Oil* v. *Sun International*,[2] where it was held that it constituted authority for the United Kingdom to restrict exports of oil products to Israel. It does in fact lay down a consultation procedure with regard to such restrictions, but in its judgment in the *Bulk Oil Case*, the European Court held that an alleged failure to follow this consultation procedure could not be invoked in disputes between private traders.

The other legislation from that period which is still extant is Council Decision 69/494[3] on the renewal or extension of agreements entered into by the Member States. This effectively is the provision which enables gaps in the common policy to be plugged by the Council's authorization of Member States' own agreements with third countries in commercial policy matters. However, the Council's authorization of such extensions or renewals is given subject to strict time limits, and nowadays the authorization is stated to be applicable only insofar as the agreements in question are not contrary to the common commercial policy and with regard to areas *not* covered by agreements between the Community and the third countries concerned,[4] which means in effect that the scope of

---

[1] JO 1969, L 324/25.
[2] Case 174/84 [1986] 2 All ER 744.
[3] JO 1969, L 326/39.
[4] See e.g. Council Dec. 87/229 (OJ 1987, L 95/25).

the authorization can only be ascertained by comparison with the specific rules of the common commercial policy legislation.

With regard to imports, the legislation which was adopted in 1970 set a pattern which has been followed ever since of distinguishing between imports from State-trading countries and imports from other countries, although the importance of the distinction has begun to diminish in the light of the series of agreements made with East European countries from 1988.[5] Regulation 109/70[6] set out common rules for imports from State-trading countries, and Regulation 1025/70[7] set out general common rules for imports from all other countries. It must be said, however, that both of them were rather limited in the range of products which they covered.

Leaving aside the free-trade agreements with European and Mediterranean countries, and the special arrangements under the successive Lomé Conventions with African, Caribbean, and Pacific countries, there is nowadays a complex and reasonably coherent pattern of commercial-policy legislation. It should, however, be noted at the outset that this legislation is derived from very different sources; some of it reflects agreements concluded by the Community itself, some of it represents an adoption by the Community of what were formerly national policies of the different Member States, and some of it represents unilateral Community legislation.

The basic legislation with regard to imports is currently Regulation 288/82.[8] This is notable for defining what it does not apply to rather than what it does apply to. Essentially, it does not apply to imports of products governed by other more specific legislation. So, it does not apply to the products imported from State-trading countries which remain subject to separate legislation; it does not apply to textile products, which again are subject to more specific legislation; and it does not derogate from the legislation governing the Common Agricultural Policy, although it may add to it. Indeed, most common organizations of agricultural markets regulate in great detail the importation and exportation of the products in question, and in particular endeavour to govern the relationship between world prices and Community prices for those products. For products not falling within more specific legislation, however, Regulation 288/82 lays down a basic principle of importation free from quantitative restrictions. This basic principle is subject to a considerable list of exceptions contained in Annex 1 of the Regulation when the products in question are imported

---

[5] The first being the agreement with Hungary, see Council Dec. 88/595 (OJ 1988, L 327/1).

[6] JO 1970, L 19/1.

[7] JO 1970, L 124/6.

[8] OJ 1982, L 35/1. Its Annexes were replaced by Council Regulations 196 and 197/91 (OJ 1991 L21/1 and 76).

into the Member States listed in that Annex; however, the basic principle does remain that of unrestricted entry. Nevertheless, the Regulation provides for Community surveillance where there is a threat of injury to Community producers. Products which are subject to prior surveillance may be put into free circulation, that is, admitted to free movement between the Member States, only on production of an import document issued by the relevant Member State.

With regard to the products imported from State-trading countries, it is necessary to distinguish between the People's Republic of China and other State-trading countries. The reason is that the treatment of imports from China results from a series of trade agreements reached with China,[9] whereas the treatment of imports from the other State-trading countries constituted, until agreements began to be negotiated in 1988,[10] a set of unilateral Community measures. However, both Regulations[11] are drafted on the same basis, which is the opposite from that on which the basic Regulation 288/82 is drafted: only products specifically listed in the Regulations may be imported free of quantitative restrictions and there is no general principle of unrestricted import. No doubt further differences in treatment will emerge from the agreements which have been and are being negotiated with individual East European countries since 1988.[12]

However, the products of State-trading countries which are subject to quantitative restrictions on import into the Member States of the Community are in fact specifically listed in Council Regulation 3420/83,[13] which again makes it clear that it does not apply to the products subject to liberalization or to products subject to the special textiles rules. Although this is a Community instrument, it must be said that many of the restrictions which it imposed were in fact merely the continuation of restrictions that had previously been applied by the Member States as such. A clear example of this may be found in *Mikx*,[14] which was concerned with a restriction on the importation of hunting cartridges from Czechoslovakia, and where it was common ground that this restriction had been reproduced from a previous Benelux bilateral arrangement with Czechoslovakia.

The regulation of imports of textiles into the Community reflects the Community's membership of the multifibre arrangement and the bilateral agreements negotiated within the context of that arrangement.

---

[9] See Council Reg. 2616/85 (OJ 1985, L 250/1).
[10] See n. 1 above.
[11] Reg. 1766/82 (OJ 1982, L 195/21) (China); Reg. 1765/82 (OJ 1982, L 195/1) (other State-trading countries).
[12] Following Council Dec. 88/345 on relations with COMECON (OJ 1988, L 157/34). See n. 5 above.
[13] OJ 1983, L 346/6.
[14] Case 90/85, [1986] ECR 1695.

The results of the negotiation of a series of agreements were consolidated in Regulation 4136/86 on common rules for imports of textiles.[15] On the one hand, this Regulation specifically lists the products which may be imported into the Community free of quantitative restrictions and the countries from which those products may be imported into the Community free of quantitative restrictions, and on the other hand, it also specifically sets out the products which are subject to quantitative restrictions, the countries from which imports of those products are subject to quantitative restrictions, and the Member States in which the quantitative restrictions apply. Hence, again, the Community rules treat different Member States differently, thus giving rise to problems which will be considered later in this chapter. However, the Regulation does contain a provision[16] enabling the transfer within certain limits of unused shares of a quota relating to one Member State to the quota relating to another Member State. It may be hoped that in the long term such techniques may lead to the creation of genuine Community quotas as opposed to national quotas contained in Community legislation.

Unlike the general rules on imports, the special rules concerned with the import of textiles apply both to the products of State-trading countries and to the products of market-economy countries, although there are more specific Community Regulations such as those dealing with the import of certain textile products from the People's Republic of China[17] and from the USSR.[18]

Unfair Trading Practices

As well as the regulation of what might be termed 'normal trade', the Community has from the outset also concerned itself with protection against what might be regarded as unfair international trading practices. So, for example, the Community has had its own anti-dumping rules for as long as it has had its own common customs tariff. The original anti-dumping legislation was introduced by Regulation 459/68[19] giving effect to the GATT Anti-dumping Code which came into force on 1 July 1968, the same day as the Common Customs Tariff entered into force. From the outset, the anti-dumping legislation has been drafted in terms of injury to *Community* producers; similarly, from the outset the legislation has provided for the imposition of anti-dumping duties by the Community authorities on goods which are entered for Community

---

[15] OJ 1986, L 387/42.
[16] Art. 7.
[17] Council Reg. 2135/89 (OJ 1989, L 212/1).
[18] Council Reg. 1925/90 (OJ 1990, L 177/1).
[19] JO 1968, L 93/1.

consumption. The current version of the Community's anti-dumping legislation is contained in Regulation 2423/88.[20] Changes have been introduced to take account of the interpretation of the relevant GATT rules by the EEC's major trading partners, as reflected in their legislation or established practice, and also to develop clearer rules on the determination of the 'normal' value of dumped goods and the methods of constructing such a normal value. The retention of such a concept in dumping legislation may be contrasted with its replacement by the transaction value for the purposes of customs valuation in 1980.[21] The 1988 Regulation also takes account of 'screwdriver' operations, that is, the assembly in the Community of products the direct importation of which would be subject to anti-dumping duties.[22]

Many of the concepts used in the anti-dumping legislation were taken up in Council Regulation 2641/84[23] on the 'strengthening' of the Common Commercial Policy. This is concerned with laying down procedures under which the Community's rights may be enforced with regard to illicit commercial practices. The Community's rights in this context mean those international trade rights of which the Community may avail itself either under international law or under generally accepted rules, and illicit commercial practices are defined as 'any international trade practices attributable to third countries which are incompatible with international law or with the generally accepted rules'.

Under this Regulation, a complaint about such practices, which must also include proof of injury, may be submitted to the Commission on behalf of Community producers by any natural or legal person or even by an association having no legal personality, and a similar complaint may also be referred to the Commission by a Member State. Proof of injury is defined in terms analogous to those used in anti-dumping legislation, and involves, amongst other things, an examination of the volume of Community imports or exports, an examination of the prices charged by the Community producers' competitors, and the consequent impact on Community industry. In particular, it involves consideration of whether a threat of injury will develop into actual injury. If sufficient evidence is produced, the Commission may initiate an examination procedure during which the parties may be heard and may be given the opportunity to meet. The procedure may terminate, if the third country involved takes satisfactory measures, but otherwise, if it is found to be a harmful illicit commercial practice, the Regulation permits any commercial policy measures to be taken which are compatible with existing international obligations and procedures. These measures include the suspension or withdrawal of concessions, the raising of customs duties

---

[20] OJ 1988, L 209/1.
[22] See p. 11 above.

[21] See p. 8 above.
[23] OJ 1984, L 252/1.

or the introduction of other charges on imports, insofar as that may be possible under GATT rules, and the introduction of quantitative restrictions.

Nevertheless, the Regulation expressly recognizes the Community's international obligation to follow specific consultation or settlement procedures. The question might well, therefore, be asked as to what, if any, useful purpose is served by this Regulation. The answer seems to be that it provides a procedure under which trading undertakings can request the Commission to take up their complaints in the relevant international framework, without that undertaking having to go through its national government in order to seek a remedy. What is, however, now clear is that this remedy will not be used simply as a method of protection against unwelcome imports: the first complaint to be received by the Commission under this Regulation was made by a European undertaking whose products had been kept out of the United States by an American producer invoking industrial property rights before a trade court, which had no jurisdiction to determine whether or not the claims relating to the industrial property rights were in fact justified or valid.[24] A GATT panel eventually upheld this complaint.[25]

The most recent measure in this line of legislation is Council Regulation 3842/86[26] which prohibits the release for free circulation within the Community of counterfeit goods. Counterfeit goods are defined as 'any goods bearing without authorization a trademark which is identical to a trademark validly registered in respect of such goods in or for the Member State in which the goods are entered for free circulation, or which cannot be distinguished in its essential aspect from such a trademark'. Increasingly, therefore, this represents an attempt by the European Community to enable trading regulations to be used to protect industrial property rights.

Powers of the Member States

The question then arises as to the extent to which this development of a common commercial policy by the European Economic Community has affected the powers of the Member States with regard to commercial policy. The simple answer is that within the scope of the common commercial policy, Member States no longer have any autonomous powers, but that there may be questions still as to the precise extent of

---

[24] Complaint by the Dutch Akzo company in relation to the sale of aramid fibre in the United States (OJ 1986, C 25/2). See Denton, 'The New Commercial Policy Instrument' (1988), 13 E.L. Rev. 3.

[25] [1989] 1 CMLR 715.

[26] OJ 1986, L 357/1.

the common commercial policy. The basic principle was laid down by the European Court in *Opinion* 1/75,[27] when the Court was asked for its opinion under Article 228 of the EEC Treaty, as to the compatibility with that Treaty of a so-called draft understanding on a local cost standard in relation to exports on credit terms negotiated under the OECD. The real question put to the Court was whether it was for the Community to negotiate that understanding, or for the Member States to do so. The Court noted that Article 112 of the Treaty expressly required harmoniza-tion of the systems by which Member States grant aid for exports to third countries. After further observing that commercial policy is made up of a combination and interaction of internal and external policies, and having noted the provisions of Article 113 which provide an express mechanism enabling the Community to negotiate agreements with third countries, the Court came to the conclusion that this particular understanding did fall within the scope of the common commercial policy, and hence within the scope of the Community's powers. It then went on to hold that the concept of a common commercial policy was incompatible with the freedom to which Member States could lay claim by invoking a concurrent power so as to ensure that their own interests were separately satisfied in external relations.

The fundamental concept underlying the Court's view appears to be that there could not be a common commercial policy if each Member State was still free also to pursue its own commercial policies. This view was reaffirmed in *Donckerwolcke* v. *Procureur de la République de Lille*,[28] with regard to certain French restrictions on the import of textiles from third countries. The Court there stated that since full responsibility in the matter of commercial policy was transferred to the Community under Article 113, then even though there was not at that stage a fully comprehensive common commercial policy, nevertheless measures of commercial policy of a national character were only permissible after the end of the transitional period by virtue of specific authorization by the Community.

This view was also followed with regard to restrictions on exports in the *Bulk Oil* v. *Sun International*,[29] where the Court held that national restrictions on exports were similarly only permissible once the transitional period had ended by virtue of a specific authorization from the Community.

Whilst the principle of exclusive Community competence may be well established, questions remain as to its substantive scope. A fairly broad view was taken in *Opinion* 1/78[30] in relation to the international agreement on natural rubber then being negotiated under the aegis of the United Nations Conference on the Trade and Development

[27] [1975] ECR 1355.
[28] Case 41/76 [1976] ECR 1921.
[29] Case 174/84 [1986] 2 All ER 744.
[30] [1979] ECR 2871.

(UNCTAD). The vital feature of the proposed agreement was a buffer-stock intended to stabilize the balance between supply and demand, and the concept of a stabilization arrangement hardly appears in the list of commercial measures mentioned in Article 113 of the EEC Treaty. However, the Court held that although liberalization of trade may have been a dominant idea at the time when the Treaty was drafted, the Treaty nevertheless did not prevent the Community from developing a commercial policy aimed at the regulation of the world market for certain products rather than at a mere liberalization of trade. This Opinion also illustrates the fine line between Community competence and the competence of the Member States; with regard to the funding of the stabilization scheme, the Court held that if the scheme was to be financed by the Member States as such, that would imply their participation in the agreement; on the other hand, if the Community contribution to this financing was to be through the Community budget, the matter would remain within the competence of the Community. It is perhaps because of the difficulties of drawing this line that the widespread use of 'mixed' agreements[31] has developed. On the other hand, Council Decision 74/393,[32] which merely requires that a consultation procedure should be followed when so-called co-operation agreements are negotiated between Member States and third countries, would appear to imply that co-operation agreements as such do not fall within the Community's exclusive competence. However, it is palpably clear that the Community itself has actually negotiated a number of agreements labelled 'co-operation agreements'.[33]

Measures Equivalent to Quantitative Restrictions

A particular difficulty relates to the extent to which a Member State may still impose measures equivalent to quantitative restrictions[34] on goods whose import is not subject to any quantitative restrictions as such. Here, there is a terminological difference between the free-trade agreements with other European countries and the successive Lomé Conventions on the one hand, and the general rules governing imports on the other. In the free-trade agreements, there is indeed an express

---

[31] See O'Keeffe and Schermers (eds.), *Mixed Agreements* (1983).

[32] OJ 1974, L 208/23.

[33] While some of these are in fact also trade agreements, such as the recent agreement with Poland on trade and economic and commercial co-operation (Council Dec. 89/593, OJ 1989, L 339/1), others are not. See e.g. the Co-operation Agreements with Sweden (OJ 1983, L 185/22) and Switzerland (OJ 1985, L 58/22) on research and development in the field of wood as a renewable raw material.

[34] For a discussion of this concept in the context of the internal trade of the Community, see Chap. 4 below.

prohibition on measures having effect equivalent to quantitative restrictions, but there is no such express prohibition in the general rules on imports. When it considered the matter in the light of the 1974 version of the common rules on imports,[35] the Court held[36] that the Treaty provisions on commercial policy did not lay down any obligation on the part of the Member States to extend to trade with third countries the binding principles governing the free movement of goods between Member States, and in particular the prohibition of measures having effect equivalent to quantitative restrictions. Having noticed the different drafting of the free-trade agreements, the Court stated that the binding commitments undertaken by the Community with regard to certain countries could not automatically be extended to others. The case in fact involved the use of trademark rights by a trading undertaking to keep out direct imports from the United States. In this context the Court had no difficulty in holding that the principles governing the common commercial policy did not prevent the owner of the trademark from exercising his rights in order to prevent the importation of similar products bearing the same mark coming from a third country. However, it should be observed that in discussing the differences between the general rules on imports and the specific rules governing the free-trade agreements, the Court talked in terms of the commitments undertaken by the Community with regard to imported goods and did not talk in terms of the powers left to the Member States. In any event, even where a free-trade agreement does expressly prohibit not only quantitative restrictions but also measures having effects equivalent to quantitative restrictions, it is clear that the same interpretation of that phrase need not be given in the context of trade with a non-member State as will be given in the context of trade between States, since there is no intention to create a single market under free-trade agreements.[37]

Free Circulation and National Quotas

The fundamental consequence for the internal market of the existence of a Common Customs Tariff is that goods imported from non-Member States which have paid the Common Customs Tariff duties are treated under Articles 9 and 10 of the EEC Treaty as being in free circulation within the Community, and are hence able to take advantage of the rules on the internal free movement of goods.[37A] Unfortunately, the theory

[35] Council Reg. 1439/74 (OJ 1974, L 159/1).
[36] *EMI* v. *CBS*, Case 86/75, [1976] ECR 871, pp. 905–6.
[37] *Polydor* v. *Harlequin*, Case 270/80, [1982] ECR 379. The rules prohibiting measures equivalent to quantitative restrictions in trade between Member States are discussed in Chap. 5 to 7 below.
[37A] Goods imported on a commercial basis must be accompanied by the documents

does not wholly correspond to practice, since as has already been noted, many of the instruments of the common commercial policy create distinctions between the Member States in so far as different quotas are allocated to different Member States. Furthermore, Article 115 of the EEC Treaty appears on the face of it to empower the Commission to authorize Member States in certain circumstances not to grant Community treatment to goods imported from a non-Member State which are in free circulation in another Member State.[38]

In so far as national quotas are created by Community instruments, it would appear that the fact that goods are imported into the Community under such a quota does not in itself prevent those goods benefiting from the principle of free circulation. The matter first came before the Court in *Commission* v. *Council*,[39] where the Court held that the division of a global Community tariff quota into national quotas would only be compatible with the Treaty if it did not hinder the free movement of the goods forming part of the quota after they had been admitted into free circulation.

The problem occurred in rather more concrete terms in *Commission* v. *Ireland*.[40] The proceedings here related to an Irish order prohibiting the importation into Ireland of potatoes produced in non-Member States unless a licence was granted. This order followed the importation into Ireland of Cyprus potatoes originally imported into the United Kingdom under a Community tariff quota allocated to the United Kingdom. After repeating the well-established case-law to the effect that agricultural products for which a common organization or market has not been established, such as potatoes, are subject to the general rules of the EEC with regard to importation, exportation, and movement within the Community,[41] and after also citing the case-law holding that the rules governing the internal free movement of goods are applicable without distinction to products originating in the Member States and to those coming from non-Member States which have been put into free circulation in the Community,[42] the Court held that goods imported into the Community under a quota allocated to a particular Member State are to be treated as products which are in free circulation in that State once they have been properly imported, so that it must be possible for them to be imported without hindrance into the other Member States.

Just as a Member State cannot prevent the import of goods originally

required by Community transit legislation, Case C–117/88 *Trend-Moder v. HZA Emerich* (7 March 1990), but a private traveller is required only to make a declaration of origin, unless there are suspicious circumstances, Case C–85/89 *Houben* (22 March 1990).

[38] See p. 25 below.
[39] Case 218/82, [1983] ECR 4063.
[40] Case 288/83, [1985] ECR 1761.
[41] *Charmasson*, Case 48/74, [1974] ECR 1383.
[42] *Donckerwolcke* v. *Procureur de la République, Lille*, Case 41/76, [1976] ECR 1921.

imported into another Member State under a quota allocated to that State, so also the State to which the quota has been allocated may not prevent the export of those goods to another Member State. This was expressly decided by the Court on a reference from an Italian court[43] in relation to a Community tariff quota for frozen beef of which a specific quantity was allocated to Italy. The defendants before the Italian court were accused of exporting some of this beef from Italy to Germany, thus using it for a purpose other than that for which its importation was authorized. The Italian court asked the European Court quite simply whether the allocation of a quota to a particular Member State meant that the products subject to the quota were to be consumed and marketed only in that State without any possibility of re-exportation to another Member State. The Court emphasized that the quota was a Community quota even though it was allocated between the Member States, and indicated that its division between the Member States was intended simply to facilitate the fair distribution of the quota between traders in different Member States. The Court also took the view that subsequent trade between Member States could not be affected by the fact that the meat subject to the quota could only be imported into the Community under an import licence valid solely in the Member State which issued it; the Court repeated that the division of a global tariff quota into national quotas was compatible with the Treaty only in so far as it did not hinder the free movement of the goods forming part of the quota after they had been admitted into free circulation.

The Court has now made a more direct attack on the subdivision of EEC tariff quotas into national quotas, holding in *Commission* v. *Council*[44] that it was unlawful to allocate EEC quotas among Member States unless there were compelling circumstances of an administrative, technical, or economic character which made it impossible to do otherwise. Subsequent legislation on generalized tariff preferences has made express reference to this case-law.[45] It remains to be seen whether the same view will be taken with regard to protective quotas.

Restrictions on Free Circulation

A Member State may still be able to prevent the import of goods in free circulation in another Member State where it itself is a beneficiary of a quota, and it has authorization from the Commission to protect that quota under Article 115 of the EEC Treaty. This provision might appear

---

[43] *Migliorini and Fischl*, Case 199/84, [1985] ECR 3317.
[44] Case 51/87, [1988] ECR 5459.
[45] See e.g. Council Reg. 4257/88 (OJ 1988, L 375/1).

hardly to be compatible with the idea either of a single internal market or of a common commercial policy. It provides that

in order to ensure that the execution of measures of commercial policy taken in accordance with this Treaty by any Member State is not obstructed by deflection of trade . . . the Commission shall recommend the methods for the requisite cooperation between Member States. Failing this the Commission shall authorise Member States to take the necessary protective measures, the conditions and details of which it shall determine.

If, of course, the Community were treated as a single unit by all instruments of the common commercial policy, Article 115 would be redundant; however, the Community is not so treated, and Article 115 is not yet redundant.

The first question to ask is whether a Member State can still have any commercial policy measures of a national type to protect under Article 115. The answer was given in the *Donckerwolcke* case,[46] which has already been noted. The Court there stated that since full responsibility in the matter of commercial policy was transferred to the Community under Article 113, measures of commercial policy of a national character were permissible after the end of the transitional period only by virtue of specific authorization by the Community. That Community legislation may authorize national measures of commercial policy is illustrated by *Cayrol* v. *Rivoira*.[47] There, in relation to French restrictions on imports of Spanish table grapes, it was found that the 1970 agreement between the Community and Spain prohibited quantitative restrictions on fresh table grapes between 1 January and 31 March of each year, and that the market organization measure then in force, Council Regulation 2513/69,[48] permitted Member States to impose quantitative restrictions on imports of table grapes for the period between 1 July in each year and the following 31 January. Putting these two provisions together, the Court worked out that a Member State could impose quantitative restrictions on imports of Spanish table grapes during the period 1 July–31 December in each year. However, even if a Member State is empowered to take measures of commercial policy, it cannot enforce those measures of commercial policy against goods in free circulation in other Member States unless the Commission has given express authorization under Article 115.

The background to the *Rivoira* case arose from the importation into France of Spanish table grapes in free circulation in Italy at a time when France claimed to be able to restrict imports of Spanish table grapes, and in a reference made in subsequent French criminal proceedings,[49] the

[46] See n. 28 above.
[47] Case 52/78, [1977] ECR 2261.
[48] JO 1969, L 318/6.
[49] *Procureur de la République, Montpellier* v. *Rivoira*, Case 179/78, [1979] ECR 1147.

Court stated quite simply that even if France was entitled to have the policy of restricting imports of Spanish table grapes, it could not enforce that policy unless it had received an authorization from the Commission in accordance with Article 115 of the Treaty, which would appear not to have been the case in this particular instance.

Whilst on the face of it Article 115 might appear to be designed only to authorize the Commission to permit the protection of measures taken by Member States themselves albeit with Community authorization, in fact the Court has now held that it can also be used to protect quotas allocated to Member States under instruments of the common commercial policy. This appears from the *Tezi Textiel* cases.[50] Here the Commission, acting under Article 115, authorized the Netherlands not to grant Community treatment to, that is, not to permit the import of, men's and boys' cotton trousers originating in Macao, and in free circulation in Italy. The Commission's decision was issued to enable the Netherlands to protect the quota allocated to the Benelux countries within the context of the Community quota for the relevant products originating in Macao set by Regulation 3589/82,[51] which was the general regulation at that time governing imports of textiles into the Community. In determining whether a decision under Article 115 could be used to protect a quota granted under Community legislation as part of the common commercial policy, the Court distinguished between what it called 'genuine' common commercial policy instruments and those which did not create a 'genuine' common commercial policy. The basis for this distinction would appear to be that it was only if the Community legislation created a genuine common commercial policy that Article 115 would ceased to play a role; on the other hand, if the Community legislation treated the Member States differently, then the objectives of Article 115 were still relevant and Article 115 could still be used. The Court in fact took the view that whilst the Regulation on the import of textiles was a step towards the establishment of a common policy based on uniform principles, it in reality maintained, albeit to a limited extent, some of the existing disparities, and did not standardize everything all at once. Hence, in the view of the Court, the Commission retained its power to grant a Member State authorization under Article 115 to adopt protective measures. It may be wondered how far this approach may be reconciled with the Court's more recent view expressed in *Commission* v. *Council*,[52] that tariff quotas, as opposed to protective quotas, should not in principle be subdivided between Member States. It was, however, stated in *Tezi Textiel* that in the context of commercial policy legislation such as Regulation 3589/82, the Commission might only authorize

---

[50] Cases 59/84 and 242/84, [1986] ECR 887.
[51] OJ 1982, L 374/106.
[52] Case 51/87, [1988] ECR 5459.

protective measures under Article 115 for serious reasons and for a limited period, provided the measures chosen were those which would cause the least disruption of trade between the Member States.

By way of conclusion, it may be stated that the Community now is clearly an actor in its own right on the stage of international trade. However, the situation still has to be reached where the Community's common commercial policy is able to treat all the Member States as a single unit; there still remain differences in treatment which in turn may preclude imported goods from obtaining the full benefit of the single Community market.

3

Internal Trade: Customs Duties and Charges Having Equivalent Effect

Structure of the Treaty Provisions

The link between the external customs union and the internal free movement of goods was made clear in the previous chapter. By virtue of Article 9(1) of the EEC Treaty, the Community is based upon a customs union which covers all trade in goods, and which involves the prohibition between Member States of customs duties on imports and exports and of all charges having equivalent effect, and the adoption of a common customs tariff in relations with third countries.

The mechanism used to achieve the elimination of intra-Community customs duties and charges having equivalent effect was a combination of a standstill clause and the progressive removal of existing charges. The standstill clause contained in Article 12 of the Treaty applied generally to customs duties as such and to charges having equivalent effect, whether imposed on imports or on exports, requiring Member States to refrain from introducing between themselves any new customs duties or equivalent charges, and to refrain from increasing those which they already applied. The removal of existing duties and charges was, however, treated differently depending on whether they affected imports or exports.

Under Article 13(1) of the EEC Treaty, customs duties on imports were to be abolished during the transitional period according to a timetable laid down by the Treaty itself, and under Article 13(2) charges equivalent to customs duties on imports were also to be abolished during the transitional period but, under one of the few provisions of the EEC Treaty to confer original legislative competence on the Commission, it was left to the Commission to determine by directives the timetable for such abolition.

On the other hand, with regard to customs duties and charges having equivalent effect on exports, Article 16 of the Treaty required their abolition by the end of the first stage of the transitional period, that is, by 1 January 1962. Hence, although there was a correlation between the

Treaty provisions on the introduction of the Common Customs Tariff and on the elimination of customs duties and charges having equivalent effect on imports in trade within the Community, there was no such correlation with regard to the elimination of customs duties on exports.

Furthermore, as was explained in the previous chapter, the Common Customs Tariff was in fact introduced in July 1968, eighteen months before the end of the transitional period, and by the same 'Acceleration Decision',[1] the Council agreed to eliminate customs duties in trade between Member States from the same date. While the removal of national customs duties was the necessary corollary to the introduction of a common tariff, it did not on the face of it alter the date by which charges equivalent to customs duties on imports should be abolished, a matter which was ultimately resolved by the European Court of Justice. The view taken by the Court was that where the Commission had issued a directive under Article 13(2) requiring a Member State to eliminate a specific charge by 1 July 1968, the prohibition was directly effective from that date,[2] but that where no such directive had been issued, the prohibition on charges equivalent to customs duties on imports only gave rise to rights enforceable by individuals from 1 January 1970, the end of the transitional period.[3] Whatever the complexities to which this lack of co-ordination might theoretically have given rise, they do not appear to have arisen in practice.

Before turning to a separate consideration of customs duties and of charges having equivalent effect to customs duties, there are certain fundamental points which they have in common. The first is that by virtue of Article 9(2) of the Treaty these provisions apply not only to products originating in the Member States but also to products coming from third countries which are in free circulation in Member States (that is, products which have complied with import formalities and which have paid relevant Common Customs Tariff duties)[4]—hence the importance of the link with the development of a common system of external protection. The second is that these are fundamental provisions of the Treaty from which the institutions may not authorize derogations.

This is illustrated in *Ramel* v. *Receveur des Douanes*,[5] where France imposed levies on imports of Italian wine, claiming to be so authorized under a Council Regulation[6] on the common organization of the market in wine. Whilst one provision of that Regulation repeated the basic Treaty prohibition on the levying of charges equivalent to customs duties, another contained a derogation purporting to allow producer

---

[1] Council Dec. of 26 July 1966 (JO 1966, p. 2971/66).
[2] *SACE* V. *Italian Ministry of Finance, Case 33/70, [1970] ECR 1213.*
[3] *IGAV* V. *ENCC,* Case 94/74, [1975] ECR 699.
[4] See p. 6 above.
[5] Cases 80 and 81/77, [1978] ECR 927.
[6] Reg. 816/70 (JO 1970, L 99/1).

Member States to take measures to limit imports from another Member State to avoid disturbances on their markets, whilst all the administrative mechanisms necessary for the management of the market in wine were not in application. The French view was that the relevant administrative mechanisms were not in aplication in Italy, and therefore the question faced by the European Court was whether the provision in the Regulation was compatible with the Treaty. After considering the agricultural provisions of the Treaty (Articles 39–46), the Court found that there was nothing which expressly or by necessary implication provided for or permitted such charges, and concluded that, at all events after the end of the transitional period, the Community institutions' powers should be used with the unity of the market in mind, to the exclusion of measures breaching the prohibition on customs duties and quantitative restrictions and charges and measures having equivalent effect. It therefore held that the provision in the Regulation, in so far as it permitted Member States to levy charges equivalent to customs duties in trade with other Member States, was incompatible with Article 13(2) and hence invalid.

Customs duties as such

The current situation with regard to customs duties in internal Community trade may be stated very simply: since 1 July 1968 no Member State has purported to introduce or maintain customs duties as such with regard to products falling within the scope of the EEC Treaty,[7] with the exception of new Member States acting under transitional arrangements consequent to their accession. Nevertheless, the impact of the Treaty provisions on customs duies stricto sensu does remain of legal significance, since it was in this context that the European Court first developed the concept of 'direct effect', in *Van Gend en Loos* v. *Nederlandse Administratie der Belastingen*,[8] The background to that case was that in 1960 Van Gend en Loos imported some ureaformaldehyde from West Germany into the Netherlands, and were charged an import duty of 8 per cent, whereas they claimed that at the date of entry into force of the Treaty in 1958, the duty had been 3 per cent. The question, therefore, arose as to whether they could invoke the standstill provision, Article 12, against the Dutch authorities before the Dutch courts. In the words of the European Court:

The wording of article 12 contains a clear and unconditional prohibition which is

---

[7] For the situation under the ECSC Treaty see *Mabanaft* v. *HZA Emmerich* Case 36/83 [1984] ECR 2497, discussed in Usher, 'The Single Market and Goods Imported from Third Countries' (1986), YEL 159, pp 161–2.

[8] Case 26/62, [1963] ECR 1.

not a positive but a negative obligation. This obligation, moreover, is not qualified by any reservation on the part of States which would make its implementation conditional upon apositive legislative measure enacted under national law. The very nature of this prohibition makes it ideally adapted to produce direct effects in the legal relationship between Member States and their subjects. . . . Article 12 must be interpreted as producing direct effects and creating individual rights which national courts must protect.

The importance of this concept of direct effect for the subsequent development of the free movement of goods within the EEC can hardly be over-emphasized.

Charges Equivalent to Customs Duties: The Basic Concept

To determine the nature of a charge equivalent to a customs duty requires some analysis of the nature of a customs duty as such. It may be suggested that it is a sum of money, levied by reason of goods crossing a frontier, payable as a matter of law, collected by the State authorities, and traditionally protective in nature; it therefore self-evidently restricts trade between States. Nevertheless, whilst there is case-law of the European Court which makes reference to the protective nature of charges equivalent to customs duties (more usually speaking of their 'discriminatory' effect, however),[9] the definition which it has most frequently used refers only to the fact of such a charge being levied by reason of crossing a frontier[10]—it need not be for the benefit of the State, and it need not be protective in nature.

This was made clear in *Commission* v. *Italy*,[11] where the Court was faced with a charge of 10 lira imposed under Italian law on all imported goods for the purpose of a statistical survey:

Any pecuniary charge, however small and whatever its designation and mode of application, which is imposed unilaterally on domestic or foreign goods by reason of the fact that they cross a frontier, and which is not a customs duty in the strict sense, constitutes a charge having equivalent effect within the meaning of articles 9, 12, 13, and 16 of the Treaty, even if it is not imposed for the benefit of the State, is not discriminatory or protective in effect and if the product on which the charge is imposed is not in competition with any domestic product.

What is, therefore, objectionable in the eyes of Community law is the hindrance to trade caused by the fact of having to make a payment, and in that perspective the Court was able to apply the same definition both with regard to imports and with regard to exports. Indeed, it has held

---

[9] See e.g. *Commission* v. *Luxembourg and Belgium* Cases 2 and 3/62, [1962] ECR 425.

[10] See e.g. *Sociaal Fonds voor Diamantarbeiders* v. *Brachfeld*, Cases 2 and 3/69, [1969] ECR 211, p. 244.

[11] Case 24/68, [1969] ECR 193.

that the phrase has the same meaning when used in secondary legislation in the context of the Common Agricultural Policy[12] and when used in the context of the external trade of the Community,[13] even though the objective there is to prevent the common level of protection of the Common Customs Tariff being unilaterally altered.[14]

However, the emphasis on crossing a frontier means that a charge which is also genuinely levied on goods which do not cross the frontier cannot be a charge equivalent to a customs duty. Hence, when France imposed a levy on photocopiers, for the benefit of the publishing industry, the fact that the vast majority of photocopiers sold in France were imported did not make the levy a charge equivalent to a customs duty since the 1 or 2 per cent of photocopiers actually made in France also bore the levy.[15] On the other hand, a charge imposed by national law only on imported or exported goods will always be unlawful, even if it is to pay for an inspection justified under Article 36 of the EEC Treaty[16] for the protection of health,[17] unless it falls within a narrow range of exceptions.

There are three categories of exceptional cases recognized in the case-law of the European Court: charges which meet the cost of sevices rendered to the importer or exporter,[18] charges which meet the cost of inspections and so on required by Community law or which promote the purposes of Community law,[19] and charges which in reality fall within the scope of internal taxation.[20] These will be considered in the following sections of this Chapter.

Charges for Services Rendered

Whilst the European Court has frequently stated that charges to meet the cost of services rendered are lawful, it has been extremely reluctant to hold that a charge levied by reason of crossing a frontier did in fact meet the cost of a service. The example might be taken of *Cadsky* v. *Istituto Nazionale per il Commercio Estero*.[21] This involved the imposition by the Italian authorities of inspections to ensure the quality control of salad vegetables exported from Italy, for which a charge was levied. The

---

[12] *Variola* v. *Italian Finance Administration*, Case 34/73, [1973] ECR 981.
[13] Ibid.
[14] *Simmenthal* v. *Italian Finance Administration*, Case 70/77, [1978] ECR 1453.
[15] *Commission* v. *France*, Case 70/79, [1981] ECR 283.
[16] See p. 77 below.
[17] See e.g. *Denkavit Futtermittel*, Case 251/78, [1979] ECR 3369 and *Commission* v. *Denmark*, Case 158/82, [1983] ECR 3573.
[18] *Donner*, Case 39/82, [1983] ECR 19.
[19] See e.g. *Commission* v. *Germany*, Case 18/87, [1988] ECR 5427.
[20] *Capolongo* v. *Maya*, Case 77/72, [1973] ECR 611.
[21] Case 63/74, [1975] ECR 281.

exporter claimed that this was a charge equivalent to customs duty on export, whereas the Italian authorities argued that the quality controls improved the reputation of Italian produce in foreign markets and were therefore of benefit to all exporters. Although it accepted that a charge could be made if a service was rendered, the European Court took the view that the benefit received by any individual exporter was too remote for the inspection of his goods to be regarded as a service rendered to him personally.

A couple of more recent examples may be given. In *Ford España* v. *Spain*,[22] the Spanish authorities argued that it was a service to the importer to allow customs formalities to be carried out at the place of destination rather than at the frontier, but the European Court did not accept that the charge made related to a specific service to that importer, since it was on a flat-rate basis. In *Commission* v. *Italy*,[23] it was argued that to allow frontier formalities to be carried out outside certain defined times was a service for which a charge could be made. Unfortunately for the Italian authorities, it emerged that certain of the times for which they wished to make a charge were times at which, by virtue of Community legislation, their customs posts should have been open in any event. Consequently, the European Court took the view that to allow formalities to be carried out at such times was not a service for which an importer could be charged.

Despite its general reluctance to accept that a standard charge may be payment for a service rendered, the Court did show itself sympathetic to such an argument in *Donner*.[24] There, an importer of books (a former judge of the European Court, Professor Donner) was faced with a charge demanded by the Dutch Post Office for having dealt with the payment of value-added tax on the importation on his behalf, and argued that it constituted a charge equivalent to a customs duty. Here the European Court suggested that the national court should investigate how realistic it was for an individual recipient of a postal packet to deal with the payment of value-added tax himself, and how much it would cost him. If in the light of this, the charge made by the Post Office was reasonable, then it could indeed be regarded as payment for a service rendered.

Charges Relating to Requirements of Community Law

The distinction between charges on import or export under national law alone, which are always unlawful even if they relate to inspections which are themselves justifiable, and charges relating to inspections

---

[22] Case 170/88 (11 July 1989).
[23] Case 340187 (30 May 1989).
[24] Case 39/82, [1983] ECR 19.

required under Community law was made in the context of a reference from a Dutch court in proceedings brought by a cattle dealer to recover fees paid for veterinary public-health inspections carried out by the Dutch authorities on the export of certain animals.[25] Some of the fees were paid for inspections carried out under requirements of a Council Directive, and some were paid for inspections under national law alone.

With regard to the inspections carried out under the Directive, the Court pointed out that the measures in question were not prescribed by each Member State to protect some interest of its own but by the Council in the general interest of the Community. They could not, therefore, be regarded as unilateral measures which hinder trade, but rather as operations intended to promote the free movement of goods, since they removed the obstacles to free movement caused by national measures under Article 36. Fees charged for inspections required by Community law before export did not constitute charges equivalent to customs duties, provided they did not exceed the actual cost of the inspection at issue. On the other hand, with regard to the charges for inspections carried out under Dutch law alone, the Court held that such inspections constitute unilateral obstacles to the free movement of goods, and the same considerations, therefore, do not apply. Those charges are to be treated as equivalent to customs duties.

The underlying theory is that since inspections under Community law obviate the need for unilateral national inspections, they promote the free movement of goods and therefore Member States are permitted to recover the real cost of carrying them out. The same approach has also been taken with regard to inspections required under international conventions to which all the Member states are party, at least to the extent that the need for unilateral national inspections is again removed: in *Commission* v. *Netherlands*[26] it was held that fees (not exceeding the actual cost) could be charged for phytosanitary inspections carried out under the 1951 International Plant Protection Convention, to which all the Member States were party, since these inspections were not unilateral measures but were intended to assist the free movement of goods.

The Commission has attempted to persuade the Court to take a different approach, but the result was a reaffirmation of the previous case-law.[27]

---

[25] *Bauhuis* v. *The Netherland*, Case 46/76, [1977] ECR 5.
[26] Case 89/76, [1977] ECR 1355.
[27] See n. 19 above.

Charges falling within the scope of Internal Taxation

The legal rules relating to internal taxation will be considered in a later Chapter. However, it may be noted that it has been consistently held since the early 1960s that the same charge cannot both be regulated by the rules relating to charges equivalent to customs duties and by the rules relating to internal taxation.[28] Essentially this is because if a charge is equivalent to a customs duty it is unlawful in its entirety, whereas internal taxation is unlawful only to the extent that it is discriminatory or protective;[29] moreover, the dates at which the relevant provisions entered into force were different.[30] Nevertheless, the distinction is not always easy to make, and there is some authority for saying that certain charges which appear to be internal taxation nevertheless constitute charges equivalent to customs duties.

The problem arose in the context of the Italian paper and cellulose industry, where a charge ostensibly levied on both imported and domestic products was allegedly used to benefit the domestic product. In *Capolongo* v. *Maya*,[31] after reciting the usual definition of a charge equivalent to a customs duty and after mentioning that the same charge could not be both equivalent to a customs duty and internal taxation, the Court stated that where a charge is levied both on imports and on domestic products, it can nevertheless constitute a charge equivalent to a customs duty when it is intended exclusively to support activities which specifically benefit the taxed domestic product; in a later judgment[32] it was stated that this was so where the the domestic tax was made good 'wholly or in part'. It might be observed that a partial reimbursement of the tax paid by the domestic product does not mean that the tax is borne only by the imported product, so that it hardly seems to make the charge equivalent to a customs duty, and in fact the Court later refined its definition to make it clear that it was only where the tax on the domestic product was compensated in full that such a classification would be appropriate. In *Cucchi* v. *Avez*,[33] it was stated that apparent internal taxation can only constitute a charge equivalent to a customs duty 'if it has the sole purpose of financing activities for the specific advantage of the taxed domestic product; if the taxed product and the domestic product benefiting from it are the same; and if the charges imposed on the domestic product are made good in full'. While this may be explicable as a matter of theory, it may be doubted whether

---

[28] See e.g. *Lütticke* v. *HZA Saarlouis*, Case 57/65, [1966] ECR 205.

[29] *IGAV* v. *ENCC*, Case 94/74, [1975] 699.

[30] Art. 95 on internal taxation required implementation by the end of the first stage of the transitional period, i.e. 1 Jan. 1962.

[31] See n. 20 above.

[32] See n. 29 above.

[33] Case [1977], ECR 987.

such a situation is in fact likely to be encountered. In the meantime, it has now been made clear that the much more likely situation of a tax on imported and domestic products which gives a partial benefit to the taxed domestic product does in fact constitute discriminatory internal taxation, on the basis that it is of such a nature as indirectly to impose a heavier burden on products from other Member States than on domestic products.[34]

There is one further problem in the relationship between charges equivalent to customs duties and internal taxation: it has been suggested by the Court that a charge only constitutes internal taxation if it is levied on the same chargeable event both for imports and domestic products. The comment was made in *Denkavit Loire* v. *France*,[35] which involved a French charge on the import of lard which was claimed by the French authorities to equate to a domestic charge on the slaughter of a pig. It is self-evident that in this case there was no real correlation, so that the charge on the lard could be regarded as equivalent to a customs duty, but it may be doubted if the remark about the same chargeable event was meant literally, because the Community's own system of value-added tax treats importation as such as a chargeable event.[36]

[34] *Commission* v. *Italy*, Case 73/79, [1980] ECR 1533.
[35] Case 132/78, [1979] ECR 1928.
[36] See p. 45 below.

4

Internal Taxation

Relationship to other rules on the Free Movement of Goods

Although, like the rules on customs duties and charges having equivalent effect, the EEC Treaty provisions on internal taxation are intended to eliminate restrictions of a fiscal nature on trade between Member States, they involve a number of fundamental differences from the other free-movement-of-goods rules.

The first, and most obvious, difference is that the provisions on internal taxation are set out in Article 95 of the Treaty, which is contained in the chapter on tax provisions in Part III of the Treaty, whereas the rules on customs duties and charges having equivalent effect and on quantitative restrictions and measures having equivalent effect are set out in Chapters 1 and 2 of Title I of Part II of the Treaty. The importance of this is that on a literal reading of Article 9(2) of the Treaty, it is only provisions falling within those two chapters which are expressly stated to apply not only to products originating in Member States but also to products coming from third countries which are in free circulation in Member States. Indeed, Article 95 itself only refers in terms to products 'of' other Member States. There was, therefore, doubt as to whether products in free circulation could benefit from the provisions on internal taxation, and in the context of external trade the European Court went so far as to say that the EEC Treaty did not prohibit discrimination in the application of internal taxation to products imported from non-member countries, subject to any treaty which may be in force between the Community and the country of origin of the product.[1] This hardly seemed consonant with the concept of the Common Customs Tariff,[2] and faced with a case actually involving third-country goods in free circulation in the Community, the Court took a different approach and used the opportunity to interpret Article 95 so as to parallel the other free-movement-of-goods rules. This was in *Cooperativa Co-Frutta*,[3] which involved Italian taxation of bananas imported through other Member States. The Court invoked the

---

[1] *Hansen* v. *HZA Flensburg*, Case 148/77, [1978] ECR 1787.
[2] See Usher: 'The Single Market and Goods Imported from Third Countries' (1986), YEL 159, p. 167.
[3] Case 193/85, [1987] ECR 2085.

principles underlying the Common Customs Tariff and the Common Commercial Policy, which are intended to ensure both uniform treatment of goods imported from third countries and to enable such goods to circulate freely within the Community once they have been legitimately imported, to hold that the Treaty prohibitions on discriminatory and protective internal taxation under Article 95 must also apply to such goods.

The second distinctive feature of the rules on internal taxation is that, according to the usual definition, internal taxation comprises financial charges within a general system applying systematically to domestic and imported products according to the same criteria.[4] There is, therefore, nothing inherently offensive to Community law in its being imposed: it only breaches Community law to the extent that it discriminates against products imported from other Member States or it protects domestic production, as is reflected in the wording of Article 95 itself. In this it differs from the prohibition of charges equivalent to customs duties and the prohibition of measures equivalent to quantitative restrictions where, as has been seen with regard to the former and as will be seen with regard to the latter, it is not necessary to show a discriminatory effect.

The final difference between Article 95 on internal taxation and the other free-movement-of-goods rules is that, whilst there is an express requirement to eliminate customs duties and charges having equivalent effects on exports[5] as well as on imports, and there is an express requirement to eliminate quantitative restrictions and measures having equivalent effect on exports[6] as well as on imports, Article 95, by referring in terms to taxation on 'the products of other Member States', appears to relate only to imports. The way in which it has been extended to exports will be considered in the last section of this Chapter, but it may be observed at this stage that the European Court has held that the principles underlying Article 95 may also be applied to exports,[7] that is, internal taxation which discriminates against exports is regarded as being in breach of the Treaty.

Concepts of Discrimination and Indirect Protection

Two distinct requirements are contained in the first two paragraphs of Article 95 of the EEC Treaty. The first paragraph states that 'no Member State shall impose, directly or indirectly, on the products of other

---

[4] See e.g. *Capolongo* v. *Maya*, Case 77/72, [1973] ECR 611.
[5] Art. 16.
[6] Art. 34.
[7] *Statenskontrol* v. *Larsen*, Case 142/77, [1978] ECR 1543.

Member States any internal taxation of any kind in excess of that imposed directly or indirectly on similar domestic products', and the second states that 'no Member State shall impose on the products of other Member States any internal taxation of such a nature as to afford indirect protection to other products'. The difference between their consequences was noted at an early stage in *Fink-Frucht* v. *HZA München-Landsbergerstrasse,*[8] where it was said that whilst the first paragraph only prohibits taxation in so far as it exceeds a clearly defined level, the second paragraph is based on the protective effect of the taxation in question to the exclusion of any exact standard of reference. The ease or otherwise of the calculation will depend on how close the relationship is between the competing domestic and imported goods at issue.

This leads on to what might be termed the material difference between the two paragraphs in question. In general terms, the first paragraph is regarded as relating to the situation where the imported and domestic products are the same or so similar as to be treated the same way, and the second paragraph relates to the situation where the products are not the same but they may nevertheless be regarded as competing in the same market.[9] This is an area of the law where alcoholic beverages have loomed large, no doubt because many governments tax them heavily for social or revenue-raising reasons. In the matter of such drinks, similarity may be deduced from, *inter alia*, method of manufacture, taste, strength, and organoleptic qualities.[10]

Hence, similarity has been found between whisky and gin, on the one hand, and cognac and armagnac on the other,[11] between fruit wine and wine,[12] and between sparkling wine matured in the cask and sparkling wine matured in the bottle.[13]

By way of contrast, what is perhaps the most complex analysis of what constitutes competing, rather than similar, products is to be found in the comparison of wine and beer in *Commission* v. *United Kingdom,*[14] where it was held that, in order to determine the existence of a competitive relationship, it was necessary to consider not only the present state of the market, but also possible developments regarding the free movement of goods within the Community 'and the further potential for the substitution of products for one another which might be revealed by intensification of trade, so as fully to develop the complementary features of the economies of the Member States'. It was

---

[8] Case 27/67, [1968] ECR 223.
[9] See, *Commission* v. *France*, Case 168/78, [1980] ECR 347.
[10] *Commission* v. *Denmark*, Case 106/84, [1986] ECR 833.
[11] See n. 9 above.
[12] See n. 10 above.
[13] *Commission* v. *Italy*, Case 278/83, [1985] ECR 2503.
[14] Case 170/78, [1983] ECR 2265.

further pointed out that, for the purpose of measuring the possible degree of substitution between wine and beer, attention should not be confined to consumer habits in a Member State or in a given region. Those habits should not be regarded as immutable, and a Member State's tax policy must not, therefore, crystallize given consumer habits. Working out the basis on which a comparison could be made between the tax burden on wine and the burden on beer was, however, more difficult. After requesting further information, the Court concluded that the competitive relationship must be established by reference to the lightest and cheapest varieties of wine, and that fiscal comparisons should be made by reference to the alcoholic strength or to the price of the two beverages in question. In the result the relative tax burden on wine in the United Kingdom was reduced, and it would appear that consumption of wine has increased—but whether one is the cause of the other is not for the lawyer to say.

The question of whether products compete with each other arises in other areas of Community law, notably in determining the relevant market in the context of anti-competitive conduct under Articles 85 and 86,[15] and it has to be said that the case-law is not wholly consistent as between these different areas. To take the simple example of bananas, in the context of Article 95 it was held that they compete with apples, peaches, and the like, so that Italian taxation which bore more heavily on bananas than on other fruit breached Article 95;[16] yet in the context of an alleged abuse of a dominant position in the market in bananas, it has been held that they constituted a market separate from that for other fruit.[17]

There remains the problem of whether it is discriminatory or protective to tax an imported product for which there is no domestic equivalent. To pose the question in this way in effect answers it, since if there is nothing to protect and nothing to discriminate in favour of, there cannot be a breach of Article 95. This was the view taken by the European Court in *Fink-Frucht* v. *HZA München-Landsbergerstrasse*,[18] which involved the import of Italian sweet peppers into Germany where they were not grown commercially. It was stated categorically that Article 95 does not prohibit Member States from imposing internal taxation on imported products when there is no similar domestic product, or any other domestic products capable of being protected.

It is, however, notorious that Member States which do not produce motor cars, for example, tend to tax them more heavily than do producer States. Whether this is a breach of Community law depends, it

---

[15] See p. 236 below.
[16] *Cooperative Co-Frutta*, Case 193/85, [1987] ECR 2085.
[17] *United Brands* v. *Commission*, Case 27/76, [1978] ECR 207.
[18] See n. 8 above.

may be suggested, on whether it really is internal taxation, the definition of which requires the charge to fall within a general system applying systematically to domestic and imported products according to the same criteria.[19] If the tax, by reason of its rate or basis of charge, falls outside the generally applied system then, since it will apply only to imported goods, it may well constitute a charge equivalent to a customs duty on import.

Finally there is one important factor which both substantive paragraphs of Article 95 have in common. Under the third paragraph, any national provisions which breached Article 95 had to be repealed by the beginning of the second stage of the transitional period, that is, 1 January 1962, and it has long been held that at least from that date both main paragraphs produce direct effects and create individual rights which national courts must protect.[20]

Prohibited conduct

RATES OF TAX

Whilst it is obviously unlawful to impose a different rate of tax on an identical product simply because it is imported, such a blatant breach of Article 95 is rarely, if ever, encountered. Much more common is the situation where different rates of tax are imposed on products between which there are some differences, and the real argument will be over whether the products in question are sufficiently similar or compete with each other so as to trigger the application of one of the paragraphs of Article 95, and even then it must be shown that the difference in treatment operates against imports. Hence, in *John Walker*,[21] which involved Danish taxation of spirits, although virtually all the relevant imports fell into the higher band of duty, it was shown that a substantial volume of Danish production also fell into that category, so that it could not be said that the difference in treatment discriminated against imports. On the other hand, French legislation which imposed a higher duty on grain-based spirits than on fruit-based spirits did breach Community law, since the grain-based spirits (whisky, gin, and so on) were imported, and French production was of fruit-based spirits.[22] Similarly, UK taxation of wine at a higher rate than beer offended against Article 95 on the basis that wine was an imported product and

[19] See n. 4 above.
[20] *Lütticke* v. *HZA Saarlouis*, Case 57/65, [1966] ECR 205 with regard to the first paragraph, *Fink-Frucht* v. *HZA München-Landbergerstrasse*, Case 27/67, [1968] ECR 223 with regard to the second paragraph.
[21] Case 243/84, [1986] ECR 875.
[22] See n. 9 above.

beer was a domestic product,[23] as did Italian taxation of sparkling wine fermented in the bottle at a different rate from that fermented in the cask, when the result was that a higher rate of duty was paid by French champagne.[24] So also was it a breach of Article 95 for Italy to tax bananas at a higher rate than apples and peaches when bananas were largely imported but apples and peaches were home-grown.[25]

In comparing the tax burden on imports and domestic products, it is now clear that it is only tax payments as such on the domestic product which may be taken into account. This appears from *HZA Flensburg* v. *Andresen*,[26] where the German tax on imported spirits was intended both to compensate the internal tax element and the payment made in Germany as a contribution to the running costs of the German alcohol monopoly. It was held that the latter was not internal taxation, and therefore could not be taken into account in determining whether the tax charged on imports was discriminatory.

Particular problems arise with regard to graduated scales of taxation. It may be that the graduations themselves amount to discrimination, as with the the French system of taxation of cars by reference to the engine size. It emerged that the highest rate applied to vehicles of a power which were not manufactured in France, so that it applied only to imports; it was therefore held to breach Article 95.[27] A more delicate situation arose in *Bobie* v. *HZA Aachen-Nord*,[28] which involved the German system of taxation of beer, which was designed to benefit small-scale, specialist producers. Essentially, the small-scale producer paid a lower percentage-rate of duty (and would have a lower volume on which to pay it) and the large-scale producer paid a higher percentage-rate (on, by definition, a higher volume of production).

The system provided for a median rate to be paid on imports. It was, however, argued that if beer was imported into Germany produced by a small-scale Belgian brewery, the application of the median rate would mean that a higher rate of tax would be paid than would be payable by a small-scale German producer. The Court agreed with this argument, and held that discrimination against importers must be avoided, and if it was not possible administratively to apply the graduated scale to imports (because of the difficulty of obtaining production figures), then the lowest rate must be applied to all imports, as the only way of

[23] *Commission* v. *United Kingdon*, Case 170/78, [1983] ECR 2265.
[24] See n. 13 above.
[25] See n. 16 above.
[26] Case 4/81, [1981] ECR 2835.
[27] *Humblot*, Case 112/84, [1985] ECR 1367. But contrast *Commission* v. *Greece*, Case C–132/88 (5 Apr. 1990), where the highest rate of tax applied to cars of an engine size not manufactured in Greece, but the next two bands down also comprised only imported cars, and the banding was held legitimate.
[28] Case 127/75, [1976] ECR 1079.

ensuring that there was no possible discrimination. This approach could, of course, mean that imported goods are treated more favourably than domestic goods, but in this area of Community law it is clearly established that reverse discrimination is not objectionable.[29]

BASIS OF ASSESSMENT

Discrimination may involve not just the rates of taxation, but also the way in which the tax is assessed. An example may be found in *FOR* v. *VKS*,[30] where Italian machinery was imported into Germany and installed in a factory there. The German authorities charged what was then turnover-equalization tax both on the import and on the installation, and they included the value of the machinery again in the second calculation. In effect, therefore, tax was charged twice on the machinery, whereas it was clear that within Germany there would have been just one taxable operation at the time of the installation. It was held that the imported machinery must be taxed on the same basis as German machinery, and tax should therefore be charged on the basis of one taxable operation.

OTHER ASPECTS

Other features of a tax system may well affect the relative tax burden of imported and domestic products. If different deductions were allowed, this would obviously contravene the Treaty rules, but even to allow what are apparently the same deductions may also breach Article 95 if the different situation of an importer and of a domestic producer with regard to the national tax system mean that the ultimate burden is in fact different.[31] Similarly, to require payment from importers immediately or within a very short period when domestic taxpayers are allowed a longer period is regarded as imposing an additional burden on imported products.[32]

In order to avoid indirect discrimination or protection, the scope of Article 95 has been extended beyond direct taxation of the goods to taxation of services ancillary to the supply of the goods. This became apparent in *Schöttle* v. *FZA Freudenstadt*,[33] in the context of a German tax on the transport of goods by road. It was held that if the tax was charged on a different basis for the international carriage of goods and for purely domestic transport, and, for example, in certain circumstances the

---

[29] *Peureux* v. *Directeur des Services Fiscaux de la Haute-Sâone*, Case 86/78, [1979] ECR 897.
[30] Case 54/72, [1973] ECR 193.
[31] *Pabst & Richarz* v. *HZA Oldenburg*, Case 17/81, [1982] ECR 1331.
[32] *Commission* v. *Ireland*, Case 55/79, [1980] ECR 481.
[33] Case 20/76, ECR 247.

national product might be transported the same distance without being subject to the tax, while transport of an imported product would be subject to the tax simply because the border had been crossed, then there would be a breach of Article 95. The Court stated that it was irrelevant that, as a tax on the international transport of goods by road, it applied also to exports from Germany; the comparison was between the taxation of goods from other Member states and the taxation of similar domestic products in that Member State. Indeed, although the Court did not discuss the point, it may be suggested that to impose a heavier burden on goods exported from Germany than on those sold on the domestic market would itself be a breach of the principles underlying Article 95 which have been held to apply also to exports.[34]

Justifiable Difference in Treatment

Community law does not in principle prohibit domestic tax laws from imposing or permitting different rates of tax on different products, or indeed on products which may serve similar economic ends.[35] What it does object to is differential taxation of similar or competing products where the category of goods paying the higher rate is composed largely or exclusively of imported goods. Examples which have already been given include the French taxation of cars on the basis of engine size,[36] the French distinction between grain-based spirits and fruit-based spirits,[37] and the Italian distinction between sparkling wine fermented in bottle and in cask.[38]

There is, however, a line of case-law which accepts that higher taxation may coincide with a category of products which is largely imported where such differentiation is on the basis of objective criteria, such as the nature of the raw materials used or the production processes employed, where it pursues economic-policy objectives which are themselves compatible with the requirements of Community law, and where the detailed rules are such as to avoid any form of discrimination, direct or indirect, with regard to imports from other Member States, or any form of protection of competing domestic products.[39] It may be wondered how the last requirement may be reconciled with higher taxation affecting only imports. The cases involved Italian taxation of

---

[34] See n. 7 above.
[35] *Commission* v. *Italy*, Case 21/79, [1980] ECR 1.
[36] *Humblot*, Case 112/84, [1985] ECR 1367.
[37] See n. 9 above.
[38] See n. 13 above.
[39] *Chemical Farmaceutici* v. *DAF*, Case 140/79, [1981] ECR 1 at p. 15, *Vinal* v. *Orbat*, Case 46/80, [1981] ECR 77 at p. 93. The principle was reaffirmed in *Commission* v. *Greece*, Case C–132/88, (5 Apr. 1990).

denatured synthetic alcohol (that is, alcohol manufactured from petroleum derivatives) at a higher rate than denatured alcohol obtained by
fermentation (that is, alcohol maufactured from agricultural products).
The Court stated that this was a legitimate choice of industrial policy,
and that it could not be considered discriminatory since, on the one
hand, imports of agricultural alcohol from other Member States received
the same tax treatment as Italian agricultural alcohol and, on the other,
although the rate for synthetic alcohol had the effect of restraining the
importation of synthetic alcohol from other Member States, it had an
equivalent economic effect within Italy in so far as it also hampered the
establishment of profitable production of synthetic alcohol there.

While these statements are not easy to reconcile with the judgments
mentioned above—after all, the higher taxation of grain spirits in France
would presumably deter their production in that country—the core of
these decisions would appear to lie in the acceptance that the higher
taxation of synthetic alcohol represented 'a legitimate objective of
industrial policy'. In the light of the oil-supply crisis of the 1970s,
national measures which had the effect of limiting oil consumption were
no doubt looked upon with particular favour. There appear to have been
no subsequent examples of justifiable differentiation until 1990, when
the Court found that the Greek special consumption tax on cars, the
highest rate of which applied only to imported vehicles, nevertheless
did not constitute a measure which favoured Greek-produced cars.[40]

Relationship to the system of Value-Added Tax

While Article 95 is essentially negative in character, prohibiting certain
conduct on the part of Member States, Article 99, even as originally
drafted,[41] envisaged the possible harmonization of aspects of indirect
taxation. The most important consequence of this was the development
of the Community system of value-added tax, which is currently largely
regulated by the Sixth VAT Directive.[42] This sets out a common basis for
the tax but, in particular, leaves the rates to be fixed by the Member
States. Its essential feature is that a supplier of goods or services is liable
for tax assessed on the value of the product when he disposes of it, and
may set off against this liability the tax paid on the value of the product
when he acquired it, in other words the net liability is to pay tax on the
added value.

If it were a truly Community system, it would operate in this manner

---

[40] See n. 27 above.
[41] It was amended by the Single European Act to make it more specific, but it still requires
unanimity in the Council.
[42] Council Dir. 77/388 (OJ 1977, L 145/1).

even in trade between Member States, so that a trader liable for tax in one State could set off the tax paid in another Member State. However, there are obvious difficulties in establishing a clearing-house system between Member States, particularly when national rates of tax differ widely (the set-off could conceiveably be greater than the liability, for example), and so the value-added tax system only operates in its classic form in trade within a Member State. In trade between Member States, therefore, sale for export is exempt from the tax and qualifies for reimbursement of the tax paid, and import is a chargeable event. This means that in a transaction between taxable persons, the tax borne in the country of export is repaid, and tax is payable on the whole value at the rate applicable in the country of importation. The system is generally regarded as economically neutral, in that goods finally sold in a particular Member State will all have borne tax at the rate applicable in that Member State whatever their origin, although it inevitably means that importation and exportation involve considerable amounts of paperwork, and its very existence appears to contradict the concept of 'an area without internal frontiers' envisaged in Article 8A of the EEC Treaty.

However economically neutral it may be for commercial transactions, legal problems have arisen from the fact that import is always a chargeable event whatever the status of the importer, so that VAT may be levied where the goods were not originally intended for export or where the goods were acquired second-hand. This was the background to the *Schul* cases,[43] where in two judgments in references in the same national action the Court endeavoured to reconcile this aspect of the VAT system with the requirements of Article 95. The dispute involved the importation into the Netherlands of a boat purchased second-hand in France. The importer was charged VAT on the import, under Dutch legislation giving effect to the Directive, even though no VAT would have been payable on a second-hand sale in the Netherlands.

At first sight, this might appear to be a clear breach of Article 95 but, quite apart from the fact that such a finding would have upset an essential element of the VAT legislation, the European Court started from a subtly different perspective: it took the view that, even though no VAT may be charged on the sale of a second-hand boat in the Netherlands, the second-hand price would reflect a residual element of the VAT paid when it was new, and that therefore the Community legislation should, if possible, be interpreted in such a way as to ensure that a second-hand boat imported into the Netherlands from another Member State reflected that same element. In effect, the French VAT element had to be replaced by a corresponding Dutch element. To do

---

[43] *Schul* v. *Inspecteur der Invoerrechten*, Cases 15/81 and 47/84, [1982] ECR 1409 and [1985] ECR 1491.

this, it was held that in calculating the value of the boat for tax purposes on importation, an element reflecting the French VAT paid when the boat was new should be deducted—it was suggested that this should be the same proportion of the second-hand price as the original VAT had been of the new price (but it could not exceed the VAT actually paid if the second-hand price was higher than the new price, which appears to have been the situation in this case). The Dutch VAT should then be calculated on the second-hand price minus the residual French VAT. Furthermore, the residual French VAT (not exceeding the amount actually paid) should then be deducted from the Dutch VAT due. The overall effect should be a tax burden on the boat the same as that borne by a boat which had originally been bought in the Netherlands.

This may seem an operation of some complexity, and indeed the Court acknowledged that it was doing something that should have been done by legislation. The case does, however serve to highlight the point that, for the purposes of Article 95, it is not the fact that a charge is levied by reason of importation which is objectionable but the fact that the charge discriminates against imports or protects domestic products.

Exports

As has already been mentioned, Article 95 is silent with regard to exports. Since there is, however, an express provision with regard to charges equivalent to customs duties in Article 16, it might have been wondered whether that might be the appropriate measure to deal with fiscal discrimination against exports. However, with one lapse, the European Court has also applied to exports its view that the same duty cannot both be equivalent to a customs duty and part of a scheme of internal taxation. The point first arose in *Demag* v. *HZA Duisburg-Sud*,[44] when Germany introduced a 'special turnover tax' on exports, apparently in an attempt to reduce its balance-of-payments surplus with the rest of the Community. It was claimed that this was a charge equivalent to a customs duty on exports, but the Court repeated the need to distinguish such charges from internal taxation, and held that the German tax in fact fell within the system of internal taxation (it amounted to a removal of an exoneration from tax for exports), and therefore could not contravene Article 16.

The lapse occurred when the Court held in a subsequent judgment[45] that the same charge on exports could both breach Article 16 and the principles underlying Article 95—but at least it was the first time the possibility of a breach of those principles by a charge on exports had

---

[44] Case 27/74, [1974] ECR 1307.
[45] *Hulst* v. *Produktschap voor Siergewassen*, Case 51/74, [1975] ECR 79.

been recognized. The problem was finally resolved in *Statenskontrol* v. *Larsen*,[46] where it was said that the aim of the Treaty was to guarantee generally the neutrality of systems of internal taxation with regard to intra-Community trade whenever an economic transaction going beyond the frontiers of a Member State at the same time constituted the chargeable event giving rise to a fiscal charge within the context of such a system. It was therefore necessary, according to the Court, to interpret Article 95 as meaning that the rule against discrimination which forms the basis of that provision also applies when the export of a product constitutes such a chargeable event. The Court concluded that it would be incompatible with the structure of the tax provisions in the Treaty to allow Member States, in the absence of an express prohibition, to apply internal taxation in a discriminatory manner to products intended for export to other Member States. Here again, therefore, a legislative gap has been filled by the Court.

[46] See n. 7 above.

5

Quantitative Restrictions and Measures having Equivalent Effect: General Issues

Introduction—the Treaty provisions

In practice, the rules prohibiting quantitative restrictions and measures having equivalent effect in trade between Member States have emerged as the most general and most important of the Treaty provisions relating to the free movement of goods, and have given rise to a copious literature.[1] The structure of these provisions in many respect parallels that of those governing customs duties and charges having equivalent effect, and like those rules they are expressly stated to apply not only to Community goods but also to third-country goods in free circulation in the Community by virtue of Article 9(2).[2] Article 30 sets out the basic prohibition of quantitative restrictions and charges having equivalent effect on imports, and Article 34(1) does the same for exports. A standstill was imposed by Article 31(1), which prohibited Member States from introducing any new quantitative restrictions and charges having equivalent effect, and Article 32(1), which prohibited making existing quotas and charges having equivalent effect more restrictive. With regard to the elimination of existing restrictions and measures having equivalent effect, Article 32(2) required those on imports to be abolished by the end of the transitional period, under a timetable set out in Article 33, and Article 34(2) required those on exports to be abolished by the end of the first stage of the transitional period, that is, 1 January 1962.

As in the context of customs duties and charges having equivalent effect, Article 33(7) gave the Commission original power to issue directives establishing the procedure and timetable for the abolition of measures equivalent to quotas (a term which in this part of the Treaty appears to be interchangeable with 'quantitative restrictions'); Directive 70/50[3] issued under this power retains some importance, and will be discussed in the next Chapter.

[1] The major works in English are Gormley, *Prohibiting Restrictions on Trade within the EEC* (1985) and Oliver, *Free Movement of Goods in the EEC* (2nd edn., 1988).
[2] See *Donckerwolcke* v. *Procureur de la République, Lille*, Case 41/76, [1976] ECR 1921.
[3] JO 1970, L 13/29.

The texts of Articles 31(2) and 33(6) take as their starting point the degree of liberalization already achieved pursuant to a 1955 decision of the Council of the Organization for European Economic Co-operation (now the Organization for Economic Co-operation and Development) to raise the basic minimum level of liberalization to 90 per cent of the value of imports. This meant that there was relatively little to be done to eliminate quotas as such pursuant to the EEC Treaty, and the 1966 Acceleration Decision[4] recorded that quotas had already disappeared in trade between Member States. So far as the Treaty timetable is concerned, the standstill provision, like that relating to customs duties and charges having equivalent effect, was held to be directly effective in *Salgoil* v. *Italian Ministry of Foreign Trade*,[5] but the requirement to eliminate existing restrictions with regard to imports has been held to produce enforceable individual rights only since the end of the transitional period.[6]

It should finally be observed that this section of the Treaty contains two provisions, Articles 36 and 37, which have no parallel in the rules on customs duties and charges having equivalent effect. Article 36 permits restrictions on imports, exports, or goods in transit if they are justified on a number of specified grounds, provided they do not constitute a means of arbitrary discrimination or a disguised restriction on trade between Member States. The implications of this will be considered in later Chapters of this book, but the fact that there is no parallel justification for charges equivalent to customs duties means that, as has been seen, while it may be justified to carry out an inspection of imported or exported goods under national law on grounds of protection of health, to charge for such an inspection will always be unlawful as a charge equivalent to a customs duty.[7]

Article 37, on the other hand, requires State monopolies of a commercial character to be 'adjusted' so as to ensure that no discrimination exists between nationals of Member States with regard to the conditions under which goods are procured and marketed. The fact that it is included in this part of the Treaty has led the Court to interpret it as a specific aspect of the requirement to abolish quantitative restrictions and measures having equivalent effect,[8] so that, in effect, a national monopoly cannot be a monopoly with regard to imports or exports.

---

[4] Council Dec. of 26 July 1966 (JO 1966, p. 2971/66).
[5] Case 13/68, [1968] ECR 453.
[6] See n. 2 above.
[7] See e.g. *Denkavit Futtermittel*, Case 251/78, [1979] ECR 3369.
[8] *Pubblico Ministero* v. *Manghera*, Case 59/75, [1976] ECR 91.

Quotas as such

For the reasons mentioned above, quotas as such have not been encountered in internal Community trade since the 1960s, except in the context of Accession transitional arrangements for new Member States.

There are, nevertheless, instances where it has been held that a national provision constituted a quantitative restriction as such and not merely a measure equivalent thereto, most notably in *R.* v. *Henn and Darby*.[9] There, a prohibition on the import of indecent or obscene articles into the United Kingdom was held to be a quantitative restriction on imports (albeit justified under Article 36), a finding which takes on a certain irony in view of the fact that in the English Court of Appeal (Criminal Division) it had been suggested that where there was a total prohibition this could not be a 'quantitative' restriction, because there was no restriction by reference to a quantity.[10] The European Court's holding that a total prohibition on imports may amount to a quantitative restriction is supported by the wording of Article 36 itself, which refers to 'prohibitions or restrictions' on imports, exports, or goods in transit.

While quotas in trade between Member States may have disappeared, it should not be forgotten that under the Common Commercial Policy, Community legislation still accords different quotas to different Member States with regard to goods imported from third countries,[11] or may authorize Member States to maintain national measures of commercial policy.[12] To the extent that it benefits from such a quota,[13] or from such an authorization,[14] a Member State may request the Commission to take a decision under Article 115 of the EEC Treaty permitting that State not to grant Community treatment to goods in free circulation in another Member State if their import would threaten or breach that quota or measure. To that extent, therefore, quotas in trade with third countries may be reflected by a prohibition of import into a Member State of goods in free circulation in the Community, but this may only be done by virtue of a Commission decision under Article 115 which, according to the Court, should only be given for serious reasons and for a limited period, and provided the measures chosen are those which will cause the least disruption of trade between the Member States.[15]

---

[9] Case 34/79, [1979] ECR 3795.
[10] [1978] 3 All ER 1190, per Lord Widgery, CJ.
[11] See p. 17 above.
[12] See p. 14 above.
[13] *Tezi Textiel* v. *Commission*, Case 59/84, [1986] ECR 887.
[14] *Cayrol* v. *Rivoira*, Case 52/77, [1977] ECR 2261.
[15] See n. 13 above.

Measures Equivalent to Quantitative Restrictions

DEFINITION OF THE CONCEPT

Although the prohibition on measures equivalent to quantitative restrictions was routinely reproduced in regulations enacted in the 1960s creating common organizations of agricultural markets,[16] it would appear that the European Court was not faced with defining the concept until its judgment in *Procureur du Roi* v. *Dassonville*.[17] The definition there given has been repeated word-for-word ever since: 'All trading rules enacted by Member States which are capable of hindering, directly or indirectly, actually or potentially, intra-Community trade are to be considered as measures having an effect equivalent to quantitative restrictions.'

This is self-evidently a very wide statement, which in its reference to indirect and potential effect on trade between Member States borrows from the wording of the first judgment on the competition rules of the Treaty, *Consten and Grundig* v. *Commission*.[18] There is, however, one respect in which the *Dassonville* test is relatively narrow, which is in its reference to 'trading rules'. While this avoids fiscal measures being included in the otherwise compendious concept of a measure equivalent to a quantitative restriction—it had already been held that internal taxation could not be classified as such a measure,[19] and was soon held that a charge equivalent to a customs duty could not also be a measure equivalent to a quantitative restriction[20]—it has to be said that other financial or exchange-control restrictions may be regarded as constituting such measures. The matter came to light in *Commission* v. *Italy*,[21] in relation to an import deposit scheme. Under Italian law, in order to deter currency speculation, importers paying for goods in advance of their release from customs clearance had to lodge an interest-free security or guarantee. Although this involved a payment to the public authorities by reason of importation, it was held that it could not be a charge equivalent to a customs duty because the money was eventually returned to the importer. Since it was undeniably a hindrance to trade, however, it was classified as a measure equivalent to a quantitative restriction.

The essence of the *Dassonville* test is that, as a matter of law, a

[16] A practice described by Advocate General Warner in his Opinion in *Ramel* v. *Receveur des Douanes*, Cases 80 and 81/77, [1978] ECR 927 as otiose once the transitional period had ended and the Treaty provisions had been held to be of direct effect.
[17] Case 8/74, [1974] ECR 837.
[18] Cases 56 and 58/64, [1966] ECR 299.
[19] *Fink-Frucht* v. *HZA München-Landsbergerstrasse*, Case 27/67, [1968] ECR 223.
[20] *Ianelli and Volpi* v. *Meroni*, Case 74/76, [1977] ECR 557.
[21] Case 95/81, [1982] ECR 2187.

hindrance to trade might occur, and the purpose or intent behind the measure does not seem to be relevant. Indeed, taken at face value, the test would in itself prohibit any difference in national legislation which had the effect that goods sold in one Member State could not be sold in another Member State. However, without pre-empting the debate as to how far, if at all, a measure must be discriminatory to be prohibited as being equivalent to a quantitative restriction,[22] it may be noted that *Dassonville* itself was concerned with a measure affecting only imports (Belgian rules concerning certificates of origin for imported Scotch whisky), and that when the Court openly addressed the question of measures applying equally to imported and domestic products in the *Cassis de Dijon* case,[23] it in effect added a number of limitations to the basic rule in *Dassonville*.[24]

WHAT ARE 'MEASURES'?

To answer this question it is necessary to consider whether Articles 30 and 34 relate only to legislation or to other conduct as well, and whether they bind only the State and public authorities or extend also to other subjects of the law. These considerations are to some extent interrelated: does the fact that Articles 30 and 34 may restrict the use of legal rights by individuals mean that they bind individuals or that they bind the State which created the legal rules?[25] The problem has arisen particularly in the context of the exercise of intellectual and industrial property rights,[26] and was starkly presented in the leading cases which established the principle that the Treaty rules impose on holders of industrial property rights the duty not to use those rights so as to prevent the importation into a Member State of goods lawfully marketed in another Member State by the holder of the property right himself or with his consent.[27] The bulk of the imports in question were from the United Kingdom to the Netherlands, and Article 42(2) of the 1972 Act of Accession provided that, in trade between the Community as originally constituted and the new Member States, existing measures equivalent to quantitative restrictions on imports and exports should be abolished by 1 January 1975 (that is, after the date of the judgments, which were delivered in 1974). The national court therefore asked whether the Treaty rules could be invoked before that date with regard to imports originating in the United Kingdom. The Commission argued that the measure equivalent

---

[22] See p. 60 below.
[23] *Rewe* v. *Bundesmonopolverwaltung für Branntwein*, Case 120/78, [1979] ECR 649.
[24] See p. 65
[25] See Gormley, op. cit., p. 262, Oliver, op cit., p. 55.
[26] The substance of which is treated in Part III of this book.
[27] *Centrafarm* v. *Sterling Drug*, Case 15/74, [1974] ECR 1147; *Centraform* v. *Winthrop*, Case 16/74, [1974] ECR 1183.

to a quantitative restriction would be a judgment of a Dutch court enforcing the industrial property rights, which would be a 'new' measure, not an existing one, and therefore not protected by Article 42(2).[28] Advocate General Trabucchi, on the other hand, stated in his Opinion that it was the Dutch legislation which constituted the measure having equivalent effect, and that it could not be required to be eliminated before 1975.[29] The response given by the European Court reflects neither of these views: it stated that the timetable in Article 42(2)

can only refer to those measures having an effect equivalent to quantitative restrictions which, as between the original Member States, had to be abolished at the end of the transitional period. . . . It therefore appears that art.42 of the Act of Accession has no effect upon prohibitions on importation arising from national legislation concerning industrial and commercial property.[30]

Apart from the obvious implication that there have, from the outset, been different types of measure equivalent to a quantitative restriction, this statement can only be understood in the light of one of the Court's earlier decisions on industrial property rights, *Deutsche Grammophon* v. *Metro-SB-Grossmärkte*,[31] in which it has been held that it was not the existence of industrial property rights which might conflict with the Treaty, but their exercise, and hence it would appear that in its 1974 judgments in the *Centrafarm* cases the Court was referring in reality to prohibitions upon importations arising from the exercise of industrial property rights under national legislation. If this is the case, the distinction the Court was making was between measures having equivalent effect to quantitative restrictions for which Member States as such are responsible, and measures which are in reality acts of individuals (albeit involving the use of legal remedies).[32]

While the Court has consistently maintained its case-law on the exercise of industrial and intellectual property rights, its subsequent dicta in other areas are not always easy to reconcile. In *Dansk Supermarked* v. *Imerco*,[33] in the context of alleged unfair trading practices, it was stated that 'it is impossible in any circumstances for agreements between individuals to derogate from the mandatory provisions of the Treaty on the free movement of goods'. On the other hand, in *Officier van Justitie* v. *Van de Haar*,[34] a comparison was made between Articles 30 and 85[35]in which it was suggested that the competition rules are addressed to undertakings and associations of undertakings, whereas the free-movement-of-goods rules seek to eliminate measures taken by Member States, and a similar view was expressed in *Vlaamse Reisbureaus*.[36]

---

[28] [1974] ECR, pp. 1158–9, 1191.

[29] [1974] ECR, pp. 1178–9.

[30] [1974] ECR, pp. 1166–7, 1197–8.

[31] Case 78/70, ECR 487.

[32] See Usher, 'Duties imposed on individuals under the EEC Treaty' in Lasok (ed.), *Fundamental Duties* (1980), pp. 148–50.

[33] Case 58/80, [1981] ECR 181.

[34] Cases 177 and 178/82, [1984] ECR 1797.

[35] See p. 217 below.

[36] Case 311/85, [1987] ECR.

It may be suggested that these views were obiter, particularly in the second case, which involved the application of the competition rules to a supply of services, and that the situation remains that actions by an individual may be subject to Articles 30 and 34, at least where they involve the use of legal rights and remedies. However, an individual acting outside a legal context is almost certainly not subject to those rules, as appears from *Apple and Pear Development Council* v. *Lewis*.[37] It was there indicated that, whilst it might be a breach of Article 30 for a publicly financed body to promote national products on the basis of their national origin, greater liberty could be enjoyed by producers themselves or producers' associations of a voluntary character with regard to their advertising. The other necessary consequence of this, however, is that action by, or promoted by, the public authorities may be regarded as a measure equivalent to a quantitative restriction even though it does not take the form of legislation.

Furthermore, the actions of an association or organization which controls the activities of a particular profession may be subject to Articles 30 and 34, even if it is not a public authority and its actions are not legislative in nature. This results from *R.* v. *Royal Pharmaceutical Society*,[38] which concerned the compatibility with Article 30 of rules of the Society which required pharmacists, when faced with a prescription naming a branded medicine, to supply only that branded product, and not a generic equivalent. It was held that those rules did breach Article 30, since they amounted to a restriction on the importation of equivalent drugs from other Member States (although they were held to be justified under Article 36). The reason why they were found to be measures equivalent to quantitative restrictions would appear to be that pharmacists had little option but to observe the rules, and those rules governed the activities of the whole profession, so the effect was like that of action by the public authorities.

PROHIBITED MEASURES

Certain parallels can be traced between charges equivalent to customs duties and measures equivalent to quantitative restrictions. So, just as in *Cadsky*,[39] to charge for a quality-control inspection carried out only on exports was held to be a charge equivalent to a customs duty on exports, so also in *Procureur de la République, Besançon* v. *Bouhelier*,[40] actually to carry out a quality control only on exports, and not on goods sold on the domestic market, was held to be a measure equivalent to a quantitative restriction on exports. Again, just as a minimal charge may be

---

[37] Case 222/82, [1983] ECR 4083.
[38] 18 May 1989.
[39] *Cadsky* v. *Istituto Nazionale per il Commercio Estero*, Case 63/74, [1975] ECR 281.
[40] Case 53/76, [1977] ECR 197.

prohibited as equivalent to a customs duty,[41] so in *International Fruit* v. *Produktschap voor Groenten en Fruit*,[42] a requirement to obtain an import licence which would be granted automatically in trade with other Member States was held to be equivalent to a quantitative restriction because of the inconvenience involved in applying for it, and the same view has been taken with regard to export licences which were said to be granted automatically in trade with other Member States.[43]

The fact that statistically imports have not been reduced does not appear to be relevant, given that the test is the legal one of potential to hinder trade, as is shown in the 'Buy Irish' case.[44] This involved a government-supported campaign in Ireland to persuade people to buy Irish goods (and incidentally confirms that action by the public authorities falling short of legislation may breach Article 30). Such a promotion of national products is regarded as a potential restriction on imports, but the Irish government argued that in fact the volume of imports had increased during the campaign, so that there was no breach of Article 30. The answer of the European Court was that imports might have increased even more without the campaign! More generally, it is a measure equivalent to a quantitative restriction for a body established by the public authorities and financed by a compulsory charge to promote national products on the basis of their national origin, although it is apparently permissible to promote goods typical of national production by reference to their inherent virtues.[45]

While it is obviously discriminatory to require an indication of origin only on imported goods,[46] the very fact of requiring indications of origin has been held to discriminate against imports on the basis that it will reinforce consumers' natural preference for domestic products.[47] *A fortiori*, a measure which is not just an encouragement but a requirement to buy the national product will breach Article 30, as in *Campus Oil*.[48] There, the Irish government required that importers of petroleum products should purchase a certain proportion of their supplies from Ireland's one and only oil refinery.[49] Other measures may equally

---

[41] *Commission* v. *Italy*, Case 24/68, [1969] ECR 193.

[42] Cases 51 and 54/71, [1971] ECR 1116.

[43] *Commission* v. *France*, Case 68/76, [1977] ECR 515. However, in subsequent national proceedings, in which the Conseil d'État awarded damages against the relevant minister, it was claimed that exports to Italy had in fact been prevented (*Alivar*, *Conseil d'État*, 23 Mar. 1984).

[44] *Commision* v. *Ireland*, Case 249/81, [1982] ECR 4005.

[45] See n. 37 above.

[46] *Commission* v. *Ireland*, Case 113/80, [1982] ECR 1625.

[47] *Commission* v. *United Kingdon*, Case 207/83, [1985] ECR 1201. It may be wondered how realistic that view is when, in the United, certain well-known electrical retailers use Japanese-sounding names on their 'own brand' goods.

[48] Case 72/83, [1984] ECR 2727.

[49] Although this measure was ultimately held to be justified under Article 36. See p. 83 below.

effectively, though less obviously, discriminate against imports, such as a requirement to have a local agent in the State of import before the product may be sold there.[50] A particularly striking example is *Commission* v. *Ireland*.[51] This involved a public works contract for a water supply which required tenderers to bid on the basis of using pipes meeting a particular Irish standard. The only pipes to be approved under the Irish standard were manufactured by a producer in Ireland, so the effect was to prevent foreign pipes being used. Whilst this was obviously discriminatory at one level, it could hardly be held that no standards at all had to be met, and the way the Court dealt with the problem was to hold that there was a breach of Article 30 to the extent that tenderers were prevented from proving that pipes imported from another Member State were of an equivalent standard.

Before turning in the next Chapter to consideration of the extent to which measures applying equally to domestic products and imported products may be prohibited as equivalent to quantitative restrictions, it may be noted that such measures were first discussed in the context of national price controls, and that the initial approach of the European Court was to search for indirect discrimination or protection. In *Tasca*,[52] in the context of Italian controls on the maximum price of sugar, it was stated that a maximum price might have an effect equivalent to a quantatitive restriction when it was fixed at a level such that the sale of imported products became, if not impossible, at least more difficult than that of domestic products. This would, in particular, be so where the price was fixed at such a low level that dealers wishing to import the products in question into the Member State concerned could do so only at a loss. The same approach, that is, to ask whether importation is more difficult or may only be undertaken at a loss, was taken in the context of price freezes, in a judgment delivered *after* the modern principles on other equally applicable measures had been established.[53] It may, therefore, be suggested that price-control cases represent a special category.

The question of minimum prices was encountered in *Van Tiggele*,[54] which involved Dutch legislation on the minimum price and profit margins of old genever. It was there said that imports may be impeded by such legislation where they either cannot be profitably marketed in the conditions laid down, or because the competitive advantage conferred by lower prices is cancelled out.[55]

On the other hand, price legislation is compatible with Community

---

[50] *Commission* v. *Germany*, Case 247/81, [1984] ECR 1111.
[51] Case 45/87, [1988] ECR 4929.
[52] Case 65/75, [1976] ECR 291.
[53] *Danis et al*, Cases 16–20/79, [1979] ECR 3327.
[54] Case 82/77, [1978] ECR 25.
[55] This approach was confirmed in *Cullet*, Case 231/83, [1985] ECR 305.

law where the legally enforced price is one freely chosen by the manufacturer or importer, as with the Belgian requirement to sell tobacco at the price appearing on the tax label.[56] However, this is not the case where, as occurred in France with regard to the price of books, the legally enforced price was not chosen by the individual importer but by the principal distributor.[57] This meant that any other importer could not charge the price in France that he considered appropriate in the light of his costs.

Limits on Prohibited Measures

At this stage it may be asked if there is any national legislation or conduct that could not be treated as being equivalent to a quantitative restriction, other than those falling under other Treaty provisions. The first indication that there were such limits was given in *Blesgen* v. *Ministre des Finances*,[58] in the context of a Belgian law prohibiting the offer for sale of spirits in public places. Whilst obviously this would reduce the overall consumption of spirits, the Court took the view that the measure had no connection with the importation of the products and was not of such a nature as to impede trade between Member States. In essence, it seems to have been regarded as a legitimate matter of social policy. The decision has been heavily criticized,[59] and it has been suggested that it would have been better for the Court to hold that the Belgian law did breach Article 30 but that it was justified on grounds of public policy or public health.[60] However, a similar approach was taken with regard to English Sunday-trading rules in *Torfaen Borough Council* v. *B&Q plc*,[61] where it was said that such rules reflected certain political and economic choices and were not designed to govern the patterns of trade between Member States. They would, therefore, not breach Article 30 unless their restrictive effects were disproportionate to their purpose. How these cases may be distinguished from other examples of equally applicable rules will be considered in the next Chapter, though it may be observed that the Commission in its submissions in the B&Q case suggested that measures which restrict the circumstances under which goods may be sold or used do not prevent the importation or marketing of goods from other Member States. Such an approach was expressly adopted by the Court in *Quietlynn and Richards* v. *Southend Borough Council*,[62] with regard to the licensing of sex establishments. It was held that national legislation prohibiting the sale of sex articles from unlicensed sex establishments 'does not constitute an

---

[56] *GB-Inno* v. *ATAB*, Case 13/77, [1977] ECR 2115.

[58] Case 75/8, [1982] ECR 1211.					[57] *Leclerc*, Case 229/83, [1985] ECR 1.

[60] See Gormley, op. cit., pp. 55–6 and 252.					[59] See Oliver, op. cit. pp. 157–9.

[61] 23 Nov. 1989.					[62] 11 July 1990.

absolute prohibition on the sale of the products in question, but merely a rule regarding their distribution, regulating the outlets through which the products may be marketed'. The Court then expressly followed *Blesgen*,[63] to hold that such a measure was not of such a nature as to impede trade between Member States. In principle it seems, therefore, that measures of social policy of this type will not be regarded as being equivalent to quantitative restrictions.

DIFFERENCE BETWEEN IMPORTS AND EXPORTS

It has been shown above that, so far as discriminatory measures are concerned, the concept of what is equivalent to a quantitative restriction is the same whether imports or exports are affected. However, while the rules on imports have gone on to be applied to equally applicable measures (and it is restrictions on imports that represent the real threat to the single Community market), the rules on exports have been held to apply only to measures which are actually aimed at exports. Otherwise, to put it very simply, any restriction on national production would run the risk of breaching Community law.

The point was first made in *Groenveld*,[64] with regard to Dutch legislation prohibiting sausage manufacturers from stocking or processing horsemeat, which obviously meant that they could not export horse-meat sausages. The Court, however, held that Article 34 concerned national measures which had as their specific object or effect the restriction of patterns of exports, and thereby the establishment of a difference between the domestic trade of a Member State and its export trade in such a way as to provide a particular advantage for national production or for the domestic market of the State in question. The same form of words has been repeated with regard to German legislation prohibiting night work in bakeries,[65] though that also raised the same kind of social policy issue as *Blesgen* and *B&Q*, and in the context of Dutch legislation on minimum standards for enclosures for fattening calves.[66]

---

[63] [1982] ECR 1211.
[64] Case 15/79, [1979] ECR 3409.
[65] *Oebel*, Case 155/80, [1981] ECR 1993.
[66] *Holdijk*, Cases 141 to 143/81, [1982] ECR 1299.

6

Quantitative Restrictions and Measures Having Equivalent Effect: Equally Applicable Measures

The Debate

There are generally said to be three main currents of thought with regard to the scope of the prohibition on measures equivalent to quantitative restrictions.[1] The narrow view, put forward in particular by German writers, is that only measures which discriminate against imports are prohibited, and that measures which apply equally to domestic and imported products (henceforth 'equally applicable' measures) could not fall within the scope of the prohibition. In its most restrictive form, it was argued that to be prohibited a measure had to be not only discriminatory but also act as a direct barrier to trade across frontiers.[2] The wider view, put forward initially by Professor VerLoren van Themaat,[3] who later became an Advocate General at the European Court, is that equally applicable measures fall in principle within the scope of Article 30 whenever they constitute an obstacle to imports or exports, unless they are justified under Article 36 or governed by some other provision of the Treaty.

The approach taken first by the Commission then by the Court falls somewhere in between, though the Commission's Directive 70/50[4] follows a a somewhat narrower view than the Court's *Cassis de Dijon* case-law.[5] In essence, the Commission Directive treats overtly discriminatory measures as prohibited, but provides that equally applicable measures are prohibited only where their restrictive effects are disproportionate, whereas the *Cassis de Dijon* judgment treats equally applic-

---

[1] Conveniently summarized in Oliver, op. cit., pp. 82–91, and Gormley, op. cit., pp. 8–19 and 262–5.

[2] Ehle and Meier, *EWG-Warenverkehr* (1971), p. 159 *et seq.*

[3] (1967) 15 SEW, 632.

[4] JO 1970, L 13/29.

[5] *Rewe-Zentral* v. *Bundesmonopolverwaltung für Branntwein*, Case 120/78, [1979] ECR 649.

able measures which hinder trade between Member States as prohibited if they are not necessary to satisfy 'mandatory requirements' which Member States are entitled to protect. In this it may be regarded as a step back from the basic definition of a measure equivalent to a quantitative restriction in the *Dassonville* case[6] as any trading rule capable of directly or indirectly, actually or potentially, hindering intra-Community trade, which, taken out of its context, could have been regarded as supporting the wider approach mentioned above. On the other hand, it may be recalled that in the context of price controls, the Court seems to have regarded it as necessary that there should be an element of discrimination against imports in order for there to be a breach of Article 30;[7] furthermore, it has regarded certain measures of social policy as falling outside the scope of the prohibition on measures equivalent to quantitative restrictions.[8]

Commission Directive 70/50

Although the expressed purpose of Directive 70/50[9] was to abolish those measures equivalent to quantitative restrictions which were operative at the date of entry into force of the EEC Treaty, and although it must be read subject to the directly effective terms of Article 30 itself,[10] it remains of interest both as a catalogue of certain types of prohibited conduct and as an illustration of the Commission's attitude at the time of its enactment.

Its most substantial provision is its Article 2, which relates to measures other than those applicable equally to domestic or imported products. At the outset, a difference from the case-law of the Court may be noted, in that Article 2(2) refers to conditions 'other than a formality' to which only imported products are subjected, whereas it was made clear in *International Fruit* v. *Produktschap voor Groenten en Fruit*[11] that even a purely formal requirement to obtain an import licence which would be automatically granted constituted a measure equivalent to a quantitative restriction.

There are, nevertheless, numerous instances of the discriminatory conduct listed in Article 2 coming before the European Court. Article 2(3)(g) prohibits national measures which make access of imported products to the domestic market conditional upon having an agent or representative in the territory of the importing Member State, the

---

[6] *Procureur du Roi* v. *Dassonville*, Case 8/74, [1974] ECR 837.
[7] See *Tasca*, Case 65/75, [1976] ECR 291.
[8] See *Blesgen* v. *Ministre des Finances*, Case 75/81, [1982] ECR 1211.
[9] JO 1970, L 13/29.
[10] See Opinion of *Advocate General Warner in Commission* v. *Germany*, Case 12/74, [1975] ECR 181, p. 208.
[11] Cases 51 and 54/71, [1971], ECR 1116.

situation at issue in *Commission* v. *Germany*,[12] where German law in effect required foreign pharmaceutical undertakings to have recourse to a subsidiary, branch, or representative established in Germany in order to sell pharmaceutical products there. Similarly, the prohibition on measures which 'encourage, require or give preference to the purchase of domestic products only' in Article 2(3)(k) encompasses precisely the conduct at issue in cases which have concerned encouragement to buy Irish goods[13] or English apples and pears,[14] or a requirement to buy oil refined in Ireland.[15]

Some cases have turned on the precise terminology of the Directive: an example may be found in *Commission* v. *Germany*[16] with regard to Article 2(3)(s), which prohibits measures which 'confine names which are not indicative of origin or source to domestic products only'. Under German legislation, the expression '*Sekt*' could only be used of a sparkling wine produced in Germany or a country of which German was the official language. The expression '*Prädikatsekt*' could only be used of a '*Sekt*' containing 60 per cent German grapes, and the expression '*Weinbrand*' could only be used of a brandy meeting certain quality requirements produced in a country of which German was the official language. These were the common German words for the products in question, and the equivalent foreign products had to be called respectively '*Schaumwein*', '*Qualitätsschaumwein*', or '*Qualitätsbranntwein aus Wein*'. In the view of the Commission, these latter names were unknown to or held in lower esteem by the German consumer, and the effect of the legislation was to favour domestic production to the detriment of imported goods. Germany argued, however, that the names in question were indirect indications of origin and so not prohibited under Article 2(3)(s) of the Directive. On this, the Court took a strict line. It held that an area of origin which was defined on the basis either of the extent of national territory or a linguistic criterion could not constitute a geographical area within the meaning of the Directive capable of justifying an indication of origin, particularly as certain of the products in question might be produced from grapes of indeterminate origin , and it could not be accepted that the use of 60 per cent German grapes in *Prädikatssekt* conferred a particular flavour on it. The Court therefore agreed with the Commission's view that the legislation in question was calculated to favour the disposal of the domestic product on the German market to the detriment of the products of other Member States.

[12] Case 247/81, [1984] ECR 1111.
[13] *Commission* v. *Ireland*, Case 249/81, [1982] ECR 4005.
[14] *Apple and Pear Development Council*. Case 222/82, [1983] ECR 4083.
[15] *Campus Oil*, Case 72/83, [1984] ECR 2727.
[16] Case 12/74, [1975] ECR 181.

It may, nevertheless, be observed that conduct prohibited by Article 2(3) of the Directive in so far as it affects imported products only has in fact been held to have an effect equivalent to a quantitative restriction when it affects domestic products as well. Article 2(3)(a) prohibits measures which lay down 'for imported products only' minimum or maximum prices below or above which imports are prohibited, reduced, or made subject to conditions liable to hinder importation, whereas the cases in which the European Court has held maximum price legislation[17] or minimum price legislation[18] to breach Article 30 of the Treaty have involved legislation applying both to imported and domestic goods, even though the Court appears to have looked for indirect discrimination against imports in such cases.[19] Equally applicable measures as such are mentioned only in Article 3 of the Directive, which prohibits measures governing the marketing of products which deal, in particular, with shape, size, weight, composition, presentation, identification, or putting up, and which are equally applicable to domestic and imported products but only where the restrictive effect of such measures on the free movement of goods exceeds the effects intrinsic to trade rules, in particular where the restrictive effects on the free movement of goods are out of proportion to their purpose or where the same objective can be attained by other means which are less of a hindrance to trade. In principle, therefore, equally applicable trading rules only breach Article 3 of the Directive if they have disproportionately restrictive effects on imports, and it should be said at once that this is not the approach followed by the European Court; rather than holding equally applicable trading rules to be prohibited only if they produce disproportionately restrictive effects on trade, its *Cassis de Dijon*[20] case-law rests on the basis that an equally applicable national trading rule which hinders the import of a good lawfully sold in another Member State is prohibited unless it may be justified as protecting a 'mandatory requirement'[21] or under the terms of Article 36 of the Treaty, and the question of proportionality or reasonableness goes to its justification as a mandatory requirement[22] or as a measure falling under Article 36.[23] The example may be given of *Rau*,[24] which involved Belgian legislation requiring margarine to be packed in cubic blocks, allegedly to enable purchasers to distinguish it from butter, thus preventing the importation of oblong blocks or round tubs from other Member States. Clearly this involved shape and presentation as mentioned in Article 3 of the Directive, but rather than looking at the proportionality of the restriction as such, the Court looked

---

[17] See n. 7 above.
[18] *Van Tiggele*, Case 82/77, [1978] ECR 25.
[19] See p. 57 above.
[20] See n: 5 above.
[21] See p. 65 below.
[22] See e.g. *Gilli*, Case 788/79, [1980] ECR 2071.
[23] See e.g. *Commission* v. *United Kingdom*, Case 124/81, [1983] ECR 203.
[24] Case 261/81, [1982] ECR 3961.

to see if it could be justified as a mandatory requirement (in this case to protect consumers), and considered whether the restriction was proportionate in that context (holding that it was not).

On the other hand, the Court does apply a proportionality test to see whether a measure may be regarded as breaching Article 30 in those cases where the measure itself is not regarded as being connected with importation or exportation.[25] To take the example of *Torfaen Borough Council* v. *B & Q plc*,[26] where the Sunday-trading rules in England were at issue, it was first stated that such rules reflected certain political and economic choices and were not designed to govern the patterns of trade between the Member States. The Court then went on to refer expressly to Article 3 of the Directive in order to hold that the rules would not breach Article 30 of the Treaty unless their restrictive effects exceeded what was necessary to achieve the aim in view and exceeded the effects intrinsic to trade rules. Whether they did was held to be a question of fact for the national court to determine.

Finally, it may be observed that in at least one instance a national measure relating to weight, which had the effect of restricting imports from other Member States, has been held to be justified under Community secondary legislation: *Union Laitière Normande* v. *French Dairy Farmers*[27] involved, *inter alia*, United Kingdom legislation requiring milk to be sold in pint units, which meant that French milk packaged in litres could not be imported. However, special transitional arrangements had been made for the United Kingdom under the relevant weights-and-measures Directive,[28] which had still not expired, and it was held that by virtue of these arrangements the United Kingdom could still provide that milk should be packaged in pints. The judgment does not, however, discuss the question of proportionality under Article 3 of Directive 70/50, or the relationship between the weights-and-measures Directive and the general rule of Article 30 of the Treaty, or whether that Directive could be regarded as designed to improve the free movement of goods;[29] it may perhaps, therefore, be regarded as exceptional.

The Recognition of Mandatory Requirements

Although it had, in 1974, formulated its definition of a measure equivalent to a quantitative restriction as 'all trading rules enacted by

---

[25] See p. 58 above.   [26] Case 145/88 (23 Nov. 1989).
[27] Case 244/78, [1979] ECR 2663.   [28] Council Dir. 75/106 (OJ 1975 L42/1).
[29] Cf. *Bauhuis* v. *The Netherlands*, Case 46/76, [1977] ECR 5, where to charge for an inspection required by Community law was held not to constitute a charge equivalent to a customs duty since such Community inspections helped the free movement of goods. See Chap. 3 above.

Member States which are capable of hindering directly or indirectly, actually or potentially, intra-Community trade',[30] and hence capable of including not only measures discriminating against imports or exports but also measures applying equally to domestic products, the Court did not have to give detailed consideration to equally applicable measures (except in the rather special matter of price controls)[31] until its 1979 judgment in *Rewe* v. *Bundesmonopolverwaltung für Branntwein.*[32] This arose from the attempted importation into Germany of French *Cassis de Dijon* (hence the name of this line of cases). The problem was very simple: under German law, fruit liqueurs were required to have an alcoholic strength of at least 25 per cent, whereas *Cassis de Dijon*, a blackcurrant liqueur, had an alcoholic strength of between 15 per cent and 20 per cent. On a literal application of the 1974 *Dassonville*[33] formula, the German legislation clearly directly hindered trade with France; however, the Court recognized that, in the absence of Community legislation on the matter, it was for Member States to regulate all matters relating to the production and marketing of alcohol and alcoholic beverages on their own territory. It then set out in general terms the extent to which restrictions on the free movement of goods arising from such national legislation had to be tolerated:

obstacles to movement within the Community resulting from disparities between the national laws relating to the marketing of the products in question must be accepted in so far as those provisions may be recognized as being necessary in order to satisfy mandatory requirements relating in particular to the effectiveness of fiscal supervision, the protection of public health, the fairness of commercial transactions and the defence of the consumer.

On the other hand, if the national measures did not serve to protect such a mandatory requirement, there was no valid reason why alcoholic beverages which had been lawfully produced and marketed in one of the Member States should not be introduced into any other Member State.

By an act of what it would hardly be an exaggeration to call judicial legislation, the European Court therefore confirmed that non-discriminatory measures could indeed be treated as measures equivalent to quantitative restrictions, but only to the extent to which they were not justified to satisfy mandatory requirements. It may be observed that these mandatory requirements do not necessarily coincide with restrictions expressly permitted by Article 36 of the EEC Treaty,[34] that they may only be invoked in favour of national measures which are genuinely non-discriminatory,[35] and that, as has subsequently appeared,

---

[30] See n. 6 above.
[32] See n. 5 above.
[35] *Kohl* v. *Ringelhan*, Case 177/83, [1984] ECR 3651.

[31] See p. 57 above.
[33] See n. 6 above.
[34] See p. 72 below.

the list is not closed.[36] In practice, it has not been easy to show that a measure is justified as a mandatory requirement. In *Rewe* itself, the German government invoked the protection of health, claiming that beverages with a low alcohol content may more easily induce a tolerance towards alcohol; this did not convince the Court, which pointed out that beverages sold with a high alcohol content are often consumed in a diluted form. The German government also invoked consumer protection, but the Court held that it was a simple matter to ensure that suitable information is conveyed to the purchaser by requiring the display of the alcohol content on the packaging of products.

The same formulation was repeated a year later in *Gilli*,[37] in relation to Italian legislation requiring vinegar to be made from wine, thus preventing the sale of German cider vinegar: it could hardly seriously be argued that cider vinegar constituted a threat to health, and the Court took the view that consumers could be protected by labelling. In the light of this reaffirmation, the Commission issued its 1980 Communication on the consequences of this case-law,[38] emphasizing the underlying general principle of free movement rather than the concept of mandatory requirements. It stated that any product lawfully produced and marketed in one Member State must, in principle, be admitted to the market of any other Member State, but added that technical and commercial rules equally applicable to national and imported products may create barriers to trade only where those rules are necessary to satisfy mandatory requirements and to serve a purpose which is in the general interest and for which they are an essential guarantee. In the light of this, the Commission announced a new policy with regard to the legislative proposals it would put forward for the harmonization or approximation of national law: henceforth it would be directed to the removal of barriers to trade arising from national provisions which are admissible under the criteria set by the Court, and it would concentrate on sectors deserving priority because of their economic relevance to the creation of a single internal market. It may, therefore, be suggested that this is the genesis of the approach taken in the subsequent White Paper[39] on completing the internal market and in the internal-market provisions of the Single European Act which rest on the theory that the internal market may be completed through the enactment of a relatively small amount of Community legislation. The underlying assumption, derived from this and similar case-law in other sectors, is that most national restrictions on intra-Community trade were already prohibited under Community law, and that specific legislation was therefore only required to remove or replace those few (and identifiable) national restrictions that were still justifiable in Community law.

---

[36] *Commission* v. *Denmark*, Case 302/86, [1988] ECR.   [37] See n. 22 above.
[38] OJ 1980, C 256/2   [39] June 1985.

Be that as it may, this interpretation of Article 30 of the EEC Treaty has continued to be widely applied. Perhaps the most contentious example was in *Commission* v. *Germany*,[40] with regard to sixteenth-century German legislation on beer purity. This required beer to be made from a limited number of natural ingredients, and had the incidental effect of preventing beers made in other Member States which contained various additives or preservatives from being sold in Germany. The essential argument was as to whether the German legislation could be regarded as serving the mandatory requirements of protection of health or protection of consumers; on the former question, the Commission was able to show that all the preservatives or additives at issue were permitted under German law to be used in other foodstuffs, and the Court concluded that they did not therefore constitute a threat to health in beer (despite the German government's arguments as to the high consumption of beer by German drinkers), and on the latter, the Court again took the view that consumers could be protected by labelling (even on the pump handle if it was draught beer).

Many more examples could be given: German law requiring only Franconian wine to be sold in the *Bocksbeutel* shape of bottle could not be used to prevent the import of Italian wine which was normally and lawfully sold in that shape of bottle on its home market;[41] Italian law requiring pasta to be made from durum wheat could not prevent the importation of pasta containing soft wheat (even though the Court recognized that Italian consumers would be unlikely to eat it),[42] and German law on the meat content of sausages could not be enforced against imported sausages where there was no threat to health and consumers could be informed of the contents by labelling.[43] Similarly, French legislation restricting the use of the word 'yoghurt' to a live product could not stop the sale of frozen yoghurt,[44] and rules on the minimum fat content of Edam cheese could not stop the sale as Edam of imported cheese with a lower fat content.[45]

Turning more specifically to the mandatory requirements originally listed in *Rewe*,[46] the effectiveness of fiscal supervision has rarely been discussed. However, the protection of public health has been frequently invoked, and its use raises difficult question as to the relationship between this case-law and the express terms of Article 36 of the Treaty, which permit restrictions on imports or exports justified, *inter alia*, on grounds of 'the protection of health and life of humans, animals or plants', provided they do not constitute a means of arbitrary discrimination

---

[40] Case 178/84, [1987] ECR 1227.
[41] *Prantl*, Case 16/83, [1984] ECR 1299.
[42] *Zoni*, Case 90/86, [1988] ECR 4285.
[43] *Commission* v. *Germany*, Case 274/87 [1989] ECR 229.
[44] *Smanor*, Case 298/87, [1988] ECR 4489.
[45] *Deserbais*, Case 286/86, [1988] ECR 4907.

or a disguised restriction on trade between Member States.[47] Whilst there is an obvious substantive overlap, the formulation adopted in the *Cassis de Dijon* case-law would appear to mean that an equally applicable measure which is justified on health grounds does not constitute a measure equivalent to a quantitative restriction, whereas the formulation in Article 36 would appear to mean that a measure equivalent to a quantitative restriction may be permitted where it is justified for the protection of health. However, the distinction has gradually been eroded: the more recent case-law in the *Cassis de Dijon* line refers to the mandatory requirements as justifying a measure likely to hinder trade between the Member States,[48] and on the other hand it has long been established that for a measure relating to imports to be justified under Article 36, effective measures for the same purpose must be taken with regard to domestic production,[49] which is not far short of requiring the measure to be equally applicable. Hence, the cases mentioned above which involved measures claimed to be for the protection of health have generally also involved a discussion of Article 36, at least since *Melkunie*,[50] where Dutch legislation relating to the presence of active coliform bacteria and active micro-organisms in milk products was at issue. It was held that this equally applicable legislation was *prima facie* a measure having equivalent effect to a quantitative restriction in so far as it prohibited the marketing of goods lawfully produced and marketed in the exporting Member State, but that it was justified on health grounds under Article 36.

On the other hand, the fairness of commercial transactions and the defence of the consumer are not expressly mentioned in Article 36 and are not regarded by the Court as falling within its scope.[51] They may, therefore, only be invoked with regard to measures that are genuinely equally applicable;[52] hence in *Schützverband gegen Unwesen* v. *Weinvertriebs-GmbH*[53] it was held that German legislation requiring foreign wine-based beverages to be produced according to the local rules and to be capable of being marketed in the State of production could not be used as a measure for the protection of consumers to keep out of Germany Italian vermouth containing less alcohol than required under Italian law for vermouth marketed in Italy. The German legislation by definition applied only to imports, and the Court pointed out that consumer protection could only be invoked to exclude Article 30 where

---

[46] See n. 5 above.
[47] See p. 72 below.
[48] *Wurmser*, Case 25/88 (11 May 1989), paras. 10 and 11.
[49] *Rewe-Zentralfinanz* v. *Landwirtschaftskammer Bonn*, Case 4/75, [1975] ECR. 843.
[50] Case 97/83, [1984] ECR 2367.
[51] E.g. as matters of public policy. See *Wurmser* (n. 48 above), para. 10.
[52] See n. 35 above.
[53] Case 59/82, [1983] ECR 1217.

the the legislation governed the marketing of national and imported products uniformly. The same approach applies where a measure which appears to be equally applicable is nevertheless regarded as discriminating against imports. In particular, national legislation requiring goods to be labelled with an indication of their origin has been held to prompt consumers to give preference to national goods and therefore to be discriminatory, so that the protection of consumers could not be invoked as a justification.[54] It is also clear that a measure which is not regarded as effective to protect consumers will not be justified as fulfilling a mandatory requirement.[54A]

There are a few instances of restrictions being held justified to protect consumers.[55] In *Robertson*,[56] it was held that Belgian legislation requiring silver-plated goods to bear a special hallmark was capable of affording effective protection to consumers and of promoting fair trading and could be enforced against imports unless they were already hallmarked in an equivalent and intelligible manner. In *Buet*,[57] it was held that French legislation prohibiting the doorstep selling of educational material was justified as a measure to protect consumers (purchasers of educational material being treated as particularly vulnerable), even though it may be regarded as a restriction on the importation of such material from other Member States, and in *Oosthoek's Uitgeversmaatschappij*,[58] Dutch legislation which prohibited the giving of free gifts in the form of books to purchasers of an encyclopaedia was held to be justified because 'the offering of free gifts as a means of sales promotion may mislead consumers as to the real prices of certain products and distort the conditions on which genuine competition is based'. More obviously, in *Diensten Groep* v. *Belle*,[59] Dutch rules prohibiting the passing-off of an almost-identical product were held to be justified for the protection of consumers and fairness in commercial transactions. On the other hand, the fact that Belgian jenever contains

---

[49] *Rewe-Zentralfinanz* v. *Landwirtschaftskammer Bonn*, Case 4/75, [1975] ECR. 843.

[50] Case 97/83, [1984] ECR 2367.

[51] E.g. as matters of public policy. See *Wurmser* (n. 48 above), para. 10.

[52] See n. 35 above.

[53] Case 59/82, [1983] ECR 1217.

[54] *Commission* v. *United Kingdon*, Case 207/83, [1985] ECR 1201. See p. 56 above.

[54A] Case C–67188 *Commission v. Staly* (21 November 1990), in the context of an Italian requirement that sesame oil be added to all vegetable oils other than olive oil.

[55] It may be observed that the protection of consumers has also been held to justify restrictions in the context of the freedom to provide services under the Treaty. In *Commission* v. *Germany*, Case 205/84, [1986] ECR 3755, it was held that with regard to direct insurance effected through intermediaries, Germany was justified in requiring insurance undertakings established in other Member States to comply with its authorization requirements (notably with regard to its technical reserves) in so far as they were necessary to ensure the protection of policy-holders and insured persons.

[56] Case 220/81, [1982] ECR 2349.   [57] Case 382/87 (16 May 1989).

[58] Case 286/81, [1982] ECR 4575.   [59] Case 6/81, [1982] ECR 707.

less alcohol than Dutch jenever and therefore is subject to a lower rate of taxation when sold in the Netherlands has been held not to constitute unfair competition,[60] and it was accepted that consumers of that product could be adequately informed of its alcohol content by labelling. Furthermore, it was held in *GB-INNO-BM* v. *Confédération du Commerce Luxembourgeois*,[61] that Luxemburg legislation prohibiting advertisements of offers for sale at a reduced price from indicating the duration of the offer or the previous price was not only not justified as a measure to protect consumers, but was contrary to Community policy on the protection of consumers, which was based on the idea of providing as much information as possible for consumers. The Luxemburg authorities could not, therefore, stop a Belgian supermarket from indicating how long its offer lasted and what price it had previously charged for the goods.

Whilst *Rewe*[62] itself listed only four examples of mandatory requirements, it is clear from *Commission* v. *Denmark*[63] that national legislation designed to protect the environment may also be regarded as justifying restrictions on trade between Member States. The case involved Danish legislation which in essence required drinks to be sold in returnable containers, so as to help reduce the problem of litter, and the Court held this to be justifiable in principle, even though it prevented, for example, the import of drinks in cans from other Member States; it was, however, held that certain of the details of the scheme were unnecessarily restrictive. Another possible extension occurred in *Cinéthèque*,[64] in the context of French legislation prohibiting the sale or hire of video-cassettes of a film within a fixed period from the film's release in the cinema. The Court found that this did restrict the importation of video-cassettes from other Member States, but none the less held the restriction to be justified, without stating a category for this justification. In its arguments, the Commission had indicated some sympathy for the idea of protecting cultural policy, which might be an appropriate categorization; on the other hand, *Cinéthèque* is cited as a precedent in *Torfaen Borough Council* v. *B & Q plc*,[65] which has been treated in this book as an example of a measure which does not constitute a measure equivalent to a quantitative restriction in the first place.[66] However, it was there cited as an example of the proportionality rule, that the restriction was not compatible with the principle of the free movement of goods 'unless any obstacle to Community trade thereby created did not exceed what was necessary in order to ensure the attainment of the objective in view and unless that objective was justified with regard to

---

[60] *Miro*, Case 182/84, [1985] ECR 3731.
[61] Case C–362/88, (7th Mar. 1990).
[62] See n. 5 above.
[63] See n. 36 above.
[64] Cases 60 and 61/84, [1985] ECR 2605.
[65] See n. 26 above.
[66] See pp. 58 and 64 above.

Community law'. It is submitted that this is a criterion which must be met by any measure which is claimed to be justified to protect a mandatory requirement,[67] and that *Cinéthèque* is authority for the proposition that cultural policy may justify restrictions on trade.

Be that as it may, it is now clear that, just as in the case of express exemptions under Article 36 of the Treaty, a national measure may be justified as protecting a mandatory requirement only if the matter at issue is not already regulated by Community law. This is clear from the original judgement in *Rewe*,[68] which refers to 'the absence of common rules relating to the production and marketing of alcohol' as enabling the Member States to have rules on the matter, and it was expressly reaffirmed by the Full Court in *Wurmser*,[69] although, as will be seen, Article 100A(4) of the EEC Treaty, introduced by the Single European Act, appears to be intended alter this principle,[70] albeit to a limited extent.

[67] See p. 63 above.   [68] See n. 5 above.
[69] See n. 48 above.   [70] See p. 85 below.

7

Quantitative Restrictions and Measures Having Equivalent Effect: The Express Exceptions

The Treaty Provisions

Apart from the general safeguard provisions of the EEC Treaty,[1] restrictions on the free movement of goods in internal Community trade are only envisaged in Articles 36 and 115 of that Treaty. Article 115 essentially provides a mechanism under which third-country goods in free circulation in the Community may be denied Community treatment by a Member State in order to protect a quota enjoyed by that State, and it has been considered in the context of the Common Commercial Policy.[2] Article 36, on the other hand, allows restrictions to be imposed for a wide range of reasons, but imposes overriding limitations on these restrictions. It reads:

The provisions of arts. 30 to 34 shall not preclude prohibitions or restrictions on imports, exports or goods in transit justified on grounds of public morality, public policy or public security; the protection of health and life of humans, animals or plants; the protection of national treasures possessing artistic, historic or archaeological value; or the protection of industrial and commercial property. Such prohibitions or restrictions shall not, however, constitute a means of arbitrary discrimination or a disguised restriction on trade.

The case-law on the protection of industrial and commercial property has developed in a very specific way and is treated in this book as an aspect of the competition rules of the EEC Treaty. Certain general observations may be made about the rest of this provision. Above all, it has been made clear from a very early stage that Article 36 is concerned with protecting non-economic interests.[3] As it was stated more recently in *Campus Oil* v. *Minister for Industry and Energy*,[4] 'a Member State cannot

---

[1] Notably Art. 103 (conjunctural policy), Arts. 108 and 109 (balance-of-payments difficulties), and Arts. 223 to 225 (military products, and internal disturbances or threat of war etc.)

[2] See p. 25 above.

[3] See *Commission* v. *Italy*, Case 7/61, [1961] ECR 317, p. 329.

[4] Case 72/83, [1984] ECR 2727, p. 2752.

be allowed to avoid the effects of measures provided for in the Treaty by pleading the economic difficulties caused by the elimination of barriers to intra-Community trade'. Secondly, the burden of proving that a measure falls within Article 36 rests on the party which relies on that provision, usually the national authorities.[5] Thirdly, in order to avoid being categorized as arbitrary discrimination, it must be shown that effective measures to protect the same interest have been taken with regard to domestic products, and not just with regard to imports or exports.[6] Finally, even if a measure complies with all these require-ments, it may still be regarded as a disguised restriction on trade if it goes beyond what is necessary for the effective protection of the general interest at issue, and in particular if that objective could be achieved by means less restrictive of intra-Community trade.[7] In other words, a test of proportionality or reasonableness[8] is applied, and in determining what is reasonable account must be taken of the information or means of proof available to an importer or exporter.[9]

Turning to the specific justifications for restrictions on intra-Commun-ity trade listed in Article 36, it may be noted that the protection of national treasures possessing artistic, historic, or archaeological value has rarely been at issue—perhaps surprisingly in view of the way in which Member States tend to regulate such trade. The matter was raised in *Commission* v. *Italy*,[10] in the context of a tax on the export of such articles from Italy. *Inter alia*, the Italian government invoked Article 36, claiming that a levy would disturb the functioning of the common market less than the application of prohibitions or export restrictions. On this issue, the European Court held that Article 36 does not appply in the context of customs duties and charges having equivalent effect.[11] However, it added that the effect of the Italian legislation was to render more onerous the exportation of the products in question, without ensuring the attainment of the object of protecting the artistic, historic, or archaeological heritage; the implication appears to be that, to be justified under Article 36, a measure to protect national treasures must restrict trade in such products in a way which is capable of achieving that objective.

On the other hand, there have been many examples of the protection

---

[5] *Denkavit Futtermittel*, Case 251/78, [1979] ECR 3369, p. 3392. The same rule would appear to apply with regard to the invocation of 'mandatory requirements' under the *Cassis de Dijon* case-law, *Wurmser*, Case 25/88 (11 May 1989).

[6] *Rewe-Zentralfinanz* v. *Landwirtschaftskammer Bonn*, Case 4/75, [1975], ECR 843, *Conegate* v. *HM Customs and Excise*, Case 121/85, [1986] ECR 1007.

[7] See e.g. *Commission* v. *United Kingdom*, Case 124/81, [1983] ECR. 203, and *Wurmser* (see n. 5 above).

[8] *De Peijper*, Case 104/75, [1976] ECR 613.

[9] Ibid., and see also *Wurmser* (n. 5 above).

[10] Case 7/68, [1968] ECR 423.

[11] See p. 28 above.

of health, and of restrictions claimed to be justified on grounds of public policy, and these will be considered separately.

Protection of Health

SUBSTANTIVE ISSUES

The protection of health and life of humans, animals, and plants under Article 36 may conveniently be divided into a study of the substance of the health measures which may be enforced and a study of the procedures which may be used to enforce those measures. The fundamental substantive requirement is that there must be a 'seriously considered health policy', which was found not to be so in *Commission* v. *United Kingdom*,[12] with regard to the British policy adopted in 1981 imposing a prohibition on imports into Great Britain of poultry-meat and eggs from all other Member States except Denmark and Ireland. The expressed aim of this prohibition was to enable Newcastle disease (of which the last recorded outbreak in Great Britain had been in 1978 and the last outbreak in France in 1976) to be dealt with by a slaughter policy, and the import restrictions were intended to ensure that imports could only be accepted from Member States (that is, Denmark and Ireland) which were totally free from Newcastle disease, which prohibited the use of vaccine, and which imposed compulsory slaughter requirements in the event of an outbreak of the disease. The Court doubted whether this was a seriously considered health policy, because it was introduced in a matter of days (whereas the previous change to a policy of vaccination in 1964 had been preceded by elaborate reports and studies), it followed domestic pressure to restrict the growing imports of French poultry products, it was timed to exclude French turkeys from the 1981 Christmas market, and because the prohibition on French imports was not lifted when the French changed their policy so as to accord with the three conditions set out by the British authorities. In any event, the Court took the view that the United Kingdom had not shown that a total prohibition on imports was the only possibility open to it, and concluded that less stringent measures could have been used.[13]

Another example may be found in *Commission* v. *France*,[14] which involved French legislation prohibiting the marketing of milk substitutes; here the French government based two arguments on the

---

[12] Case 40/82, [1982] ECR 2793.
[13] This judgment gave rise to a claim for damages before the English courts in *Bouguoin* v. *MAFF*, [1985] 3 All ER 585, which was settled on payment of £3.5 million to the French turkey producers (*Hansard*, 23 July 1986, vol. 102, no. 156, col. 116).
[14] Case 216/84, [1988] ECR 793.

protection of health, claiming that milk substitutes had a lower nutritional value, and that they were harmful to particular groups of the population. On the first point, the European Court held that given the choice of foodstuffs available to consumers in the Community, the mere fact that an imported product had a lower nutritional value did not pose a real threat to human health, and on the second point it was noted that milk products themselves also pose risks to people suffering from certain diseases, and that labelling would provide consumers with appropriate information. Hence, the French measures could not be justified on grounds of the protection of human health. Similarly, it has been held that German legislation, which prohibited the import from other Member States of meat products manufactured from meat not coming from the country of manufacture of the finished product, could not be justified on health grounds since there was no reason to think that the risk of contamination increased simply because the fresh meat crossed a Community frontier prior to being processed,[15] Finally, in *Commission* v. *France*,[16] the French government endeavoured to justify restrictions on the advertising of grain spirits such as whisky and gin (which were largely imported) on grounds of the protection of health, in particular its campaign against alcoholism, but the Court pointed out that other alcoholic beverages (notably fruit and wine-based spirits, which happen to be produced in France) were not subject to any advertising restrictions even though they had the same harmful effects from the point of view of public health in the event of excessive consumption. The legislation, therefore, constituted arbitrary discrimination in trade between Member States.

By way of contrast, if the measure does pursue a genuine aim of health policy, it is not necessary to show that there is unanimity of scientific opinion on the matter, provided there is a serious doubt. The point first appears to have arisen in *Kaasfabriek Eyssen*,[17] in the context of Dutch legislation prohibiting the use of nisin in processed cheese. It was found that while some Member States took the same view as the Netherlands, others allowed its use without restriction or subject to prescribed maximum levels, and it was also noted that studies had been undertaken by the Food and Agriculture Organization of the United Nations and by the World Health Organization which had not established absolutely certain conclusions. It was held that such a measure did fall within the scope of Article 36, and that 'in view of the uncertainties prevailing in the various Member States regarding the maximum level of nisin which must be prescribed in respect of each preserved product intended to satisfy the various dietary habits', it did

---

[15] *Commission* v. *Germany*, [1979] ECR 2555.
[16] Case 152/78, [1980] ECR 2299.
[17] Case 53/80, [1981] ECR 409.

not constitute arbitrary discrimination or a disguised restriction on trade, even though the prohibition did not apply to cheese intended for export. A convenient formulation of this approach was set out in *Sandoz*:[18]

in so far as there are uncertainties at the present state of scientific research it is for the Member States, in the absence of harmonization, to decode what degree of protection of the health and life of humans they intend to assure, having regard however for the requirements of the free movement of goods within the Community.

Thus, it has been held that Belgian legislation requiring the use of a colorant to be entered on a national positive list by a procedure involving reference to a committee of experts could be enforced against an importer of black and red lumpfish roe coloured with indigotin and cochineal-A red from Germany, where those colorants were authorised under national law.[19] Similarly, in *Mirepoix*,[20] French legislation prohibiting the use on, *inter alia*, onions of maleic hydrazide, a growth inhibitor, was held to be a measure justifiable under Article 36, which could be invoked with regard to the importation into France of Dutch onions treated with that substance. It was agreed that this substance left residues which did not disappear entirely during the normal marketing period, and the Court stated that the fact that the quantities absorbed by the consumer could therefore neither be predicted nor controlled justified strict measures intended to reduce the risks faced by the consumer. It concluded that:

in so far as the relevant Community rules do not cover certain pesticides,[21] the Member States may regulate the presence of residues of those pesticides on foodstuffs in a way which varies from one country to another according to the climatic conditions, the normal diet of the population and their state of health.

On the other hand, in the light of the reference to 'normal diet', it should be remembered that in the German beer case,[22] the fact that beer is consumed on a large scale by German drinkers was held not to justify the prohibition in beer of additives and preservatives permitted in other foodstuffs.

Finally, it is clear that Member States may adopt different approaches to the same safety issue. *Commission* v. *France*[23] concerned French legislation on woodworking machines which, in effect, required them to

---

[18] Case 174/82, [1983] ECR 2445, p. 2463.
[19] *Motte*, Case 247/84, [1985] ECR 3887.
[20] Case 54/85, [1986] ECR 1067.
[21] In 1986, the year in which this judgment was given, the Council enacted Dir. 86/362 and 86/363 (OJ 1986, L 221/37 and 43) on the maximum levels of pesticide residue in cereals and in foodstuffs of animal origin.
[22] *Commission* v. *Germany*, Case 178/84, [1987] ECR 1227.
[23] Case 188/84, [1986] ECR 419.

be designed so as to protect their users from their own mistakes. The Commission argued that in other Member States, notably Germany, a different philosophy was followed, requiring workers to be trained so as to respond correctly if the machine malfunctioned, and that France should not be allowed to prevent the importation of machines designed in accordance with a different approach which nevertheless was proved to provide the same level of safety. However, the Court took the view that, on the evidence, it had not been shown that machines in free circulation in other Member States provided the same level of protection—indeed no such claim had been made by the manufacturers who had complained to the Commission—and that Member States are not required to allow into their territory dangerous machines which have not been proved to afford users on their territory the same level of protection. Therefore France could enforce its rules, provided that its approvals procedure was not operated in a discriminatory manner.

PROCEDURES

The procedures adopted to protect a genuine measure of health policy must, as has been indicated, be necessary for that purpose, proportionate to the objective being pursued, and must not constitute arbitrary discrimination or a disguised restriction on trade. To a large extent these considerations tend to be interlinked, but possible discrimination was clearly the main issue in *Rewe-Zentralfinanz* v. *Landwirtschaftskammer Bonn*.[24] This case arose from a requirement of German law that imported apples, in this case from France, should be subject to phytosanitary inspection on entry, when no such compulsory examination was imposed on home-produced apples. The case thus posed, at a time when many commentators thought that only discriminatory measures breached Article 30 in the first place,[25] the problem of how to reconcile such a measure with the second sentence of Article 36, requiring health measures not to constitute a means of arbitrary discrimination. Indeed, the Court expressly recognized the inspections as being discriminatory within the meaning of Article 2(2) of Directive 70/50.[26] Its approach was first to investigate the objective of the inspections, which it found to be to control San José Scale, and held that this was in principle justified under Article 36. It then turned to the question whether there was nevertheless arbitrary discrimination, and reached a conclusion which is still of relevance:

The different treatment of imported and domestic products, based on the need to prevent the spread of the harmful organism could not, however, be regarded

[24] See n. 6 above.
[25] See p. 60 above.
[26] JO 1970, L 13/29. See p. 00 above.

as arbitrary discrimination if effective measures are taken in order to prevent the distribution of contaminated domestic products and if there is reason to believe, in particular on the basis of previous experience, that there is a risk of the harmful organism's spreading if no inspection is held on importation.

Therefore it may be possible to justify a discriminatory measure under Article 36 on health grounds, but only if effective measures serving the same purpose are taken with regard to the equivalent domestic product. It has already been suggested that this does not fall very far short of holding that only equally applicable measures may be justified under Article 36.[27]

The issues of necessity, reasonableness, and proportionality arose in the context of the protection of human health in *De Peijper*.[28] Under Dutch legislation, certain information had to be supplied to the relevant authorities before pharmaceutical products could be marketed, and this information was of a type which could only be supplied by the manufacturer (or, in practice, an importer authorized by the manufacturer). The accused was prosecuted for marketing products in the Netherlands which had been bought in the United Kingdom, without supplying the requisite information to the Dutch authorities. Those products were very similar to, if not identical with, products already marketed in the Netherlands by the same manufacturer or an authorized importer, and with regard to which the relevant information had already been supplied. It was first held that rules which mean that only traders authorized by the manufacturer may effect imports in principle breach Article 30, and in this context the Court thought it particularly important that parallel imports should not be placed at a disadvantage, since they are usually lower priced, and 'the effective protection of health and life of humans also demands that medicinal preparations should be sold at reasonable prices'. However, while recognizing that 'health and life of humans rank first among the property or interests protected by article 36', the Court held that restrictive measures are compatible with the Treaty only to the extent to which they are necessary for the effective protection of health and life of humans. Measures are not necessary if health and life could be protected by other measures which restrict trade to a lesser extent; in particular, Article 36 cannot justify practices explained primarily by a concern to lighten the burden on the administration or reduce public expenditure, unless this burden or expenditure would otherwise clearly exceed the limits of what could reasonably be required.

In the light of these general considerations, the Court held it was not necessary for a second trader who imported a medicinal preparation in every respect the same as one with regard to which the necessary

---

[27] See p. 68 above.   [28] See n. 8 above.

information had already been given by another trader to supply that information again. With regard to the conformity of individual batches with the general information already received, it was held that a trader could not be required to produce documents to which he did not have access, when national authorities could require manufacturers or their agents to produce information, or they could co-operate with the authorities of other Member States. Following this judgment, Dutch law was amended to provide a simplified procedure for registration designed to ascertain whether the product which the parallel importer proposed to import was the same or practically the same as the product already registered, and in *Kortmann*[29] its validity seems to have been accepted.[30]

It may be observed that the reasonableness test in *De Peijper* relates not just to the burden on the trader but also to the burden on the public authorities, and this aspect was raised again in *Commission* v. *Italy*.[31] This involved Italian legislation which regulated the importation of grapefruit, requiring grapefruit to be imported only through named ports, at which they would undergo a health inspection. This meant that grapefruit could not be imported by land into Italy, which was clearly a *prima facie* breach of Article 30. Italy claimed that its measures were justified to protect the health of its own citrus fruit harvest, and that to have inspectors available at land crossing-points or at the point of destination of a cargo would be difficult to organize and expensive. The Court, however, took the view that Italy had not shown that it was impossible to organize inspections at other points, and took account of the fact that until 1985 health inspections of grapefruit had been carried out at other points of entry, and that Italy had not shown there was any specific factor which justified no longer allowing grapefruit to be imported through a land crossing-point.

Just as the judgment in *De Peijper* hinted that Member States should take account of information held by other Member States, a more general doctrine has developed in the matter of health inspections, that Member States cannot invoke Article 36 to duplicate on importation inspections already carried out by another Member State on exportation, such duplication not being necessary to protect health. This was first established in *Denkavit Futtermittel*,[32] where it was held that both to require a certificate from the exporting Member State and to carry out systematic inspection of the goods on import went beyond what was justified under Article 36 if health could be protected as effectively by measures that were not so restrictive of trade. Similarly, it has been held

[29] Case 32/80, [1981] ECR 251.
[30] The case was largely concerned with the validity of the registration fees charged.
[31] Case C–128/89, (12 July 1990).
[32] See n. 5 above.

that whilst a Member State is entitled to require a plant-protection product with a toxic constituent, which has already received approval in another Member State, to undergo a fresh procedure of examination and approval, its authorities may not 'unnecessarily . . . require technical or chemical analyses or laboratory tests where those analyses and tests have already been carried out in another Member State and their results are available to those authorities, or may at their request be placed at their disposal'.[33]

An inspection system going beyond mere duplication was at issue in *United Foods* v. *Belgium*.[34] This involved Belgian legislation on the health inspection of fish, which required 24 hours' notice to be given of the importation. Whilst to carry out such inspections was held in principle to fall within Article 36, it was suggested that it would be a disguised restriction on trade to require 24 hours' notice to be given of the importation of a highly perishable commodity like fresh fish. On the question of duplication of inspections, it appeared that the export inspections were those laid down by Belgian law, so that 'control on importation must in all cases be limited to measures designed to counter the risks arising from transportation or from any handling following the inspection carried out on dispatch'.

Perhaps the clearest example of import controls being regarded as disproportionate is *Commission* v. *United Kingdom*,[35] which concerned the United Kingdom rules on the importation of UHT milk. These rules contained two main elements. The first was a requirement to obtain an import licence, which in principle has long been held to breach Article 30,[36] claimed by the United Kingdom to be necessary in effect to police health requirements. The Court held this to be disproportionately restrictive, suggesting that the objectives in question could be attained by, for example, requiring declarations from importers, accompanied if necessary by the appropriate certificates. The second element was that UHT milk should be packed in a dairy approved by the competent local authority, that is, that it should be packed in premises within the United Kingdom. In practice this meant that the milk had to be re-treated in the United Kingdom, since the original packs could not be opened without losing the benefits of the UHT treatment. Re-treatment would make importation uneconomic, so the requirement amounted to a total prohibition on imports. In the view of the Court, the United Kingdom could protect the health of consumers by a requirement that importers

---

[33] *Frans-Nederlandse Maatschappij voor Biologische Producten*, Case 272/80, [1981] ECR 3277, p. 3291.

[34] Case 132/80, [1981] ECR 995.

[35] See n. 7 above.

[36] *International Fruit* v. *Produktschap voor Groenten en Fruit*, Cases 51 and 54/71, [1971] ECR 1116. See p. 56 above.

produce certificates issued by the competent authorities of the exporting Member States, coupled with controls by means of samples.[37]

The dividing-line between sampling and systematic analysis has been a matter of some debate. It has been held to be disproportionate for the French authorities to analyse three out of four consignments of Italian wine, in the absence of evidence of fraud or irregularities;[38] such action was also found to be discriminatory in view of the fact that no similar practice existed in relation to French wine. In an order for interim measures in that case,[39] the Court ordered that analyses should be restricted to a maximum of 15 per cent of the consignments. On the other hand, in *Rewe-Zentrale* v. *Landwirtschaftskammer Rheinland*,[40] inspection of up to one in three consignments was held to be valid as sampling; such a level of inspections was in fact laid down in a Directive,[41] and the question at issue was whether the provisions of the Directive contravened the principles of Articles 30 and 36. The view taken by the Court was that the Council had not exceeded the limits of its discretion, although the very incomplete nature of the harmonization effected by the directive was emphasized.

Import regulation of a rather different nature was encountered in the form of German legislation which allowed importation of pharmaceutical products from other Member States only by pharmacists or wholesalers in Germany, effectively prohibiting the private importation of such products. However, in the context of the importation by a private citizen of a product purchased from a pharmacy in France, and which could be purchased without prescription from a pharmacy in Germany, it was held that this rule went beyond what was necessary for the protection of health.[42] It would appear that the Court regarded the sale by a pharmacy in another Member State as a adequate protection.[43]

In summary, it would appear that procedures which amount to a prohibition on importation will not normally be regarded as necessary for the protection of health under Article 36,[44] except to enforce a legitimate prohibition on the use of certain additives, preservatives, or pesticides.[45] In so far as inspections or analyses are a permissible method of protecting health, they should not duplicate those carried out

[37] The matter of UHT milk has subsequently been regulated by Council Dir. 85/397 (OJ 1985, L 226/13) on health and animal-health problems affecting intra-Community trade in heat-treated milk.

[38] *Commission* v. *France*, Case 42/82, [1983] ECR 1013.

[39] Case 42/82R, [1982] ECR 841.

[40] Case 37/83, [1984] ECR 1229.

[41] Council Dir. 77/93 (OJ 1977, L 26/20) on protective measures against the introduction into the Member States of harmful organisms of plants or plant products.

[42] *Schumacher* v. *HZA Frankfurt am Main-Ost*, Case 215/87, (7 Mar. 1989).

[43] It noted that the profession of pharmacist was regulated by Council Dir. 85/432 and 85/433 (OJ 1985, L 253/34 and 37).

[44] See n. 7 above.

[45] See e.g. *Mirepoix*, Case 54/85, [1986] ECR 1067.

in other Member States,[46] and should also take account of information obtained in other Member States[47] (a similar rule applying also where there is a requirement to declare information).[48] In principle, it would appear that compliance with health requirements should be ensured by random sampling,[49] if inspections are an appropriate method.

Public morality, public policy, and public security

The general issues of necessity, proportionality, and non-discrimination are the same as in the context of the protection of health, and there are certain parallels in the case-law. The question of public morality first arose in *R. v. Henn and Darby*,[50] a criminal prosecution following an attempt to import pornographic literature from Denmark into the United Kingdom. It was argued that the United Kingdom customs legislation governing such imports could not be invoked because the equivalent domestic English and Scottish provisions were different from the customs legislation and from each other, so that to enforce special rules for imports would constitute discrimination. The Court, however, took the view that although there may have been differences in detail, there was no lawful domestic trade in such literature, so that to prohibit imports did not amount to arbitrary discrimination. While the decision has been criticized as allowing measures to be applied against imports which are different from those applying to domestic products, it in fact follows the same approach as was taken with regard to the protection of health in *Rewe-Zentralfinanz*,[51] where the Court held that inspections of imports to prevent San José Scale were permissible even though domestic products were not inspected in the same way, provided other effective measures were taken with regard to domestic products; in other words, it is not necessary that exactly the same measures are taken for domestic products as for imports, provided the same overall policy is pursued by effective means. On the other hand, if effective measures are not taken to prevent domestic trade, then imports cannot be prohibited on grounds of public morality. This situation occurred in *Conegate* v. *H.M. Customs and Excise*,[52] where it was held that the United Kingdom could not prevent the importation of life-size inflatable female dolls when (subject to certain limits) there was no prohibition on manufacturing or marketing such objects within the United Kingdom.[53] In both these public-morality cases, however, it was accepted that 'it is for each

---

[46] See n. 5 above.   [47] See n. 33 above.   [48] See n. 8 above.
[49] See n. 38 above.   [50] Case 34/79, [1979] ECR 3795.
[51] See n. 6 above, and p. 77 above.   [52] Case 121/85, [1986] ECR 1007.
[53] There is a clear link here with the public policy rules which affect the free movement of persons, as was recognized by Advocate General Slyn in his Opinion, [1986] ECR, p. 1011. See *Adoui and Cornuaille* v. *Belgium*, Cases 115 and 116/81, [1982] ECR 1665.

Member State to determine in accordance with its own scale of values and in the form selected by it the requirements of public morality in its territory'.

At the time of writing, there has only been one example of the protection of public policy.[54] This was *R. v. Thompson and others*,[55] which involved a breach of the United Kingdom rules then in force prohibiting the importation of gold coins and the export of silver-alloy coins minted before 1947. The judgment is of particular importance to the extent that it established a distinction between 'goods' and 'means of payment', the free-movement-of-goods rules not applying to 'means of payment'. While the criteria used by the Court have been heavily criticized,[56] it took the view that since the silver-alloy coins minted before 1947 were not legal tender, they were not a 'means of payment' and could be designated as goods. The question of the application of Article 36 therefore arose, and the Court started from the premise that it is for Member States to mint their own coinage and to protect it from destruction. Being informed that, in the United Kingdom, the melting down or destruction of national coins was prohibited even if they were no longer legal tender, the Court held that a ban on exporting such coins which was imposed to prevent their being melted down or destroyed in another Member State was justified on grounds of public policy under Article 36.

There has also been one example of the protection of public security. The issue at stake in *Campus Oil*[57] was the security of oil supplies. The case involved Irish legislation requiring importers of petroleum products to buy a proportion of their requirements at prices fixed by the competent Minister from the only refinery in Ireland, which was owned by the State. Ireland's argument was that the importance of oil for the life of the country made it indispensible to maintain refining capacity on the national territory, and the system at issue was the only means of ensuring that the refinery's products could be marketed. The Court asserted that this was a matter of public security rather than public policy, accepted that an interruption of supplies of petroleum products could seriously affect public security, and further accepted that the fact that a measure justified on grounds of public security might also achieve certain economic objectives did not take it out of the scope of Article 36. The Commission argued that if there was a crisis, there would above all

---

[54] Analogous principles have, however, been applied with regard to the provision of services, despite the silence of the Treaty on the point. For example, in *Debauve*, Case 52/79, [1980] ECR 833, it was recognized that a Member State may enforce its public policy with regard to the prohibition of advertising on television against television services provided from another Member State through a cable system.

[55] Case 7/78, [1978] ECR 2247.

[56] See F. A. Mann, *Legal Aspects of Money* (4th edn., 1982), pp. 24–5.

[57] Case 72/83, [1984] ECR 2727.

be a shortage of crude oil, making the refinery unable to operate, but the Court took the view that having a refinery enabled the State to enter into long-term contracts with oil-producing countries, which would offer a better guarantee of supplies in the event of a crisis, and that it reduced the dependence of the State on the commercial policies of the major oil companies. It was held, however, that the purchasing obligation could be imposed only if no less-restrictive measure was capable of achieving the same objective, and that the quantities covered by the system must not exceed the minimum supply requirements without which the public security of the State would be affected or the level of production necessary to keep the refinery's production capacity available.

The effect of Community measures

It is clear that both under Article 36[58] and under the theory of the protection of mandatory requirements,[59] national measures may only be justified where the matter at issue is not governed by provisions of Community law. The question then arises as to how specific the Community legislation has to be before it precludes national legislation. Many of the cases cited above involved Community legislation which was found to be incomplete or not relevant.[60] As a further illustration, in *Denkavit Futtermittel*[61] it was held that, where Directives regulated the composition and preparation of animal foodstuffs but did not regulate health inspections of those products, Member States could still justify national health inspections under Article 36. In some instances,[62] Community law itself may permit or require Member States to carry out inspections or take other measures, but it is now clear that the Council or Commission may not authorize a Member State to take measures which go beyond those which would be justified under Article 36.[63]

On the other hand, a Member State may not invoke its own legislation where EEC Directives expressly require a Member State to allow the marketing of goods which comply with the provisions of those Directives,[64] and more generally, national legislation will not be justified if the Community legislation is intended to regulate the matter at issue in a comprehensive manner. This was clearly shown in *Commission* v.

---

[58] See n. 5 above, pp. 3388–9.
[59] *Rewe* v. *Bundesmonopolverwaltung für Branntwein*, Case 120/78, [1979] ECR 649, p. 662. Reaffirmed for both situations in *Wurmser* (n. 5 above).
[60] See e.g. *Mirepoix* (n. 45 above).
[61] Case 73/84, [1985] ECR 1019.
[62] See e.g. *Rewe*, Case 37/83, [1984] ECR 1229.
[63] *Commission* v. *Italy*, Case C–128/89, (12 July 1990), para. 17.
[64] *Ratti*, Case 148/78, [1979] ECR 1629, which concerned directives on the labelling of paints and varnishes.

Germany,[65] where the animal-foodstuffs Directives, which, as men
tioned in the previous paragraph, had been held not to preclude health
inspections under national law,[66] were found to create a comprehensive
system with regard to the composition and preparation of animal
foodstuffs, so that Germany could not lay down its own rules on
minimum and maximum levels of certain ingredients. Similarly, where
Community law sets up a comprehensive system of health controls on
export, as in trade in fresh poultry-meat, the importing Member State
may no longer impose systematic checks on importation under its own
law.[67] Community legislation may be comprehensive without necessarily dealing with the precise point raised by the Member State, and may
therefore have the effect of 'freezing' the situation. This occurred in
Commission v. *United Kingdom*,[68] with regard to motor-vehicle headlights. The United Kingdom introduced legislation requiring the fitting
of a 'dim-dip' device, invoking safety grounds, but it was held that the
EEC Directives on motor-vehicle headlights regulated the matter in an
exhaustive manner, so that a Member State could not require a form of
lighting which was not listed in those Directives.

This line of case-law would appear to be challenged by the wording of
Article 100A(4) of the EEC Treaty, introduced by the Single European
Act. Article 100A provides that harmonization of national legislation for
the purpose of establishing the internal market by the end of 1992 may
be achieved by 'measures' (rather than directives alone, as under Article
100) adopted by a qualified majority. However, where such measures
are adopted by a qualified majority, Article 100A(4) provides that 'a
Member State which deems it necessary to apply national provisions on
grounds of major needs referred to in Article 36, or relating to protection
of the environment or the working environment' shall notify such
provisions to the Commission, and the Commission may confirm them
after having verified that they are not a means of arbitrary discrimination or a disguised restriction on trade between Member States. If it
considers that a Member State is making improper use of the powers
provided for in this paragraph, the Commission (or another Member
State may invoke an accelerated enforcement procedure against the
Member State. The obvious intention of this provision is to override the
Court's case-law and empower Member states to legislate on matters
covered by Community legislation, at least where that legislation is
enacted under Article 100A. It does, nevertheless, give rise to both
procedural and substantive difficulties. Procedurally, does it apply

---

[65] Case 28/84, [1985] ECR 3097.
[66] See n. 61 above.
[67] *Moormann*, Case 190/87, [1988] ECR 4689; *Commission* v. *Germany*, Case 186/88, (28 Nov. 1989).
[68] Case 60/86, [1988] ECR 3921.

whenever Article 100A is used, or only if a qualified majority vote is taken? If, as appears likely, it only applies to the latter case, can it be invoked by any Member State or only by a Member State which voted against the legislation? The further problem then arises as to whether the Commission's confirmation is to be obtained before or after the entry into force of the national measures.[69]

In the present context, however, it is the substantive problem which is perhaps of greater interest. Article 100A(4) speaks of 'major needs referred to in Article 36', yet the provisions of Article 36 make no reference to 'major needs'. A perusal of the French text shows that it uses the phrase *'exigences importantes'*, which appears to bear a family resemblance to the phrase *'exigences impératives'* used in the French texts of judgments following the *Cassis de Dijon*[70] case-law and rendered into English as 'mandatory requirements'. It may, therefore, be wondered if the drafting of Article 100A(4) does not betray some confusion between that concept and Article 36. Be that as it may, the limitation by reference to Article 36 means that Article 100A(4) cannot be used, for example, to protect consumers,[71] although it may be used to protect health, and the specific reference to the environment means that it may also be used in that context. Nevertheless, perhaps because of the procedural problems outlined above, Article 100A(4) does not yet appear to have been invoked by any Member State, despite the fears expressed at the time the Single European Act was signed that it would destroy the Court's achievements in this sphere.[72] More positively, Article 100A(4) may be seen as the price to be paid for the acceptance of a system of decision-making which may lead to the enactment of Community legislation in areas still subject to national measures. Article 100A has in fact been used in the context of measures relating to health, such as food additives,[73] in the context of consumer protection, such as the indication of prices,[74] and in the context of the protection of the environment, as in the legislation on air-pollution by gaseous emissions from motor vehicles,[75] to give examples from important areas that could otherwise be subject to national legislation which would have the effect of hindering the free movement of goods.

It would, however, be a mistake to think that Community legislative activity in this area is only a recent phenomenon. In 1980, just after the *Cassis de Dijon*[76] judgment, the United Kingdom Department of Trade

---

[69] See Flynn, 'How will art. 100A(4) work?' (1987) 24 C.M.L.Rev., 689.

[70] [1979] ECR 649. See p. 65 above.

[71] See e.g. *Commission* v. *Ireland*, Case 113/80, [1981] ECR 1625, p. 1638.

[72] Pescatore, 'Observations critiques sur l'acte unique européen' in Louis (ed.), *L'acte unique européen* (1986), p. 39 at p. 45.

[73] See e.g. Council Dir. 89/107 (OJ 1989, L 40/27).

[74] Council Dir. 88/314 and 88/315 (OJ 1988, L 142/19 and 23).

[75] Council Dir. 88/76 and 88/436 (OJ 1988, L 36/1 and L 214/1).

[76] See n. 70 above.

and Industry reported that there were more than 140 harmonization directives in the industrial sector and about forty concerning foodstuffs.[77] Food-additive legislation, involving the famous 'E' numbers, dates back to 1962,[78] but there is also a long series of directives on motor-vehicle construction, generally drafted in very great detail and even including diagrams,[79] some of which were at issue in the 'dim-dip' headlights case.[80]

However, as has been noted,[81] following the *Cassis de Dijon* case-law a change of policy occurred, and the Commission announced[82] that it would concentrate its efforts on proposing the harmonization of national laws in those areas (that is, 'mandatory requirements' and matters governed by Article 36) where national rules could still legitimately be used to hinder trade between Member States. This was largely reflected in the Council Resolution of 7 May 1985 on a new approach to technical harmonization and standards,[83] which emphasizes that legislative harmonization in that context should be limited to the adoption of the essential safety requirements. It also states that drawing up technical specifications should be entrusted to organizations competent in the standardization area: the specifications would not be mandatory, but products manufactured in confirmity with them would be presumed to conform to the essential requirements of the Directive. Legislation enacted under Article 100A concerned with the free movement of goods, therefore, largely follows the same approach. To take the example of Council Directive 88/378 on the safety of toys,[84] 'the harmonization to be achieved should consist in establishing the essential safety requirements to be satisfied by all toys if they are to be placed on the market'. Whilst it sets its own basic objective of ensuring that 'toys may be placed on the market only if they do not jeopardize the safety and/or health of users or third parties',[85] the Directive provides that, as envisaged in the Council Resolution, harmonized standards are to be set by the European Committee for Standardization (CEN) and the European Committee for Electrotechnical Standardization (CENELEC) on a remit from the Commission in accordance with Council Directive 83/189[86] on the provision of information in the field of technical standards and regulations. That Directive, it may be noted, also provides a mechanism for draft national standards to be communicated

---

[77] *British Business*, (4 July 1980), pp. 322–7.
[78] Council Dir. of 23 Oct. 1962 on colouring matters (JO 1962, p. 2645).
[79] See e.g. Dir. 79/795 on rear-view mirrors (OJ 1979, L 239/1).
[80] *Commission* v. *United Kingdom*, Case 60/86, [1988] ECR 3921.
[81] See p. 66 above.
[82] Communication of 3 Oct. 1980 (OJ 1980, C 256/3). See p. 00 above.
[83] OJ 1985, C 136/1.
[84] OJ 1988, L 187/1.
[85] Art. 2.
[86] OJ 1983, L 109/8.

to the Commission, and enables the entry into force of such standards to be delayed to allow for amendment to remove or reduce barriers which they might create to the free movement of goods, or to allow the Commission to propose a directive on the subject.

Reference to standards set by CEN and CENELEC is not in fact new,[87] but formal guide-lines for co-operation between them and the Commission were signed in November 1984.[88] While the Toy Safety Directive does not, therefore, set its own detailed standards, it sets out in an annex three pages of 'essential safety requirements for toys'. Compliance with these requirements is presumed if the manufacturer follows the harmonized standards, and Member States may appoint 'approved bodies' to carry out 'EC type-examination' of models of toys which do not follow the harmonized standards to see if they nevertheless meet those requirements, other Member States being in principle required to accept that determination. It may be wondered whether this is in reality simpler than setting detailed Community standards.[89]

[87] See Dir. 73/23 on low-voltage electrical equipment (OJ 1973, L 77/29).
[88] As stated in the recitals to the Directive.
[89] See, however, Commission Communication of 16 October 1990 on the development of European Standardization (OJ 1991 C20/1).

PART II

Free Movement of Persons

8
Structure and Scope of the Law

Introduction

There can be no doubt that freedom of movement for labour is an essential element of a common market. Without it, the market would be distorted, since workers would not be able to move from countries where there is unemployment and wages are low to those where there is a labour shortage and consequent high wages. Moreover, the concept of a common market also requires that businessmen should be able to carry on their activities in whatever country they deem most attractive; likewise, professionals and other self-employed persons should be able to open an office wherever there is a call for their services. None of this is possible without freedom of movement for the persons concerned.

However, it is not necessary for this purpose to have freedom of movement for *everybody*: all that is required is that what Community officials call 'economically active' persons should be able to move freely in order to carry on their activities in other Member States. This is why the EEC Treaty does not give the right of free movement to everyone, but only to certain categories of persons—workers, self-employed persons and providers of services. The absence of a general right of free movement, and the consequent categorization of the persons who benefit from it, is one of the basic features of the Community law on this subject.

At this point, it is necessary to confront a fundamental question regarding the nature of the Community: are its objectives economic only—as the name 'European Economic Community' suggests—or does it also have objectives in the social and even political spheres? If the former view is correct, the free movement of persons cannot be regarded as a Community objective in its own right, but merely as a means to an end. In such a case, there can be no such thing as Community social policy (except to the extent that this serves economic ends), but only Community economic policy.

If we look just at the EEC Treaty, especially if we concern ourselves only with the Treaty in its original form, the economic viewpoint predominates. Most Treaty articles are concerned with economic matters and deal with social questions only to the extent that they are relevant to the attainment of economic objectives.[1] The provisions in the Treaty that appear to contradict this are largely concerned with laying down general principles and rarely contain any hard law. With few exceptions, they do not appear to be directly effective or to confer legislative power on the Council or Commission.[2] One can conclude, therefore, that the authors of the EEC Treaty regarded the Community as predominantly an economic organization.

However, though the initial objectives of the Community were almost entirely economic, its nature has changed over the years. Today it is widely accepted, not least by the Community institutions themselves, that the Community has a social dimension. It is thought that the Community should concern itself more with the individual than it has in the past, and the concept of a 'People's Europe' is intended to give expression to this idea.[3] This new thinking is evidenced both in the Single European Act and in some of the more recent pieces of Community legislation. The best examples of the latter are three directives passed in 1990 granting rights of free movement to three categories of persons whose only common characteristic is that they are *not* economically active—students, retired persons and persons of independent means.[4] Other examples may be found in the field of sex discrimination.[5] Thus, though the Community law on the free move-

---

[1] At first sight the provision concerned with sex discrimination, Art. 119 EEC, might seem an exception to this. However, it contains a very interesting feature: it does not prohibit sex discrimination in general; it merely provides for equal pay for equal work. In other words, it does not prevent employers from discriminating with regard to appointment, promotion or dismissal: an employer is not obliged to employ women, but if he does, he must pay them the same salary as men. This suggests that the purpose of Art. 119 is not so much to help women achieve equality as to prevent unfair competition between manufacturers in different Member States: apparently employers in Member States which already had equal-pay legislation when the Treaty was being negotiated were afraid that they would be at a disadvantage if manufacturers in other Member States could employ cheap female labour. Art. 119, therefore, can also be regarded as supporting the economic thesis.

[2] Examples are Art. 50, which requires the Member States to encourage the exchange of young workers; Art. 117, which states that the Member States agree upon the need to promote improved working conditions and an improved standard of living for workers; and Art. 118, which gives the Commission the task of promoting close co-operation between Member States in the social field, especially with regard to certain specified matters. (Despite its wording, the European Court has in fact held that Art. 118 gives the Commission implied legislative powers: see *Germany* v. *Commission*, Cases 281, 283–5, 287/85, [1987] ECR 3203.)

[3] See the reports of the Committee on a People's Europe (Adonnino Committee) presented to the European Council in March and June 1985, summarized by the Commission in COM (88) 331 (7 July 1988).

[4] Dir. 90/366, OJ 1990, L 180/30 (students); Dir. 90/365, OJ 1990, L 180/28 (retired persons); and Dir. 90/364, OJ 1990, L 180/26 (which purports to give a general right of residence, but which in fact was aimed at persons of independent means).

[5] See Dir. 76/207 (usually known as the Equal Treatment Directive), which makes good the deficiencies of Art. 119 of the Treaty by extending the prohibition against sex discrimination to cover appointment, promotion and dismissal, and Dir. 79/7, which

ment of persons was originally adopted for the purpose of attaining economic objectives, in particular the establishment of the common market, its nature has changed, together with that of the Community itself: freedom of movement for the citizens of the Community is now regarded as an objective in its own right.

Persons Covered

Title III of Part Two of the EEC Treaty contains three chapters concerned with the free movement of persons:[6] Chapter 1 deals with workers; Chapter 2 with the right of establishment; and Chapter 3 with services.[7] Workers, persons enjoying the right of establishment and providers of services are, therefore, the three basic categories of persons covered by Community law. Community legislation has added further categories— receivers of services, students, retired persons, persons of independent means and the families of any of the above. Taken together, these categories add up to almost, but not quite, the whole population.[8] However, the law is still fragmented, with different provisions applying to different categories and, though the rights given to each category are usually similar, it is still necessary to start any discussion of the law with an analysis of the categories of persons to whom rights are given. In doing this, it should be remembered that the meaning of concepts employed by Community law is solely a matter for Community law itself. National rules defining, for example, a 'worker' are of no relevance.[9]

WORKERS

Chapter 1 uses the term 'workers', but does not define it. However, Community legislation and the case-law of the European Court make clear that a 'worker' is any employed person, irrespective of whether he performs managerial or manual functions. If we examine this concept

provides for equal treatment of men and women in matters of social security. Both these directives, it should be noted, apply generally to all women, not just to immigrants, and the latter is not confined to workers.

[6] There is also a fourth chapter, dealing with the free movement of capital.

[7] Title III of the Treaty bears the heading, 'Free Movement of Persons, Services and Capital', thereby implying that only Chaps 1 and 2 are concerned with the free movement of persons. However, services cannot move by themselves, and Chap. 3 in fact gives the person providing the service the right to pursue his activity in another Member State.

[8] Persons who are unable to support themselves (and who are not members of the families of persons covered) are excluded. Examples are tramps, beggars and persons dependent on supplementary benefit.

[9] See, for example, *Hoekstra* v. *Bestuur der Bedrijfsvereniging voor Detailhandel en Ambachten*, Case 75/63, [1964] ECR 177.

more carefully, it becomes apparent that its exact meaning depends on the context. In other words, it may have a more extended meaning for some purposes than for others. The best way of looking at it is to think in terms of a core concept and an extended concept. The core concept is that of a person in permanent employment in a Member State other than that of which he is a national. Such a person is a 'worker' in the fullest sense and has all the rights granted by Community law.

The extended concept covers the following:

1. *Temporary workers.* These are persons whose job in the country to which they have migrated is intended to last only a limited time (less than twelve months);[10]

2. *Frontier workers.* These are persons who live in their own country but work in another, returning home each day or at least once a week;[11]

3. *Work-seekers.* These are persons who do not have (and never have had) a job in the country to which they have migrated, but who have come to look for work;

4. *Involuntarily unemployed workers.* These are persons who previously had a job in the country to which they have migrated, but have become unemployed through circumstances beyond their control. (If they voluntarily gave up their job with no intention of taking another, they are not covered by Community law);[12]

5. *Temporarily incapacitated persons.* These are persons who previously worked in the country to which they have migrated, but are temporarily incapable of work due to illness or injury;

6. *Permanently incapacitated persons and retired persons.* These are persons who previously worked in the country to which they have migrated, but have permanently ceased work either because they are permanently incapable of working due to illness or injury, or because they have reached the age of retirement;

7. *Family Members.* Members of an immigrant's family are covered even if they are not workers. This means that they can accompany the worker and reside with him (or her). The following qualify as members of the family:[13]

   (*a*) the spouse (wife or husband);

   (*b*) children, grandchildren and other descendants, provided they are either under 21 or dependent[14] on the worker;

   (*c*) parents, grandparents and other ascendants, provided they are dependent on the worker.

---

[10] See Dir. 68/360, Arts 6(3) and 8(1)(a).
[11] See Dir. 68/360, Art. 8(1)(b).
[12] For a fuller discussion of the meaning of this concept, see p. 119 below.
[13] Dir. 68/360, Art. 1 together with Reg. 1612/68, Art. 10(1).
[14] On the meaning of 'dependent', see p. 152 below.

All the persons covered by the extended concept enjoy rights under Community law, but these rights are usually more limited than those of persons within the core concept.

Self-Employed Persons

Chapter 2 covers self-employed persons, such as members of the professions, businessmen, tradesmen, craftsmen, writers, artists, performers, and so on. It only applies, however, to persons wishing to establish themselves on a permanent basis in the new country. Those going on a temporary basis come under Chapter 3.

The core concept under Chapter 2 is that of a person permanently established in his occupation in the country to which he has migrated. The extended concept is similar to that in Chapter 1, but is more limited: temporary immigrants and, it seems, the self-employed equivalent of frontier workers are excluded: they both come under Chapter 3.

It also appears that Chapter 2 does not cover formerly self-employed persons whose business or profession has failed.[15]

The persons within the extended concept are:

1. *Prospective self-employed persons.* These are persons who wish to establish themselves in the country of immigration but have not yet done so.
2. *Temporarily incapacitated self-employed persons.* This is the same as the equivalent category under Chapter 1.
3. *Permanently incapacitated and retired self-employed persons.* This is the same as the equivalent category under Chapter 1.
4. *Family Members.* Members of the families of any of the above are covered. The definition of the family is the same as in the case of workers except that descendants other than children (for example, grandchildren) are covered only if they are dependent. Thus a financially independent grandchild of a self-employed person is not covered even if he is under 21.[16]

In one respect, Chapter 2 is more extensive than Chapter 1: it covers legal persons (companies) as well as natural persons (individuals).[17] This means that if a company incorporated in England wishes to do business in Germany by establishing a branch there, its right to do so is granted by Chapter 2. However, if it wants to send over some of its English employees to staff the branch, their right to enter Germany and reside there comes from Chapter 1, since they are workers, not self-employed persons.

---

[15] There is no equivalent in Dir. 73/148 to Art. 7 of Dir. 68/360.
[16] Dir. 73/148, Art. 1(1)(c) and (d).

SERVICES

Chapter 3 is the only one of the three chapters to define the concept on which it is based. Article 60 EEC states:

Services shall be considered to be 'services' within the meaning of this Treaty where they are normally provided for remuneration, in so far as they are not governed by the provisions relating to freedom of movement for goods, capital and persons.

'Services' shall in particular include:
(a) activities of an industrial character;
(b) activities of a commercial character;
(c) activities of craftsmen;
(d) activities of the professions.

Without prejudice to the provisions of the Chapter relating to the right of establishment, the person providing a service may, in order to do so, temporarily pursue his activity in the State where the service is provided, under the same conditions as are imposed by that State on its own nationals.

Though far from ideal as a definition, this provision makes clear that a service is an activity of a kind that is normally provided on a commercial basis (thus excluding, for example, charitable and religious activities or state education);[18] it also implies that any activity covered by Chapter 1 or Chapter 2 is automatically excluded. It is implicit that there must be some transnational (cross-border) element in the activity. The result is that one can define a service as a transnational activity of a kind normally performed for remuneration, carried out on a short-term basis by a self-employed person.[19]

Article 60 expressly grants immigration rights to the provider of a service in order to pursue his activity in another Member State. This will usually be the State where the recipient resides, but may be a third State—for example, where a free-lance journalist resident in England goes to France to research an article for a newspaper in Holland. In addition, Article 1(1)(b) of Directive 73/148 grants immigration rights to the recipient of the service: he may, therefore, travel to the provider of the service, or they may meet in a third country.

A complication is introduced by the definition in Article 59 EEC, which refers to the provision of services by nationals of Member States who are established in a State of the Community other than that of the person for whom the services are intended. This could be regarded as excluding from Chapter 3 the case where both provider and recipient are

---

[17] See Art. 58 EEC.

[18] *Humbel*, Case 263/86, [1989] CMLR 393 (discussed below in Chap. 13).

[19] It will be remembered that temporary activities performed by self-employed persons are not covered by Chap. 2.

resident in the same State, but the service is performed in another State. Examples of such a situation are a British free-lance journalist reporting on events in France for a British newspaper, or a British architect designing a house in Italy for a British client. Notwithstanding the provision of Article 59, however, one can expect the European Court, in view of its policy of expanding the ambit of the Treaty wherever possible, to hold that the above examples are covered by Chapter 3. In other words, Chapter 3 probably covers all cases where there is a transnational element, even if the provider and recipient of the service live in the same country.

Is it possible to perform a service for oneself? Take the case of an English author who goes to Holland to promote his new book. It could be argued that he is performing a service for his publishers, but he will not be paid by them for making the trip: the reward he hopes to obtain is increased sales and higher royalties. Another example is a businessman who goes to look for business—perhaps new customers or sales outlets, perhaps new suppliers, perhaps new investment opportunities. Again, one could hardly say that he is performing a service for the people concerned. Yet both examples concern commercial activities which should be covered by heading (b) in the second paragraph of Article 60: there is little doubt that the European Court would so hold. It seems, therefore, that the existence of a recipient may not—despite the terms of Article 59 EEC (quoted above)—be necessary for an activity to be covered by Chapter 3.

Since the migration rights covered by Chapter 3 are for a specific purpose and a limited period, there can be no question of an 'extended concept'. Once the service has been performed, the immigration right is at an end: no rights are given to retired, unemployed or incapacitated providers of services.[20] Family members (both of the provider and the recipient) are, however, covered. The definition of the family is the same as that in the case of the right of establishment.[21]

In terms of numbers, the most important group of persons entitled to immigration rights under this head are tourists, who are covered on the basis that they are recipients of services.[22] This means that they are

---

[20] Advocate General Lenz appears to believe that providers (and recipients?) of services can claim the right to remain (*Cowan*, Case 186/87, [1989] ECR 195 at para. 16 of the Opinion), but this cannot be correct, despite the reference in Art. 1 of Dir. 75/34 to Art 1 of Dir. 73/148: the title, preamble and operative provisions of Dir. 75/34 all refer—in sharp contrast to those of Dir. 73/148—to establishment only. However, the boundary between establishment and services—that is, between permanent and temporary activities—is fluid, and one could perhaps say that if a person resides long enough in the country concerned to qualify for the right to remain, that is itself a strong indication that he is established there.

[21] Dir. 73/148, Art. 1(1)(c) and (d).

[22] *Luisi and Carbone*, Cases 286/82, 26/83, [1984] ECR 377.

entitled to both immigration rights (in practice, never a serious problem) and the right to equal treatment in the country they visit.[23]

Companies are covered by Chapter 3; so the right of a British advertising agency to handle the account of a Danish manufacturer comes under Chapter 3. Again, the right of employees of the company to travel to Denmark to meet the client would come under Chapter 1.

It could be difficult to know whether a case is covered by Chapter 2 or Chapter 3 where it is not certain in which country the person is established. Two examples, both based on decided cases, will make this clear. In the first example, the person works from home. His home (office) is in Belgium but his clients are in the Netherlands. He is clearly established in Belgium and performs services for his various Dutch clients. Chapter 3 gives him the right to travel to Holland and carry on his activities there under the same conditions as persons resident there.[24]

The second example is that of an insurance broker who is resident in Belgium and works in the Netherlands. In contrast to the previous case, his office is also in the Netherlands. It could be argued that he is established in the Netherlands and therefore comes under Chapter 2. (He would be the self-employed equivalent of a frontier worker.) However, in *Coenen* v. *Sociaal-Economische Raad*,[25] the European Court dealt with the case under Chapter 3. It did not, however, make much difference which Chapter applied, and the point was not really a contentious issue.

Others

Put together, Chapters 1–3 cover all economically significant activities, provided there is some Community element.[26] This fulfils the economic objectives of the EEC Treaty.[27] As was said previously, it is now widely considered that the objectives of the Community extend beyond the establishment of a common market, and the Commission has been working for some time to extend the scope of Community migration law

---

[23] *Cowan* (see n. 20 above).

[24] *Van Binsbergen*, Case 33/74, [1974] ECR 1299.

[25] Case 39/75, [1975] ECR 1547.

[26] Chaps 1–3 do not apply to situations which have no Community element: *R.* v. *Saunders*, Case 175/78, [1979] ECR 1129; *Morson and Jhanjan* v. *The Netherlands*, Case 35, 36/82, [1982] ECR 3723; *Moser* v. *Land Baden-Württemberg*, Case 180/83, [1984] ECR 2539.

[27] For the position of workers in the industries covered by the ECSC and Euratom Treaties, see Art. 69(1) ECSC and Art. 96 Euratom, together with the Dir. of 5 Mar. 1962, OJ (Special English Edn) 1959/62, p. 245 (Euratom); Dec. 74/494, OJ 1974, L 269/25 (ECSC); Art. 11 of Dir. 68/360; and Art. 42(1) of Reg. 1612/68. The result of these provisions is that such workers almost certainly have the same rights as those covered by the EEC Treaty. See, further, Hartley, *EEC Immigration Law* (1978), pp. 137 and 140.

to cover almost everyone who might want to move to another Community country, irrespective of whether or not they are going for a purpose which could be regarded as 'economic'. In 1979 the Commission submitted a draft directive to the Council to bring this about,[28] but the Council failed to adopt the draft and in 1989 the Commission withdrew it, replacing it with proposals for three new directives covering persons of independent means, retired persons and students. These were adopted by the Council on 28 June 1990, acting (in all three cases) under Article 235 EEC; the deadline for their implementation is 30 June 1992.[29]

An important feature of these directives is that they are intended to be purely supplementary: they do not apply if the person concerned comes within one of the categories previously mentioned of persons enjoying rights of free movement under Community law.[30] This is of special significance in the case of Directive 90/364, which at first sight seems to give a general right of residence. However, since it applies only to nationals of Member States 'who do not enjoy this right under other provisions of Community law', and then only if they are able to support themselves, it becomes clear that it applies only to persons of independent means. This was in fact the intention behind it.

The idea behind each of the directives is that the persons concerned should be entitled to rights under Community law provided they (and their families) have sufficient financial resources to avoid their becoming a burden on the social-security system of the Member State to which they migrate.[31] They must also be covered by medical insurance.[32]

These are the only requirements for benefiting from the rights conferred by Directive 90/364 (persons of independent means). To be covered by Directive 90/365 (retired persons), the applicant must, in

---

[28] Proposal for a Council Directive on a right of residence for nationals of Member States in the territory of another Member State, OJ 1979, C 207, p. 14.

[29] Dir. 90/364, OJ 1990, L 180/26 (persons of independent means); Dir. 90/365, ibid., p. 28 (retired persons); and Dir. 90/366, ibid., p. 30 (students).

[30] This is expressly stated in Art. 1 of Dirs 90/364 and 90/366 respectively. It is not expressly stated in Dir. 90/365, which concerns retired people. Such persons would only rarely come within one of the other categories—they might do so as members of the family of an economically active person—and it was probably considered unnecessary to state expressly that the directive was only supplementary.

[31] In Dirs 90/364 and 90/365 it is stated that the resources of the applicant will be deemed sufficient if they are higher than the level below which the Member State may grant social assistance to its nationals, taking into account the personal circumstances of the applicant and, where appropriate, the members of his family. Where this test cannot be applied, the level of the minimum social security pension provides the appropriate criterion.

[32] It is not entirely clear whether this requirement applies in the case of the United Kingdom. It could, however, be argued that if such migrants do not take out private medical insurance, they would become a burden on the taxpayer if they became ill and had to resort to the National Health Service.

addition, be in receipt of a pension.[33] To come within the scope of Directive 90/366 (students), the additional requirement is that the applicant must be enrolled in a recognized educational establishment for the principal purpose of following a vocational training[34] course.[35]

The members of the families of persons falling into these three categories are also covered, even if they would not otherwise come within the scope of Community law.[36]

International Scope

The international scope of the Community provisions must be considered under two heads—the international personal scope and the international territorial scope. The international personal scope relates to the persons who benefit from the Community rights; the international territorial scope is concerned with the territory within which the rights may be exercised. As a matter of principle, the two should be linked: if the inhabitants of territory X are obliged to compete for jobs with immigrants from territory Y, it is only right that they themselves should be entitled to migrate to territory Y and work there. In other words, the beneficiaries of the rights should be the inhabitants of the territories over which the rights extend. Though not enshrined in the Treaties, this equivalence between the personal and the territorial scope is, as will be seen below, largely respected in Community law.

TERRITORIAL SCOPE[37]

Article 227 EEC lays down the general principle that the Treaty applies to the Member States (which means that it operates within the territory of the Member States)[38] and then sets out a number of special provisions

---

[33] This may be an invalidity or early retirement pension, old-age benefit, or a pension in respect of an industrial accident or disease. The amount must be sufficient to avoid the person's becoming a burden on the social-security system of the Member State.

[34] The meaning of this phrase is discussed in Chap. 13 (pp. 179–81): it covers most, but not quite all, university courses.

[35] It is not expressly stated that the course must be a full-time one, but if it did not occupy a substantial portion of his time, the would-be student might find it difficult to establish that his 'principal purpose' in migrating was to follow the course.

[36] In the case of Dirs 90/364 and 90/365, the definition of 'family' is the same as for self-employed persons (see above); in the case of students, it is narrower: only the student's spouse and dependent children are covered. This is presumably because the student's sojourn in the country concerned will be of limited duration. In all cases, family members need not be Community nationals.

[37] For a more detailed discussion of this topic, see Hartley, *EEC Immigration Law*, Chap. 2.

[38] See Arts 48(1), 48(3)(b), 48(3)(c), 48(3)(d), 52 and 58 EEC; see also Reg. 1612/68, Arts 1 and 47; Dir. 68/360, Art. 2; Reg. 1251/70, Art. 1; Dir. 73/148, Arts 1. 3, 4 and 5, and Dir. 75/34, Art. 1.

(some of which are now out of date) which qualify this principle.[39] The most important points to note are the following:

1. The French overseas departments (which are constitutionally a part of France) are covered;[40]
2. The 'overseas countries and territories', which are dependencies of the Member States outside Europe,[41] are excluded as far as workers are concerned;[42]
3. Hong Kong, which is not an overseas country or territory, is excluded by virtue of Article 227(3), the second paragraph of which provides that the EEC Treaty does not apply to dependencies of the United Kingdom which are not on the list of 'overseas countries and territories';
4. Greenland and the Faroes, both linked to Denmark, are excluded;[43]
5. The Channel Islands and the Isle of Man are excluded;[44]
6. Gibraltar is included by virtue of Article 227(4), which provides that the EEC Treaty applies to 'the European Territories for whose external relations a Member State is responsible';
7. The United Kingdom Sovereign Base Areas in Cyprus[45] are excluded.[46]

---

[39] For example, the reference to Algeria in Art. 227(2) is no longer operative since Algeria, once part of France, is now an independent state.

[40] Art. 227(2) EEC together with Decs 64/350 and 68/359.

[41] They were originally listed in Annex IV to the EEC Treaty (see Art. 227(3) EEC). However, the European Court held in *Lensing* v. *Hauptzollamt Berlin-Packhof*, Case 147/73, [1973] ECR 1543, that once a territory on the list gains independence, it automatically ceases to be a 'country' or 'territory' for the purposes of the EEC Treaty. Updated lists of the countries and territories have been set out in a series of decisions adopted by the Council under Art. 136 EEC. The most recent list is contained in Annex I to Dec. 86/283.

[42] Art. 135 EEC states that 'freedom of movement . . . within the countries and territories for workers from Member States shall be governed by agreements to be concluded subsequently with the unanimous approval of Member States'. No such agreements have been concluded. For the position regarding establishment and services, see Art. 176 of Dec. 86/283 and *Kaefer and Procacci* v. *France*, Cases C–100, 101/89, judgment of 12 December 1990, *The Times*, 25 February 1991, where it was held that Art. 176 provides immigration rights in connection with establishment and services, but that such rights are subject to the same restrictions as apply to immigrants who are citizens of the Member State of which the country or territory is a dependency. They are also subject to a condition of reciprocity.

[43] Greenland decided to leave the Community, a decision given effect to in a Treaty signed in Brussels on 13 Mar. 1984. Under this, Greenland is now an overseas country or territory: see Art. 136A EEC. The Faroes are excluded by Art. 227(5)(a) EEC: no declaration under that provision was made by Denmark by the date specified.

[44] See Art. 227(5)(c) EEC and Protocol 3 to the Act of Accession of 1972.

[45] These are British military bases in Cyprus which remained under British sovereignty when Cyprus became independent.

[46] Art. 227(5)(b) EEC.

International Personal Scope[47]

The basic criterion for determining the international personal scope of the Community provisions is nationality—that is to say, the beneficiaries of the Community rights are the citizens of the Member States. This is made clear by the Treaty as regards establishment[48] and services,[49] and by Community legislation as far as workers are concerned.[50] As a result, someone who is not a citizen of a Member State cannot benefit from Community immigration rights even if he is lawfully resident within the Community: admission to one Member State does not carry with it the right to reside in any other Member State.[51] This contrasts with the general principle regarding free movement of goods: normally goods from outside the Community which have been lawfully admitted to one Member State can thereafter move freely to other Member States. The reason for the difference is simple: there are common Community rules regulating imports of goods from outside the Community (the Common External Tariff), but no common rules regulating the entry of people. Community immigration rules apply only to immigration within the Community: immigration from outside the Community is a matter for each Member State.[52] If non-Community citizens admitted by one Member State could settle anywhere they wanted in the Community, the result would be that the Member State with the most lenient immigration rules would in effect determine immigration policy for the whole Community.

There are, therefore, good reasons for using nationality as the criterion. However, in spite of the fact that the term 'Community nationality' is often used, it must be understood that this is not an autonomous concept of Community law. Each Member State has its own nationality legislation and is free to decide for itself who its citizens are. Community citizenship is merely a bundle of autonomous Member State citizenships: anyone who, according to the law of a Member State, is a citizen of that Member State, is a Community citizen.

The use of Member State citizenship to define the scope of Community rights has potentially far-reaching consequences, since a Member State could, at least in theory, unilaterally extend the international scope of Community law simply by expanding the scope of its own nationality law. If a country has abnormally wide nationality legislation when it

---

[47] For a more detailed discussion of this topic, see Hartley, *EEC Immigration Law*, Chap. 3.

[48] Art. 52 EEC.

[49] Art. 59 EEC.

[50] Reg. 1612/68, Art. 1.

[51] However, recent proposals by the Commission would, if adopted, make it difficult to enforce the law in this regard: see pp. 134–6 below.

[52] See pp. 108–9 below.

joins the Community, its membership will produce a corresponding anomaly in the scope of Community law.

Germany is a case in point. When the Federal Republic of Germany (West Germany) was constituted after the war, it did not enact its own citizenship legislation. Instead, it continued to apply pre-existing German nationality law, which dates back to a statute passed in 1913.[53] (The failure to adopt a new citizenship law was an indication of the refusal to treat the division of Germany as permanent.) This meant that persons who had previously been German citizens were regarded as citizens of West Germany. The result was that, even in the days of the Berlin Wall when the Communists were in power, most citizens of East Germany were, in West German eyes, (West) German citizens; consequently, they were Community citizens, entitled to benefit from Community immigration rights. Thus, because West Germany had chosen to regard this wide group of people as its citizens, other Member States were obliged to accept them as Community citizens.[54] While the Wall stood, this made little practical difference because few East Germans were able to avail themselves of their Community rights; nevertheless, it shows how the law of a Member State can determine who benefits from Community rights. When unification occurred, the territory of the Community was automatically increased and, with it, the territorial scope of Community Law.

British nationality raises particular problems. Before 1948, the main form of British nationality was that of a British subject, a status enjoyed by most inhabitants of the Commonwealth (including the United Kingdom).[55] By 1948 some Commonwealth countries—for example, Canada—had adopted their own nationality legislation; Britain then did the same by creating a new citizenship, that of the United Kingdom and

---

[53] The *Reichs- und Staatsangehörigkeitsgesetz* of 22 July 1913.

[54] This was recognized by the other Member States when the EEC Treaty was signed: see the Declaration by the German Government on the definition of the expression 'German national', which provides, 'All Germans as defined in the Basic Law of the Federal Republic of Germany shall be considered nationals of the Federal Republic of Germany'. It should be noted that under Art. 116, para. 1, of the Basic Law, the concept of a 'German' is wider than that of a German citizen, since it includes certain categories of ethnic Germans not possessing German citizenship. These too are beneficiaries of Community immigration rights.

[55] This status was retained under the British Nationality Act 1948, but was redefined. Previously it depended on Unitd Kingdom law alone, but the 1948 Act provided that anyone who was, under the law of any independent Commonwealth country (including the United Kingdom), a citizen of that country would thenceforth be a British subject. Under the 1948 Act, the term 'Commonwealth citizen' could be used interchangeably with 'British subject'. As a result of the British Nationality Act 1981, however, 'Commonwealth citizen' is now the only term used for this purpose. 'British subject' now has the meaning given to it by Part IV of the 1981 Act, being applied to persons previously known as 'British subjects without citizenship', who are, by definition, not citizens of any Commonwealth country.

Colonies, which lumped the United Kingdom and the Colonies together in one citizenship unit.[56]

When a colony became independent, the persons who were citizens of the United Kingdom and Colonies by virtue of birth in (or some other connection with) that colony normally became citizens of the new state and ceased to be citizens of the United Kingdom and Colonies. In some cases, however, they did not obtain such citizenship and were allowed to retain their former citizenship.

Citizenship of the United Kingdom and Colonies was thus broadly made up of three main categories:

1. Persons connected with the United Kingdom;
2. Persons connected with a colony;
3. Persons connected with a former colony who had not obtained citizenship of that country when it became independent.

Under legislation passed in 1971,[57] persons in the second and third categories were not generally entitled to enter the United Kingdom and reside there as of right: they did not have the 'right of abode'.

This was the position when the United Kingdom joined the Community in 1973. At the request of the other Member States, the United Kingdom adopted a Nationality Declaration[58] specifying who should be regarded as a British national for Community purposes. This contained a complicated definition, but, broadly speaking, it restricted Community citizenship to citizens of the United Kingdom and Colonies having a link with either the United Kingdom or Gibraltar, these being the only parts of the United Kingdom and colonies within the territorial scope of the EEC Treaty.[59]

In 1981 British nationality law was again recast.[60] Citizenship of the United Kingdom and Colonies was abolished and replaced with three new concepts:

1. British citizenship;
2. British Dependent Territories citizenship;
3. British Overseas citizenship.

The basic idea behind these three categories of citizenship is that persons connected with the United Kingdom are British citizens;[61] persons connected with a colony or other dependency are British Dependent Territories citizens;[62] and persons who previously were

[56] See the British Nationality Act 1948.

[57] Immigration Act 1971; for earlier legislation, see the Commonwealth Immigrants Acts 1962 and 1968.

[58] This was made in 1972 when the Treaty of Accession was signed.

[59] For the details, see Hartley, *EEC Immigration Law*, pp. 64–76.

[60] See the British Nationality Act 1981.

[61] When the 1981 Act came into force, approximately 57 million persons became British citizens, most of them resident in the United Kingdom.

[62] Approximately 3 million persons (of whom 2.5 million lived in Hong Kong) acquired this status when the Act came into force.

citizens of the United Kingdom and Colonies by reason of a connection with a former colony are British Overseas citizens.[63] Of these three, only British citizenship automatically gives the right to enter the United Kingdom and reside there (the right of abode); British Dependent Territories citizens and British Overseas citizens can normally enter only with leave. However, any British Dependent Territories citizen or British Overseas citizen who is given leave to settle in the United Kingdom, and resides there for five years, is entitled to obtain British citizenship by registration.[64]

As a result of this legislation, the United Kingdom adopted a new Nationality Declaration, which replaced the earlier one as from 1 January 1983. This states that, for Community purposes, British citizens, together with British Dependent Territories citizens who acquired their citizenship through a connection with Gibraltar, are to be regarded as nationals of the Unitedd Kingdom.[65]

It is now possible to go through the list of territories connected with the Member States in order to see whether their inhabitants come within the international personal scope of the Community provisions.

1. *The French overseas departments.* These territories are within the territorial scope of the Community provisions. Their inhabitants are (mainly) French citizens; consequently they are within the personal scope of Community law.

2. *The 'overseas countries and territories'* It was said previously that these territories are outside the territorial scope of the Community provisions, at least as regards workers. In so far as these territories are British, their inhabitants will be (mainly) British Dependent Territories citizens[66] and, as such, outside the personal scope of Community law. The inhabitants of territories dependent on a Member State other than the United Kingdom may possess the citizenship of that state but, in the case of workers, they will nevertheless be excluded by virtue of Article 135 EEC, which states

[63] When the Act came into force, approximately 210,000 persons acquired British Overseas Citizenship as their only nationality. A larger number were British Overseas citizens in addition to being citizens of another country.

[64] For further details, see Evans, *Immigration Law* (2nd edn, 1983), pp. 72–90.

[65] There is also a third category consisting of persons who are British subjects by virtue of Part IV of the British Nationality Act 1981 and who have the right of abode in the United Kingdom and are therefore exempt from United Kingdom immigration control. British subjects under Part IV of the 1981 Act are persons who were previously British subjects without being citizens of the United Kingdom and Colonies or any other Commonwealth country. They are an anomalous and diminishing group, mainly of Indian ancestry (including Tamils from Sri Lanka). They enjoy Community rights only if they are exempt from United Kingdom immigration control, a condition very few of them can meet.

[66] The Falkland Islands (which are an overseas country or territory) are an exception. Their inhabitants are British citizens by virtue of a special Act of Parliament, the British Nationality (Falkland Islands) Act 1983. In so far as they are workers, however, they are excluded from the personal scope of the Community provisions by virtue of Art. 135 EEC.

that freedom of movement within the Member States for 'workers from the countries and territories' would be governed by subsequent agreements. Such rights were never granted.[67]

3. *Hong Kong.* This is outside the territorial scope of the Community provisions and, as its inhabitants are (mainly) British Dependent Territories citizens, they are outside the personal scope of Community law.

4. *Greenland and the Faroes.* Both these territories are outside the territorial scope of the Community provisions. Their inhabitants are (mainly) Danish citizens and, as such, potentially within the international personal scope of the provisions. However, Greenland is now an overseas country or territory; so workers from there cannot benefit from the Community provisions.[68] As far as the Faroes are concerned, Article 4 of Protocol 2 to the Treaty of Accession of 1972 excludes Danish nationals resident in the Faroes from the international personal scope of the Community provisions.

5. *The Channel Islands and the Isle of Man* These are outside the territorial scope of the Community provisions. Their inhabitants are (mainly) British citizens and would, therefore, qualify as Community citizens; however, Article 2 of Protocol 3 to the Act of Accession of 1972 provides that they will not benefit from the Community provisions relating to the free movement of persons and services.[69]

6. *Gibraltar* This is within the territorial scope of the Community provisions. Under the British Nationality Declaration, Gibraltarians are Community citizens;[70] consequently, they benefit from the Community provisions.

It will be seen that the territorial scope and the international personal scope of the Community provisions largely coincide. The principle of equivalence is respected.

It might be wondered why some territories are included and others excluded. The answer is that there appears to be a general principle that territories in Europe are included and those outside Europe excluded, a principle which might be thought to follow from the European nature of the Community. This explains the status of most of the territories considered. The French overseas departments are probably the only non-European territories within the scope of the provisions. Since they are an integral part of France, they could hardly have been excluded.

The European territories expressly excluded—the Channel Islands,

---

[67] On the position regarding establishment and services, see Hartley, *EEC Immigration Law*, pp. 58–60.

[68] See above.

[69] The new British Nationality Declaration states that the reference in Protocol 3 to 'any citizen of the United Kingdom and Colonies' is to be understood as referring to 'any British citizen'.

[70] See above.

the Isle of Man, Greenland and the Faroes—all appear to have been excluded at their own request: they did not want to be obliged to accept Community immigrants. The price they had to pay for this was exclusion from the personal scope of the migration provisions of the Treaty.

All the exceptions to the principle of nationality mentioned so far have been cases in which nationals of Member States are denied benefits under Community law. The most important exception in the opposite direction is the rule that members of the family of a person entitled to Community immigration rights are entitled to benefit from the Community provisions even if they are not nationals of a Member State: it is sufficient if the person entitled to the primary right (the worker, and so on) is a national.[71] It should also be mentioned that in 1964 the Member States made a Declaration that they would consider the entry of refugees with 'special favour'.[72] It is doubtful whether this confers any legal rights on refugees who are not Community citizens; however, refugees (and stateless persons) who *are* admitted by a Member State enjoy the same social-security rights as Community citizens.[73]

The Uniform Passport

In 1981 the representatives of the governments of the Member States, meeting in the Council, adopted a resolution laying down the format for a uniform passport for their nationals.[74] This passport is issued by each Member State to its own citizens and cannot, therefore, be called a Community passport in the true sense. However, the fact that all Community citizens will eventually[75] have passports of the same colour—burgundy red—and of a common design with the words 'European Community' on the cover,[76] should, according to the resolution, 'strengthen the feeling among nationals of the Member States that they belong to the same Community'. On the other hand, the choice of a resolution by the representatives of the Member States as the

[71] Reg. 1612/68, Arts 10–12; Dir. 68/360, Arts 1 and 4(4); Reg. 1251/70, Arts 1 and 3; Dir. 73/148, Art. 1(1)(c) and (d) and Art. 1(2); Dir. 75/34, Arts 1 and 3.

[72] JO 1964, No. 78, p. 1225.

[73] Reg. 1408/71, Art. 2(1).

[74] Resolution of 23 July 1981, OJ 1981, C 241, p. 1.

[75] The resolution called upon Member States to 'endeavour' to issue the passport by 1 Jan. 1985, though they were permitted 'if necessary' to continue to issue the old type of passport.

[76] This will be followed by the name of the state issuing the passport and its emblem. The information on the cover will be in the language of the state issuing the passport, but the more important information on inside pages will also be given in English and French or, in some cases, in all the official languages of the Community.

means of introducing the uniform passport indicates that the matter is regarded as being outside Community jurisdiction.

Immigration from Non-Member States

Community law is concerned only with migration by Community nationals.[77] Immigration by nationals of third countries is outside Community jurisdiction and is governed by the law of the individual Member States, which are free to pursue their own policies and to determine for themselves whom they will admit.[78] In spite of this, the Community has a limited interest in third-country migration, not least because an increase in the number of non-Community migrants permitted by a Member State to work within its territory would mean more competition in the job market for Community migrants. Thus, though the EEC Treaty has no provision dealing with third-country migration, the Commission has nevertheless succeeded in obtaining for itself a limited legislative and executive power on this subject by resort to Article 118 EEC, which gives it the task of promoting close co-operation between the Member States in the social field, in particular in matters relating to (among other things) employment, labour law, and working conditions. Acting under this power, the Commission has adopted a decision[79] requiring Member States to consult it and the other Member States before making major changes in their policy regarding third-country migration. This measure emerged largely (but not completely) unscathed from an annulment action brought by five of the Member States.[80]

More serious problems are caused by illegal migrants from third countries who work in the Community. Living in constant fear of deportation, they pay no taxes or social-security contributions. This allows them to survive on a lower salary, but means that they get no sick pay or unemployment benefit. Their employers pay no social-security contributions on their behalf, which makes them cheaper to employ than legal migrants. They are rarely members of a trade union, and if they cause trouble their employer can report them to the police, which normally leads to their deportation. As a result, they do the dirtiest jobs and get the lowest pay.[81]

Partly for humanitarian reasons, but mainly (one suspects) because they bring down wage levels, illegal immigrants have been the subject of

[77] The limited exceptions to this were discussed above at p. 107.
[78] *Germany* v. *Commission*, Cases 281, 283–5, 287/85, [1987] ECR 3203.
[79] Dec. 85/381.
[80] *Germany* v. *Commission* (n. 78 above).
[81] There are relatively few illegal immigrants in Britain (because of its strictly enforced immigration laws) but there are many in some Continental Member States.

concern on the part of labour leaders in a number of Member States. This led the Commission to propose a draft directive to combat illegal migration and illegal employment,[82] the main provision of which required Member States to make it a criminal offence to 'organize, aid and abet or participate in illegal immigration and illegal employment'; another provision had the aim of ensuring that, if an illegal employee was deported, the employer paid the costs of deportation. This measure would have discouraged employers from giving jobs to illegal migrants; however, the Council proved reluctant to adopt it and eventually it was withdrawn.

A rather different reason for Community interest in third-country migration arises out of the Community's power to enter into international agreements. The European Court has held that association agreements with non-member States, concluded by the Community under Article 238 EEC, may contain provisions dealing with immigration.[83] This means that an association agreement may give the citizens of such a country the right to migrate to any Member State and work there. The European Court has ruled that the relevant provisions of the association agreement with Turkey—probably the only one to grant immigration rights—are not directly effective.[84] However, decisions of the Association Council set up under that agreement can be directly effective.[85]

---

[82] Submitted to the Council on 5 Apr. 1978: see OJ 1978, C 97, p. 9.

[83] *Demirel*, Case 12/86, [1987] ECR 3719. The result is that the Community has international jurisdiction (treaty-making power) in this field, even though it lacks internal jurisdiction—the reverse of the more normal situation. So far, however, no one has suggested that the doctrine of 'parallelism' should apply in reverse. (On this, see Hartley, *The Foundations of European Community Law* (2nd edn 1988), pp. 156–162.)

[84] Ibid.

[85] *Sevince*, Case C–192/89 (20 Sept. 1990).

9

Immigration Rights

This chapter is concerned with the right of a migrant to leave his own Member State, enter another, and reside there. These rights are conferred in broad terms by the EEC Treaty[1] and in detail by Community legislation.[2] All these provisions are directly effective.[3]

A general point regarding the structure of these provisions should be made at the outset. This is that they give migrants a wide range of rights, defined in the directives in fairly precise terms, but they make all the rights subject to a proviso that enables Member States to restrict them on grounds of public policy, public security or public health. Each Member State determines for itself what its public policy, public security or public health requires, though Community legislation imposes limitations on this power. This restriction on Community migration rights, which will be discussed in the next chapter, must be borne in mind when the rights are discussed.

The Right to Depart

This is the right of a migrant to leave his own (or any other) Member State. Though taken for granted in Western countries, the right of emigration is an essential prerequisite to immigration. The right to depart, which could be regarded as implicit in the relevant Treaty provisions, is expressly granted by the directives.[4] The latter make clear that it applies only to migrants who wish to enter another Member State in order to carry on activities covered by Community law, in particular as employed or self-employed persons or as providers or recipients of

---

[1] See Art. 48(3) (workers), Art. 52 (establishment) and Art. 60 (services).
[2] The most important measures are Dir. 68/360 (workers) and Dir. 73/148 (establishment and services). Arts 2, 3, 6(1) (a), 6(2) and 9 of Dir. 68/360 apply *mutatis mutandis* to the beneficiaries of Dirs 90/364 (persons of independent means) and 90/365 (retired persons); Arts 2, 3, and 9 of Dir. 68/360 apply to the beneficiaries of Dir. 90/366 (students): see Art. 2(2) of each of the latter directives.
[3] *Watson and Belmann*, Case 118/75, [1976] ECR 1185 (first para. of the Ruling). It is interesting to contrast the blanket assertion of direct effect in this case with the cautious approach adopted less than two years earlier in *Van Duyn* v. *Home Office*, Case 41/74, [1974] ECR 1337.
[4] Art. 2(1) of Dir. 68/360 and of Dir. 73/148.
[5] Family members are covered, even if they do not intend to carry on these activities.

services.[5] Someone who wishes to migrate to a non-member state, or for purposes not covered by Community Law, cannot invoke the right.

The directives do not lay down any specific exceptions to the right to depart, but there clearly must be some: a convict in jail, for example, cannot demand the right to leave the country. The exact scope of these exceptions—and whether they should be regarded as based on the public policy proviso or on some more general principle—is, however, unclear.

The directives also grant the Community migrant the right to a travel document. In most Member States this may be either a passport or an identity card, but in the United Kingdom the latter is not available. British citizens, therefore, have a right to a passport, which must be valid for at least five years and allow travel to all the Member States. On leaving the country, an emigrant cannot be required to produce any document other than his passport (or identity card); no exit visa may be demanded.[6]

The Right to Return

This is the right of a migrant to return to his own country. It is given by Article 3(4) of Directive 64/221, which requires the Member State which granted the passport or identity card on which the migrant travelled to allow him to re-enter its territory, even if the document is no longer valid or the nationality of the holder is in dispute. This provision seems intended, first and foremost, to benefit other Member States, rather than the migrant himself. Its purpose is to provide what is sometimes called a 'guarantee of returnability'. It can happen that a country might wish to deport an alien, but be unable to do so because no other state can be found to which he can be sent. This may occur if he is stateless, if his

Art. 2(1) of Dir. 68/360 is clumsily worded in this regard, but there can be no doubt that this is what was intended. The beneficiaries of Dirs 90/364, 90/365 and 90/366 are also covered: see n. 2, above.

[6] These rights are all laid down in Art. 2 of the directives. It is noteworthy that in United Kingdom law there is no absolute legal right to a passport, since passports are issued under the royal prerogative: see *R . v. Secretary of State, ex parte Everett* [1989] 2 WLR 224 (CA). In practice, passports are normally given to everyone entitled to them. The limited exceptions to this principle were spelled out in a statement made in the House of Commons on 15 Nov. 1974: see H.C.Deb. vol. 881, col. 265. These include minors, if their parents object to the proposed trip, persons for whom a warrant of arrest has been issued, persons whose activities are so demonstratively undesirable that the grant of a passport would be contrary to the public interest and persons who were repatriated from abroad at public expense and who have not repaid the debt. Community law could, therefore, be regarded as giving British citizens a right they did not have before, though this right is of little practical importance because it is subject to the public-policy proviso, which would probably allow the Government to impose the same restrictions as before. See, further, Hartley, *EEC Immigration Law*, pp. 203–5.

nationality is in dispute, or if the country of which he is a citizen will not accept him. In such a case, the country in which he is resident may have no option but to allow him to remain. In order to avoid this situation, most states will, therefore, refuse entry to any immigrant if there are doubts regarding his returnability. Article 3(4) appears to have been adopted in order to avoid this problem in the case of Community migrants. The result is that if a migrant presents himself at a port of entry, and shows a passport or identity card issued by a Member State which indicates that he is a Community citizen,[7] the immigration authorities will have no reason to deny him entry on grounds of non-returnability, since the Member State which issued his travel document will always accept him back. This will be the case even if the passport or identity card was issued to him by mistake.

The Right to Enter

The right to enter is the right to cross the frontier and enter the new Member State. Must a migrant worker already have an offer of employment before he can enter the country? This appears to have been the intention of the authors of the Treaty. Article 48(3) EEC reads:

[Freedom of movement for workers] shall entail the right . . .
(a) to accept offers of employment actually made;
(b) to move freely within the territory of the Member States for this purpose . . .

The phrase 'for this purpose' in sub-paragraph (b) must refer back to sub-paragraph (a): the right of free movement is granted for the purpose of accepting offers of employment 'actually made'.[8] However, when Directive 68/360 was adopted by the Council, a statement was recorded in the minutes (which are not officially published) that persons without job-offers will be allowed to enter another Member State for a period of three months in order to look for work, provided they can support themselves without recourse to public assistance. The statement makes clear that migrant workers may be deported if they fail to find a job by the end of three months; they may also be deported within this period if they become a burden on public funds.[9]

A statement of this kind cannot create law and in *R.* v. *Immigration*

---

[7] The right to return does not, therefore, apply to those British passport-holders whose passports indicate that they are not British nationals for Community purposes. (For the meaning of this, see pp. 103–5 above.) Thus a migrant travelling on, for example, a British Overseas citizen's passport would have no right under Community law to enter the United Kingdom.

[8] The word 'actually' is a not very happy translation of the French *'actuellement'*, which means 'at the present time'. The idea is that the offer must be open at the time when the worker migrates.

[9] For the text of the statement, see *Levin*, Case 53/81, [1982] ECR 1035 at p. 1043.

Appeal Tribunal, ex parte *Antonissen*[10] the European Court held that it cannot be used to interpret Community legislation. It thus has no legal significance.[11] The Court nevertheless went on to hold that Community law gives immigrants seeking employment the right to enter another Member State and stay there for a sufficient period of time to appraise themselves of employment opportunities corresponding to their qualifications and, where appropriate, to take employment. Under United Kingdom law,[12] the relevant period is six months.

The European Court held that this is not in principle unreasonable; it ruled, however, that if, after the expiry of this period, the immigrant provides evidence that he has a genuine chance of obtaining employment, he should not be subject to immediate deportation.

In the case of self-employed persons, this question is expressly covered by Directive 73/148, which gives the right of entry to migrants who wish to establish themselves in another Member State; it is not necessary that they should already be established before entry.[13]

Migrants entitled to the right to enter must be admitted on the production of a valid passport or identity card. No visa or equivalent document may be demanded, except in the case of family members who are not nationals of a Member State.[14]

The Right to Reside

The right to reside is the right to stay in the new country after entry.[15] Community law distinguishes between the full right to reside, which lasts indefinitely unless something happens to terminate it, and temporary rights of residence, which end automatically. The former is much more important: it is the right most immigrants will want to acquire.

Since most Community immigration rights are granted for a specific purpose, it is not surprising that the acquisition of the right to reside depends on fulfilling that purpose. In order to obtain the right to reside, therefore, the migrant must obtain employment, establish himself in a self-employed capacity, provide (or receive) a service or enroll at a recognized educational establishment. Retired persons and persons of independent means are exceptions.

To obtain the full right to reside, a worker must obtain permanent

[10] Case C–292/89 (judgment of 26 February 1991), *The Times*, 27 February 1991.

[11] The Court also held that Art. 69(1) of Reg. 1408/71, O J 1983, L 230, p. 6 (which lays down a three-month period for certain purposes) was irrelevant.

[12] Immigration Rules (H C Paper 169 of 1982/83), *Control of Entry*, Rule 70.

[13] See Art. 1(1) (a), read with Art. 3(1).

[14] Art. 3 of Dir. 68/360 and of Dir. 73/148. On the meaning of 'visa or equivalent document', see *R.* v. *Pieck*, Case 157/79, [1980] ECR 2171, discussed below at pp. 132–3.

[15] The main provisions of Community law dealing with the right to reside are Arts 4–9 of Dir. 68/360 and Arts 4–7 of Dir. 73/148; see also Dirs 90/364, 90/365 and 90/366.

employment. If his employment is only temporary (for twelve months or less), he obtains only a temporary right to reside, which lasts only for the expected duration of the employment.[16] (If the period of employment is more than three months, he is entitled to a temporary residence permit.)

Persons who live in one country and work in another—known as frontier workers—are also entitled to the right to reside, though in their case it effectively means the right to come and go. They may be given special residence permits.[17]

A self-employed person obtains the full right to reside once he is permanently established in his occupation.[18] Self-employed persons who pursue their activity on only a temporary basis in the country to which they have migrated are not covered by the right of establishment. They are regarded as providers of services. Providers and recipients of services have a temporary right to reside, lasting for the period during which the service will be provided. Where this is for more than three months, they are entitled to a temporary residence permit (called a 'right of abode').[19]

Students have a temporary right to reside which lasts for the duration of their course. They are entitled to a residence permit limited to that period (or to one year, if the course lasts longer). Retired persons and persons of independent means have a right to reside which continues indefinitely.[20] They are entitled to a full residence permit.

A full residence permit is valid for at least five years[21] and is automatically renewable. This means that persons entitled to it—persons with the full right to reside—can reside indefinitely, unless some event occurs which terminates their right. The right to reside is effective throughout the territory of the country concerned.[22]

A residence permit granted under Community law is different in form

[16] The Commission is not happy with this, and wants to amend Dir. 68/360 to ensure that a worker who has held a series of temporary jobs is entitled to the full right to reside and can claim a full residence permit: *Guidelines for a Community Policy on Migration*, Bull. EC, Supp. 9/85, p. 8.

[17] Dir. 68/360, Art. 8(1)(b).

[18] Dir. 73/148, Art. 4(1).

[19] Ibid., Art. 4(2).

[20] All three categories, however, lose their right to reside once they cease to be covered by Community law: see pp. 99–100 above.

[21] Member States may, however, require the revalidation of a residence permit issued to a retired person or a person of independent means at the end of the first two years of residence: see Art. 2(1) of Dirs 90/364 and 90/365 respectively.

[22] See Dir. 68/360, Art. 6(1)(a) and Dir. 73/148, Art. 5. The former applies also to retired persons and persons of independent means, but not to students (see Art. 2(2) of Dirs 90/364, 90/365 and 90/366 respectively). This omission must have been deliberate; so it is possible that Member States may have the power to limit a student's right of residence to certain parts of the country, though paradoxically the second para. of Art. 2(2) allows a student's spouse and dependent children to take up an employed or self-employed activity anywhere within the territory of the Member State.

from one granted to non-Communityimmigrants.[23] Though the right to reside does not depend on the permit,[24] Member States may require immigrants to possess one and impose fines on those that do not.[25]

What Constitutes Employment

From what has been said, it will be appreciated that, for most immigrants, the key to gaining rights under Community law is obtaining employment or becoming established in a self-employed capacity. The meaning of temporary employment has already been discussed. In *Levin*,[26] the question of part-time work came before the European Court. Mrs Levin was British and her husband was South African. They wanted to live in Holland. They entered the country and resided there for a time, but the Dutch authorities were apparently not willing to allow them to stay permanently. When Mrs Levin applied for a residence permit under EEC law, this was refused because she was not working. She took a job as a chambermaid, working half days (twenty hours a week), and for this she was paid 130 guilders a week, something in the region of £25. The Dutch authorities were not prepared to accept this as 'employment' for the purposes of Community law, because her income from the job was not sufficient to live on: it was below the minimum wage laid down by Dutch legislation for full-time workers. She argued that this did not matter because she had private means to supplement her earnings.[27] The Dutch authorities also maintained that she had not come to the Netherlands in order to work but because she and her husband wanted to live there. It seemed that she had taken the job only in order to obtain the right to reside.

The European Court overruled both these objections. It ruled that the Dutch minimum-wage legislation was irrelevant because the definition of 'worker' cannot depend on national law; otherwise, Community rights could be frustrated by a unilateral change in the law of a Member State. The Court refused to give a restrictive interpretation to the concept of a worker. It held that part-time workers are covered, even if their income falls below national minima. However, only 'effective and genuine' employment is covered. Community law does not recognize

---

[23] For workers, the form is laid down in the Annex to Dir. 68/360; for self-employed migrants, the only requirement is that it must be entitled 'Residence Permit for a National of the European Communities': see Art. 4(1) of Dir. 73/148.

[24] Though some provisions of the directives may suggest the contrary, the European Court has ruled that the right to reside arises automatically; the function of the residence permit is merely evidentiary: *Royer*, Case 48/75, [1976] ECR 497 (paras 32–7).

[25] See pp. 134, n. 47 below.

[26] See n. 9 above.

[27] At the time of the case persons of independent means were not, as such, entitled to Community immigration rights.

'activities on such a small scale as to be regarded as purely marginal and ancillary'. The Court also held that the motives which prompted a worker to seek employment in another Member State are of no account. This means that it does not matter that the worker took the job solely in order to get a residence permit: Community law is concerned with the fact of work, not the worker's reasons for taking the job.

The European Court gave no examples of activities which would be so marginal as not to constitute work, but *R. v. Secchi*,[28] an earlier English case, may provide one. Secchi was a young Italian, who abandoned his studies to wander across Europe. He entered the United Kingdom, where he found squatting accommodation. He made no attempt to get a regular job but occasionally took casual work, such as washing dishes in a restaurant. Did he have a right to reside under Community law? According to the magistrate before whom he pleaded guilty to a charge of indecent exposure, and who was considering whether to recommend his deportation, Secchi could not be regarded as a worker and had no rights under Community law. Though the case is of little authority—no reference was made to the European Court—and was decided before *Levin*, the result may nevertheless be consistent with Community law.

In *Levin*, the European Court held that a worker is not deprived of his status merely because the income from his employment is less than what is generally regarded as the minimum necessary to ensure a reasonable standard of living. The Court said that it makes no difference whether the worker supplements his wages through a private income, obtains support from another member of the family, or is content to live at a low level. But what if he applies for assistance from public funds? This question arose in *Kempf*,[29] where a German immigrant in the Netherlands found employment as a part-time music teacher, giving twelve hours of lessons a week. His income was below the Dutch minimum wage and he applied for the Dutch equivalent of supplementary benefit to make up the difference. The European Court held that this did not affect his status as a worker or his right to reside in the Netherlands.[30]

In *Lawrie-Blum*,[31] a case concerning a British immigrant in Germany, the European Court held that a trainee teacher is a worker for Community purposes, even if, under the law of the country in question, it is necessary to serve in this capacity for a given period in order to

---

[28] [1975] 1 CMLR 383.

[29] Case 139/85, [1986] ECR 1741.

[30] It will be remembered that the statement of the Council on the admission of immigrants looking for work provided that an application for public assistance is a ground for deportation, but this applies only to immigrants who have *not* found work. Once the immigrant has obtained the right to reside, such an application cannot deprive him of that right.

[31] Case 66/85, [1986] ECR 2121.

qualify as a teacher. Under German law, a trainee in the position of Ms Lawrie-Blum received a salary and was required to teach up to eleven hours of classes per week, at first under supervision and later independently. This judgment means that pupillage (barristers), service of articles (solicitors), internship (doctors) or similar systems in the professions, as well as apprenticeship, all constitute employment for the purpose of Community law, at least if—as is normally the case—the person concerned receives a salary.

The case also laid down a general definition of employment. Its essential characteristic, said the Court, is that, during specified hours, the employee performs services for the employer under his direction and in return for remuneration. This definition must be read in conjunction with the rule that the work performed must be real and effective.

Two subsequent cases have further clarified the question. In *Steymann*,[32] the European Court had to consider the position of an immigrant from Germany who joined a religious community, the Bhagwan community, in the Netherlands. The community secured its economic independence through various commercial activities, such as a discothèque, a bar and a launderette. Work seemed to play an important part in the life of the community and members were normally expected either to participate in the community's commercial activities or to help with domestic tasks. Members were not paid directly for their work: the community provided for their material needs and supplied them with pocket money, regardless of the nature and extent of the work done. Steymann, a plumber by trade, did plumbing work in their building, carried out general domestic tasks and assisted in their commercial activities. He was supported by the community.

The Dutch court had found that his work was genuine and effective, but was this sufficient in view of the fact that he received no direct pay for it? The European Court held that it could be: in a case of this kind, if work constitutes an essential element of membership of the community, the benefits which the community gives its members could be regarded as an 'indirect countervailing advantage for their work'. It is for the national court to decide whether this is the case. In deciding this, the member's motive for working cannot presumably be taken into account.

The other case, *Bettray*,[33] also concerned a rather unusual situation, which arose from Dutch legislation intended to help people who, for one reason or another, are incapable of holding down a normal job. The legislation provided for what was called 'social employment', by which was meant jobs specially created for such people in order to support them, rehabilitate them or increase their capacity for normal work. This

---

[32] Case 196/87, [1989] 1 CMLR 449.
[33] Case 344/87, *The Times*, 16 June 1989.

was done through state-financed work associations specifically created for the purpose.

Bettray was a German immigrant in the Netherlands who was given 'social employment' in the context of his treatment for drug addiction. He applied for a residence permit, but was refused on the ground that he was not a genuine worker. The European Court held that the essential characteristic of the employment relationship existed in his case since he was receiving remuneration. It was irrelevant that the productivity of persons in such schemes was very low or that their wages were indirectly paid by the state. However, the Court ruled that activities cannot be regarded as real and effective if they are carried out as part of a scheme for retraining or rehabilitation. The jobs in question were reserved for persons unable to take normal employment. The persons concerned were not selected by reason of their capacity to do a particular job: the jobs were created to fit their capacity to work; moreover, the work associations were set up solely in order to provide them with employment. The result was that Bettray had no right under Community law to reside in the Netherlands.

Loss of the Right to Reside

A temporary right to reside terminates automatically when the purpose for which it was granted has been attained. The full right to reside, on the other hand, is (in principle) of indefinite duration. Community law makes no express provision for the loss of the right to reside; the directives deal with the question only indirectly and in a negative way: they simply state that certain facts are not grounds for withdrawal of a residence permit. From this it may be deduced that the right to reside is not lost by reason of those facts; inferences may also be drawn as to facts which may cause the right to be lost.

DEPARTURE

The directives provide that absence from the country for not more than six months (or a longer period, if it is for the purpose of military service) shall not affect the validity of a residence permit.[34] From this one may deduce, first, that such absence does not terminate the right to reside

---

[34] Dir. 68/360, Art. 6(2) and Dir. 73/148, Art. 4(1). The former provision applies also to retired persons and persons of independent means, but not to students (see Art. 2(2) of Dirs. 90/364, 90/365 and 90/366, respectively). This omission was presumably deliberate; so any absence may in theory deprive a student of his right to reside. In practice, however, he could normally claim a new right on his return, provided he still fulfilled the necessary conditions.

and, secondly, that absence for more than six months (other than on military service) does have this effect.

UNEMPLOYMENT

Since employment (or self-employment) is, in most cases, the foundation of the right to reside, it would be reasonable to expect that unemployment would result in the loss of the right. The position in this regard is different for workers and self-employed persons. As far as workers are concerned, Article 7(1) of Directive 68/360 provides that a residence permit may not be withdrawn from a worker solely on the ground that he is no longer in employment, either because he is temporarily incapable of work as a result of illness or accident, or because he is involuntarily unemployed. Again, one can deduce that neither of these two facts can affect the right to reside. One can also deduce that permanent incapacity for work as a result of illness or accident, or voluntary unemployment, will terminate the right to reside.

A worker who is permanently incapable of work will, however, be entitled to the 'right to remain' (discussed below), provided he has resided continuously in the country for more than two years by the time he is forced to give up working; if his incapacity is the result of an accident at work or an occupational disease entitling him to a state pension, the two-year residence requirement does not apply.[35]

There is no doubt that voluntary unemployment leads to the loss of the right to reside, though precisely what constitutes voluntary unemployment is not always easy to determine. The obvious case is where the worker voluntarily gives up his job and makes no effort to find another. Such a person may be deported. More difficult problems arise where the worker gives up his job, but tries to find another, perhaps in another place, at higher pay or in a different kind of work. Assuming that his efforts are genuine and not unreasonable, can he be said to be voluntarily unemployed? A worker who loses his job through no fault of his own—as a result of redundancy or the bankruptcy of his employer—is involuntarily unemployed; but does his unemployment continue to be involuntary if he does not make reasonable efforts to find another job? An even more difficult question is whether a worker who loses his job through misconduct can be regarded as voluntarily unemployed. The answers to these questions will have to await a decision of the European Court.

A further provision concerning unemployment is contained in Article 7(2) of Directive 68/360. This states that when the residence permit is renewed for the first time, the period of residence may be restricted—

[35] Reg. 1251/70, Art. 2(1)(b). For other cases in which the residence requirement does not apply, see ibid., Art. 2(2).

but not to less than twelve months—if the worker has been *involuntarily* unemployed for more than twelve consecutive months.[36] The directive does not say what happens if the worker is still unemployed when the additional period expires, but it is a reasonable assumption that he may then be deported. Involuntary unemployment may, therefore, lead to the loss of the right to reside, but only in these restricted circumstances. It will be remembered that a normal residence permit must be valid for at least five years. This means that once an immigrant has found permanent employment and thus obtained the right to reside, if he then becomes involuntarily unemployed, he can have up to six years to find another job—five years until his permit has to be renewed (assuming he loses his job immediately after obtaining his permit) and at least one year thereafter.[37] The worst situation would be to lose his job exactly one year before his residence permit is due to expire: in this case he would have only two years to get another job. On the other hand, if he has a job at any time within one year of the renewal date, he is safe. Moreover, since Article 7(2) applies only when the residence permit is renewed for the first time, the right to reside will not be affected by involuntary unemployment once his permit has been renewed, provided it is renewed for the normal period.

As might be expected, the rights of self-employed persons are less favourable in these circumstances. The only rule laid down by Directive 73/148 is found in Article 4(1), which provides that a self-employed person's residence permit may not be withdrawn solely on the ground that he is no longer in employment, if this is due to the fact that he is temporarily incapable of work as a result of illness or injury. He does, however, have the same right as a worker to remain in the country concerned if his incapacity for work is permanent.[38] It seems, therefore, that a self-employed person loses the right to reside if he ceases to carry on his occupation for any reason other than incapacity as a result of illness or injury.

The Right to Remain

The right to remain is the right to stay on in the country after ceasing to work. The main situations in which it applies are where the worker or self-employed person retires, either because he has reached the age laid down by the law of the country concerned for entitlement to an old-age

---

[36] This presumably means twelve consecutive months immediately prior to the date on which the permit has to be renewed.

[37] The Commission feels that even this is not good enough, and wants to amend Dir. 68/360 to allow involuntarily unemployed workers to stay beyond their sixth year: *Guidelines for a Community Policy on Migration*, Bull. EC, Supp. 9/85, p. 8.

[38] Dir. 75/34, Art. 2(1)(b).

pension, or because he is permanently incapable of work.[39] Incapacity has been discussed above; where the worker or self-employed person retires on grounds of old age, he is entitled to the right to remain if, when his employment ceases, he has worked (or been self-employed) for at least the previous twelve months and has in addition been resident continuously in the country concerned for more than three years. In certain cases, these requirements are relaxed.[40]

Family Rights

As was mentioned in the previous chapter, Community law also grants immigration rights to the members of the family, even if they are not Community nationals.[41] We therefore have two kinds of rights— independent immigration rights (which are granted to a worker, self-employed person, provider or recipient of services, student, retired person or person of independent means) and dependent immigration rights (which are granted to the family of such a person). The essential difference between the two kinds of rights is that the latter cannot exist without the former. If a migrant has an independent right to be in the country, this cannot be affected by the actions of any other person; but if he has only a dependent right, this will be lost if the person with the independent right loses it or gives it up; it will also be lost if the relationship ends.

An example will make the position clear. Assume that H, an Indian citizen, marries W, a West German citizen, and they migrate to England, where W gets a job. As a Community national with a permanent job, W obtains the right to reside in England. H is not a Community national, but he is a member of W's family and as such has a dependent right to reside in England. Assume that the couple then separate and W returns to Germany. H will automatically lose his right under Community law to reside in England.[42] H will also lose his right if his marriage is terminated by a decree of divorce or nullity, even if W remains in England.[43] However, if the couple decide to live apart without obtaining a divorce, H will retain his right to reside in England so long as W

---

[39] See Reg. 1251/70 (workers) and Dir. 75/34 (self-employed). The right to remain does not apply to providers and recipients of services or to students. Retired persons covered by Dir. 90/365 and persons of independent means covered by Dir. 90/364 do not need it.

[40] See Art. 2(2) of Reg. 1251/70 and of Dir. 75/34. For further details on the right to remain, see Hartley, *EEC Immigration Law* (1978), pp. 118–26.

[41] For the definition of 'family', see pp. 94–5 above.

[42] See *In re Sandhu*, *The Times*, 10 May, 1985 (HL). The position would be the same if W lost her right to reside—for example, by becoming voluntarily unemployed.

[43] This seems to be implicit in *Diatta*, Case 267/83, [1985] ECR 567 (see para. 20 of the judgment and *per* Advocate General Darmon at pp. 572–3). If H had been a citizen of a Community country, he could obtain an independent right if he got a job.

remains there.[44] This means that W cannot bring about H's deportation by throwing him out of the house.

Article 10(3) of Regulation 1612/68 contains a provision, which applies only in the case of workers (not self-employed migrants, or providers or recipients of services), that the immigration rights of the family are dependent on the worker's having adequate housing available for them. This must be of a standard considered normal for local workers in the region concerned. In *Commission* v. *Germany*,[45] the European Court held that this requirement applies only when the family member first arrives. If the housing is adequate at this point, the family member cannot be deported if it subsequently becomes inadequate—for example, because a child is born. Article 10(3) goes on to state that the application of the provision must not give rise to discrimination between national workers and workers from the other Member States, though it is not entirely clear what this proviso means:[46] it cannot mean that the provision will apply only if the Member State in question has a rule that national workers without suitable housing are prohibited from having their families with them.[47] In any event, the United Kingdom does not apply the provision.[48]

The only case in which the rights of the family are not dependent on those of the primary migrant is where the latter dies. In such a situation, the family obtain an independent right to remain if they were residing with the primary migrant in the country concerned when he died, and he had himself acquired the right to remain or—if he died during his working life—he had resided there continuously for at least two years.[49]

In *Netherlands* v. *Reed*[50] it was argued that an unmarried couple living together in a stable relationship should be treated as husband and wife for the purpose of immigration rights under Community law. Ann Reed was a British citizen who was living with her boyfriend in the Netherlands. He was also a British citizen, but had obtained the right to reside in the Netherlands through employment there. Could Ann Reed obtain a dependent right to reside there through her relationship with

---

[44] *Diatta* (n. 43 above).

[45] Case 249/86 (18 May 1989—not yet reported).

[46] For the background to the provision, see Hartley, *EEC Immigration Law*, pp. 133–4.

[47] It also cannot mean that Member States must not discriminate against Community immigrants as regards the provision of public housing, since this is already provided for in Art. 9 of Reg. 1612/68.

[48] Immigration Rules (H.C. Paper 169 of 1982/83), Control on Entry, para. 68; Control after Entry, para. 140(c).

[49] Art. 3 of Reg. 1251/70 and of Dir. 75/34. The two-year residence requirement does not apply if the primary migrant died from an accident at work or an occupational illness, nor does it apply if the surviving spouse was a national of the country concerned but lost her nationality on marriage.

[50] Case 59/85, [1986] ECR 1283.

him? She argued that social developments in the Netherlands had reached the point where a stable relationship of this kind could be equated with marriage. The European Court, however, ruled that social developments in one Member State alone cannot affect the interpretation of Community law; relationships outside marriage cannot, therefore, give rise to dependent rights of residence under Community law. However, there was a rule of Netherlands immigration law that the non-Dutch boyfriend or girlfriend of a Dutch citizen could in similar circumstances obtain a right to reside under Dutch law; consequently, if Ann Reed's boyfriend had been Dutch, she would have had a right of residence under Dutch law. The European Court held that the Community principle of non-discrimination (discussed in Chapter 11 below) required the Dutch authorities to give the same right to Ann Reed.[51] She therefore won her case, but on a ground which will not assist migrants in a similar situation in countries with no equivalent rule.

Article 11 of Regulation 1612/68 grants the wife (or husband) and children[52] of an immigrant Community worker or self-employed person the right to take employment throughout the territory of the Member State, even if they are not Community nationals.[53] The spouse and dependent children of a person of independent means, a retired person or a student have a similar right under Directives 90/364, 90/365, 90/366 respectively.[54]

The significance of this rule is illustrated by *Gül*,[55] a case concerning a doctor of Cypriot nationality, married to a British citizen. He and his wife immigrated to Germany where he trained as a specialist in anaesthesiology. After completing his training, he wanted to settle in Germany and practise there. The German authorities were unwilling to allow him to practise, since, when he commenced his specialist training, he had undertaken to return to his own country after qualifying. On the facts so far mentioned, he had no rights under Community law. However, there was an additional fact: his wife was employed in Germany as a hairdresser. Being a Community national, she thereby gained the right to reside in Germany. As her husband, he was entitled to a dependent right to reside and to carry on any occupation as an employed person. The European Court held that a person in his position had to be allowed to practise medicine, provided he had the appropriate

---

[51] This aspect of the case is discussed further at p. 153 below.

[52] The children must be either under 21 or dependent on the primary migrant.

[53] There does not appear to be any provision of Community law giving family members the right to carry on an activity as a self-employed person.

[54] See Art. 2(2) (second para.) of each of the directives. These provisions also give the family member the right to carry on an activity as a self-employed person. Reg. 1612/68 gives no equivalent right to the families of workers and self-employed persons, though they may possibly be able to benefit from Art. 2(2) of Dir. 90/364. It would be anomalous if they were worse off than the families of persons of independent means.

[55] Case 131/85, [1986] ECR 1573.

qualifications and observed the rules governing the profession, which had to be applied to him in the same way as to a German national. The interesting point about this case is that his wife's earnings were apparently insufficient to provide a decent living for the family. In view of the Court's previous judgments, this obviously did not matter. The result was that the great bulk of the family income came from his earnings; however, she could never give up work, since their right to reside in Germany depended on her having a job (or otherwise qualifying for the right to reside).[56] It is paradoxical that the principal wage-earner can be the person with the dependent right.

[56] In time, he would no doubt acquire a right to reside under German law, perhaps by becoming a naturalized German citizen.

10

Public Policy and Immigration Control

The previous chapter contained a description of the rights given to migrants by Community law. In this chapter, we will change focus from the rights of the migrant to the powers of the Member States. We will also consider questions of procedure and remedies. These further dimensions must be added in order to give a full picture.

The Public-Policy Proviso

It was mentioned at the beginning of the previous chapter that all the immigration rights given by Community law are subject to what is usually called the public-policy proviso. This is a formula, found in various provisions in the Treaty and Community legislation, which gives Member States extensive powers to override Community rights.[1] The exact terms vary slightly in different provisions, but the essence is always the same: Member States are permitted to restrict the rights granted to migrants by Community law 'on grounds of public policy, public security or public health'. These three phrases, which are identical in all the provisions, constitute the key to the Member States' powers. Each Member State decides for itself what its public policy, public security, or public health requires; so the power is to a large extent open-ended. Potentially, the existence of the public-policy proviso constitutes a serious threat to the realization of Community objectives; in practice, however, Member States normally exercise restraint, and its effect is only marginal. It can, therefore, be regarded as a reserve power, used only in exceptional situations.[2]

Public policy is the least clearly defined of the three concepts. It is

---

[1] See Art. 48(3) EEC (workers); Art. 56(1) EEC (establishment; extended to services by Art. 66 EEC); Art. 10 of Dir. 68/360; Art. 8 of Dir. 73/148 and Art. 9 of Dir. 75/34. Interestingly, it is not found in Reg. 1251/70. (Reg. 1251/70 is the equivalent for workers of Dir. 75/34; unlike the directives, it was enacted by the Commission.)

[2] The European Court has always emphasized that the absence of public-policy objections is not a condition precedent to the acquisition of immigration rights under Community law: see e.g. *Royer*, Case 48/75, [1976] ECR 497 (para. 29).

concerned with the fundamental interests of society, and the power granted by the proviso may be exercised only if the immigrant's presence in the country constitutes a sufficiently serious threat to those interests.[3] The French term is *'ordre public'*. This should not be translated as 'public order', a much narrower concept which normally refers to the absence of disturbances and violence in public places: avoiding public disorder is simply one of the fundamental interests of society. Nor is it limited to activities which are contrary to the criminal law, though if the activity in question is not a criminal offence the Member State must have taken other 'genuine and effective' measures to combat it.[4]

It has already been stressed that each Member State decides for itself what its public policy is: the public-policy proviso is not concerned with Community public policy, which could very well be different from that of the Member States, since it places greater emphasis on freedom of movement. It follows that public policy is not the same in every Member State;[5] moreover, public policy can, and does, change over time.

A good example is Scientology, a quasi-religious cult invented by a former science-fiction writer from California. In the late Sixties and Seventies the British Government regarded Scientology as contrary to public policy on the ground that it was socially harmful. According to a Government statement in 1968, it alienated members of families from each other, its practices were a potential menace to the personality of its followers and its methods could be a serious danger to the health of those who submitted to them.[6] Scientology was never illegal in Britain and was openly practised by its many British adherents; however, the Home Office used its powers under the immigration laws to keep foreign Scientologists out. After the United Kingdom joined the Community, the question arose whether this policy was compatible with Community law. It appears that the Scientologists engineered a test case. Yvonne van Duyn, a Dutch citizen, arrived at Gatwick Airport and told the immigration officer that she was coming to take a job with the Scientology organization at its headquarters in East Grinstead, Sussex. She was refused entry. Legal action followed, but the European Court upheld the United Kingdom's right to regard Scientology as contrary to public policy. This meant that her right of entry under Community law could be overridden.[7] Interestingly, the Government

---

[3] *R. v. Bouchereau*, Case 30/77, [1977] ECR 1999.

[4] See *Adoui and Cornuaille*, Cases 115–16/81, [1982] ECR 1665 (para. 1 of the Ruling), discussed further below.

[5] See *Adoui and Cornuaille* (n. 4 above), where the European Court said (para. 8) that Community law does not impose upon the Member States a uniform scale of values as regards the assessment of conduct which may be considered as contrary to public policy.

[6] See the statement by the Minister of Health in the House of Commons on 25 July 1968, H.C.Deb., vol. 769, col. 189.

[7] *Van Duyn* v. *Home Office*, Case 41/74, [1974] ECR 1337.

has now reversed its policy and no longer attempts to exclude Scientologists.

Public security is more limited in scope. It relates to the protection of the country from terrorism, crime, espionage, insurrection, destabilization and revolution. It overlaps with public policy: anything contrary to public security is also contrary to public policy, but the converse is not true.

Public health is the least subjective of the three, since public-health issues can to some extent be settled by expert medical opinion. It is invoked as a ground for refusing entry to migrants suffering from infectious diseases. Article 4 of Directive 64/221, however, imposes two important limitations on its use: it provides that entry may be refused on grounds of public health only in the case of a limited number of diseases specified in the directive; and it prohibits the deportation of immigrants by reason of diseases contracted after their first residence permit has been issued.[8] The Annex to the directive, which contains the list of diseases, makes clear that drug addiction and mental illness come under public policy or public security, not public health.

According to the Treaty provisions, the public-policy proviso should cover all the immigration rights given by Community law.[9] However, in *Rutili*,[10] the European Court ruled that it does not apply to the right of free movement *within* a Member State. The Court, however, said that a Member State could impose restrictions on the internal free movement of Community migrants, provided they were treated in the same way as its own nationals. This means that if the internal free movement of nationals may be restricted—for example, by arrest, imprisonment, bail conditions or a probation order—the internal free movement of Community immigrants may be restricted in the same way.

It will be clear from what has been said that the entire Community system of free movement could be undermined if the public-policy proviso were abused. For this reason, the Council adopted Directive 64/221, which imposes limitations on the exercise of the power. The first limitation, laid down in Article 2(2), is that the proviso may not be invoked to serve economic ends.[11] A Member State cannot, therefore, ban the entry of immigrant workers in order to relieve unemployment among its own citizens.

The second limitation is that measures taken under the proviso must be 'based exclusively on the personal conduct of the individual

---

[8] The European Court will probably interpret this as prohibiting deportation by reason of diseases contracted after the migrant has gained the right to reside.

[9] See Arts 48(3) and 56(1) EEC.

[10] Case 36/75, [1975] ECR 1219.

[11] The English text actually says 'service economic ends', an example of the translation errors that sometimes occur in Community documents.

concerned'.[12] This is an important provision. Personal conduct implies voluntary action; consequently, the national authorities cannot base their decision on circumstances beyond the control of the individual concerned. Thus, for example, place of birth, race, sex or physical characteristics cannot be taken into account. If, through circumstances beyond his control, an immigrant is unable to support himself—through involuntary unemployment or illness, for example—this fact cannot be used as a reason for invoking the proviso.[13] The limitation, however, applies only to measures taken on grounds of public policy or public security, not to measures taken on grounds of public health. The reason is obvious: infection with a disease is not usually voluntary; consequently, if the limitation applied to public health, Member States would not be able to refuse entry to immigrants suffering from infectious diseases.

In *Van Duyn* v. *Home Office*,[14] the question arose whether association with an organization—the Church of Scientology—could constitute conduct within the meaning of the directive. Except where the person is forced to do so, joining an organization is obviously personal conduct, and the same would be true of voluntary association with an organization. This is what the European Court held; however, it also said that past association—as distinct from present association—cannot, in general, justify a decision denying the right of free movement. This latter statement seems hard to accept: if the British Government has reason to believe that, two years ago, an immigrant was associated with a terrorist organization, should this not be sufficient reason to deny him entry? Past conduct is still conduct, and the directive does not require the conduct to be continuing. Of course, if the immigrant is able to supply convincing evidence that he has not only left the organization but has completely disassociated himself from its activities, the Government might decide to take no action. This decision, however, is one for the Government to take: they have the responsibility of weighing the evidence and deciding whether, in view of all the facts, the presence of the individual concerned constitutes a threat to public policy or public security.

The third limitation states that previous criminal convictions cannot 'in themselves' constitute grounds for taking measures under the

---

[12] Art. 3(1).

[13] Art. 3(1) applies only to deportations under the public-policy proviso. Therefore, if the immigrant has no rights under Community law—for example, because he immigrated in order to look for work but did not find a job within a reasonable period of time—he can be deported without recourse to the proviso. In such a case, the fact that he was unable to support himself without assistance from public funds may be used as a ground for deporting him.

[14] See n. 7 above.

proviso.[15] This provision applies both to convictions in a foreign country and to those in the country concerned. What it means is that the mere fact of the *conviction* alone is not a sufficient justification; it does not, however, prevent the immigration authorities from taking account of the *actions* of the immigrant that constituted the crime. Member States may not lay down a blanket rule that no one with a conviction may be allowed to enter: each case must be looked at individually in order to ascertain whether the conduct of the individual is a sufficiently serious threat to public policy to justify his exclusion. The criteria applicable in such an appraisal will not necessarily be the same as those applied by the court in convicting him of the offence.[16] No account will be taken of a minor offence, nor, in the case of a conviction in a foreign country, of some act which, though a crime in the foreign country, is not contrary to public policy in the country which the migrant wishes to enter.

In *Bonsignore*,[17] the European Court had to consider in greater detail the justification for deporting a migrant who has been convicted of a crime. Bonsignore was an Italian immigrant in Germany. He had illegally obtained a pistol, with which he accidentally shot his brother. He was convicted of two offences under German law, illegal possession of a firearm and negligent homicide. The German authorities wanted to deport him, and he brought proceedings in the German courts to challenge the deportation order. The German court ruled that, in view of the anguish he had suffered at his brother's death, it was very unlikely that he would ever commit a similar offence again; therefore, if the purpose of the deportation order was individual deterrence—preventing him from committing another offence—it was unjustified. However, if its purpose was general deterrence—deterring others from committing a similar crime—it could be justified. This judgment meant that, under German law, the deportation order could be upheld only on the latter ground. The question then arose whether general deterrence is an acceptable ground under Community law. The European Court ruled that it is not.

In a later case, however, the European Court held that individual deterrence is not the only legitimate objective in deporting a migrant who has been convicted of a criminal offence. This was in *R. v. Bouchereau*,[18] where the Court said that a criminal conviction can be taken into account only if 'the circumstances which gave rise to that conviction are evidence of personal conduct constituting a present threat to the requirements of public policy'. The Court went on to say: 'Although, in general, a finding that such a threat exists implies the existence in the individual concerned of a propensity to act in the same way in the future, it is possible that past conduct alone may constitute

[15] Art. 3(2).
[17] Case 67/74, [1975] ECR 297.

[16] *R. v. Bouchereau*, Case 30/77 [1977] ECR 1997.
[18] See n. 16 above.

such a threat to the requirements of public policy.' This means that in exceptional cases a migrant may be deported even if there is no risk that he will commit another crime.[19]

The fourth limitation laid down in the directive is that the expiry of the passport or identity card used by the migrant to enter the country and obtain a residence permit cannot justify his deportation.[20] This rule does not, however, prevent a Member State from refusing entry to an immigrant who does not have a valid passport or identity card,[21] nor does it prevent a Member State from imposing a fine on a migrant resident in the country who allows his passport or identity card to expire without renewing it.[22]

It will be remembered from the discussion of *Van Duyn* v. *Home Office*[23] that, at the time when the case arose, foreigners wishing to work for the Church of Scientology were banned from entering the United Kingdom, even though no restrictions were placed on the right of British Scientologists to take such employment. It might be thought that such discrimination was contrary to Community law;[24] however, since a country cannot refuse entry to its own citizens, a rule prohibiting Member States from discriminating in the exercise of the proviso would effectively prevent them from invoking it at all. For this reason, the European Court in the *Van Duyn* case upheld the United Kingdom's right to exclude foreign Scientologists on public-policy grounds, even though this involved an element of discrimination.

In a later case, however, the European Court introduced a significant qualification to this ruling. This was in *Adoui and Cornuaille*,[25] where, after referring to the principle laid down in *Van Duyn*, it said that Member States nevertheless cannot apply an 'arbitrary distinction to the detriment of nationals of other Member States'.[26] It went on to rule that Member States may not invoke the proviso with regard to an activity which, when carried on by their own nationals, does not give rise to

---

[19] See the opinion of Advocate General Warner, where he said that in exceptional cases a migrant's conduct may cause such deep public revulsion that public policy would require his departure, even if he is unlikely to commit a similar crime in the future.

[20] Art. 3(3).

[21] Art. 3(1) of Dir. 68/360 and of Dir. 73/148 makes clear that a valid identity card or passport must be produced on entry. It is uncertain whether the migrant may be deported after entry but before he has obtained the right to reside. The wording of Art. 3(3) of Dir. 64/221 suggests that he is liable to deportation until he has obtained a resident's permit (see also Art. 4(3) of Dir. 68/360 and Art. 6 of Dir. 73/148, which require production of an identity card or passport in order to obtain a residence permit). However, the European Court might be reluctant to accept this.

[22] See pp. 133–4 below.

[23] See pp. 126–7 above.

[24] See Arts 7 and 48(2) EEC, which prohibit discrimination on grounds of nationality (discussed in the next chapter).

[25] Cases 115, 116/81, [1982] ECR 1665.

[26] Para. 7.

'repressive measures or other genuine and effective measures' intended to combat it.[27] This means that the activity must either be a criminal offence or subject to other genuine and effective measures which apply irrespective of nationality. It is not clear exactly what would constitute such 'genuine and effective measures', but it is doubtful whether they existed in the *Van Duyn* case.[28]

Immigration Control

Immigration control is the mechanism used by states to ensure that their immigration laws are observed. Broadly speaking, it may be divided into two categories, control on entry and control after entry. The former is intended to prevent the entry of persons who have no right to immigrate; the latter is aimed at discovering (and normally removing) illegal immigrants already in the country.[29] Control on entry normally takes the form of requiring immigrants to enter the country only at specified points of entry, requiring them to present themselves to an immigration officer, show a passport and answer questions. Sometimes a visa, or other authorization, must be obtained in advance. Control after entry may include requiring the immigrant to register his address with the police and requiring him to apply, after a specified period of time, for an extension of his leave to enter the country.

In order to explain the legal basis for immigration control in the United Kingdom, it is necessary to say something about the principles of British immigration law. The basic principle laid down by the Immigration Act 1971 was that persons having what was called the 'right of abode' were free to come and go as they pleased, but other persons could enter, reside and work only with leave.[30] The right of abode was given to British citizens and certain other limited categories of persons, but not to Community citizens;[31] consequently, when the United Kingdom joined the Community, citizens of other Community countries were required by United Kingdom law to obtain leave to enter.[32] The Government tried to reconcile this situation with the requirements of Community law by instructing immigration officers to give Community citizens leave to enter in all cases where they had such a right under

---

[27] See the first paragraph of the Ruling.

[28] It would normally be for the national court to decide this question.

[29] In this context, 'illegal immigrants' refers both to illegal entrants (persons whose original entry was illegal) and to persons who entered legally but overstayed their time limit or otherwise infringed the law.

[30] Immigration Act 1971, s. 1.

[31] Immigration Act 1971, s. 2, as substituted by British Nationality Act 1981, s. 36.

[32] Irish citizens were (and still are) in a special position: see n. 52 below.

Community law.[33] The result was that, though Community migrants were required under United Kingdom law to obtain leave to enter, immigration officers were obliged to give them leave.

This, however, was not good enough for the European Court, which held in *R. v. Pieck*[34] that, where a migrant has a right to enter under Community law, giving leave to enter is not only unnecessary, but also illegal.[35] As a result of this case, immigration officers are no longer permitted to take any step, such as stamping the immigrant's passport,[36] which could be regarded as giving him leave to enter.[37] This means that, in the case of Community migrants, immigration-control measures (such as an obligation to report to the police) cannot, as in the past, be imposed by means of conditions attached to the grant of leave to enter.

What immigration-control measures does Community law allow? There can be little doubt that Member States are permitted to require immigrants to enter only at specified points of entry[38] and to show their passports or identity cards.[39] The *Pieck* judgment seems implicitly to allow such additional measures (for example, asking questions) as are reasonably necessary to establish whether the immigrant comes within the internal personal scope of the Community provisions, that is, whether he is a worker, self-employed person, and so on.[40] In *Pieck*, the Court said that the public-policy proviso cannot 'justify administrative measures requiring in a general way formalities at the frontier other than simply the production of a valid identity card or passport'.[41] This could be interpreted as outlawing any additional measures taken to ascertain whether entry should be denied on grounds of public policy, but the better view is that such measures may not be imposed *as a matter of*

---

[33] This was done by means of an amendment to the Immigration Rules: see H.C. Paper 169 of 1981/82, paras 66–72 (Control on Entry) and 139–147 (Control after Entry).

[34] Case 157/79, [1980] ECR 2171.

[35] The European Court held that requiring leave to enter constituted an infringement of Art. 3(2) of Dir. 68/360, which provides that Member States may not demand any 'entry visa or equivalent document' from the migrant. It rejected the United Kingdom's contention that this provision is concerned only with documents which have to be obtained prior to arrival. In view of the versions of Art. 3(2) in the other Community languages, the phrase 'equivalent document' should probably have been 'equivalent requirement': cf. Art. 3(2) of Dir. 73/148. In spite of this, however, it is by no means self-evident that the United Kingdom's contention was wrong.

[36] The Commission takes the view that *any* stamping of a migrant's passport, even if simply to record the date of entry, is contrary to Community law (see Press Release IP(88) of 8 June 1988), though it is hard to see the logic in this.

[37] United Kingdom immigration law has now been amended to bring it into line with the Court's ruling: under s. 7(1) of the Immigration Act 1988, a person entitled to enter under Community law no longer requires leave.

[38] This is implicit both in the Community legislation and in the judgments of the European Court: see e.g. *Royer*, Case 48/75, [1976] ECR 497.

[39] This is recognized by Art. 3(1) of Dir. 68/360 and of Dir. 73/148.

[40] See Wyatt, (1980) 5 E.L.Rev. 380 at 384; see also Commission Document V/526/81 (12 June 1981), p. 4 (para. 3) and p. 6 (para. 2).

[41] Para. 19.

routine: if the immigration authorities already have grounds for suspicion, there is no reason why they should not question the immigrant to ascertain whether their suspicions are justified.[42]

As far as control after entry is concerned, Member States are entitled to require immigrants to register with the police[43] and to obtain a Community-type residence permit,[44] but they may not require immigrants to obtain an ordinary (non-Community) residence permit.[45]

An important rule laid down by the European Court is that the infringement of an immigration-control requirement cannot in itself lead to deportation.[46] This means that if an immigrant enters illegally—for example, by landing at night on a deserted beach from a small boat—he cannot be expelled on that ground. The same applies to an immigrant who fails to register with the police or to obtain a residence permit. Such a person may, of course, be deported if he is not covered by Community law, or if, for reasons other than his breach of the immigration-control requirement, public policy requires his expulsion.

What sanctions may be imposed for violation of immigration-control requirements? Where he has not yet entered the country, an immigrant may be refused entry if he does not comply with control-on-entry requirements—for example, if he does not have a valid passport or identity card. Once he is in the country, however, the only acceptable

[42] Wyatt, op. cit., pp. 386–8; Commission Document V/526/81 (12 June 1981), p. 6, para. 3.

[43] *Watson and Belmann*, Case 118/75, [1976] ECR 1185. This case concerned an Italian law which provided that immigrants had to report their presence within three days and that persons giving accommodation to an immigrant had to report the immigrant's presence within twenty-four hours. The European Court said that provisions of this kind are compatible with Community law provided that the time limits are reasonable. However, in *Messner*, Case C–265/88 (12 Dec. 1989—not yet reported), the Court held that the three-day time limit was unreasonably short, in view of the fact that the immigrant has to travel from the frontier to his final destination and then make inquiries as to the competent authorities. The Italian law was, therefore, held to be contrary to Community law. The Court, however, acknowledged that a similar requirement with a longer time limit would be acceptable.

[44] This is the document provided for in Art. 4(2) of Dir. 68/360 (workers) and Art. 4(1) of Dir. 73/148 (self-employed). The requirement can, of course, be imposed only in the case of those immigrants who are entitled to a residence permit. In *Commission* v. *Belgium*, Case 321/87, [1989] ECR 997, the European Court was asked to give a ruling on a Belgian decree requiring Community immigrants (and other foreigners) to have their residence permits on their persons at all times and to produce them on demand to the appropriate authorities. Similar requirements were imposed on Belgian citizens with regard to their identity cards. In both cases, the only penalty was a small fine. The European Court held that the decree was not contrary to Community law, despite the fact that such checks were sometimes carried out at frontiers (though this was not done on a regular basis, nor were Community immigrants refused entry for failure to be in possession of their residence permits). The Court said, however, that frontier checks of this kind could constitute a violation of Community law if carried out systematically, arbitrarily or to no useful purpose. It would also be contrary to Community law if failure to produce a residence permit could lead to denial of entry.

[45] *Sagulo*, Case 8/77, [1977] ECR 1495.

[46] *Royer* (see n. 38 above), para. 3 of the ruling.

penalty appears to be a modest fine: imprisonment seems no longer to be permitted.[47]

The effect of these rules, which are almost entirely the work of the European Court, is that immigration control over Community migrants is somewhat tenuous: immigration-control measures are permitted, but the sanctions for their violation are of limited effectiveness. The Commission, moreover, wants to go further and abolish all entry controls at internal frontiers in the Community.[48] Under their plan, migrants could move from one Community country to another without having to show their passports or being subject to any other form of control: travelling from Germany to England would be the same as travelling from Scotland to England. Entry controls would still apply— and might even be strengthened—on migrants entering from outside the Community, but there would be no checks on travel within the Community.[49] Substantive Community migration law would remain the same,[50] but would be enforced only by control after entry.

The Commission considers that the abolition of intra-Community border controls is necessary in order to make the Community a reality for its citizens. It also argues that it is required by Article 8A of the EEC Treaty, which was inserted by Article 13 of the Single European Act.

[47] The European Court's position on this question has evolved over several cases. In *Watson and Belmann* (n. 43 above) the Court said that the penalties must not be 'disproportionate to the gravity of the offence' (para. 2 of the Ruling); it also said that they must be 'comparable to those attaching to infringements of provisions of equal importance by nationals' (para. 21). The latter statement was used by Advocate General Reischl to argue in *Sagulo* (n. 45 above) that the penalty imposed on an immigrant whose identity card, passport or (Community) residence permit is no longer valid should be no greater than that applicable to a citizen of the country concerned whose identity card has expired. (The case concerned immigrants in Germany, a country where all citizens are obliged to have identity cards.) The European Court, however, rejected this argument. It also pointed out that in some Member States (for example, the United Kingdom) citizens are not required to possess identity cards; in the case of such countries, therefore, there would be no standard of comparison. This judgment could be regarded as a repudiation of the second statement in *Watson and Belmann*, though the first statement in that case was expressly affirmed. In *Pieck* (n. 34 above), however, the Court said that failure to obtain a (Community) residence permit may be punished only if the penalties are 'comparable to those attaching to minor offences by nationals' (para. 19); moreover, it expressly ruled out imprisonment.

[48] It might be thought that the United Kingdom had only one internal Community frontier, that between Northern Ireland and the Republic of Ireland, but the Commission has a wider concept of what 'internal frontier' means: it regards a journey by sea or air from one Member State to another as a crossing of an internal frontier (see, for example, Art. 9 of the Commission proposal for a directive on the easing of controls and formalities applicable to nationals of the Member States when crossing intra-Community borders, the original version of which was published in OJ 1985, C 47, p. 5, and the amended version in OJ 1985, C 131, p. 5).

[49] For an outline of the Commission proposals, see Commission Document (88) 640 of 7 Dec. 1988. These proposals are intended to supersede the earlier plan contained in the draft directive mentioned in the previous footnote.

[50] The Commission also wanted to recast Community migration rights, but in the end had to settle for the limited extension provided by Dirs 90/364, 90/365 and 90/366: see pp. 98–100, above.

After providing for the establishment of the internal market by 31 December 1992, this states: 'The internal market shall comprise an area without internal frontiers in which the free movement of goods, persons, services and capital is ensured in accordance with the provisions of this Treaty.' The Commission's position is that the concept of an area without internal frontiers implies the abolition of all entry controls. However, the free movement of persons is to take place in accordance with the provisions of the Treaty, and the Treaty provides for free movement only within certain limits; therefore, it could be argued that sufficient controls must remain to ensure that these limits are respected: all that is required is that persons entitled to Community immigration rights should not be hindered in the exercise of those rights when they cross an internal frontier.

The Commission proposal has met with opposition from the United Kingdom. Its most serious defect concerns migrants who are not Community citizens. Their immigration rights would continue to be a matter for each Member State, but it would be much more difficult to enforce the law since they too would be free from control when entering from another Community country. As intra-Community travellers would no longer be required to show their passports or identity documents, there would be no way of distinguishing Community citizens from non-Community citizens; consequently, it would not be possible to retain entry controls for the latter alone. The result would be that a migrant from a non-Community country who wished to enter the United Kingdom could quite easily evade United Kingdom immigration control by entering the Community via another Member State where immigration controls on non-Community migrants are lax.

Another undesirable consequence of the Commission proposal is the effect it would have on the fight against terrorism and drug-smuggling; it could also mean the end of Britain's attempt to prevent the spread of rabies. Moreover, the abolition of exit controls could make it easier for criminals to escape prosecution by fleeing the country. The Commission's answer to these objections is to stress the need for common policies and co-operation on such matters as drugs, visas, refugees, extradition and terrorism; it does not, however, consider that it would be necessary to attain complete uniformity of policy among the Member States as regards the immigration rights of non-Community nationals.

The Commission also argues that entry controls are in any event of limited effectiveness and that control after entry is sufficient. This latter argument raises particular problems for the United Kingdom because it has traditionally relied much more on entry controls (as distinct from control after entry) than have Continental countries,[51] and British public

[51] This is partly because entry controls are much more effective in the case of Britain than they are in the case of countries with land frontiers. The land frontier in Ireland is covered by the common travel area : see n. 52, below.

opinion would be reluctant to accept the measures that would be necessary to make control after entry effective. These would probably include compulsory identity cards for the whole population and an obligation for citizens and aliens alike to register their address with the police.[52] At the present time it is impossible to tell whether the Commission's proposals will be adopted. It is, however, significant that France, Germany and the Benelux countries have already agreed to the eventual abolition of entry controls at their common borders.[53]

Remedies

In this final section we shift the focus back to the viewpoint of the migrant and consider the remedies available to him when his rights under Community law are infringed.

Articles 5–9 of Directive 64/221 contain several provisions of a procedural nature,[54] the most important being Articles 8 and 9. Article 8 is what may be called an 'equality' provision. It provides that Community migrants must be given the same right to challenge immigration decisions[55] as nationals have to challenge administrative acts in general. In the English context, this means that immigration decisions must be subject to judicial review, which has in fact always been the case.

Article 9 is not an equality provision, but a 'minimum standards' provision. Article 9(1) benefits only immigrants who have already acquired a residence permit.[56] It states that if the law of the Member

---

[52] It should be noted that entry controls have never existed between the United Kingdom and the Republic of Ireland, which, together with the Channel Islands and the Isle of Man, form a common travel area. This is made possible by the fact that these countries have a common policy with regard to immigration from third countries and co-operate closely in immigration matters. See s. 9 of the Immigration Act 1971.

[53] The first step was taken on 14 June 1985, when representatives of the five countries met in the little Luxembourg village of Schengen to sign a treaty in which they agreed to relax controls at their common frontiers. (This was preceded by the Saarbrucken Agreement of 13 July 1984, which was between France and Germany only.) Schengen was also the place where a second treaty was signed in 1990. This made provision for the abolition of all frontier controls and for increased police co-operation, as well as granting police from one country the right to cross into another in pursuit of criminals.

[54] Art. 5(1) lays down a time limit for reaching a decision on an application for a residence permit; Art. 5(2) is concerned with requests to another Member State for a migrant's police record; Art. 6, which applies when the public-policy proviso is invoked, entitles the immigrant to know the ground on which the decision was taken, unless this would be contrary to state security; and Art. 7 is concerned with the notification of decisions to the migrant and the time period within which he must leave the country. For a fuller discussion of the procedural provisions of Dir. 64/221, see Hartley, *EEC Immigration Law* (1978), pp. 169–81.

[55] It covers decisions concerning entry, the issue or renewal of a residence permit and expulsion.

[56] It covers decisions refusing to renew a residence permit or providing for the deportation of a holder of such a permit.

State does not make provision for an appeal to a court of law on the merits (as distinct from judicial review),[57] the immigration authority must (except in cases of emergency) consult what is called a 'competent authority' before taking the decision. The competent authority must be separate from the authority taking the decision, and the migrant must have 'such rights of defence and of assistance or representation as the domestic law of that country provides for'. This rather unclear provision probably grants the immigrant the right to be legally represented and the rights generally subsumed under the rubric of natural justice. After the hearing, the competent authority gives its opinion and the immigration authority then takes its decision. It appears not to be bound by the opinion, though it must take it into consideration.

A similar procedure is laid down in Article 9(2), which covers decisions refusing to grant a residence permit or ordering the deportation of a migrant who has not yet obtained a permit. In these cases, however, the competent authority is consulted *after* the decision has been taken. Presumably the decision has to be reviewed if it is not supported by the competent authority.[58] The European Court has held that the procedure under Article 9 has suspensory effect, by which is meant that the immigrant cannot be deported until it has been completed.[59] The only exception is in cases of urgency.[60]

In the United Kingdom, an immigrant normally has a right of appeal against immigration decisions to a person called an adjudicator and then to the Immigration Appeal Tribunal.[61] Appeals to an adjudicator and the Immigration Appeal Tribunal cover issues of fact, law and the exercise of discretion; so the merits of the decision are fully reviewed. In conducting his case, the immigrant has all the rights normally associated with proceedings in a court of law. For these reasons, the appeal procedure appears to satisfy the requirements of Article 9 in those cases in which it applies.[62]

There are two situations, however, in which this procedure does not apply. The first concerns those (rare) cases in which the Home Secretary

[57] The appeal must also have suspensory effect, that is, the deportation of the immigrant must be suspended until a decision on the appeal is given.

[58] For further details on the appointment of the competent authority and the procedure before it, see *Adoui and Cornuaille*, Cases 115–16/81, [1982] ECR 1665.

[59] *Pecastaing*, Case 98/79, [1980] ECR 691. Proceedings under Art. 8, on the other hand, do not have suspensory effect unless this is normally the case under national law; the immigrant must, however, be allowed to remain in the country long enough to commence proceedings and must be allowed to remain longer if this is necessary to allow him to put his case effectively: ibid.

[60] The national authorities decide when the case is one of urgency: *Pecastaing* (n. 59 above).

[61] See Part II of the Immigration Act 1971. (For the procedure, see SI 1984, No. 2041). Decisions of the Immigration Appeal Tribunal are subject to judicial review for error of law.

[62] It would probably constitute an appeal to a court of law within the terms of Art. 9(1).

considers that the immigrant's presence is not conducive to the public good, normally for reasons of national security.[63] In these cases, the immigrant is allowed to make representations to a person, or persons, nominated by the Home Secretary. Their opinion is considered by the Home Secretary, but is not binding on him.[64] Here the immigrant's procedural rights may be severely curtailed for security reasons. Whether this procedure would satisfy the 'competent authority' requirements of Article 9 would probably depend on the way it operated in the particular case.

The other situation in which the normal system does not apply is where the immigrant is deported as a result of having been convicted of a criminal offence.[65] Here the court which convicts him may make a recommendation that he be deported. If such a recommendation is made, the Home Secretary may make a deportation order. There is no right of appeal against the Home Secretary's decision to make the deportation order, but the court which made the recommendation could be regarded as the 'competent authority' required by Article 9. In *R. v. Secretary of State*, ex parte *Santillo*,[66] the European Court accepted this There is, however, a further problem. If the accused is sentenced to a term of imprisonment, he will not normally be deported until he has served his sentence. There could, therefore, be a lapse of several years between the appeal and the deportation order. This is what happened in *Santillo's* case. He was convicted of serious sexual offences and sentenced to eight years' imprisonment. The court recommended that he be deported. He petitioned the Court of Appeal for leave to appeal against his sentence and against the recommendation for deportation, but leave was refused. He then went to prison. Four years later, when the time for his release was drawing near,[67] the Home Secretary decided to make the deportation order. Santillo challenged this in proceedings for judicial review and the case went to the European Court, which held that a lapse of time amounting to several years between the recommendation and the Home Secretary's decision 'is liable to deprive the recommendation of its function as an opinion within the meaning of Article 9'.[68] It is not clear whether by this the European Court meant that a lapse of time automatically deprives the recommendation of its function as an opinion, or whether it meant that it can do so if there has

---

[63] See the Immigration Act 1971, ss. 13(5). 14(3), 15(3) and 15(4). The normal appeals procedure is also not applicable to exclusion orders under s. 7 of the Prevention of Terrorism (Temporary Provisions) Act 1989.

[64] This procedure is extra-statutory, except in the case of exclusion orders, where provision is made for it by the Prevention of Terrorism (Temporary Provisions) Act 1989, s. 4(4) and Sched. 2, para. 3.

[65] See the Immigration Act 1971, s. 3(6).

[66] Case 131/79, [1980] ECR 1585.

[67] He had earned remission for good conduct.

been a change of circumstances in the intervening period. When the proceedings recommenced in England, the Divisional Court adopted the latter interpretation. Since it considered that no new facts had arisen, it refused to set the deportation order aside.[69] This decision was upheld by the Court of Appeal.[70]

[68] Para. 3(b) of the Ruling.
[69] [1980] 3 CMLR 212; [1981] 2 All ER 913.
[70] [1981] QB 778.

11

Equal Treatment for Migrants

The rule that all its citizens must be treated equally is one of the fundamental principles of the Community. According to the European Court, the prohibition against discrimination on grounds of nationality is itself the expression of an even wider principle, that of equality, which is a general principle of Community law.[1] The prohibition against discrimination on grounds of sex is another application of this general principle.

The prohibition against discrimination on grounds of nationality is laid down in general terms in Article 7 of the EEC Treaty; equal treatment for migrants is expressly required by Article 48(2) EEC, which prohibits discrimination on grounds of nationality in the employment field, and by Articles 7–9 of Regulation 1612/68; it is implicit in many other provisions.

In view of the fundamental status accorded to the principle of equality, the European Court interprets these provisions in a broad way. It has also held that they prohibit indirect discrimination: it has ruled that the principle of equal treatment forbids not only overt discrimination on grounds of nationality, but also 'all covert forms of discrimination which, by the application of other criteria of differentiation, lead in fact to the same result'.[2] In spite of the words used by the Court, it is not necessary that the result should be exactly the same, only that the effect should be in practice more or less the same. Thus, discrimination on grounds of residence will normally be treated as an indirect form of discrimination on grounds of nationality.[3] One important difference betwen direct and indirect discrimination, however, is that the latter is not prohibited absolutely, but only if there is no objective reason for it, by which is meant some rational ground, not inconsistent with the principles of Community law, on which it might be justified.

A good example of indirect discrimination is provided by *Südmilch* v. *Ugliola*,[4] a case which concerned a German law granting benefits to

---

[1] *Frilli* v. *Belgium*, Case 1/72, [1972] ECR 457 (para. 19); *Sotgiu* v. *Deutsche Bundespost*, Case 152/73, [1974] ECR 153 (para. 11). See further, Hartley, *The Foundations of European Community Law* (2nd edn), Chap. 3.

[2] This definition was first put forward in *Sotgiu* (see n. 1 above), para. 11, and has been repeated in subsequent cases.

[3] Ibid.

[4] Case 15/69, [1969] ECR 363.

workers called up on military service. If the law had granted the benefits only to workers who were German citizens, it would clearly have discriminated on grounds of nationality. It did not do this. It did, however, apply only to service in the German army. In other words, a foreign worker in Germany who for some reason served in the German army would obtain the benefits, but a German worker who served in a foreign army would not. In practice, of course, both these situations would be rare. Consequently, the practical effect of differentiating on the basis of the nationality of the army was almost the same as that of differentiating on the basis of the nationality of the worker. The European Court held, therefore, that the German law discriminated indirectly on the basis of nationality.

It was clearly necessary for the European Court to create the concept of indirect discrimination in order to ensure the effectiveness of the Treaty provisions; otherwise, it would have been easy for unscrupulous Member States to find ways of evading the law. The European Court has, however, never made quite clear whether it is necessary to establish a subjective intention to discriminate, or whether it is sufficient to show that there is no objective reason for the provision in question.[5] In practice, perhaps, these two alternatives may come to almost the same thing.

Article 7 EEC

The first paragraph of Article 7 EEC provides: 'Within the scope of application of this Treaty, and without prejudice to any special provisions contained therein, any discrimination on grounds of nationality shall be prohibited.' There is no doubt that this provision, which must of course be understood as applying only to discrimination against Community nationals, is directly effective to the extent that it binds Member States, though it is less clear whether it imposes directly effective obligations on private individuals.[6] Its basic intent is fairly clear: it prohibits discrimination on grounds of nationality within those areas covered by the Treaty, subject to any special provisions in the Treaty dealing with particular cases.

An example of a 'special provision' which overrides the general

---

[5] The doctrine of indirect discrimination also applies in the area of sex equality and it is here that this issue has caused problems: see *Jenkins* v. *Kingsgate (Clothing Production), The Times*, 8 July 1981 (EAT) and compare *Jenkins* v. *Kingsgate*, Case 96/80, [1981] ECR 911.

[6] In its second paragraph, Art. 7 goes on to empower the Council to adopt 'rules designed to prohibit such discrimination', which implies that the discrimination is not fully prohibited by Art. 7 as it stands. See further, Brita Sundberg-Weitman, *Discrimination on Grounds of Nationality* (1977), Chap. 3 and the article by the same author in (1973) 10 C.M.L.Rev. 71.

prohibition is to be found in the public-policy proviso in Articles 48(3) and 56(1) EEC. It will be remembered[7] that this allows Member States to restrict the immigration rights of Community citizens on grounds of public policy, public security or public health. However, since a Member State's own citizens are not subject to such restrictions, the application of the proviso necessarily results in discrimination on grounds of nationality. In *Van Duyn* v. *Home Office*,[8] the European Court held that this is neverthelesss not against the Treaty. Presumably the Treaty Articles embodying the public-policy proviso are to be regarded as 'special provisions'.[9] Another example is contained in Article 48(4) EEC (discussed below),[10] which states that the provisions of Article 48 do not apply to employment in the public service.[11] Since Article 48 prohibits discrimination in employment, the effect of Article 48(4) is to permit Member States to restrict many civil-service posts to their own citizens. Article 7 does not prevent this: it is overridden by Article 48(4), even though the latter does not expressly refer to Article 7.

In *Sagulo*,[12] the European Court went further and held that Community legislation can also constitute a 'special provision' in terms of Article 7 EEC.[13] The point at issue in the case was whether an immigrant who fails to renew his identity card when it expires may be punished more severely than a national in the same position. The case arose in Germany, a country in which all citizens are obliged to possess identity cards. German legislation provided for a fairly lenient penalty in the case of German citizens who failed to renew their identity cards, but a much heavier one in the case of immigrants. The European Court held that this was permissible, and squared its ruling with Article 7 EEC by stating that Directive 68/360, which requires immigrants to be in possession of a valid passport or identity card, is a 'special provision' under Article 7. In the case of the United Kingdom, the discrimination is even more striking, since British citizens are not required to carry identity documents. Immigrants must nevertheless have a valid passport or identity card and, where applicable, a Community residence permit.[14]

---

[7] See pp. 125–31 above.

[8] Case 41/74, [1974] ECR 1337.

[9] The European Court has, however, tried to limit such discrimination to the minimum necessitated by the proviso: see pp. 130–1 above.

[10] See pp. 155–6.

[11] See also Art. 55 EEC (activities connected with the exercise of official authority).

[12] Case 8/77, [1977] ECR 1495.

[13] This ruling conflicts with the terms of Art. 7 EEC in its English version, which provides, 'Within the scope of application of this Treaty and without prejudice to any special provisions contained therein . . . '. This clearly requires the special provision to be contained in the Treaty. In its French version, however, Art. 7 reads, 'Dans le domaine d'application du présent traité, et sans préjudice des dispositions particulières qu'il prévoit . . . '. A better translation of this would be, ' . . . without prejudice to any special provisions *envisaged* therein . . . '. On the basis of the French text, therefore, the Court's ruling is quite correct.

[14] For further developments in this regard, see above, p. 134 n. 47.

Deciding what comes within the scope of the Treaty involves more difficult problems. Is Article 7 applicable only to those areas covered by Treaty provisions giving lawmaking power to the Community or laying down rules binding on the Member States? Or does it apply to any area that is the subject of a Treaty provision, no matter how vague? In particular, is it possible for Article 7 to apply to an area which remains within the legislative jurisdiction of the Member States? These questions arise in a particularly acute form with regard to education, a topic which forms the subject of Chapter 13. The only Treaty provisions dealing with education are Article 128 EEC, which empowers the Council, acting on a proposal from the Commission, to 'lay down general principles' for implementing a common vocational-training policy, and Article 118, which gives the Commission the task of promoting close co-operation between the Member States with regard to 'basic and advanced vocational training'. It might be thought that these provisions, which do not deprive the Member States of jurisdiction in the field, were insufficient to trigger Article 7. The European Court, however, decided otherwise, and in a series of cases which will be discussed in Chapter 13, it ruled that Article 7 prevents Member States from charging higher tuition fees to students from other Community countries than apply to local students. It also held that Article 7 requires Member States to give the same grants for tuition fees to Community students as are available to their own students. Paradoxically, however, the Court has ruled that Article 7 EEC does not prevent Member States from restricting *maintenance* grants to their own citizens.

The cases on education are enough to demonstrate that policy, rather than legal principle, is the dominant consideration in this area. This may be further illustrated by the Court's judgment in *Cowan*,[15] a case concerning a British tourist who was mugged as he left the Paris Metro. French legislation provided for government compensation for the victims of criminal violence, but applied only if the claimant was a French citizen, a foreigner in possession of a French resident's card or a citizen of a country having a reciprocal agreement with France on this matter. Mr Cowan did not fall into any of these categories, so it looked as though he would have to go uncompensated. It might be thought that Article 7 could not apply because the French legislation concerned criminal law and procedure, an area outside Community jurisdiction. The European Court, however, ruled that, as a tourist, he was a recipient of services, and consequently within the scope of the EEC Treaty. It then said that when Community law gives someone the right of free movement, that right implies, as a necessary corollary, that he must be protected against physical violence and, if it nevertheless occurs, given compensation to the same extent as a citizen.

[15] Case 186/87, [1989] ECR 195.

From a policy point of view this decision is admirable; nevertheless, it raises serious questions regarding the interpretation of Article 7. If all that is required is that the individual in question should be covered by the Treaty (even if the subject-matter is outside its scope), it is hard to see how Community law could permit a migrant worker, or other person within the free movement provisions of the Treaty, ever to be denied a right available to nationals. Taken to its logical conclusion, this would mean that such a person should be given the right to vote, and to stand as a candidate, in elections to the national parliament. No one has yet suggested that the European Court would go this far, but there is no *legal* distinction between the two situations.[16] In policy terms, of course, they are easily distinguishable.

In view of the wide scope of Article 7, it might be thought that the more specific provisions on discrimination were of no importance. However, the European Court prefers to base its decisions on these provisions where they are applicable, reserving Article 7 for use in those cases which would not otherwise be covered. Moreover, the precise terms of these provisions can affect the way the prohibition operates. We will now look at some of the more important areas in which the prohibition applies, and consider the specific provisions relevant to each area.

Employment

Employment is the area in which the prohibition against discrimination applies most strongly. Article 48(2) EEC provides that the principle of freedom of movement entails the abolition of any discrimination based on nationality between workers of the Member States as regards employment, remuneration and other conditions of work. This is further amplified by Article 7(1) of Regulation 1612/68, which also prohibits discrimination as regards dismissal and, where the worker becomes unemployed, reinstatement or re-employment.

Articles 1–6 of Regulation 1612/68 spell out in detail the principle that

[16] Advocate General Lenz tried to provide a legal basis for the application of Art. 7 in *Cowan* by arguing that the French legislation constituted a restriction on the free movement of tourists. He sought to justify this rather far-fetched conclusion on the ground that a tourist wishing to enjoy the same protection as a national of the country concerned would have to take out insurance, thereby diminishing the funds available for his touristic activities. The unreality of this argument is exposed by the fact that insurance covering the consequences of criminal assault alone does not seem to be generally available, while a more general policy would be a wise precaution in any event. An equally strained argument was adopted by the Court in an earlier decision, *Commission* v. *Italy*, Case 63/86, [1988] ECR 29, in which it held that Italy could not withhold publicly funded housing assistance from self-employed immigrants because this would distort competition between them and local citizens carrying on the same trade or profession, since, if they had to spend more money on housing, they would have less to devote to their businesses.

Community workers must be given the same opportunities as national workers to look for a job. This applies both before and after the worker has moved to the new country: discrimination on grounds of residence is prohibited. Community immigrants must be given the same assistance by employment offices as national workers. Special recruitment procedures or restrictions on advertising are prohibited if they make it more difficult for immigrants to obtain employment; quotas for immigrants are expressly forbidden. Restrictions are illegal, even where not based on nationality, if their principal aim or effect is to keep immigrant workers away from the employment offered.[17]

Under Article 3(1) of the Regulation it is permissible to stipulate that applicants for a post must have attained a given level of proficiency in a particular language, provided this is 'required by reason of the nature of the post to be filled'. In Ireland there is a rule that applicants for certain posts must possess a certificate of proficiency in the Irish language. The compatibility of this rule with Community law was considered by the European Court in *Groener* v. *Minister for Education*,[18] a case concerning a Dutch woman who was barred from appointment as an art teacher at a college of marketing and design in Dublin because she was unable to obtain the certificate. Was the requirement justified by the nature of the post? In answering this question, the European Court noted that, under the Irish Constitution, Irish is the first official language of the Republic. For many years, successive Irish Governments have followed a policy of promoting its use as a means of expressing national identity and culture. Irish is a compulsory subject in primary schools. The Court held that the EEC Treaty does not prohibit the promotion by a Member State of its national language, provided the measures taken to implement it are not disproportionate[19] to the objective pursued and do not discriminate against nationals of other Member States. The Court therefore concluded that, in view of the important role that teachers could play in the promotion of Irish, a knowledge of the language could be regarded as required by the nature of the post in the case of teachers at public educational institutions. Such a requirement must, however, be applied in a non-discriminatory manner, and the level of knowledge to be attained must not be excessive in relation to the objective pursued.[20]

Whatever doubts there may be regarding Article 7 of the Treaty, Articles 1–7 of the Regulation clearly impose directly applicable obligations not only on national governments, but also on private

---

[17] This is an example of indirect discrimination.

[18] Case 379/87 (judgment of 28 Nov. 1989), *The Times*, 1 Dec. 1989.

[19] This is an application of the doctrine of proportionality, one of the general principles of law applied by the European Court: see Hartley, *The Foundations of European Community Law*, pp. 145–7.

[20] This would be for the national court to decide.

employers and trade unions.[21] This means that if a private employer refuses to employ a worker because he is a citizen of another Member State, the worker can claim that his rights under Community law have been infringed. The precise nature of the remedy might, however, depend on national law.[22]

Business and the Professions

The provisions discussed above do not apply to self-employed persons, but the European Court has derived similar principles from other provisions of the Treaty, especially Article 52, which provides (in part): 'Freedom of establishment shall include the right to take up and pursue activities as self-employed persons . . . under the conditions laid down for its own nationals by the law of the country where such establishment is effected . . . '. This provision (which is directly effective)[23] precludes a Member State from restricting membership of a given profession—for example, solicitors—to its own citizens.[24] It would also prohibit a professional organization (or any other body having the power to regulate any trade, profession or other occupation) from applying a similar restriction. If it is impossible (or more difficult) to practise a given profession without being a member of the appropriate professional organization (for example, the Law Society), exclusion from membership on grounds of nationality would equally be against Community law.[25]

[21] Apart from the fact that provisions contained in regulations are generally directly applicable both against governments and private individuals, Art. 7(4) of the Regulation expressly provides that any clause in a collective or individual agreement is null and void in so far as it authorizes discrimination against workers who are citizens of other Member States.

[22] See *Von Colson and Kamann*, Case 14/83, [1984] ECR 1891 and *Harz*, Case 79/83, [1984] ECR 1921. In both these cases, however, the probition (which concerned discrimination on grounds of sex) was contained in a directive, not a regulation. In Britain, the victim of discrimination on grounds of nationality can bring proceedings before an industrial tribunal under the Race Relations Act 1976. This remedy exists quite apart from Community law, but since Community law prevails over British law, it could be used to override exemptions or restrictions in the British legislation. Examples of this occur frequently in the case of sex discrimination: see e.g. *Macarthys Ltd* v. *Smith* [1979] 3 All ER 325 (CA, before reference to ECJ); Case 129/79, [1980] ECR 1275 (ECJ); [1981] 1 All ER 111 (ECJ) and 120 (CA, after reference to ECJ).

[23] *Reyners*, Case 2/74, [1974] ECR 631.

[24] For an English decision on this point, see *Haug* v. *Registrar of Patent Agents*, [1976] 1 CMLR 491 (Comptroller of the Patent Office).

[25] See *Walrave and Koch*, Case 36/74, [1974] ECR 1405, where the Court held that the prohibition against discrimination applies not only to the actions of public authorities, but also to 'rules of any other nature aimed at regulating in a collective manner gainful employment and the provision of services'. (Para. 17.) This ruling does not expressly mention self-employed activities because they were not relevant on the facts of the case, but there can be no doubt that it applies to them: see the cases on the recognition of qualifications discussed in Chap. 12, below.

Services

The European Court has held that Article 59 EEC, which provides for the abolition of restrictions on the freedom to provide services, has the effect of applying the same rules to the provision of services.[26] It is, therefore, equally illegal to discriminate against providers of services on the ground of their nationality.

Since the essence of the concept of a service in Community law is that it is transnational—it assumes that a self-employed person established in one Community country carries on his activity on a temporary basis in another Community country—it does not require much imagination to see that a restriction based on residence would totally negate the right given by the Treaty.[27] For this reason, it is illegal for Member States to discriminate on grounds of residence against the providers or recipients of services.[28]

There may, however, be exceptions to this rule where the provider of the service, while residing in one country, habitually or exclusively carries on his activity in another country. *Van Binsbergen*[29] is a case in point. This concerned a person who, though not a qualified lawyer, carried on the profession of 'legal representative', appearing on behalf of claimants before Dutch social-security tribunals. He was a Dutch citizen and his entire practice appeared to be in Holland, but he had moved his residence to Belgium. A Dutch statute provided that legal representatives had to be resident in Holland and, as a result, his right to appear before Dutch tribunals was challenged. The European Court, however, ruled that a residence restriction of this kind is contrary to Articles 59 and 60 EEC unless it is 'objectively justified by the need to ensure observance of professional rules of conduct'. In Holland, legal representatives were not subject to any professional regulation nor were any qualifications required. In view of this, the European Court ruled that the residence restriction could not be justified with regard to that profession.

A similar problem arose in *Coenen*,[30] a case concerning a Dutch insurance broker who carried on his profession in the Netherlands while residing in Belgium. This case differed from the previous one in that his professional office was in the Netherlands. The Court held that a Member State can impose a residence requirement in order to prevent a

---

[26] Ibid. The relevant part of Art. 59 EEC is directly applicable: *Van Binsbergen*, Case 33/74, [1974] ECR 1299.

[27] Arts 59 and 60 EEC.

[28] Since restrictions based on residence could affect frontier workers and temporary immigrants, they would also be illegal (under Art. 1(1) of Reg. 1612/68 and possibly also as a form of indirect discrimination) in so far as they applied to employed persons.

[29] See n. 26 above.

[30] Case 39/75, [1975] ECR 1547.

person whose activities are entirely or chiefly directed towards its territory from evading the professional rules which would apply to him if he resided in that state. However, it said that this may be done only if less restrictive means of achieving this objective are not available: if the person has a *bona fide* place of business in the state where he practises, this will normally be sufficient. It seems, therefore, that a residence restriction will be permitted only in exceptional cases.

Professional Sport

Sport is covered by the EEC Treaty to the extent that it constitutes an economic activity, that is to say when it is carried on professionally or semi-professionally.[31] In such a case, the rules discussed above are binding on national sports federations and other bodies controlling sporting activities. However, the European Court has held that it is permissible to apply a nationality criterion for eligibility to play in a particular match if the reason is non-economic—for example, to ensure that the team playing for a particular country really represents that country. Consequently, it is not against Community law to have a rule that only British citizens are eligible to play for England. Whether nationality restrictions are permissible at club level is more doubtful.[32] In any event, nationality restrictions cannot apply to persons who are not members of the team—for example, a trainer or coach.[33]

Trade-Union Activities

Article 8 of Regulation 1612/68 deals with discrimination in the area of trade-union activities. It provides that workers from other Member States have a right to equal treatment as regards trade-union membership and the rights that go with it, including the right to vote and to be eligible for appointment to administrative posts in the union. They must also be eligible for appointment to workers' representative bodies in the undertaking. Article 8, however, provides that immigrant workers may be excluded from taking part in the management of bodies governed by public law and from holding an office governed by public law. This

[31] *Donà* v. *Mantero*, Case 13/76, [1976] ECR 1333.
[32] Compare the views of Advocate General Trabucchi in *Donà* v. *Mantero* (supra) with the more cautious statement by the Court.
[33] *Walrave and Koch* (n. 25 above); see also *UNECTEF* v. *Heylens*, Case 222/86, [1987] ECR 4097.

presumably refers to statutory bodies with public functions, the composition of which includes trade-union representatives.[34]

Housing

Article 9 of Regulation 1612/68 gives immigrant Community workers the right to equal treatment with regard to housing, including public housing. This would clearly bar any rule precluding them from putting their name down for council housing, or giving them lower priority on account of their nationality. It would also bar a requirement based on residence in the country as a whole.[35] Whether it would bar a rule based on residence in the local area, if such a rule applied equally to national workers, is less certain.[36]

Article 9 applies to the right to own a house and would cover legislation giving council-house tenants a right to buy their property. A rule precluding Community workers from owning land in a particular part of the country would be illegal;[37] the same would be true of a rule making it easier for the government to expropriate land owned by citizens of other Member States or providing them with less favourable compensation.

Article 9 of the Regulation does not apply to self-employed persons, but the European Court has derived similar principles from Article 52 of the Treaty.[38] *Fearon* v. *Irish Land Commission*[39] is an interesting example of the interaction of policy and principle in this area. For many years, the Republic of Ireland has had a policy of trying to ensure that agricultural holdings are not too small to be economical and that the land is owned by those who work it. Effect was given to this policy by the Land Acts of 1933 and 1965, which set up the Irish Land Commission and gave it powers of compulsory acquisition of land. It was, however, provided that these powers could not be used against persons who had resided for more than a year within three miles of the land. If the land was owned by a corporation, all the shareholders had to fulfil the residence requirement.

The land in question was owned by a company, the shareholders of

[34] The rule that equality of treatment does not extend to public functions ties in with the 'public service' exception in Art. 48(4) EEC and the 'official authority' proviso in Art. 55 EEC: see pp. 155–156 below.

[35] This would fall under the doctrine of indirect discrimination.

[36] This would depend on whether the European Court considered that there was an 'objective reason' for the rule: see p. 140 above.

[37] If imposed for reasons of military security, it might possibly be justifiable under the public-policy proviso (see pp. 154–5 below), but even this is doubtful.

[38] See *Commission* v. *Italy*, Case 63/86, [1988] ECR 29.

[39] Case 182/83, [1984] ECR 3677.

which were British nationals who did not meet the residence requirement. The Irish Land Commission decided to acquire the land compulsorily, but the company argued that this would contravene Community law. Was the residence restriction a form of discrimination against citizens of other Member States? It was argued by the company that it was an indirect way of discouraging foreigners from owning Irish land. The European Court, however, held that no discrimination existed in view of the fact that the residence rule also applied to Irish citizens. The result would almost certainly have been different, however, if there had been reason to believe that the purpose of the rule was to exclude foreigners.[40]

Social Advantages

Article 7(2) of Regulation 1612/68 provides that immigrant Community workers must be given the same social advantages as national workers.[41] This provision has given rise to extensive case law.[42] The wording of Article 7(2) clearly suggests that it covers only advantages given to the worker himself; it might also be thought that it applies only to advantages given to the worker in his capacity as such. In the beginning, this was the view taken by the European Court. In *Michel S*[43] it held that Article 7 of the Regulation applied only to rights 'connected with employment' which 'benefit the workers themselves': it did not cover benefits for the worker's family.[44] The question before the Court was whether the mentally retarded son of an immigrant Italian worker in Belgium could benefit from Belgian legislation granting various benefits, including physiotherapy and occupational training, to the handicapped. The legislation originally applied only to Belgian citizens, but was later extended to foreigners, provided that the incapacity was first diagnosed after the person concerned had become resident in Belgium. Michel S did not meet this condition and was, therefore, excluded. The European Court held that no violation of Article 7(2) had occurred.[45]

[40] See *Minister for Fisheries* v. *Schonenberg*, Case 88/77, [1978] ECR 473 and *Commission* v. *Ireland*, Case 61/77, [1978] ECR 417.

[41] An analogous right applicable in social security matters is given by Art. 3 of Reg. 1408/71.

[42] Art. 7(2) also gives immigrant Community workers the right to the same tax advantages as national workers, but all the cases have concerned social advantages. *Biehl*, Case C–175/88 (8 May 1990), may be regarded as an exception, though it was decided primarily on the basis of Art. 48(2) EEC. In it, the European Court held that Luxembourg not make entitlement to a tax refund conditional on residence in the country, an application of the doctrine of indirect discrimination.

[43] Case 76/72, [1973] ECR 457.

[44] Para. 9 of the judgment.

[45] The Court, however, held that Art. 12 of Reg. 1612/68 (discussed below at pp. 188–9)

Three years later, the Court did an about-turn and held that Article 7(2) could apply to benefits for the family of a worker. This was in *Cristini*,[46] a case concerning a French law granting families with three or more children the right to travel on the French railways at a reduced rate.[47] Could the wife and children of a deceased Italian worker claim the benefit, even though the legislation limited it to French citizens? The European Court held that they could, ruling that Article 7(2) applied to all social advantages, whether or not attached to the contract of employment.[48]

The new policy was further solidified in *Reina*,[49] where the Court held that a government scheme to provide couples with interest-free loans on the birth of a child could not be limited to citizens of the country concerned (Germany), even though its purpose was to counter the falling birth-rate: measures intended to prevent a decrease in the national population must be extended to immigrant workers.

It makes no difference if the benefit is claimed by the family member in his own right, independently of his relationship to the worker, and paid directly to him. *Castelli*[50] concerned an Italian who had worked in Belgium and subsequently retired there, having acquired the right to remain under Community law.[51] His widowed mother, who lived with him and was financially dependent on him (and was therefore part of his family as defined by Community law),[52] claimed the right to benefit from a Belgian law providing a guaranteed minimum income for the aged. Her claim was rejected by the Belgian authorities because she was not a Belgian citizen. The European Court, however, held that Article 7(2) entitled her to the same rights as a Belgian: though she had never worked in Belgium and did not enjoy the status of a worker under Community law, she could invoke Article 7(2) because she was a member of a worker's family.[53]

This expansion of Article 7(2) might seem at odds with the words of

applied to the Belgian legislation to the extent that it covered measures allowing the handicapped to realize or improve their aptitude for work. In a later case, *Mr and Mrs F*, Case 7/75, [1975] ECR 679, it held that Art. 3 of Reg. 1408/71 could afford a remedy in such situations.

[46] Case 32/75, [1975] ECR 1085.

[47] The legislation provided that, at the request of the head of the family, the parents and children could each receive a card entitling them to the discount.

[48] It also ruled that the right could be claimed by the widow after her husband's death by reason of the fact that she and her children enjoyed the right to remain under Reg. 1251/70 (discussed at pp. 120–1 above). Art. 7 of that regulation provides that such persons also benefit from the right to equal treatment established by Reg. 1612/68.

[49] Case 65/81, [1982] ECR 33.

[50] Case 261/83, [1984] ECR 3199.

[51] On the right to remain, see pp. 120–1 above.

[52] On the definition of the family under Community law, see pp. 94–5 above. As a member of her son's family, she too could enjoy the right to remain.

[53] See also *Frascogna*, Case 157/84, [1985] ECR 1739. Similar cases involving other welfare benefits include *Hoeckx*, Case 249/83, [1985] ECR 973, *Scrivner*, Case 122/84, [1985] ECR

the provision, but the Court's position could be supported on the ground that the worker benefits indirectly, since the effect of granting the benefit to the family member is to lessen the financial burden on the worker himself. Where the claimant is not a member of the worker's family (and is not himself a worker), he cannot benefit from Article 7(2). This was the ruling in *Lebon*,[54] a judgment of the Full Court (and consequently of greater authority).

It will be remembered from the discussion in Chapter 8[55] that under Community law the descendants (children, grandchildren, and so on) of a worker count as members of his family if they are dependent on him, even if they are over the age of majority. In *Lebon*, the European Court was asked to clarify what is meant by 'dependent': is a child dependent only if the parent is legally obliged to support him? In its answer, the Court held that a legal obligation is not necessary: it is sufficient if the parent in fact supports the child, even if the latter is fully grown and capable of getting a job. The Court also ruled that a child does not cease to be dependent for the purposes of Community law merely because he makes a claim for a social-welfare benefit. The Court's justification for this ruling was that otherwise no member of a worker's family could claim such benefits, since the mere making of the claim would automatically put the claimant outside the scope of Community law, and could even lead to deportation. It would seem to follow from this ruling that a family member would not lose his status by reason of the fact that the claim is *granted*. It is not, however, clear what would happen if the family member became wholly dependent on the welfare benefit and no longer received financial support from the working member of the family, or if he received only token support. The Court did, however, say that the family member's status is not jeopardized by the fact that he could obtain a job but chooses not to do so.

The effect of this judgment is that a Community worker can bring his parents, grandparents, children and grandchildren to the new country and, provided he supports them, they can claim the same welfare benefits as nationals. This is true even if they are not Community citizens.[56] However, if national claimants can be refused benefits where they fail to take reasonable steps to get a job, the same rule can be applied to immigrants. The result is that Community immigrants are entitled to the same welfare rights as nationals, provided they either have the status of a worker or are members of a worker's family. For this purpose, 'worker' appears to include anyone within the 'extended

1027 (both concerning the Belgian equivalent of supplementary benefit) and *Deak*, Case 94/84, [1985] ECR 1873 (unemployment benefit).

[54] Case 316/85, [1987] ECR 2811.

[55] See p. 94 above.

[56] *Deak*, Case 94/84, [1985] ECR 1873.

concept' of a worker,[57] except a work-seeker. Thus, for example, a retired worker (provided he has the right to remain)[58] or an involuntarily unemployed worker (provided he retains the right to reside)[59] is entitled to equal treatment regarding social-welfare benefits, but a person going to another Member State in order to look for work is not.[60]

The cases discussed above all concern social-welfare rights. However, the concept of 'social advantage' is wider than this, and the European Court has made clear that it can include any right which could facilitate the mobility of workers within the Community.[61] An example of this wide approach is to be found in *Netherlands* v. *Reed*,[62] a case which raised the question whether the live-in girlfriend of a British worker in the Netherlands counted as part of his family under Community law. It will be remembered from what was said in Chapter 9[63] that the European Court held that she did not. Under Dutch immigration law, however, the foreign girlfriend or boyfriend of a Dutch citizen could in similar circumstances obtain the right to reside in the Netherlands, and the European Court held that the right to reside was a social advantage in terms of Article 7(2). Consequently, the same right had to be extended to the foreign girlfriend of a Community worker.

The European Court has also held that language rights can constitute a social advantage. *Mutsch*[64] concerned a Luxembourg citizen resident in Belgium who was subject to criminal proceedings there. He claimed the right to have the case conducted in German. The official languages of Belgium are Dutch and French but, as there is a German-speaking minority in eastern Belgium, Belgian legislation provides that, in certain areas of the country, criminal proceedings will be conducted in German if the accused so requests. According to the legislation, this right applies only where the accused is a Belgian citizen, but the European Court held that it was covered by Article 7(2) and therefore had to be extended to persons such as Mr Mutsch.

Finally, a case against the trend, which, though decided some time ago, may still be good law. *Even*[65] concerned a Belgian law allowing Belgian citizens who had served in one of the Allied armies in the war to retire early on full pension. Mr Even was a French citizen, resident and working in Belgium, who had served in the French army. Service in the French army came within the terms of the law, but Mr Even was ruled

---

[57] For the meaning of this, see pp. 93–5 above.

[58] *Castelli*, Case 261/83, [1984] ECR 3199.

[59] This appears to have been the position in *Scrivner*, Case 122/84, [1985] ECR 1027.

[60] In *Lebon* the Court expressly said (paras 25–7) that work-seekers are not covered by Art. 7(2). It is possible, therefore, that a work-seeker who becomes a burden on public funds may be subject to deportation.

[61] See the definition of 'social advantage' in *Even*, quoted in note 66, below.

[62] Case 59/85, [1986] ECR 1283.

[63] See pp. 122–3 above.

[64] Case 137/84, [1985] ECR 2681.

[65] Case 207/78, [1979] ECR 2019.

out on grounds of his nationality. The European Court held that this
was not contrary to Community law, since the right in question, being
based on a scheme of national recognition, could not constitute a social
advantage under Article 7(1). The Court's reasoning was unconvincing,[66]
but it is probable that it felt that benefits for war veterans were too
sensitive a matter for full equality to be possible at the time in question:
if the Court had required Belgium to give a veteran's benefit to a
Frenchman, it might next be argued that a German veteran—perhaps
even someone who had fought against Belgium—should be given one.[67]

When Discrimination is Allowed

It will be remembered that the prohibition against discrimination
contained in Article 7 of the EEC Treaty is stated to be without prejudice
to any special provisions contained in the Treaty. Examples of such
special provisions have already been given.[68] One of them was the
public-policy proviso in Article 48(3) EEC which, the European Court
has held, allows discrimination in immigration rights. It is not clear how
far the proviso extends beyond immigration rights, in particular
whether it also permits Member States to discriminate in the employment field. It seems clear from the wording of Article 48 that the proviso
does not apply to Article 48(2) (which prohibits discrimination in
employment) and covers only the rights listed in Article 48(3). These
latter rights are all concerned with immigration, except that Article
48(1)(a) grants the right to accept offers of employment. This suggests
that Member States may be entitled to bar citizens of other Community
countries from particular jobs, but it is hard to see how it could justify
discrimination in other respects. It is rather surprising, therefore, that
there are *dicta* in two cases to the effect that the public-policy proviso in
Article 48(3) covers all aspects of discrimination in employment.[69]

In the case of establishment and services, the position is clear: Article
56(1), which contains the proviso, applies to all the provisions in the
Treaty concerning establishment and services, as well as to measures

[66] It defined social advantages as those which 'whether or not linked to a contract of
employment, are generally granted to national workers primarily because of their objective
status as workers or by virtue of the mere fact of their residence on the national territory
and the extension of which to workers who are nationals of other Member States seems
suitable to facilitate their mobility within the Community'. This is not very enlightening.

[67] This would involve ruling that the provision limiting the benefit to persons who had
fought in an Allied army was contrary to Community law, but this may well be the case:
see *Südmilch* v. *Ugliola*, Case 15/69, [1969] ECR 363 (discussed at pp. 140–1 above).

[68] See pp. 141–2 above.

[69] See *Südmilch* v. *Ugliola* (n. 67 above), paras 3 and 6, and *Marsman*, Case 44/72, [1972]
ECR 1243 (para. 4). The contrary view was expressed by Advocate General Gand in
Südmilch v. *Ugliola*, [1969] ECR 363 at p. 375.

taken in pursuance of those provisions.[70] Therefore, the right to equal treatment given to self-employed persons, providers of services and recipients of services is subject to the proviso.

The public-policy proviso has in fact been of no significance in the cases so far. A far more important provision is the so-called public-service exception, which could to some extent itself be regarded as being based on public policy and public security. This is contained in two provisions of the Treaty, Article 48(4) (workers) and Article 55 (establishment and services). The former states that Article 48 'shall not apply to employment in the public service', while under the latter, the provisions of the Treaty dealing with establishment and services 'shall not apply, so far as any given Member State is concerned, to activities which in that State are connected, even occasionally, with the exercise of official authority'.

These provisions are clearly different: Article 48(4) is based on an institutional test—whether the post in question is part of the public service—while Article 55 adopts a functional test—whether the work involves the exercise of official authority. The European Court, however, has refused to apply an institutional test under Article 48(4), saying that it does not matter whether the holder of the post has the status of a civil servant,[71] or whether the post is governed by public law or private law.[72] The reason is that, under such a test, everything would depend on national law, thus allowing each Member State to decide unilaterally which posts to exclude.

Instead, the European Court has decided to apply a functional test under both provisions. As set out in *Commission* v. *Belgium*,[73] this states that the posts covered by Article 48(4) are those 'which involve direct or indirect participation in the exercise of the powers conferred by public law and duties designed to safeguard the general interests of the state or other public authorities'. The idea seems to be to include only those officials who play a role in the exercise of governmental powers or fulfil a managerial or policy-making function. Thus, the Court has held that nurses in public hospitals, local-authority gardeners, locomotive staff on public railways, teachers in public educational institutions and researchers in public research institutions are not covered, while local-authority supervisors, stock controllers, night-watchmen and architects are.'[4] The fact that certain posts in an institution are covered by the

---

[70] Art. 56 applies only to Chap. 2 (of Title III), which covers establishment, but it is extended to Chap. 3 (services) by Art. 66.

[71] *Lawrie-Blum*, Case 66/85, [1986] ECR 2121 (para. 26).

[72] *Sotgiu*, Case 152/73, [1974] ECR 153 (paras 5 and 6).

[73] Case 149/79, [1980] ECR 3881 (para. 10).

[74] The logic regarding some of these posts is not entirely apparent. The relevant cases are *Commission* v. *Belgium*, Case 149/79, [1980] ECR 3881 and [1982] ECR 1845; *Commission* v. *France*, Case 307/84, [1986] ECR 1725; *Lawrie-Blum*, Case 66/85, [1986] ECR 2139;

exception does not justify barring foreigners from all posts in that institution: the Court has rejected the argument that it would be unfair to admit foreigners to a service in which they could not be promoted to the top.[75] It has also ruled that the exception only allows Member States to bar foreigners from certain posts; it does not permit them to pay foreigners at a lower rate, once they have been appointed.[76]

These rulings are of considerable importance since a large number of jobs in the United Kingdom, as in other Member States, are in the public sector. The great majority of them will now be open to Community immigrants, and the Commission has announced a campaign to ensure that Community law is respected.[77]

Commission v. *Italy*, Case 225/85, [1987] ECR 2625; *Commission* v. *Greece*, Case 147/86, [1988] ECR 1637; and *Alluè* v. *University of Venice*, Case 33/88 (30 May 1989) *The Times*, 16 June 1989. For a useful summary of the cases, see Handoll, 'Article 48(4) EEC and Non-National Access to Public Employment' (1988) 13 E.L.Rev. 223.

[75] *Commission* v. *France* (see n. 74 above).

[76] *Sotgiu* (see n. 72 above).

[77] See Press Release IP (87) 644 of 9 Dec. 1987. In the beginning the Commission will focus its activities on publicly-administered commercial services (public transport, electricity, gas, airlines, shipping, postal services, telecommunictions, radio and television), public health care services, teaching in state educational establishments and non-military research in public establishments.

12
Recognition of Qualifications and the Right to Work

The principle of equal treatment is not in itself always sufficient to ensure that the immigrant is able to practise his trade or profession in the new country. Recognition of his professional qualifications and admission to the appropriate professional organization may still cause problems. If he is denied the right to work on grounds of nationality, Community law will of course give him a remedy. Moreover, as we saw in the previous chapter, if the relevant authorities invent unnecessary requirements simply in order to exclude foreigners, the principle of indirect discrimination will come into operation. However, a requirement that a person should be properly qualified is not unreasonable; consequently, even in the absence of any intent to discriminate, there may be substantial obstacles to be surmounted before the migrant can begin work.

There is no directly applicable provision in the EEC Treaty requiring Member States to recognize qualifications acquired in other Member States or obliging them to allow migrants to practise a trade or profession without the appropriate qualification.[1] Article 57(1), however, makes provision for the Council to adopt directives on the mutual recognition of diplomas, certificates and other evidence of formal qualifications, and Article 57(2) provides for directives on the co-ordination of national regulations on the activities of self-employed persons. A number of directives have been adopted under those provisions. Before we discuss them, however, something should be said about the position in the absence of a directive.

General Principles

If there is no relevant directive, the migrant is likely to find that Community law is of only limited assistance to him. There is, however, a rule that if a Member State recognizes a foreign qualification as equivalent to a national one, it must give the holder the same right to

---

[1] *Auer (No. 1)*, Case 136/78, [1979] ECR 437.

practise the trade or profession in question as the holder of the national qualification. This principle is illustrated by *Patrick*,[2] a case concerning a British architect who wished to practise in France. At the time in question, there was no directive on the recognition of architectural qualifications. Under the relevant French law, a foreign architect could practise in France, provided his qualification was recognized by the French Government as equivalent to a French one and there was a reciprocal convention between France and the foreign country. As it happened, a French decree had been adopted some years previously recognizing British architectural qualifications as equivalent to French ones. However, Mr Patrick was refused permission to practise because there was no reciprocal convention with the United Kingdom. The European Court held that this refusal was contrary to Community law.[3]

In a later case, the European Court held that any decision of a national authority refusing to recognize a foreign qualification as equivalent to a national one, or otherwise barring a Community migrant from practising his trade or profession, must state the reasons on which it is based and must be subject to judicial review in the national courts.[4]

Specific Directives

Until recently, the strategy of the Commission has been to promote separate directives for each trade or profession.[5] Professions covered by directives include medicine, dentistry, nursing, pharmacy, veterinary medicine, architecture and midwifery. Directives have also been adopted concerning less regulated activities, such as hairdressing. The content of these directives varies, but the objective is always the same: to make it as easy as possible for persons practising a trade or profession in one Member State to set themselves up in the same trade or profession in another Member State. In the case of less regulated activities, the normal pattern is to provide that a person who has carried on the activity for a specified number of years in one Member State must be regarded as qualified in all other Member States. For the professions, the directives usually lay down minimum standards of professional train-

---

[2] Case 11/77, [1977] ECR 1199.

[3] See also *Thieffry*, Case 71/76, [1977] ECR 765, where the holder of a Belgian law degree was not allowed to practise as a lawyer in France, even though a French university had officially recognized it as equivalent to a French one. In this case, however, the position was complicated by the fact that recognition for academic purposes might not be the same as recognition for professional purposes.

[4] *UNECTEF v. Heylens*, Case 222/86, [1987] ECR 4097.

[5] The text of these directives is conveniently set out in Séché, *A Guide to Working in a Europe without Frontiers*, published by the Commission in 1988 and obtainable from HMSO (ISBN 92–825–8067–9).

ing, always in very general terms, and require recognition of the resulting qualifications.

There is usually a provision that where a certificate of good character, or a certificate that the person concerned has never been bankrupt, is required in a Member State as a condition for being admitted to practise, the authorities of that Member State must accept a certificate granted by the appropriate authorities of the Member State of origin.

As might be expected, the international scope of these directives is limited: they cover only citizens of a Member State[6] and apply only to qualifications obtained in a Member State. This means that an Australian citizen who qualifies as a doctor in England cannot benefit from the relevant directive if he wishes to practise in France, even though he may be fully entitled to practise in the United Kingdom. Moreover, a British citizen who qualifies in Australia is likewise excluded from the scope of the directive, even if his qualification is recognized in Britain.

On the other hand, the directives normally apply irrespective of whether the person in question carries on his trade or profession as an employed person or on a self-employed basis. Thus, a doctor qualified in another Member State can either go into private practice, obtaining remuneration from the fees he charges his patients, or he can work for a salary. Provision is also usually made for the performance of services in the Community sense of the term, that is, temporary practice in one country by a person established in another.

It is not necessary to discuss each of the directives individually; that governing medicine will be taken as an example.

Medicine

The Community regime for medicine is based on two main directives, one laying down minimum standards for medical training and the other providing for recognition of qualifications. The former, Directive 75/363, states that persons wishing to practise medicine in a Member State must hold one of the qualifications listed for each Member State.[7] It then specifies what must be covered by the course leading to such a qualification. This part of the Directive is extremely general: Article 1(1)(a), for example, requires the would-be doctor to have 'adequate knowledge of the sciences on which medicine is based and a good understanding of the scientific methods including the principles of measuring biological functions, the evaluation of scientifically established facts and the analysis of data', while Article 1(1)(d) simply

---

[6] This is true only in the case of directives granting rights of establishment. The services-of-lawyers directive (Dir. 77/249, discussed below) applies irrespective of the nationality of the lawyer, provided he is established in a Member State.

[7] The list is set out in the other directive, Dir. 75/362, Art. 3.

specifies that he must have acquired 'suitable clinical experience in hospitals under appropriate supervision'. In addition, the Directive states that a medical training course must last at least six years or comprise a minimum of 5,500 hours of theoretical and practical instruction given in a university or under the supervision of a university. Besides covering basic medical training, Directive 75/363 also lays down minimum standards for qualifications in specialized medicine. The various specializations are listed and minimum periods of study specified.

All medical schools in the Community are bound by these requirements, and degrees in medicine may be granted only where they have been fulfilled. On the other hand, the Directive does not prevent medical schools from going beyond the requirements laid down: it merely prescribes a minimum. Moreover, the Directive does not prevent Member States from recognizing qualifications obtained in a non-member State, even if the standard of medical training in that State falls below that prescribed in the Directive. Persons who have obtained such qualifications can practise in the Member State which recognizes them, but they have no right under Community law to practise in other Member States.

The second main directive is Directive 75/362. This lists the medical qualifications applicable in each Member State, including specialist qualifications, and provides that a doctor who has obtained one of these qualifications in one Member State must be given the same right to practise in another Member State as the holder of the equivalent qualification in that State. Thus someone who has obtained the qualification entitling him to be registered as a medical practitioner in Member State X can demand that he be registered in Member State Y. If, in addition, he is qualified as a gynaecologist in Member State X, he must be allowed to practise as a gynaecologist in Member State Y.

The scheme put into effect by these directives is sound in theory: if each Member State is required to ensure that its training standards are adequate, there can be no objection to requiring other Member States to recognize the resulting qualifications. Unfortunately, however, the standards are in many instances laid down in such vague terms that they constitute no guarantee of quality; moreover, the qualitative norms will be very difficult to enforce.[8] It also appears that a Member State cannot refuse to recognize a qualification from another Member State on the ground that the medical school which gave it did not meet the

---

[8] This problem does not exist with regard to the quantitative norms: a successful action under Art. 169 EEC was brought against Belium because its specialized course on tropical medicine lasted only one year, instead of the three years required by Art. 5 of Dir. 75/363. See *Commission* v. *Belgium*, Case 306/84, [1987] ECR 675.

standards laid down by the Directive.[9] The only sanction is that the Commission can bring an enforcement action under Article 169 EEC. Moreover, Member States are not allowed to require a migrant doctor to take a language test before he can practise.[10] This means that a doctor from a country with low standards of medical training, who is unable to speak English, could demand the right to practise in England. In fact, of course, such a person is unlikely to be given a hospital post and, if he sets up in private practice, is unlikely to have many patients.[11]

The doctors' directives have so far had only a fairly limited impact. The total number of doctors in the Community who go into practice in a Member State other than that in which they qualified is normally under 2,000 per year, a figure which includes doctors returning home to practise after qualification in another Member State. The main importers of doctors are Germany and the United Kingdom; the main exporter is Greece.[12]

The Services-of-Lawyers Directive

Lawyers are in a different position from the other professions mentioned so far. Although the principles of medicine and architecture are much the same in every country, those of law are not. In view of this, it is hardly surprising that progress has been much slower regarding free movement for lawyers. The only directive specifically aimed at lawyers is Directive 77/249, which is concerned, not with establishment, but with services. In other words, it does not make provision for lawyers to go into permanent practice in another Member State, but only to carry on

[9] Wägenbaur, 'The Mutual Recognition of Qualifications in the EEC', in F. G. Jacobs (ed.), *European Law and the Individual* (1976), p. 95 at p. 107. See also the Council Statement on Art. 22 of Dir. 75/362, published in OJ 1975, C 146.

[10] Art. 20(3) of Dir. 75/362 provides that Member States 'shall see to it that, where appropriate, the persons concerned acquire, in their interest and in that of their patients, the linguistic knowledge necessary for the exercise of their profession in the host country'. This seems to envisage language-training after the migrant doctor has begun to practise. See Wägenbaur, op. cit., p. 106; see also 355 HL Deb. (9 Dec. 1974), cols 503–4. In the United Kingdom, effect was given to this by Art. 2 of The European Communities (Medical, Dental and Nursing Professions) (Linguistic Knowledge) Order 1981 (SI 1981 No. 432); but see Art. 3.

[11] See also Art. 3 of SI 1981 No. 432, above.

[12] In 1986, for example, slightly under 2,000 doctors established themselves in practice in a Member State other than that in which they qualified. Over 300 of these were Greeks returning home after qualifying in another Member State (usually Italy). Germany admitted 749 migrant Community doctors to practise (175 being Greeks) and the United Kingdom admitted 445. Over 100 of the latter were Greeks, though there were also some from every Member State except Luxembourg. There were 94 British doctors who benefited from the directives: 26 went to Germany, 24 to Ireland and 19 returned home after qualifying in another Member State. Statistics on migrant doctors (and other professionals) are published each year in the Bulletin of the European Communites. Those for 1986 may be found in Bull. EC 12–1987, p. 17.

their activities on a temporary basis. For this reason, it is based on different principles from the others and applies irrespective of the citizenship of the lawyer, provided he is in practice in a Member State.

The key term in the Directive is 'lawyer'. This is defined by a list of terms, in the language (or languages) of each of the Member States, for a member of the legal profession. In England, for example, 'lawyer' means either 'barrister' or 'solicitor'; in Scotland, 'advocate' or 'solicitor'. In some Member States, however, the list does not include all the kinds of legal practitioner recognized in that State. In France, for example, the only kind of lawyer specified is an *avocat*: no mention is made of a *notaire*.

The function of this list is twofold. First of all, it indicates which practitioners are able to benefit from the rights conferred by the Directive: in England, both barristers and solicitors can benefit; in France, only *avocats*. Secondly, it defines the activities to which it applies: a lawyer covered by the Directive is able, in England, to do the work of either a barrister or a solicitor; in France, he can carry on the activities only of an *avocat*.

This is the scheme of the Directive. Anyone who counts as a 'lawyer' for the purpose of the Directive can, on a temporary basis, perform the work of a 'lawyer' in any other Member State. He must, however, use the professional title of his home country, in the language of that country. A French *avocat* must call himself *'avocat'* even when he is in England; he cannot call himself 'solicitor'. This is appropriate. To call himself a solicitor would be misleading, while use of the French title indicates to clients that his expertise is in the field of French law.

As was said above, the general principle is that a foreign lawyer can do all the work of a local lawyer. Two important exceptions to this principle have, however, been laid down. First, it is provided by Article 1(1) of the Directive that Member States may reserve to 'prescribed categories of lawyers' the preparation of documents for obtaining authority to administer the estates of deceased persons and for transferring interests in land (conveyancing). The United Kingdom implementing legislation states baldly that nothing contained in it allows EEC lawyers to do this work.[13] The second exception is that Article 5 allows Member States to require a Community lawyer wishing to represent a client in court to work in conjunction with a local lawyer. The United Kingdom legislation takes advantage of this provision by stating that an EEC lawyer who is not a barrister or solicitor (or, in Scotland, an advocate) must be instructed by, and act in conjunction with, an advocate, barrister, or solicitor entitled to practise before the court in question.[14] In 1988, however, the European Court held that this

---

[13] European Communities (Services of Lawyers) Order 1978, SI 1978 No. 1910, Art. 9.
[14] Art. 5 of SI 1978 No. 1910 (above).

exception does not apply where the law of the Member State in question does not require representation by a lawyer.[15] This appears to mean that a Community lawyer covered by the Directive cannot be obliged to work in conjunction with a local lawyer if the local law would have permitted the client to conduct his own case. If this is correct, the United Kingdom provision may be contrary to the Directive.

Although the scope of the Directive is limited, it has assisted the growing band of lawyers who advise clients in other Member States. Such lawyers normally advise on their own legal system or on Community law. In many Member States such activities are not in any event subject to restrictions, provided the lawyer does not use a professional title other than that of the country where he has been admitted to practise.

The General Directive

After a considerable number of specific directives had been adopted, the Commission changed its strategy and started working on a general directive that would apply to all professions not subject to a specific directive. After much discussion, the Council adopted Directive 89/48 in December 1988. This establishes a general system for the recognition of qualifications awarded after at least three years' university-level training. It applies to both employed and self-employed persons and it is thought that approximately a hundred professions will be covered, most notably law. (The Commission is working on a second measure to cover professions for which less advanced training is required.)[16] As might be expected, the directive is fairly complex, being the result of hard bargaining and compromises which were, in true Community fashion, sometimes left deliberately vague. It can best be understood by looking at some key concepts.

INTERNATIONAL SCOPE

Like the other directives on establishment, the General Directive benefits Community citizens only. It also applies only to qualifications awarded in a Member State, though a Council recommendation adopted at the same time urges Member States to recognize qualifications obtained by Community citizens in non-member States.[17]

---

[15] *Commission* v. *Germany*, Case 427/85, [1988] ECR 1123.
[16] For the text of the draft, see [1989] 3 CMLR 627.
[17] Recommendation 89/49, OJ 1989, L 19/24. Recommendations do not, of course, have any binding force.

Qualifications Covered

The key concept here is the term 'diploma': the Directive is concerned with the recognition of 'diplomas' as defined by Article 1(a). Under this definition, a diploma is anything which is evidence of a formal qualification or a set of formal qualifications which has the following three characteristics: first, it must have been awarded by a competent authority in a Member State; secondly, it must show that the holder has successfully completed a course of at least three years' duration (or part-time equivalent) at a university or other institution of similar level and, where appropriate, carried out the necessary professional training; and, thirdly, it must qualify the holder for the pursuit of a regulated profession in a Member State.[18] In view of the third requirement, an LL.B. degree will apparently not constitute a 'diploma' within the meaning of the directive: the person concerned must have taken the necessary professional examinations (and probably done pupillage or articles as well) before he can claim to be the holder of a 'diploma'.

It is further provided by the second paragraph of Article 1(a) that a qualification that does not meet the second requirement mentioned above must be treated as a diploma if it is awarded on the successful completion of education and training received in the Community,[19] and is recognized by a competent authority in the Member State in question as being of an equivalent level to that required in the first paragraph. This appears to cover situations where the training is of less than three years or is not in a university or equivalent institution. Qualifications received after a period of articles and part-time study not undertaken at a university-level institution are probably what is envisaged.

PROFESSIONS COVERED

The key concept here is 'regulated profession', which is defined in Article 1(c) and (d). Under these provisions, a profession is regarded as regulated if the pursuit of that profession in a Member State is dependent on the possession of a diploma (as defined by the Directive). It seems that a profession is covered even if only certain aspects of it are

[18] The training attested in the diploma must have been received mainly in the Community. However, persons who received their training outside the Community will be covered, provided their diploma is granted in a Member State and, in addition, they have had three years' professional experience certified by the Member State in question. This would presumably apply to a lawyer who did his law degree in a non-member State, but was allowed to do the bar course in a Member State. The resulting qualification would have been granted in a Member State, though the bulk of his training would have taken place outside the Community. Such persons would be entitled to benefit from the directive only after three years' practice in the Member State where they qualified.

[19] The exception mentioned in the previous footnote regarding training outside the Community does not seem to apply here.

regulated in the above sense. The Directive also makes clear that if the use of a professional designation—for example, 'chartered account-ant'—is dependent on the possession of a diploma, the profession in question is to be regarded as 'regulated'.[20]

One of the problems faced by the authors of the Directive was that, while most of the main professions on the Continent are subject to regulation (in the above sense) as a result of legislation, many professions in the United Kingdom and Ireland are self-regulating. In the latter countries, there may be no legislation relating to the profession at all. Anyone may be free to pursue it. However, there may be a professional organization, originally founded simply as a private society to promote the activity in question, which in practice exercises a considerable degree of control over the activities of the profession. This may come about because the public is prepared to deal only with members of the society or persons who are certified by the society as being competent. Should such a society be obliged to admit to membership someone who has qualified in another Member State?

The second sub-paragraph of Article 1(d) of the Directive deals with this question by stating that such a profession is to be regarded as 'regulated' if the professional society is 'recognised in a special form' by a Member State. This seems to cover professional associations in the United Kingdom which have received a royal charter. A non-exhaustive list of professional associations covered by the second sub-paragraph appears in an Annex to the Directive. This list contains five associations in Ireland and thirty-eight in the United Kingdom. The latter include a number of accountancy and engineering organizations, as well as various other bodies ranging from the Institute of Actuaries to the British Computer Society. All the bodies listed are recipients of a royal charter.

The Basic Rule

Once the provisions concerning the scope of the Directive are under-stood, the rest is fairly straightforward. The basic rule, which is contained in Article 3, is that if a Member State requires a diploma (as defined in the Directive) as a condition for exercising a regulated

---

[20] The Directive contains a further provision applicable in the case of the health-care professions. Such a profession is to be regarded as 'regulated' if, under national social-security provisions, remuneration or reimbursement is dependent on possession of a diploma. This would apply in a country where a therapist, or other health-care professional, treats the patient and then claims his fee from some health-care fund, or where he obtains the fee from the patient and the patient claims reimbursement from the fund. In either case, if the fund will pay out only if the therapist is the holder of a diploma, the profession to which he belongs will be regarded as 'regulated', even if it is not otherwise subject to control.

profession, it must accept a diploma obtained in another Member State. If a profession is not regulated in one Member State, other Member States where it is regulated must recognize someone as qualified if he has practised full-time in the former country for two years and in addition possesses certain formal qualifications specified in the Directive.

A migrant professional is entitled under the Directive to use the professional designation (for example, 'solicitor') of the Member State in which he practises, but he must use the academic title which he obtained in the country where he qualified. Thus, an English-trained solicitor who practises as an *avocat* in France may call himself '*avocat*', but may not lay claim to a French degree which he does not possess. He may put 'LL.B.' after his name (if he holds such a degree), but, if so required by the French authorities, he must add the name and location of the university which granted it.

If a given professional designation is conferred by a professional association of the kind specified in Article 1(d) of the Directive (discussed above), a migrant may not use it unless he is a member of that association. If his qualifications are entitled to recognition under the Directive, however, he cannot be refused membership on the ground that he is not qualified.

THE EXCEPTIONS

The general rule outlined above is subject to certain exceptions which apply where there is a difference between the position in the two Member States in question with regard either to the duration of the training or to its content or to the activities covered by the profession. If the training period is at least one year shorter in the Member State where the person qualified than it is in the Member State where he wishes to practise, the latter may refuse to recognize the qualification unless he has actually practised the profession for a specified period in the former country.

Where there is a substantial difference in the content of the professional training, or where there are differences in the activities pursued by the members of the profession, the Member State where the person wishes to practise may require him either to undergo an adaptation period (by which is meant a period during which he practises in the new country under the supervision of a qualified practitioner) or an aptitude test (a test of professional knowledge). Normally, the person can choose between these alternatives, but in the case of the legal profession, and possibly certain other professions in which legal advice is given, the Member State may itself decide which alternative will apply.

Conclusions

The deadline for implementing the Directive was 4 January 1991, and it is too early to tell how successful it will be. As might be expected, lawyers will not find that it removes every obstacle to practice in another Member State. An English solicitor who wishes to practise on the Continent, for example, may find that it will take him several years to gain admission. If the training period in the country where he wishes to practise is longer (by at least a year) than that in England, he may have to practise for a period in England before he can make the transition.[21] Moreover, since the content of legal education is bound to differ substantially in the two countries, the Member State in which he wishes to practise may require him to sit a professional examination ('aptitude test') or to practise for a period under the supervision of a local lawyer. The examination may well be quite stiff. It must, however, be limited to 'professional knowledge' and must take account of the fact that the candidate is a qualified professional in the Member State from which he comes. In England, the test for foreign lawyers wishing to practise as solicitors is called the Qualified Lawyers Transfer Test and is administered by the College of Law on behalf of the Law Society.

Registration and Professional Conduct

Community migrants, other than those coming on a short-term basis (services), must comply with the normal rules in the country concerned on registration and admission to the appropriate professional body. However, they cannot be refused registration or admission on any ground contrary to Community law. If they are, they cannot be penalized for practising without registration. This is illustrated by *Rienks*,[23] a case concerning the directives on veterinary medicine. Mr Rienks, a Dutch citizen, qualified as a veterinary surgeon in the Netherlands and then migrated to Italy, where he wished to practise. Under Italian law, it was a criminal offence to practise as a vet without being enrolled on the register of veterinary surgeons. Rienks applied for registration, but was refused on the ground that he was not properly qualified. His Dutch qualification should have been recognized under the directives, but Italy had failed to implement them on time. Rienks

---

[21] Art. 4(1)(a) of the Directive specifies the maximum period of practice that may be required. Where the difference in the length of training relates to the period spent in 'professional practice acquired with the assistance of a qualified member of the profession' (presumably, doing articles or pupillage), the additional period may be no more than the difference; where, however, it relates either to post-secondary studies or to a period of probationary practice *ending with an examination*, it may be as much as twice the difference.

[22] Art. 1(g).

[23] Case 5/83, [1983] ECR 4233.

was then prosecuted for practising illegally, but the European Court held that, since he had been wrongfully refused registration, the bringing of the prosecution was contrary to Community law. He was, therefore, entitled to an acquittal.[24]

Migrants must, of course, obey the rules of professional conduct laid down by the Member State in which they practise, but, in so far as these rules hinder freedom of movement, they are compatible with the Treaty only if the restrictions which they entail are 'justified in view of the general obligations inherent in the proper practice of the professions in question and apply to nationals and foreigners alike'.[25] Thus, the European Court held that a French rule obliging migrant doctors to give up their registration in their country of origin before being allowed to register in France was contrary to the Treaty.[26] The French Government argued that the rule was necessary to ensure that doctors remained on the spot to provide continuity of treatment, but the Court held that the French rule was too absolute and general to be justified.

This principle applies even if there is no directive. *Ordre des Avocats* v. *Klopp*[27] concerned a French rule that an *avocat* cannot establish chambers in more than one place. Mr Klopp was a German who had qualified as a lawyer in Germany and had opened an office there. He then re-qualified in France and applied for admission as an *avocat*, but his application was refused because he was not prepared to give up his office in Germany. Since he wished to practise on a permanent basis in France, Directive 77/ 249 (the services-of-lawyers directive) was inapplicable. At the time in question, Directive 89/48 (the General Directive) had not been adopted. The European Court, however, held that even in the absence of a directive, a Community citizen who is otherwise qualified cannot be refused the right to establish himself in a Member State merely because he is unwilling to give up his practice in another Member State.

SERVICES

Where a Community citizen lawfully established in one Member State wishes to pursue his trade or profession on a temporary basis in another Member State (the Community concept of a service), he is not normally required to obtain registration in the second Member State. There is express provision to this effect in most of the directives, and the European Court has applied a similar principle where no directive

---

[24] The principle applied in *Rienks* was first established in *Auer (No. 2)*, Case 271/82, [1983] ECR 2727, but in that case it was not entirely clear whether the person concerned had been unlawfully refused registration, since his application for registration had been made before the date on which the directives became directly effective.

[25] *Commission* v. *France*, Case 96/85, [1986] ECR 1475 (para. 11).

[26] Ibid.

[27] Case 107/83, [1984] ECR 2971.

exists. The migrant may, however, have to comply with formalities designed to inform the local professional organization of his presence and provide evidence of his qualifications.

In the case of medicine, Article 16 of Directive 75/362 lays down the general principle that doctors engaged in the provision of services are exempt from any requirement to be a member of, or to register with, a professional organization. However, Member States may require automatic temporary registration, or *pro forma* membership; alternatively, they may require a form of registration, provided that it 'does not delay or in any way complicate the provision of services or impose any additional costs on the person providing the services'.[28] In any event, the Member State may require the doctor to inform the appropriate authority. This will normally take place before the patient is treated, but in urgent cases it may be done afterwards. The doctor may also be required to provide the necessary documents to prove that he is properly qualified and in lawful practice in his home country.

A lawyer may not be required to join the local bar, or other professional organization, in the Member State in which he wishes to perform a service.[29] He may, however, be required to establish his qualifications as a lawyer[30] and, if he appears in court, he may have to be introduced to the presiding judge and, where appropriate, to the president of the local bar.[31]

Professional persons performing services in a Member State other than the one in which they are established must normally obey the rules of professional conduct of the Member State in which the services are performed (provided they are compatible with Community law). This is expressly laid down in the directives.[32] In the case of the legal profession, Directive 77/249 contains rather complicated provisions, but to a large extent lawyers must comply with the professional rules of both their home country and the host country.[33] They are subject to disciplinary proceedings in the host country,[34] (as well as in their home country).

The operation of these principles is illustrated by *Gullung*,[35] a case

[28] Amendment added by Dir. 82/76.
[29] Dir. 77/249, Art. 4(1).
[30] Ibid., Art. 7(1).
[31] Ibid., Art. 5.
[32] For doctors, see Art. 16(1) of Dir. 75/362.
[33] Art. 4, paras (2) to (4), of Dir. 77/249. Except where a lawyer is representing a client in legal proceedings or before a public authority, he is obliged to comply with the rules of the host state only if they are capable of being observed by a lawyer established in another Member State and to the extent to which their observance is 'objectively justified to ensure, in that State, the proper exercise of a lawyer's activities, the standing of the profession and respect for the rules concerning incompatibility'.
[34] Art. 7(2) of Dir. 77/249. For implementation in the United Kingdom, see SI 1978 No. 1910, Arts 15–17.
[35] Case 292/86, [1988] ECR 111.

concerning a lawyer of dual French and German nationality. Mr Gullung originally practised as a *notaire* in France but resigned following disciplinary proceedings against him. He then sought admission as an *avocat*, but was rejected on the ground that he was not of good character. His next move was to go to Germany and gain admission as a *Rechtsanwalt* (German lawyer). He then claimed that Community law gave him the right to practise in France. The local bar promptly took a decision prohibiting its members from lending him any assistance. Gullung brought legal proceedings to have this decision set aside and the case eventually came before the European Court.

After ruling that his dual nationality did not prevent his benefiting from Directive 77/249 (the services-of-lawyers directive), the Court held that members of the legal profession are obliged, when providing services, to comply with the rules relating to professional ethics in force in the host Member State. Despite the fact that Gullung's misconduct had occurred before he was admitted to practice in Germany, and thus before he was eligible to benefit from the Directive, the Court held that a lawyer cannot rely on the Directive where he has been barred from access to the profession in the host Member State for reasons relating to dignity, good repute, and integrity. Gullung could not, therefore, use Community law to escape the consequences of his misconduct or to circumvent the French rules of professional ethics.

In the case of less regulated activities, the position also seems to be that the Member State where the service is performed cannot require the provider of the service to obtain registration if he is already registered in his home country, but this is subject to the proviso that registration must fulfil the same function in the two countries. The leading authority is *Ministère Public* v. *Van Wesemael*,[36] a case in which a Belgian used a French employment agency to obtain the services of a variety artist to provide entertainment at a trade fair in Belgium. This led to his being prosecuted in Belgium because it was illegal for an employment agency not registered in Belgium to place someone in work there, unless it operated in conjunction with a registered Belgian agency. The European Court, however, held that since the agency was registered in France and subject to supervision by the relevant authority there, and since registration in France fulfilled the same functions as that in Belgium, it was contrary to Community law for the Belgian authorities to restrict the agency's right to perform services in that country. The fact that there was no applicable directive was irrelevant.

Where, on the other hand, registration fulfils a different function in the two countries, the provider of the service may have to register in the country where it is to be performed. Thus, in *Webb*,[37] the European

---

[36] Case 110/78, [1979] ECR 35.   [37] Case 279/80, [1981] ECR 3305.

Court held that a British-registered agency for the supply of temporary workers could not place people in the Netherlands without also being registered there, because registration fulfilled different functions in the two countries. In the Netherlands, it was intended to promote good labour relations and protect the interests of employees: it was apparently thought that the permanent workers in an industry might resent the presence of temporary workers. For this reason, the use of temporary workers was severely restricted. In certain industries it was entirely forbidden and, even where it was permitted, they could not be paid more than permanent employees. In the United Kingdom, on the other hand, registration was intended simply to ensure the suitability of the persons operating the agency. In view of this difference, the European Court held that Webb could not place workers in the Netherlands without being registered there.

Reverse Discrimination

Reverse discrimination occurs when a Member State treats its own citizens less favourably than those of other Member States. Whether this is contrary to Community law depends on the circumstances. If the discrimination takes place outside the Community context—if there is no element involving other Member States—Community law is not concerned with the matter. *Morson and Jhanjan*[38] is an example. This case concerned a Dutch citizen, living and working in the Netherlands, who wanted to bring her mother (who was financially dependent on her) from a non-Community country to live with her in the Netherlands. The mother, who was not a Community citizen, was refused entry by the Dutch authorities.

It will be remembered from the discussion in Chapter 9[39] that Article 10 of Regulation 1612/68 grants a worker's family the right to immigrate to the country where the worker is employed. This rule applies irrespective of the nationality of the family member, provided the worker is a Community citizen. The dependent mother of a worker counts as a member of the worker's family. However, Article 10 of the regulation applies only if the worker is employed in a Member State other than that of which he or she is a citizen; so it did not directly cover the case. Nevertheless, it was argued on behalf of the mother that, if her daughter had been a citizen of a Member State other than the Netherlands, the mother would have been entitled under Article 10 to reside in the Netherlands. The result was that the Netherlands was

[38] Cases 35 and 36/82, [1982] ECR 3723. See also *R.* v. *Saunders*, Case 175/78, [1979] ECR 1129.
[39] See pp. 121–3 above.

treating the family of a Dutch citizen less favourably than it would have treated the family of a citizen of another Community country. This constituted reverse discrimination which, it was argued, was contrary to Community law. The European Court, however, held that, since the daughter had never exercised her right of free movement within the Community, the case contained no Community element; Community law did not, therefore, prevent the Dutch authorities from excluding the mother.

The situation might have been different if the daughter had immigrated to another Member State and taken employment there. The mother would then have been entitled to enter that country. If the daughter had subsequently returned to the Netherlands, it is possible that Community law would give the mother the right to reside there: the situation would contain a Community element and it could be argued that the Netherlands would be restricting the daughter's right of free movement if it were to refuse entry to the mother.[40]

A superficially similar case has actually come before the English courts. This is *R.* v. *Secretary of State for the Home Department*, ex parte *Ayub*,[41] which concerned a Pakistani citizen who had been refused permission to enter the United Kingdom. He then went to Belgium, where he married a British citizen who had lived and worked in England up until three months before the marriage. After the marriage, she and her husband registered for work in Belgium, but left within three weeks without ever having worked there. They then returned to England, where the husband was again refused admission. He brought legal proceedings, claiming a right of entry under Community law. The English court rejected his claim without referring the case to the European Court or considering the *Morson and Jhanjan* case. However, it is doubtful whether the trip to Belgium and the rather limited efforts to find work there were sufficient to take the case outside the principle laid down in *Morson and Jhanjan*. Moreover, if (as may have been the case) the couple had had no genuine intention to work in Belgium, the whole episode being merely a subterfuge to gain entry to the United Kingdom, it is hardly conceivable that the European Court would have held that Community law gave the husband a remedy.

Two examples may be given of cases in which there was a sufficient connecting factor to bring Community law into play. The first is

---

[40] The case would not be directly covered by Art. 10 of Reg. 1612/68, but it might come under the prohibition against discrimination contained in Art. 7 EEC. A further difficulty is, however, created by the fact that Community law prohibits discrimination only against Community citizens, not against citizens of non-member States. For this reason, the mother could not claim that she had a right not to suffer discrimination. The daughter would have to argue that *she* was the victim of discrimination because she could not bring her mother into the Netherlands with her.

[41] [1983] 3 CMLR 140 (Eng. High Court, QBD).

Knoors,[42] a case concerning a plumber of Dutch nationality who married a Belgian woman and carried on his trade for a number of years in Belgium. He then returned to the Netherlands and wanted to establish his business there. The Dutch authorities refused to allow him to do so, however, because he lacked the qualifications required by Dutch legislation. An EEC Directive provided that a Community citizen who had pursued the trade of a plumber for a given number of years in one Member State had to be recognized as qualified in all other Member States. Mr Knoors had fulfilled these requirements, but the Dutch authorities refused to apply the Directive in his case because he was a Dutch citizen. This again raised a question of reverse discrimination: if Knoors had been a citizen of another Member State, his qualifications would have been recognized.

In this case, the European Court interpreted the Directive according to its plain meaning and held that Knoors's qualifications had to be recognized. It pointed out that, in view of the fairly lengthy periods laid down in the Directive,[43] there was little possibility that Dutch citizens would resort to the Directive to evade the requirements of their own law. This case clearly had a Community element, because Dutch citizens might be deterred from pursuing their trade in other Member States if they could not subsequently return home and carry on business there.

The second case, *Broekmeulen*,[44] concerned a Dutch citizen who qualified in medicine at a Dutch-language university in Belgium and then returned to the Netherlands to practise as a GP. The medical profession in the Netherlands had, however, come to consider general medicine as itself a specialization, so that medical graduates wishing to practise as GPs had to undergo an extra year's training. The Dutch authorities were willing to waive this requirement in the case of citizens of other Member States who had qualified outside the Netherlands, but they refused to do so in the case of a Dutch citizen. They were afraid that otherwise Dutchmen would attend medical school in other Member States in order to evade the Dutch requirement. The European Court, however, held that Dr Broekmeulen had to be allowed to practise.[45]

Both these decisions followed from the provisions of the relevant directive, but a Community element clearly existed in each case. Exactly how strong this element must be is not yet entirely clear. It must, however, be more than merely speculative. In one case, a German citizen who had been excluded from a teacher's training course in Germany because he was a Communist sought to bring his case within

---

[42] Case 115/78, [1979] ECR 399.
[43] These varied according to the circumstances, but six years was the minimum.
[44] Case 246/80, [1981] ECR 2311.
[45] This problem has since been solved: Dir. 86/457 now requires all Member States to provide specific training in general medicine.

the ambit of Community law by arguing that, once qualified, he might decide to work in another Member State. The European Court rejected this on the ground that a 'purely hypothetical prospect' of employment in another Member State did not establish a sufficient connection with Community law.[46]

[46] *Moser*, Case 180/83, [1984] ECR 2539 (para. 18).

13

Equal Treatment in Education[1]

Community Legislation

There can be no doubt that the authors of the EEC Treaty did not regard education, as such, as being within the scope of the Treaty. This is because education is not directly relevant to the objectives of the Treaty: even in mature federations like the United States and Germany, education is a matter for the states, not the federation. Education, therefore, features only peripherally in the Treaty. Vocational training is regarded as a matter of interest to the Community because (in the words of Article 128 EEC) it can contribute to the development of both the national economies and the common market. Article 128, therefore, obliges the Council (acting on a proposal from the Commission and after consulting the Economic and Social Committee) to lay down general principles for a common vocational-training policy.[2] In addition, Article 118 gives the Commission the task of promoting close co-operation between the Member States with regard to basic and advanced vocational training.[3] Despite the fact that these provisions have been given a wide interpretation by the European Court, neither of them can be regarded as giving the Community jurisdiction over education, even of the vocational variety. This is accepted by the European Court: in the *Gravier* case it said, 'educational organization and policy are not as such included in the spheres which the Treaty has entrusted to the Community institutions'.[4]

[1] This chapter is based on a paper, presented in Brussels to the *Association Belge pour le Droit Européen* on 9 June 1988, which was published (in French) in [1989] CDE 325 under the title 'La Libre Circulation des Etudiants en Droit Communautaire'. Much new material has, however, been incorporated.

[2] This was done in 1963: see Council Decision 63/266 of 2 Apr. 1963, OJ (Special English Edn) 1963/64, p. 25. Recently the European Court has decided to adopt a wide interpretation of Art. 128 which allows the Council to do much more than 'lay down general principles': it can now establish major programmes with significant budgetary implications. See *United Kingdom* v. *Council*, Case 56/88, [1989] 2 CMLR 789; see also *Commission* v. *Council*, Case 242/87 (30 May 1989—not yet reported). This can hardly have been intended by the authors of the Treaty, since there is no requirement in Art. 128 to consult the European Parliament, nor is there any statement as to the voting procedure to be followed by the Council (e.g. qualified majority).

[3] This has also been given a wide interpretation by the European Court: see *Germany* v. *Commission*, Case 281/85, [1988] 1 CMLR 11.

[4] *Gravier* v. *Liège*, Case 293/83, [1985] ECR 593 (para. 19 of the judgment); see also *Casagrande*, Case 9/74, [1974] ECR 773 (para. 6 of the judgment).

The only Community provisions giving clear and explicit rights to equal treatment in education are in Regulation 1612/68. Article 7(3) provides that an immigrant Community worker shall 'by virtue of the same right and under the same conditions as national workers, have access to training in vocational schools and retraining centres'. This prohibits all discrimination, but it applies only to someone who has already obtained the status of an immigrant Community worker in the Member State concerned before he begins his educational course; it also applies only to training in vocational schools and retraining centres.

Article 12 of Regulation 1612/68 provides that the children of an immigrant Community worker must be admitted to general educational courses (as well as vocational-training courses) under the same conditions as nationals of the Member State in question. To obtain this right, the child must be resident in the Member State. Article 12 covers all forms of education; but neither provision applies to someone who goes to another Member State for the sole purpose of study.

Mention should also be made of Directive 77/486, which makes provision for special educational assistance for the children of migrant workers,[5] and of various schemes providing funding for educational initiatives with a Community dimension.[6]

It will be seen from this brief survey that Community legislation is concerned with education only in limited circumstances. In particular, it gives no express rights to the student who goes to another Member State solely in order to study. The European Court, however, has enlarged the scope of Community law. Prompted, it appears, by the Commission, it has sought to establish something approaching a Community education policy and it has done this by extending the principle of non-discrimination to cover almost all students.

---

[5] Newly arrived children must be given extra teaching, particularly to enable them to learn the language of the country to which they have migrated; that country must also (in accordance with its national circumstances and legal system) take appropriate measures to promote the teaching to such children of the language and culture of their state of origin.

[6] These include Dec. 86/365, which establishes a programme of co-operation between universities and enterprises in the field of technological training (Comett), the second phase of which was put into effect by Dec. 89/27 (Comett II); Dec. 87/327, which sets up a scheme (known as 'Erasmus') to encourage student mobility by providing grants for students studying in another Member State, though these cover only the *extra* expenses involved in studying abroad (unsuccessfully challenged by the Commission on the ground that it should have been based on Art. 128 alone, not on both Art. 128 *and* Art. 235: *Commission* v. *Council*, Case 242/87 (30 May 1989—not yet reported); and Dec. 87/569 on a programme for the vocational training of young people (which was unsuccessfully challenged by the United Kingdom on the ground that it should *not* have been based on Art. 128 alone: *United Kingdom* v. *Council*, Case 56/88, [1989] 2 CMLR 789).

Policy-Making by the Court

The first case, *Forcheri* v. *Belgium*,[7] concerned a relatively limited point. The wife of a Commission official wanted to attend a course at an institution of non-university further education in Belgium, a course which seems to have been clearly of a vocational nature.[8] She and her husband were both Italians but they were resident in Belgium where he worked. Could she be required to pay an additional tuition fee not payable by Belgian students, the so-called *'minerval'*? It will be seen here that the husband could be regarded as having the status of an immigrant Community worker in Belgium. On this basis, he would have been entitled[9] to attend a vocational course on the same terms as Belgian workers. Moreover, their children would have had similar rights under Article 12 of the Regulation. Only a small extension of the law was, therefore, necessary to enable Mrs Forcheri to avoid the *minerval*. However, though the European Court ruled that Mr Forcheri enjoyed the status of an immigrant Community worker in Belgium, it did not base its decision on Regulation 1612/68 or even on Article 48 and the other provisions of the EEC Treaty dealing with immigrant workers. Instead it chose Article 7 of the EEC Treaty. This provision, which was discussed above in Chapter 11, lays down a general prohibition against discrimination on grounds of nationality within the area covered by the EEC Treaty. It might have been thought that, as education is outside the scope of the Treaty, Article 7 would not apply to it. The Court, however, ruled that, as a result of Article 128 EEC, access to education is covered, even though educational policy is a matter for the Member States. From this, it concluded that Article 7 EEC applies to prohibit the imposition of a higher fee for students from another Member State. The ruling was, however, limited to the case where the student is 'lawfully established' in the Member State in question.[10] On the question of the kind of education covered, the Court's ruling seems deliberately blurred: it referred throughout its judgment to 'educational courses relating in particular to vocational training'. Presumably the Court wanted to keep its options open; perhaps the judges were divided among themselves. It should, however, be noted that Article 128 EEC applies only to vocational training; so if Article 7 is applicable only by virtue of Article 128, it should apply only to vocational training.

---

[7] Case 152/82, [1983] ECR 2323.
[8] The educational institution in question was concerned mainly with training social workers.
[9] Under Art. 7(3) of Reg. 1612/68.
[10] The exact meaning of 'lawfully established' is unclear: it certainly covers any Community immigrant with a right under Community law to reside in the Member State in question; it might also cover a Community immigrant with a right only under national law; it certainly does not, however, cover a student who comes expressly in order to study.

Three comments may be made about this judgment. The first is that it is clearly innovative. Under a neutral interpretation of the Treaty, the Court would probably have concluded—as did Advocate General Rozès—that Community law did not apply to Mrs Forcheri. Secondly, the scope of the actual ruling was limited, since it applied only to students already in the Member State concerned. However, and this is the third point, the reasons given were very significant: once it is accepted that Article 7 applies to education—even if it is only vocational education—it could easily be argued that it covers all students, even those who come solely for the purpose of education.

This next step was in fact taken in the *Gravier* case.[11] Unlike *Forcheri*, this was a decision of the Full Court and it is probably fair to say that it represents a policy decision by the European Court to suppress the *minerval* (and similar differential fees in other countries, such as the United Kingdom) in the case of Community students taking a course of a vocational nature.

The facts of the case were that Miss Gravier, a French national who was resident in France (as were her parents), came to Belgium for the specific purpose of taking a course (on drawing strip-cartoons) at an art college in Liège. Under Belgian law she was required to pay the *minerval*. She challenged this.

She was not a worker, never having been in employment, and was not covered by any of the express provisions of Community law.[12] She relied, however, on two general provisions of the Treaty, Article 7 (which has already been discussed) and Article 59 and the other provisions regarding services. Her argument on the latter point was that education is a service and that she had rights under Community law as a recipient of that service.

The European Court did not consider the argument based on services, even though the Commission placed special emphasis on it. Instead it relied on Article 7 EEC and drew the consequences implicit in *Forcheri*. It held that, by reason of Article 128 and the steps that have been taken under it,[13] the conditions of access to vocational training fall within the scope of the Treaty. Consequently, Article 7 EEC applies to prohibit any differential fee imposed on Community students with regard to vocational training. Students like Miss Gravier, who come expressly to

---

[11] See n. 4 above.

[12] Nor was she covered by *Forcheri*, since she had not previously been resident in Belgium.

[13] In addition to Dec. 63/266, the Court referred to the general guidelines laid down by the Council in 1971, JO 1971, C 81, p. 5, the resolution of 13 Dec. 1976, JO 1976, C 308, p. 1, and the resolution of 11 July 1983, JO 1983, C 193, p. 2. For the full set of such measures, see *European Educational Policy Statements* (3rd edn, 1987), a booklet published by the Council (ISBN 92–824–0471–4), which contains the text of all Community policy statements and legislation relating to education.

study, benefit from this rule in the same way as those already resident in the country concerned. The result was to outlaw the *minerval* for Community students taking vocational courses.[14]

This, of course, raised the question of what constitutes a vocational course. In *Gravier* the Court provided a definition in two parts, compliance with either of which renders the education vocational. The first part covers 'any form of education which prepares [the student] for a qualification for a particular profession, trade or employment'; the second part covers any form of education 'which provides the necessary training and skills for such a profession, trade or employment'.[15] Though helpful, this definition is not without its difficulties. As we shall see, these featured strongly in later cases.

The Meaning of 'Vocational Training'

On 2 February 1988 the Court gave three judgments concerning the *minerval*.[16] The most important of these was *Blaizot* v. *University of Liège*,[17] in which the Court had to decide whether a university course in veterinary medicine was vocational. Eleven French students, who had come to Belgium in order to study veterinary medicine at Belgian universities, had paid the *minerval* prior to the *Gravier* case and then claimed a refund. The Belgian Government argued that university studies were incapable, by their very nature, of being vocational. This view would commend itself to many people on the basis of the general idea of a university. On the other hand, many university courses are intended to qualify the student for a particular profession. Such courses may be taught both at universities and at non-university institutions in the same Member State, or in universities in one Member State and in non-university institutions in another. For this reason the Court rejected the idea that university courses can never be vocational: the test laid down in *Gravier* must be applied in the same way to university courses as to non-university courses. In fact, the Court went so far as to say that university courses in general comply with the *Gravier* test, though this is not true with regard to courses designed for persons who want to increase their general knowledge rather than to prepare for a career. The Court also made clear that the second part of the definition in *Gravier*

[14] It should be noted that the Court was still slightly equivocal on this point. Though it referred in most passages only to vocational training, para. 19 is wider, referring 'in particular' to vocational training.

[15] See para. 30. This definition is based on that proposed by Advocate General Slynn but is somewhat wider.

[16] All three were decisions of the Full Court and in all three the advocate general was Sir Gordon Slynn.

[17] Case 24/86, [1988] ECR 379.

covers a course which provides the student with knowledge which he needs for the exercise of a particular profession, trade or employment, even if the acquisition of that knowledge is not required by any law, regulation or administrative provision.

In Belgium, the course in veterinary medicine is divided into two parts. First, there is a preliminary diploma (the *'candidature'*); if the student is successful in that, he may go on to take the second part, leading to the doctorate. It was argued that, even if the second part were classified as vocational, the first part could not be, since it did not itself provide a qualification entitling the holder to practise. The Court rejected this argument: the second part presupposes the successful conclusion of the first, so that the two parts must be considered as a whole. The result was that the whole course had to be regarded as vocational; the imposition of the *minerval* was consequently contrary to Community law.

The Court did, however, sweeten the pill by ruling that students who had paid the *minerval* prior to the date of the judgment in *Blaizot* could not reclaim it unless they had commenced legal proceedings, or made equivalent claims, before that date.[18] The reason given by the Court for limiting the effect of the judgment in this way was that the common vocational-training policy of the Community is still in the course of evolution and it is only by virtue of this continuing development that university studies can be regarded as covered by Article 7 EEC.[19] This concession by the Court spared Belgium the financial consequences of a flood of requests for refunds of the *minerval* by university students, though it did nothing to mitigate the future consequences of the ruling. Moreover, in *Barra* v. *Belgium*,[20] the second of the three cases, the Court refused to impose a similar restriction on its ruling with regard to vocational courses in non-university institutions. The Court ruled that students attending such courses could claim refunds back as far as the Belgian statute of limitations allowed.

The third of the three cases was *Commission* v. *Belgium*,[21] an action under Article 169. The judgment in this case is of no interest because the application was declared inadmissible on procedural grounds, but the opinion by Advocate General Sir Gordon Slynn contains some interest-

---

[18] This was an application of the doctrine first established in *Defrenne* v. *Sabena*, Case 43/75, [1976] ECR 455.

[19] The Court also mentioned that the Commission had changed its views on the question: its earlier view that university studies were not covered could have misled the authorities in Belgium. These considerations may well have justified the Court's ruling; nevertheless, it must be pointed out that the real quantum leap occurred in *Gravier*, rather than in *Blaizot*. It is not without interest that the English courts ruled as early as 1985 that university courses are capable of being vocational: *R.* v. *Inner London Education Authority*, ex parte *Hinde*, [1985] 1 CMLR 716.

[20] Case 309/85, [1988] ECR 355.

[21] Case 293/85, [1988] ECR 305.

ing comments on the meaning of vocational training. One situation he considered was where someone wishing to enter a particular profession is required first to obtain a university degree and then to go on to pass a professional examination. A second was where all that is required is that the student pass the professional examination, but he is exempted from part of it if he has the requisite university degree. Sir Gordon considered that in both these cases the relevant university course should be regarded as vocational. If correct, this means that a university degree in law is almost certainly vocational within the meaning of Community law. Sir Gordon also considered that a university course would be vocational if, though not formally required, it gave the student the knowledge necessary for taking a professional examination.

On the other hand, he did not consider that a general educational course could be regarded as vocational, even though an ability to read and write is necessary for most jobs: there must be a sufficiently direct link between the training and the occupation.

It could also be argued that every university course is vocational because it provides an essential qualification for being a university teacher in the subject in question. This argument was, however, rejected by Sir Gordon, though he accepted that a course on teaching skills (teachers' training course) would be vocational.

Maintenance Grants

The question of maintenance grants for students came before the Court in two cases decided on the same day, one being *Lair* v. *University of Hanover*.[22] Mrs Lair was a French national who had immigrated to Germany, and resided there for over five years. She had worked for part of this period and was unemployed for the remainder. She then enrolled for a course in Romance and Germanic languages and literature at the University of Hanover. She applied for a maintenance grant in the form of an interest-free loan, but her request was rejected on the ground that she had not been employed in Germany for at least five years prior to enrolment, a condition applicable only to foreigners. She brought proceedings claiming a right to equal treatment under Community law.

The first question considered by the European Court was whether Article 7 EEC applies to maintenance grants. The Court, after making clear that the *Gravier* principle covers only vocational training, held that, in the present state of Community law, Article 7 EEC applies only to grants covering fees required for access to education (such as enrolment fees or tuition fees) and not to maintenance grants. Its reason was that,

---

[22] Case 39/86, [1988] ECR 3161 (Full Court).

though access to vocational training comes within the scope of the EEC Treaty, other aspects of education are a matter for the Member States. Maintenance grants, said the Court, fall partly within the field of educational policy (which is not as such within Community jurisdiction) and partly within the field of social policy (which falls within national jurisdiction except to the extent that it is covered by particular provisions of the EEC Treaty).

This distinction between access to (vocational) education and educational policy has no basis in the Treaty, as will be clear from the previous discussion of the relevant provisions. Nor is it self-evident that a grant covering fees is concerned with access to education while a means-tested maintenance grant is not. This distinction must, therefore, be regarded as a compromise adopted by the Court between the conflicting requirements of European integration and educational policy.

The next question was whether Mrs Lair could rely on Article 7 of Regulation 1612/68. The Court first looked at Article 7(2), which provides that an immigrant Community worker is entitled to 'the same social and tax advantages as national workers'.[23] Could a maintenance grant be regarded as a 'social advantage'? The Court held that it could, provided the course in question was a vocational one. (Somewhat surprisingly, the German authorities did not dispute that Mrs Lair's course in language and literature was vocational.) The Court held that Article 7(2) of the Regulation entitles immigrant Community workers to equality with national workers with regard to any benefit related to obtaining a professional qualification. A maintenance grant, said the Court, is such a benefit.

It was argued before the Court that Article 7(2) should not be interpreted to cover educational grants in view of the fact that Article 7(3) expressly applies to 'access to training in vocational schools and retraining centres': it might be thought that the authors of the Regulation would not have intended Article 7(2) to overlap with Article 7(3). This argument was, however, rejected by the Court on the ground that an institution is not a 'vocational school' merely because it provides vocational training. The term 'vocational school', the Court held, applies only to institutions providing training which is either given in the course of employment or is closely linked to employment, particularly apprenticeship. A university cannot, therefore, be a 'vocational school'; so Article 7(3) cannot apply to a grant for a university course.

A maintenance grant is, therefore, a 'social advantage' within the terms of Article 7(2), but was Mrs Lair an immigrant Community worker? It was argued that a person ceases to be a worker if, being in employment, he gives up his job in order to become a student or, being

---

[23] This was discussed at pp. 150–4 above.

unemployed, he ceases to look for work in order to study. This argument was rejected by the Court, which pointed out that there are several Community provisions in which rights linked to the status of a Community worker are granted to persons who are no longer in employment.[24] Consequently, the Court ruled, a person does not cease to be an immigrant Community worker just because he gives up work in order to become a full-time student; nevertheless, the Court held that for the immigrant to retain the status of a worker, a connection must exist between the course of study and the immigrant's previous career. This appears to mean that the course of study must relate to the trade or profession previously pursued by the immigrant. (This connection is not, however, required where the immigrant is involuntarily unemployed and the state of the labour market obliges him to retrain for a new career.) The result is that a Community immigrant retains the status of a worker while engaged in full-time study, provided the course leads to a vocational qualification which is relevant (except in the case mentioned above) to his previous career.

The final question considered by the Court was whether a Member State is permitted to lay down a requirement that the immigrant must have worked for a given period of time. (It will be remembered that under German law a Community immigrant was not entitled to a grant unless he had worked in Germany for at least five years before commencing his university studies.) The European Court rejected such a notion, pointing out that the concept of an immigrant Community worker is derived from Community law and cannot depend on criteria laid down by national law. Nevertheless, the Court recognized that some Member States were concerned that the system created by the Court could be open to abuse, for example, where a person immigrated to another Member State and took a job there for a very short period solely in order to qualify for a grant; so the Court said that such an abuse would not be permitted by Community law. This somewhat cryptic statement was expanded in the *Brown* case (below).

The result of the case seems to be that Mrs Lair could claim the grant, provided she could demonstrate either that it led to a professional qualification relevant to her previous employment or that she came within the exception concerning unemployment.

The second of the two cases was *Brown* v. *Secretary of State for Scotland*,[25] which concerned a student (Mr Brown) with dual British and French nationality. His parents lived in France and he had gone to school there. He wanted to attend university in England and he was offered a place at the University of Cambridge for a course in electrical

---

[24] One example is the right to remain (on retirement) given to former workers by Reg. 1251/70, discussed at pp. 120–1, above.

[25] Case 197/86, [1988] ECR 3205 (Full Court).

engineering. The university recommended that students should have some practical experience before beginning the course, and it was obligatory to have acquired at least eight weeks practical experience before the end of the second year. Mr Brown had been accepted by an engineering firm in Scotland for what was called 'pre-university industrial training'. Such training was available only to students who had already been offered a university place. He worked for the firm for about eight months and then began his course, the firm agreeing to give him financial assistance during his studies. He also claimed a government grant to cover both his fees and his maintenance. Originally, such grants were available only to students who had resided in the United Kingdom for three years before the beginning of the course. At the time of the case, limited categories of Community students were also entitled to a grant, but Mr Brown did not fall within any of them.[26] He therefore claimed a right under Community law.

Much of the judgment in the *Brown* case covers the same ground as that in *Lair* and many passages in the two cases are identical. The Court had nothing new to say on the meaning of 'vocational training', but there can be little doubt that Mr Brown's course was covered by the *Gravier* formula. Article 7 of the EEC Treaty gave him the right to a grant to pay for tuition fees but did not help him with regard to a maintenance grant.

The Court had decided in *Lair* that Article 7(2) of Regulation 1612/68 can apply to a maintenance grant.[27] It had also made clear that Member States cannot lay down their own requirements for the attainment of the status of an immigrant Community worker. Thus, the United Kingdom rule that the immigrant must have worked for at least nine months was just as invalid as the equivalent German rule considered in *Lair*. It seems, therefore, that Mr Brown's 'pre-university industrial training' gave him the status of a worker. According to the judgment in *Lair*, he would not lose that status by becoming a full-time student: there was no doubt that the course at Cambridge was relevant to his previous employment. However, the Court ruled in *Brown* that if the immigrant obtained the employment solely by virtue of the fact that he had already been offered a university place, he will not be entitled to a grant under Article 7 of Regulation 1612/68: the employment would be merely incidental to the university course. This ruling, which in effect deprived

---

[26] Mr Brown would have been entitled to a grant if he had been employed in Scotland for nine of the preceding twelve months and he had been planning to attend a course at a 'vocational school' within the meaning of Art. 7(3) of Reg. 1612/68. He would also have been entitled to a grant if one of his parents had been employed in Scotland for at least one year during the preceding three years (a provision intended to give effect to Art. 12 of Reg. 1612/68).

[27] The Court also decided in *Lair* that Art. 7(3) of Reg. 1612/68 cannot apply to university courses; so Art. 7(2) was the only relevant provision.

Mr Brown of a maintenance grant, clearly accords with the idea behind the ruling in *Lair*, and could be regarded as illustrating one aspect of the 'abuse' referred to in that case. The *Lair* ruling seems to be premised on the theory that a student grant comes within Article 7(2) of the Regulation only if the course of study is intended to further the career already embarked on by the worker.[28] Where, on the other hand, the purpose of the employment is to assist the student in his studies, the relationship is, so to speak, reversed and the rationale of the *Lair* ruling destroyed.

INTERNATIONAL ASPECTS

Further problems arose in a later case, *Matteucci*,[29] which concerned an Italian national who had been born, and lived all her life, in Belgium, where she was a teacher of eurhythmics. She applied for a scholarship (in the form of a maintenance grant) to take a course in singing and voice-training in Germany. She felt that this would complement her training in eurhythmics. The scholarships were offered under a bilateral cultural agreement between Germany and Belgium, by which the German Government agreed to pay for a small number of Belgian citizens to study in Germany. Candidates were selected by the appropriate Belgian authority, and that authority rejected her application on the ground of her nationality. She then brought legal proceedings in the Belgian courts, claiming a right to equality under Community law.

Since the scholarships were for maintenance, Article 7 EEC was not applicable, but the European Court ruled that she could rely on Article 7(2) of Regulation 1612/68, provided her activities as a eurhythmics teacher constituted sufficiently genuine and effective employment to give her the status of a worker, a matter for the national court to decide.[30] Provided they did, she was entitled to be given the same opportunity to obtain a scholarship to further her training in another Member State as would be given to a Belgian national in her situation. The fact that the scholarship was granted under an international agreement did not affect the matter: under Article 5 EEC, Germany was obliged to assist Belgium in carrying out its obligations under Community law; therefore Germany could not refuse to accept Miss Matteucci on the ground that she was not a Belgian citizen. The Court also pointed out that the EEC Treaty takes priority over earlier agreements between the Member States.

Though the judgment in *Matteucci* is significant in showing the

---

[28] This is subject to the exception previously mentioned.
[29] Case 235/87, [1988] ECR 5589.
[30] The 'genuine and effective' test was first laid down in *Levin*, Case 53/81, [1982] ECR 1035.

lengths to which the European Court will go to protect the rights of immigrant Community workers (Miss Mateucci enjoyed this status despite the fact that she had been born in Belgium), its scope should not be exaggerated. It is important to note that her right was against Belgium, not Germany. She had no direct right against the German authorities: the extent of their obligations under Community law was to assist Belgium in carrying out *its* obligations. Consequently, if the granting of the scholarships had been a matter solely for the German authorities, it is doubtful whether she could have claimed equality of treatment under Article 7(2) of the Regulation.

This is borne out by the Court's judgment in *Humbel*,[31] a case concerning the son of a French worker in Luxemburg. The son went to school in Belgium and was obliged to pay special fees that were not payable by Belgian students. The Belgian authorities had exempted Luxembourg nationals, though it was unclear on what ground. If the education he was receiving in Belgium was regarded as vocational (a matter to be decided by the Belgian courts), the son would have been covered by Article 7 EEC. However, it was doubtful whether it was vocational. As the child of an immigrant Community worker in Luxembourg, he was entitled to equality of treatment regarding education in Luxembourg by virtue of Article 12 of Regulation 1612/68, and it was argued that, as Luxembourg students were exempt from the special fee in Belgium, he should be given the same exemption. The European Court, however, held that, since his father was not a worker in Belgium, the son had no such rights in that country: Article 12 imposes obligations only on the Member State where the migrant worker resides.[32] The same reasoning would appear to apply to Article 7(2) of the Regulation.

Problems would also arise if the treaty was with a non-Community country. Even if the Member State in which the worker resided was obliged to nominate him for a scholarship, there would be no corresponding obligation on the other country to accept a candidate who was not of the requisite nationality: Article 5 EEC does not apply to non-member States. Moreover, as Article 234 EEC makes clear, the rights and obligations of parties to treaties concluded prior to the EEC Treaty between a Member State and a non-member State are not affected by the EEC Treaty.[33]

---

[31] Case 263/86, [1988] ECR 5365.
[32] Para. 24 of the judgment.
[33] Art. 234 was raised by the French Government in the *Matteucci* case, but, as the Court pointed out, it was inapplicable in view of the fact that the treaty in that case was between two Member States.

Systems of Government Funding

In *Commission* v. *Belgium*[34] the Court considered the extent to which the system of government finance for higher education adopted by a Member State could be affected by Community law. At the time of the case, the level of government funding for universities and colleges in Belgium depended in part on the number of students at the institution in question. Subject to certain exceptions, foreign students were not, however, taken into account once they exceeded a quota of 2 per cent. Since the practical effect of this was to make Belgian universities unwilling to admit students from other Community countries once the limit had been reached, the Court ruled that (in so far as vocational training was concerned) this system was contrary to Article 7 EEC. It seems to follow from this judgment that any quota for Community students is illegal, as is any system of finance that might provide a disincentive for their admission. The consequences of this ruling for British education are considered below.

Education as a Service

In *Humbel*[35] the European Court finally ruled on the argument, first put to it in *Gravier* , that education should be regarded as a service. It held that courses provided as part of the national education system cannot be regarded as 'services' within the meaning of the Treaty, since they are not 'normally provided for remuneration', as required by Article 60(2) EEC. The fact that students pay fees does not affect this: the purpose of the state in providing education is not to obtain remuneration, but to fulfil 'its duty to its people in the social, cultural and educational fields'.[36]

Similar considerations would apply in the case of private education provided for charitable motives (for example, by a religious foundation or by a charitable trust), but there is no reason why private education provided for profit (for example, a language school) should not be regarded as a service under Community law. If this is so, any restrictions imposed by a Member State on the right of nationals of other Member States to receive such education would be contrary to Article 59 EEC. In this situation, the distinction between vocational and non-vocational education is irrelevant.

---

[34] Case 42/87, [1988] ECR 5445.
[35] See n. 31 above.
[36] See paras 18 and 19 of the judgment. For a fuller discussion of these questions, see the opinions of Advocate General Slynn in *Humbel* [1988] ECR at pp. 5377–80, and *Gravier* v. *Liège*, Case 293/83, [1985] ECR 523 at pp. 602–4.

Children of Community Workers

It will be remembered that Article 12 of Regulation 1612/68 gives the children of Community workers the right to equal treatment regarding education. The purpose of the Regulation is to ensure that migrants and their families are fully integrated into society in the country in which they work and that they have the same rights in the economic and social sphere as the local population. Article 12 plays an important part in this scheme, since Community workers might hesitate to migrate if they thought their children would not get a proper education in the new country.

Rights Covered

In *Casagrande*,[37] the first case on education it ever decided, the European Court held that Article 12 covers maintenance grants as well as fees.[38] Moreover, Article 12 expressly states that it applies to 'general educational, apprenticeship and vocational training courses', which covers all forms of education.[39] The result is that it applies to a wider range of rights than any other Community provision—both fees and maintenance grants for both vocational and non-vocational education.

As was made clear in *Humbel*,[40] Article 12 gives rights only against the Member State in which the parent works: if the child takes a course in another Member State, he cannot invoke Article 12 against the latter. In *Di Leo* v. *Land Berlin*,[41] however, the European Court held that in such a situation Article 12 can nevertheless be invoked against the Member State in which the parent resides, if that State gives financial assistance for study in other countries. This judgment, which ignores the express words of Article 12,[42] concerned the daughter of an Italian immigrant in Germany who wanted to study medicine at an Italian university. German legislation made provision for grants for Germans wishing to study abroad. This was extended to cover the children of Community workers in Germany, provided they did not study in their home country. The European Court ruled that this proviso was contrary to Community law.

---

[37] Case 9/74, [1974] ECR 723; see also *Alaimo*, Case 68/74, [1975] ECR 109.
[38] This was confirmed in *Echternach and Moritz*, Cases 389, 390/87, [1989] ECR 723.
[39] Ibid.
[40] See n. 31 above.
[41] Case C–308/89, 13 November 1990, *The Times*, 7 January 1991.
[42] Article 12 provides, 'The children of a national of a Member State who is or has been employed in the territory of another Member State shall be admitted to *that State's* general educational . . . courses . . .' (italics added). This clearly does not cover courses in *another* Member State.

PERSONS COVERED

Article 12 provides that it benefits the 'children of a national of a Member State who is or has been employed in the territory of another Member State'. This makes clear that the child's parent—it can be the father or the mother—must be (or have been) a worker in a Member State other than that of which he or she is a national. Moreover, it was held in *Brown* v. *Secretary of State for Scotland*[43] that the child must have lived with one or both of his parents in that country at that time.[44] Mr Brown's parents were French nationals who had lived and worked in Britain. They had, however, returned to France before their son was born and had not since worked in the United Kingdom. The Court held that Mr Brown could not claim rights under Article 12.

It is evident from the terms of Article 12 that the working parent need not still be in employment when the right is claimed: he may, for example, have retired or died. It seems, moreover, that the right is not lost if the parent returns to his country of origin, leaving the child behind.[45]

What if the child goes with the parent, but later returns to the country where the parent worked in order to study? This was what happened in *Echternach and Moritz*,[46] where one of the plaintiffs, Mr Moritz, had arrived in the Netherlands at the age of 5 and received his primary and secondary education there. His father was employed in the Netherlands branch of a Dutch-German uranium enrichment undertaking. When the son began his studies at a technical college in the Netherlands, the father was transferred to the German branch of the undertaking and went to live in Germany. The son went to Germany with his father, but was unable to continue his studies there because his Dutch qualifications were not recognized. He therefore returned to the Netherlands and enrolled at the technical college where he had studied previously.

The Dutch Government considered that he had forfeited his rights under Article 12 by going back to Germany, but the European Court held he was still covered. However, the Court's ruling was expressly based on the premise that the child could not continue his studies in Germany. The position might have been different, therefore, if this had not been the case or, perhaps, if he had no intention of studying when he went to Germany.

In *Matteucci*,[47] Advocate General Slynn considered whether the child

[43] See n. 45 (discussed further at pp. 183–5 above).
[44] It seems that the child need not have lived with the working parent: it is enough if he lived with one parent at a time when the other was working in the same Member State.
[45] *Per* Advocate General Slynn in *Brown* v. *Secretary of State for Scotland*, Case 197/86, [1988] ECR 3205 at p. 3234 and *per* Advocate General Darmon in *Echternach and Moritz* (n. 38 above), paras 40–50; cf. the Court's judgment in the latter case.
[46] See n. 38 above.
[47] See n. 29 above.

would lose his status either after he reached a given age or if he broke off his education to take a job.[48] He concluded that neither of these factors would affect the child's rights, though he admitted that there might be difficult cases to be decided in the future, particularly as the children of the first generation of migrant workers grow older. The Court did not consider the question.

The Present State of the Law

In the light of the cases discussed above, the present state of Community law may be summarized as follows:

1. Community law (except for Article 12 of Regulation 1612/68 and the provisions on services) applies only to vocational courses. However, this concept has been widely defined to include most, but not all, university courses.

2. In so far as vocational courses are concerned, it is contrary to Article 7 EEC to charge Community students higher enrolment or tuition fees than home students, or to deny to the former a grant available to the latter in so far as the grant covers such fees. Any other form of discrimination regarding admission, such as a quota, is also illegal. Moreover, Article 7 EEC forbids any system of government funding that provides a disincentive for universities or other educational institutions to admit Community students.

3. The same applies in the case of non-vocational courses if the student is covered by Article 12 of Regulation 1612/68.

4. It is not illegal to deny a maintenance grant to students from other Member States unless they are covered by Articles 7(2), 7(3) or 12 of Regulation 1612/68. Article 12 covers all forms of education. Article 7(3) does not apply to university courses. Article 7(2) can apply to university courses, provided they are vocational and they are relevant to the student's previous career (except where the student, after having been in employment, later becomes unemployed and is obliged to retrain for a new career).

Policy Assessment

It was said previously that these cases represent an attempt by the European Court to establish a Community education policy by judicial decision. How successful has this been? Opinions will probably differ:

---

[48] In the latter case, the child would normally be entitled to benefit from Art. 7(2) of Reg. 1612/68, but this would not help him if his proposed course was not linked to his previous employment or if he wanted to pursue studies of a non-vocational nature.

students may feel grateful that, thanks to the Court, they can now study in other Community countries under the same conditions as local students; taxpayers, on the other hand, may wonder why they have to pay for the education of foreigners. It might be thought that if there is a general exchange of students, the burden will even out in the end. However, the flow of students is unlikely to be equal: some Member States will be net 'exporters' of students and others will be net 'importers'. There are various reasons for this imbalance, but a country with a widely spoken language (for example, English) will tend to receive more students; the quality of education provided will also be important, as will the level of fees. Moreover, the real cost per student of university education varies considerably from one Member State to another. This depends, in particular, on the ratio of students to academic staff and on the facilities provided (libraries, laboratories, and so on). There are also major differences between Member States as to the extent to which the cost of educating a student is borne by the taxpayer as distinct from the student himself.[49] The result is that the *Gravier* principle throws a greater burden on some Member States than on others: in its efforts to prevent discrimination against students, the Court has created a system which discriminates against Member States (and their taxpayers).

This could have undesirable consequences, since it penalizes Member States that devote greater resources to education: the quality of education will tend to be higher in such countries or the level of fees lower; in either case, students will be attracted from countries where the reverse is true. Such Member States will have the burden of educating many students from other Community countries. On the other hand, Member States which devote only limited resources to education will be rewarded: their students will often prefer to study in other Member States, thereby shifting the burden of their education to the taxpayers in those countries.

The practical consequences of the Court's decisions in each Member State will depend on the system of government funding. In the United Kingdom, the Government has a policy that overseas students should pay the full cost of their education. Home students, on the other hand, are subsidized by the taxpayer. Undergraduates receive a twofold subsidy: their fees are below the economic cost of the education they receive, and the fees they do pay are covered by a grant from their local education authority. (This grant is available to all and is not to be

---

[49] One consequence of the *Gravier* decision has been a reported fourfold increase in the number of students from the Republic of Ireland attending universities in the United Kingdom (*The Independent*, 19 Nov. 1987, p. 17). The reason was that if they attended Irish universities they would often have had to pay their fees themselves; at British universities, on the other hand, their fees would be covered by a grant funded by the British taxpayer (see also 'Young Irish brain drain', *The Times*, 10 Apr. 1987).

confused with the means-tested maintenance grant.) In effect, their education is free. Graduates are treated less generously: they pay lower fees, but only a relatively small number are given a grant. Their education is subsidized in part only.

Understandably, the Government is not willing to put unlimited funds into education and, though the mechanisms used to ensure this have changed over the years, the effect is that universities are obliged to impose strict limits on the numbers of subsidized (low-fee) students they can accept. Since *Gravier*, EEC students (that is, students from Community countries other than the United Kingdom) have been entitled to have the cost of their education at United Kingdom universities borne by the British taxpayer to the same extent as British students: they pay the same low fees as home students and, in the case of undergraduates, are given the same grants to cover them. The result is that they now share the low-fee quota with home students.

This has two consequences. The first is that EEC students are now competing for places with British students: for every EEC student accepted, one British student must be turned away. If the number of EEC applicants continues to rise, British students could be squeezed out.

The second consequence is that EEC applicants could in some cases find it more difficult than previously to obtain admission. Once the low-fee quota is filled—and in some courses it fills quickly—there is a strong financial incentive for universities to admit high-fee, in preference to low-fee, students. The case of *Commission* v. *Belgium*[50] suggests that this is discrimination,[51] but it is discrimination between Community and non-Community students, not between United Kingdom students and those from other Community countries. The European Court has not yet had cause to consider whether such discrimination is illegal.[52] However, it is hard to see how it could be removed without a radical change in the whole system of financing higher education in the United Kingdom.

These problems illustrate the danger of policy-making by judicial decision. It would have been better if the European Court had left it to the Council to adopt a policy on migrant students.[53] Such a policy would

[50] Case 42/87, [1988] ECR 5445 (discussed at p. 187 above).

[51] If this is discrimination, it is discrimination of a peculiar kind, since it results solely from the fact that non-Community students pay higher fees and are, for this reason, financially more rewarding than United Kingdom or EEC students.

[52] Art. 7 EEC lays down a general ban on 'discrimination on grounds of nationality', without limiting it to discrimination between Community nationals. The European Court has, however, held that Community law does not prevent a Member State from discriminating *against* non-Community nationals: *Reg.* v. *Ministry of Agriculture*, ex parte *Agegate*, Case C–3/87, 14 Dec. 1989, [1990] 3 WLR 226 (ECJ); indeed, were this not the case, it would be illegal to charge higher fees to non-Community students. It remains to be seen whether the Court will decide to prohibit discrimination *in favour* of such nationals.

[53] The Erasmus scheme (n. 6 above) might be regarded as the beginning of such a policy.

no doubt take time to develop, but the end-result would probably have been preferable from the educational point of view.[54]

[54] The best way in which the Community could promote the free movement of students, and at the same time encourage educational excellence, would be to require Member States to pay the true economic cost of the education their students receive in other Community countries. An element of Community assistance could be provided to help the less affluent Member States. Such a policy would reward the Member States that attracted the most students from other Community countries, and provide an incentive for governments to improve the quality of the courses offered by their universities and other educational institutions.

PART III
Competition Law

14
Why the EEC has a Competition Policy

Introduction

The principle of free competition lies at the heart of the Community's economic order. Whether directly or indirectly, many provisions of the EEC Treaty have as their focus the creation and maintenance of conditions of free competition. Indeed, Article 3(f) of the Treaty lays down, as an express 'task' of the Community, 'the institution of a system ensuring that competition in the common market is not distorted'. This 'task' is primarily fulfilled by provisions of the Treaty which regulate the conduct of private undertakings, and it is these provisions that form the basis of this and ensuing chapters. However, the institution of a system of undistorted competition is also achieved by other provisions of the Treaty which seek to eliminate governmental barriers to free trade (for example, Articles 30 and 34) or harmonize national laws which, in their unharmonized state, have the effect of creating obstacles to free trade (for example, Articles 100 and 100A).

It must thus be remembered at all times, when considering the competition rules, that they fit into a wider mosaic of rules designed to eliminate distortions of competition. This is, of course, not to say that the sole aim of the founding fathers of the Treaties was to pursue an ideal of unadulterated competition at the expense of all other objectives. On the contrary, the Treaty (especially following the Single European Act) embraces many other wide-ranging objectives, from protection of employees to the safeguarding of the environment.

Politics, History, and Competition Law

Competition rules regulate the commercial behaviour of traders (or 'undertakings', to employ the language of Articles 85 and 86 of the EEC Treaty). They prohibit misuses of market power by, for instance, preventing undertakings which are dominant in their markets from overcharging their customers or imposing unfair trading terms and conditions upon them. Alternatively, they prohibit competing undertakings from getting together to fix the prices they will charge their customers. At one level, therefore, the purpose of competition rules seems obvious—to protect customers from their suppliers. However, such a superficial answer hides a panoply of other economic and political objectives of competition policy, and these deserve some consideration. Before considering these objectives in any depth, however, two observations should be made.

First, competition law is a fluid, dynamic instrument which has the capability of changing to meet developing economic and political situations. Thus, it is not accurate to ascribe any specific purpose as the main objective. Rather, one must view the rules of competition as serving different purposes at different points of time in history. To take an example from the anti-trust (the US term for competition law) history of the United States: in its early days (at the end of the nineteenth century and the beginning of the twentieth), American anti-trust was renowned for its vigour. Enormous fines were imposed upon companies; treble-damages suits proliferated and recalcitrant managers and directors spent time in gaol. The law started life as an instrument designed to ensure that businessmen did not, ·by private conduct, hinder the political forces seeking to integrate the vast continent of America. Railway companies that, through their trading policies, obstructed the passage of goods from coast to coast, felt the weight of the Sherman Act 1890 brought to bear upon them. Likewise, the oil companies and the inhabitants of other vital industries learned that compliance with anti-trust rules was essential. During the 1970s and 80s economists in the United States commenced a re-evaluation of the function of competition rules. The imperative of securing integration between States diminished, and economists questioned the assumptions underlying the aggressively interventionist enforcement of the rules by government authorities and the courts. The result was a radical turn-around, anti-trust policy became minimalist not maximalist. The economists, who have become known as adherents of the Chicago School, persuaded enforcement agencies and some courts that a highly interventionist policy was counter-productive; that the 'market' was a resilient creature with inherent, self-corrective abilities, and that a maximalist approach hindered the efforts of industry to compete in an increasingly global market-place. As a result of these arguments, official policy now favours regulation of only a small category of corporate behaviour. Over time, therefore, the role of competition policy has evolved.

The competition policy of the Common Market is far more youthful than its American cousin. None the less, it is still possible to identify shifts in enforcement policy and subtle changes of direction and emphasis brought about by developing patterns of European and world trade. Examples of these developing patterns include: the evolution of Japan as a major trading country; the change in emphasis in the developed economies away from the old heavy industries (the so-called 'sunset industries') towards the new high-technology industries ('sunrise industries'); and the rapid increase in importance of services to the western economies (for example, banking, insurance, and the like). All these developments, and many others, have necessitated changes in competition policy.

For instance, whereas at one time a joint venture between two large European companies might have been prohibited because of its impact on the European market, now it could receive blessing and encouragement if it enabled European companies to compete more effectively in a global market with American and Japanese counterparts. Equally, whereas at one time a licence granted by an inventor of new technology to a licensee wishing to manufacture that technology might be viewed with suspicion by the authorities if it gave the licensee exclusive rights to manufacture, now it might be viewed with favour in realization of the fact that the successful dissemination of new, and often commercially risky, technology can flourish in Europe only if licensees are encouraged to take the risk of investing in the technology by the grant of favourable terms in the licence, such as exclusivity.[1]

The second observation, which flows from the first, is that competition policy is a tool of all political parties, irrespective of their position on the political spectrum. In this context it must not be overlooked that the EEC embraces certain political assumptions about capitalism and democracy which are inherently reflected in competition rules, and indeed in all other Treaty policies. The founding fathers of the Treaty of Rome viewed the objective of an economically unified and interdependent Europe as a panacea for the devastation of the Second World War and a guarantee against its recurrence. To re-create Europe along these lines, economic, not political, forces would lead the way. The function of the Treaty of Rome, therefore, was to remove the obstacles to free trade and thereby permit normal business pressures to create European unity. Competition law was one of the Treaty's instruments of change and, as such, rests upon the political assumptions that were responsible for and underpin the Treaty. Interestingly, just as economists were beginning to challenge the seeming obsession with integration, radical political forces in Eastern Europe have forced Western politicians and economists to reaffirm its importance. Precisely what shape Community competition law will adapt into in order to meet the challenge of a changing Europe in the 1990s and beyond is impossible to predict. Should a wave of new Member States from the East be welcomed into the Community, the

---

[1] See e.g. *Hnungesser*, Case 258/78, [1982] ECR 2015.

problem of integrating them into the economics of the West will be enormous.

The Objectives of Community Competition Law

Turning, then, to the specific aims and objectives of Community competition law, it is possible to identify a number of broad currents underlying competition policy. By far the most prominent is that of the furtherance of 'integration'. This, as explained above, is an overtly political goal which employs the economics of competition and free trade as its motor force. A second, though less obvious, goal is the advancement of 'equity' or 'fairness'. A third purpose of competition law is the encouragement of 'efficiency'. The use of competition law as an instrument to encourage efficiency is, however, a (relatively) new phenomenon, but one which assumes an ever-more-important role.

Having ascribed a trilogy of objectives to competition policy, it must be said that these three notions, integration, equity, and efficiency, are not precise terms of art, and each reflects a variety of principles which are not always easy to reconcile. Having identified the three broad objectives, it is necessary to examine each in greater detail.

Integration

Broadly speaking, integration entails the process of opening up the economies of each Member State to each other. Integration is achieved by the removal of barriers to free trade. Companies are thereby encouraged to expand their operations into other Member States and to reap the benefits and economies which result therefrom. Such expansion results in consumers being offered a wider range of goods and services; workers being employed by employers of different nationalities; companies operating in co-operation with companies from other Member States. Integration does not mean that the economies of the different Member States must become the same. Rather, it means that national economies simply become open so that the interplay of market forces operates across the territory of the entire Community and not simply within the confines of a single Member State. Complete integration will have been achieved when the obstacles to trade between London and Milan are the same as those between London and Birmingham.

Whilst it is possible to describe what integration means in economic terms, it is not so easy to predict what it means in political terms. Lest the reader should fail to comprehend why economic integration is different from political integration, it is worth pointing out that politicians disagree (often vehemently) over the end-result of integration and whether it will lead to a Federal States of Europe, along the lines of the United States of America, or simply ever-increasing economic co-operation without the ceding of ultimate nationality. Crystal-ball gazing of this nature is not, however, the purpose of this text.

Competition law serves the purpose of integration by preventing undertakings from re-erecting the barriers to free trade that other Treaty provisions (for example, Article 30 on the free movement of goods) have eliminated. The Court of Justice has thus held that:

'An agreement . . . which might tend to restore the national divisions in trade between Member States might be such as to frustrate the most fundamental object of the Community. The Treaty, whose preamble and content aim at abolishing the barriers between States . . . could not allow undertakings to reconstruct such barriers. Article 85(1) is designed to pursue this aim . . .'.[2]

Competition rules thus prevent companies from thwarting integration. The European Commission has stated: 'The metamorphosis of a heterogeneous collection of isolated national markets into a single vast market could not succeed without the establishment of some basic rules.'[3] Competition law constitutes a prime example of such 'basic rules'. For example, agreements between competitors from different Member States not to trade in each other's territories (that is, market-sharing) are not tolerated. Alternatively, an agreement between a large multinational supplier and his dealers in the different Member States, whereby the dealers will not themselves sell outside their national territories or sell to anyone who intends to re-sell the goods outside the national territories, will be prohibited. Each of these examples involves companies agreeing to carve up the EEC market along national lines, thereby re-creating, by private contract, the barriers which have been eliminated by Treaty provision.

In the context described above, competition law operates in an interventionist manner to protect the process of integration by prohibiting conduct which undermines the process. More recently, an understanding of how competition law itself can hinder integration has arisen, and this appreciation has resulted in a less interventionist role in certain areas. For instance, integration may be furthered by co-operation between competitors in different Member States, but a strict application of the competition rules could result in the co-operation being prohibited. Accordingly, the European Commission, as the relevant enforcement agency, has over the past decade relaxed its stance, for instance, on certain types of joint venture and other forms of corporate

---

[2] Cases 56 and 58/64, *Consten and Grundig* v. *Commission* [1966] ECR 299, 340. See also *Sixteenth Commission Competition Report* (1986), Introduction.

[3] *Ninth Commission Competition Report* (1980), pp. 9–11.

co-operation. A criticism sometimes levelled at the Commission is that the desire to foster 'integration' plays a more pivotal role in Commission and Court of Justice decision-making than does ordinary economic principle.

Equity and Fairness

The rather amorphous concept of 'equity' or 'fairness' in the market-place is also an avowed objective of Community competition policy. The Commission has identified three strands to this objective: (i) equality of opportunity; (ii) protection of small and medium-sized enterprises (so-called 'SMEs'); and (iii) advancement of consumerism broadly defined.[4]

To take equality of opportunity first, Commission policy to achieve this end is evident in their approach to three issues: state aids, relations between the public and private sectors of the economy, and equality of application of the law to non-European traders operating within the EEC. With regard to state aid (which forms a part of competition policy in the EEC Treaty), the Commission is vigilant to ensure that governments do not favour their own commercial operators by the grant of financial and other advantages to the obvious detriment of their competitors from other Member States who do not receive such aid. This is 'fairness' or 'equity' between Member States. With regard to public and private companies, the Commission is vigilant to ensure that state enterprises do not obtain financial and other advantages when compared with their competitors (whether from the same state or, more usually, from other states). To achieve this end the Commission demands, *inter alia*, financial transparency in relations between the state and public bodies so that it can be easily verified whether the state body is competing on equal terms with its private rivals. This is 'fairness' or 'equity' between State and non-State. With regard to the treatment of non-EEC traders, the Commission ensures that such traders, whether they operate in the EEC through subsidiaries or otherwise, are subject to the same rules as are undertakings of Community origin.

Turning to the protection of small and medium-sized undertakings, the Commission perceives the need to protect and encourage SMEs as a manifestation of fairness between different market environments. Although the policy was not designed to deal with the expansion of the Community to welcome the southern states (Greece, Spain, Portugal) as full members, it is well highlighted by these states. The Community market structure is, as has been stressed elsewhere in this chapter, heterogeneous: the economies of the Member States differ, often radically; the degree of integration into the global market differs; and,

[4] Ibid.

significantly, the size and degree of sophistication of the companies and other undertakings trading in those states differs. To take a crude example, the average size of a Portuguese company is very múch smaller than its British or German counterpart. None the less, SMEs play a vital part in the economies of every Member State and of the Community itself, and hence competition law cannot afford to over-emphasize the advantages of greater size to the detriment of SMEs.

Finally, the issue of 'consumerism' broadly defined. By 'consumerism' is understood the protection of users, actual consumers, and workers. In a healthy, competitive market a balance will exist between supply and demand. Undertakings will supply goods and services at a price which gives them a reasonable reward for their efforts, and a consumer will pay a sum that is reasonable in relation to the value they place on the goods or services in question. In a market where suppliers predominate, goods or services may be offered only at excessive prices or at a quality which is either too high or too low; the supply/demand balance is distorted. In terms of competition policy, the Commission may not as a matter of law give its blessing to a restrictive agreement unless it can be established that the agreement in question, *inter alia*, ensures that 'consumers obtain a fair share of the resulting benefit' (see the language of Article 85(3) of the EEC Treaty). Thus, protection of consumers is expressly built into the Treaty provisions governing competition policy. The protection of these interests and, in particular, of workers also plays an important part in the assessment, by the Commission, of proposed state-aid schemes notified to them by Member States pursuant to Article 93 of the Treaty.

EFFICIENCY

Until the mid–1980s the concept of 'efficiency' rarely crept into the Commission's utterances on the broad objectives of competition policy. However, the radical re-evaluation of anti-trust policy which com-menced in the mid–1970s (and which is continuing) in the United States eventually forced the Commission (somewhat reluctantly) to adopt a more economic approach to the assessment of the agreements and practices that, every day, came across the desks of officials for determination. At the time of writing, the use of economic principle as a decision-making tool, and its relative importance when compared with political tools such as 'integration', remains a matter of some debate and speculation. An indication of the Commission's increased sensitivity to the relationship between competition policy and efficiency is to be found in the Introduction to the *Fourteenth Commission Report on Competition Policy*:

'When it operates satisfactorily, competition can be expected to perform three functions that help towards a harmonious development of economic activity throughout the Community: a resource allocation function, by encouraging better use of available factors of production, so that firm's technical efficiency is increased and consumers' wants better satisfied; an incentive function, by stimulating firms to better their performance relative to their competitors; and an innovative function, by encouraging the introduction of new products in markets and the development of new production processes and distribution techniques.'

As noted, the extent to which efficiency takes precedence over other objectives or is subservient to them is a matter of current debate. It will be appreciated that the single-minded pursuit of efficiency as an objective may be inconsistent with these other objectives. As the Commission itself has recognized, competition law is a policy at war with itself. If the most efficient companies are protected at all costs they will thrive at the expense of smaller, less efficient companies which, ultimately, will be eliminated. In the final outcome, competition policy will have encouraged a market-place inhabited by giant corporations. In 1980 the Commission commented with unusual elegance:

'It is an established fact that competition carries within it the seeds of its own destruction. An excessive concentration of economic, financial and commercial power can produce such far-reaching structural changes that free competition is no longer able to fulfil its role as an effective regulator of economic activity.'[5]

In response to this perceived threat, the Commission has focused upon the need to maintain a competitive market *structure* as an objective. The fulfilment of this goal may, of necessity, result in the relegation of efficiency to a second division of aims and goals. This fact is illustrated by comparing the goal of efficiency with that of encouraging SMEs (one aspect of 'fairness' or 'equity'). Clearly, an inexorable pursuit of increasing size and scale is inconsistent with adherence to a 'small is beautiful' school of thought.

The cautious approach adopted towards efficiency contrasts markedly with the Chicago School of economics that came to life in the mid–1970s in the United States and which dominated the anti-trust thinking of the 1980s. This school of thought places efficiency centre-stage in the analysis of practices and agreement, and shunts all other tests not so much to side-stage as back to the dressing-room. In brief, adherents of this school examine a company's prices in relation to its costs to determine whether it has market power. A high cost/price differential suggests the possession of market power; a low cost/price differential suggests otherwise. If the conclusion is that market power exists, the next question to ask is whether the market power is temporary or

[5] *Ninth Commission Competition Report* (1980).

enduring. Chicago School economists believe that barriers to entry to markets are (other than in exceptional cases) low, and companies have, or can readily obtain, perfect information about the costs and benefits of entering particular markets. Therefore, high prices charged by an incumbent in the market will operate as a green light to new entrants, who will enter the market and force prices down as competition reasserts itself. Furthermore, if entry barriers are low, the threat of new entry will in any event operate as a disciplining force on the incumbent and prevent it from misusing its market power to the detriment of consumers. Accordingly, the Chicago School views market power as invariably temporary, and therefore sees no reason why government should intervene. In essence, the market will rectify itself. Translated into competition-enforcement policy, this theory means that it is *prima facie* only with the traditional cartels (price-fixing, market-sharing, and so on) that competition authorities should be concerned.

The European Commission rejects this approach. It points out that the European market-place is inherently different from that of the United States. Whereas in the latter there are no real obstacles to trade within the country, in the EEC there are innate differences between the economies of the Member State which result in substantial barriers to entry. The Commission points to the legal, fiscal, currency, language, historical, and cultural differences between the EEC Member States and identifies these as obstacles that are not easily overcome in the way the Chicago economists believe. Translating this into enforcement policy, the Commission remains concerned with market structure, the vigilant control of dominance, and the methods by which companies acquire market power. This is not to say that the Commission will not change its spots. The emergence of a more genuine European market after 1992, the increasing globalization of the economy which shifts corporate vision from a European arena to a world arena, and the creeping influence of Chicago School ideas: all these factors, and others, may, in due course, result in a more minimalist approach to enforcement. Conversely, the burgeoning market economies of Eastern Europe, the prospect of new applications for membership of the EEC, and the costs of modernizing former centrally planned economies could give rise to problems of integration redolent of those confronting economists and politicians in the 1950s and 1960s.

15

The Relevance of Economics for the Application of Articles 85 and 86

In Chapter 14 it was explained how the aims and objectives of competition policy in the EEC were made up of an amalgam of political and economic constituents. In this chapter the intention is to explain how basic economic principles have become essential tools in the competition lawyer's armoury.

A simple example reveals how the economic context of a marketing practice becomes the determining factor in deciding whether that practice is anti-competitive (and hence illegal) or not. Consider the position of a company which charges its customers what are alleged to be excessive prices. If the company is a monopoly, then customers are forced to pay the prices charged or go without the goods or services in question. In such a situation there would be a good case for a competition authority to intervene in order to prevent continued exploitation of consumers by the monopolist. However, if the company is not a monopoly, there is a very much weaker case for intervention. The consumer who objects to the prices charged may seek an alternative supplier. In this latter case, the customer does not need protection from the competition authorities; the consumer may punish the over-pricing company by taking custom elsewhere. Thus it will be seen that the same practice (that is, setting a high price) may be harmful to the consumer in one economic context but not in another and therefore warrants legal control only in the monopolistic situation described. In essence it is the economic context that may determine legality.

In the text below are discussed the most important economic principles which affect competition law. In particular the following are examined:

1. The concentration spectrum and the relevance of market power;
2. The importance of entry barriers;
3. Actual and potential competition;
4. Inter- and intra-brand competition.

The Concentration Spectrum: The Relevance of Market Power

As is indicated by the example above, the attitude of competition authorities may depend upon the degree of market power held by the parties to the agreement or the company concerned. As a general rule, the more market power held by the parties or company concerned the less sympathetic will be the approach of the competition authorities; conversely, where companies hold little or no significant market power, there is no real reason why competition authorities should intervene. For the competition lawyer it is, therefore, important to be able to classify different market structures and draw legal implications from the classification. In considering this problem it is helpful to imagine market structure as a spectrum. This spectrum spans degrees of market 'concentration', that is, the amount of market power concentrated in the hands of a single company. On one side of the spectrum sits 'monopoly' power, where the market-place is dominated by a single undertaking; at the other end of the spectrum sits 'atomistic' or 'dispersed' market power, where the market-place is inhabited by a large number of different undertakings, none of which individually has the power to influence the market. Between the two extremes lie shades of market power which carry with them a range of different problems for competition authorities. For current purposes the following markers on the hypothetical spectrum will be considered: monopoly power and market dominance; duopoly; oligopoly; atomistic or dispersed.

MONOPOLY POWER AND MARKET DOMINANCE

Pure monopoly power, where a single company controls 100 per cent of the market, is relatively rare. It usually arises only where government confers the monopoly by statute, as in the case of state-owned (nationalized) industries, and thereby creates an absolute barrier to entry. In such cases the monopolist is cushioned from all sources of immediate competition. Indeed, it would be illegal for any third party to supply the goods or services that are the subject-matter of the monopoly. Given that monopolists are cushioned from competitive forces, certain tendencies may become evident: they may be technologically backward, since there is no spur of competition to encourage them to invest in new technology or undertake research and development; their product range and quality may be below par; or they may overcharge for their products or services. In the worst scenario the customer pays an excessive price for a sub-standard product. There are a number of cures for the ills of monopoly. Government may appoint a specialized regulatory agency to oversee the conduct of the monopolist.[1]

---

[1] In the UK, the Government has tended to crate regulatory bodies upon privatization.

Alternatively, it may apply competition rules stringently to the monopolist, punishing it, for example, for over-pricing with fines or price control measures.

An illustration of the application of competition rules to pure monopolists is to be found in the action commenced by the European Commission against British Leyland (BL) for excessive pricing.[2] The company enjoyed a state-created monopoly to issue certificates of conformity for left-hand drive vehicles. Initially, BL imposed a £25 charge for inspecting both right- and left-hand drive vehicles and granting the appropriate certificates. Subsequently, the charge was increased to £100 for individuals and £150 for dealers. Following criticism by the Commission, BL imposed a uniform £100 fee which was later (during proceedings) reduced to £50. The European Court held, on appeal by BL against the Commission decision that the company had abused its dominant position, that an abuse by a company in breach of the competition rules occurs: 'where it has an administrative monopoly and charges for its services fees which are disproportionate to the economic value of the service provided.'[3]

The term monopoly usually indicates absolute market power by a company *supplying* goods or services; where the company concerned is the sole *purchaser* of goods or services, then the term 'monopsony' is employed.

Dominance (discussed in Chapter 18) refers to the company which is so powerful in relation to its suppliers, competitors and customers that it may take commercial decisions without reference to the interests or pressures imposed by those other parties. However, despite its power the dominant company does have competitors, unlike the monopolist.

DUOPOLY

Duopoly describes those markets inhabited by two major players. The classic duopoly will be the market where two companies each supply 50 per cent of the demand though, in practice, an equal split of the market would be uncommon. Duopoly is in fact rare on a European scale, though it is relatively common in individual Member States. Indeed, the Monopolies and Mergers Commission (MMC) in the United Kingdom

Thus OFTEL (Office of Telecommunications) regulates British Telecom (BT) and other telecommunication companies; OFGAS (Office of Gas Regulation) regulates the gas-supply market, including British Gas plc; OFFER (Office of Electricity Regulation) regulates the privatized electricity industry, and in particular National Power and PowerGen, the successor companis to the now—defunct Central Electricity Generating Board (CEGB).

[2] See *British Leyland plc* v. *Commission*, Case 226/84, [1986] ECR 3263. See also *General Motors* v. *Commission*, Case 26/75, [1975] ECR 1367.

[3] 1986 ECR s.27. See also *General Motors v.* Commission, [1975] ECR 1367.

has considered many duopoly cases in such varied markets as white salt[4] and tampons.[5] The classic problem associated with duopoly is price leadership and followership. In this scenario one company (the price leader) will take the initiative in setting prices; the other company (the follower) follows suit. Theoretically, the more efficient company takes the lead, setting prices according to the dictates of its own cost structure. The less efficient company follows. Duopolistic markets can be competitive, but not infrequently a pattern of leadership and followership results in an unspoken non-aggression pact based upon comfortable profit margins. The end result can be prices set at supra-competitive levels.

OLIGOPOLY

This describes the market in which a small number of suppliers (or buyers, in which case the market is described as an oligopsony) supply the preponderant portion of demand. The problem associated with this market is 'mutual recognition of interdependence', which gives rise to 'conscious parallelism'. This refers to markets in which the incumbents are sensitive to the marketing of their rivals such that they must respond or lose market share. In a classic oligopoly the product is homogeneous (that is, uniform regardless of who produces it) and there is little prospect of new market entry. Take the petroleum market for illustration. Petrol supplied by different companies is for all practical purposes a substitutable product. Naturally, one would not substitute diesel for lead-free. However, within well-defined categories the motor-vehicle driver may 'fill up' at any service station regardless of brand. Price in this market is transparent, petrol stations advertise their prices on prominent hoardings by the roadside. Thus, petrol companies know that there is little consumer brand-loyalty and price is a major determinant of consumer decision-making. In a market such as this, where only a small number of well-established suppliers operate, it is unsurprising to learn that prices tend to be similar. Should one competitor attempt to increase market share by dropping prices, any gains from increased sales will, most likely, be short-lived given that rival suppliers will be forced to respond in kind in order to maintain their market share. In essence, a price reduction by one supplier will not lead to a significant increase in market share since the response rate of rivals in such a transparent market is rapid. The ultimate outcome of price cutting is that all producers sell at lower prices (and hence profit margins) but with the same market share. Over time suppliers may learn the folly of competition, and a tendency for real prices to remain static or

---

[4] Cmnd 9778 (1986).   [5] Cmnd 9705 (1986).

even increase develops. In the final outcome prices tend to rise to supra-competitive levels. Of critical importance in policy terms is the fact that, though prices may be set uniformly high and the producers act as if in concert, there is in fact no price-fixing agreement to attack.

Oligopolistic interdependence does not exist in every market inhabited by only a few suppliers. Economists explain that, for it to exist, other market conditions will invariably be present. These include: products that are homogeneous such that there is minimal distinction between different producers' products; high barriers to entry to the market, since if market access is easy the charging of high prices by producers will only encourage new entrants who will drive the price down; a relatively fixed level of demand (that is, low price elasticity of demand), such that an increase in price will not be offset by a corresponding decline in demand (motorists must still drive).

An early example of the relationship between oligopoly and price-fixing is to be found in the *Dyestuffs* case.[6] In that case the Commission investigated a suspected cartel in the market for aniline dyes. The evidence relied upon comprised a series of three general price-increases which occurred within a few days of each other in 1964, 1965, and 1967 between ten producers in different Member States. The producers held a combined market share of 80 per cent. The producers denied that they had agreed the price-rises and contended that the increases were the natural consequences of interdependent oligopoly pricing. The Commission rejected this explanation of the price-rises. They pointed to a number of factors which (in their eyes) constituted proof of collusion. In particular, they pointed out that the rates of individual price-increases were identical in all the Member States concerned with few exceptions; the price-increases were, again almost without exception, implemented on the same day; and the wording of the instructions given by the producers to their subsidiaries or representatives on the various markets were similar. The Commission stated:

'It is inconceivable that, without first meticulously working out an arrangement in concert, the major producers supplying the Common Market would have raised the price for the same products in large quantities, repeatedly and practically at the same time and at the same rate, and even in several countries, in which the market conditions for dyestuffs are different.'

To punish the producers for the cartel, the Commission imposed fines of 40,000 or 50,000 ECU (extremely modest by today's standards). The producers appealed to the Court of Justice, reiterating their argument that the parallel pricing was explicable by the oligopolistic nature of the market and not collusion.

The Commission, in a series of arguments before the Court, explained

---

[6] *ICI* v. *Commission*, Case 48/69, [1972] ECR 619.

in theoretical terms why the prices could not be referable to market conditions. They accepted that in certain circumstances parallel prices could be the consequences of the market structure. However, for this to occur the market would have to exhibit certain features: a small number of sellers with a history of interdependence; high fixed costs; a homogeneous product; transparency of prices; a limited short-term adaptability of capacity; a low price elasticity of demand; a market that was undergoing a period of depression. The Commission pointed out that the dyestuffs market did not exhibit these characteristics.

The Court upheld the Commission decision on its facts. They also accepted that, in certain market conditions, what could ostensibly appear to be price-fixing could be explained away as oligopolistic inter-dependence. However, the burden of proof of showing that parallel prices were not collusive lay on the defendants:

'[A] parallel course of conduct by the sellers raises a presumption of fact as to the existence of a concerted practice, unless, because of the special structure of the market, there is compelling economic force that determines a uniform course of conduct for the various enterprises.'

The Court stated further:

'Although parallel behaviour may not by itself be identified with a concerted practice, it may however amount to strong evidence of such a practice if it leads to conditions of competition which do not correspond to the normal conditions of the market, having regard to the nature of the product, the size and number of the undertakings, and the volume of the said market.'[7]

DISPERSED MARKETS

'Dispersed' or 'atomistic' markets exist at the competitive end of the spectrum. In these markets no single supplier or buyer can exert power over price. An increase in output by such a supplier will not result in any significant detriment to a rival supplier. In theory, in such a market there is little space for suppliers to raise prices since, with a large choice available, customers will rapidly switch from a high-priced to a lower-priced supplier. Again, theoretically, there will be no significant barriers either to entry or exit from the market. In terms of competition policy, authorities need have few concerns. A price-fixing cartel in such a market would be almost bound to fail. If five companies, out of fifty similar companies in the market, seek to raise prices by agreement, the consequence will not be the hoped-for increased profits but, rather, a decline in turnover as customers vote with their feet. Indeed, in these markets the relatively small size of the incumbents can often imply

---

[7] Ibid., para. 66.

inefficiency: scale economies are not realized; research and development is either not performed at all or duplicated wastefully; investment in new technology is a luxury that cannot be afforded. In essence, the consumer is not necessarily best served by such a small-scale market. Accordingly, competition policy may, in such circumstances, encourage certain types of co-operation where in more-concentrated markets it would be prescribed. In reality, markets rarely exhibit such classic characteristics. It is sometimes said that, when scrutinized closely, these seemingly model markets resemble clusters of micro-oligopolies. The grocery market was often referred to as showing this trend in the days before the rise of the major supermarket chains. In every locality there would be two or three small grocers' shops that would supply the local demand; customers would invariably obtain their produce from one of the local shops, rarely venturing out of the neighbourhood.

In reality, markets of the type described are extremely rare. More common would be the market inhabited by a significant number of firms with widely divergent market shares. Thus, for instance, there might exist ten firms with market shares between 0.5 per cent and 5 per cent; four firms with shares between 5 per cent and 15 per cent; and two firms with market shares exceeding 15 per cent. In such a market, the competition authorities may take the view that co-operation between the small companies was to be encouraged since it enabled them to compete effectively with the larger companies, thereby adding vigour to the market.[8] Conversely, there would be little prospect of agreements between the two larger companies being allowed.

The Importance of Entry Barriers

The subject of entry barriers is one exciting great debate amongst competition lawyers and economists. One school of thought (the so-called Chicago economists) attributes little significance to entry barriers; an opposing school (called, for the sake of convenience, the Brussels School) considers that barriers to entry are a central factor to be taken into consideration. The Chicago School claims that, in a modern 'global' economy, companies are big enough to overcome local obstacles; they can obtain the technology if necessary through licences, and the capital is available on the thriving Western banking risk and venture-capital markets. Therefore, entry barriers rarely exist as a genuine problem. The Brussels School, by contrast, says that in the EEC, entry barriers are inherent in the form of national differences in legal systems, currencies, language barriers, and cultural prejudices. Thus, entry barriers must be taken into account.

[8] See e.g. *Transocean Marine Paint Association* [1967] CMLR D9.

Stated bluntly for current purposes, an entry barrier may be defined as an obstacle to the entry of a new firm on to a market.[9] The significance of such barriers is that, if entry barriers are high and new entry therefore unlikely, the incumbent companies are protected from a source of competition, that is, the potential threat of a newcomer. Conversely, if there are few obstacles of significance hindering entry, then the incumbent companies must constantly be aware of the danger and this awareness may constitute a powerful incentive to keep prices low and the quality of service high.

It follows from the above that in a competition-law case an assessment of barriers to entry is vital. The party seeking to defend an agreement, for example a joint venture that is alleged to be anti-competitive, will endeavour to show that entry barriers are low, and the getting-together in the joint venture of two rival companies can hence pose no threat to competition. Those seeking to object to or challenge the joint venture will argue that entry barriers are high, and that the prospect of new entrants to invigorate competition in the market is limited. Depending upon the view of the entry barriers taken by the deciding authority (probably the European Commission), Article 85 may be applied strictly or liberally.

In considering economic obstacles to trade, barriers to expansion (as opposed to entry) should not be overlooked. These describe the obstacles experienced by a company which is already in the market but wishes to expand. In implementing this policy the company may encounter obstacles which are unrelated to the actual ability of the company to grow.

It is necessary to turn now to actual examples of barriers to entry. The text below operates upon the assumption, shared by the European Commission, that entry barriers often exist and can represent serious hindrances to competition. Principal examples of such entry barriers include: governmental laws and regulations; intellectual property rights; high levels of minimum capital requirements; over-capacity in the market; very strong brand loyalties enjoyed by existing companies.

GOVERNMENTAL LAWS AND REGULATIONS

If, pursuant to a particular national law, a single company is granted a monopoly right to supply a particular product or provide a specified service, then, *a fortiori*, an absolute barrier to entry exists. National law prohibits new entry; the protected monopolist may raise prices and

---

[9] Many other definitions exist. One states that an entry barrier is an obstacle encountered by a new entrant to the market that the incumbent undertaking did not have to face upon entry: see e.g. Stigler, *The Organization of Industry* (1968), p. 67.

provide inferior goods and services without fearing that its inefficiency will be punished by market forces.[10]

INTELLECTUAL PROPERTY RIGHTS

Intellectual property rights are exclusive rights conferred by law to prohibit certain acts by third parties. Thus, the holder of a patent may restrain in the courts a third party who manufactures the product covered by the patent.[11] Naturally, not every patent-holder enjoys total market power; there may be many different methods of producing a single product and a patent may only protect one such method. Alternatively, there may be many different pieces of machinery which achieve the same result and a patent will only cover one such piece of equipment. Barriers to entry may hence derive from patents, copyright, design rights, and trade-marks. Likewise, the existence of so-called 'know-how'—unpatented, secret technical information—may create an entry barrier if its possession is important to enter the market.

HIGH LEVELS OF MINIMUM CAPITAL REQUIREMENTS

Whilst the ready availability of risk capital in the western world can make financial obstacles to entry surmountable, there are many markets where the capital cost of entry is so substantial that only large corporations can afford to participate. Cost may be prohibitive, for example, in many engineering and chemical sectors, where the cost of plant is enormous. The level of required capital often operates cumulatively with other factors such as the projected return on capital. Why incur very heavy initial expenditure if profit-projections are moderate or low? Surely there will be a better use to which the capital may be put.[12]

OVER-CAPACITY IN THE MARKET

However easy the conditions of entry to a market may otherwise be, few companies will risk entering a market with over-capacity. Where supply exceeds demand then plant will lie idle or will be utilized at only a

---

[10] See e.g. *Italy* v. *Commission*, Case 41/83, [1985] ECR 873 (concerning the status of British Telecom prior to privatization); *Centre Belge d'Études de Marché Télé Marketing* v. *CLT*, Case 311/84, [1986] 2 CMLR 558.

[11] See e.g. *Hugin* v. *Commission*, Case 22/78, [1979 ECR 1869 (UK law on design copyright); *BRT-Tetrapak*, OJ 1988, L 272/27 (patents), on appeal Case 327/88.

[12] See e.g. *United Brands* v. *Commission*, Case 27/76, [1978] ECR 207. However, some economists argue that access to capital should not be treated as an entry barrier; see e.g. Bain, *Barriers to New Competition* (1956), Chap. 5.

fraction of its full capacity, and prices will be depressed (along, of course, with profit-margins) as sellers offer discounts in order to off-load surplus supplies. In such a scenario there is little to attract a corporate investor looking for a market in which investment offers acceptable returns. In the EEC, various sectors of heavy industry have experienced or are currently experiencing over-capacity: shipbuilding and shipping generally, synthetic fibres, steel, various sectors of the chemical industry. Intense, low-cost competition from the Far East has in many instances devastated these traditional European trades.

Very Strong Brand Loyalties

Where incumbents enjoy strong brand loyalty engendered through intensive advertising and promotion, a new entrant faces the challenge of establishing a brand image to compete with the existing brands.[13] Successful entry depends not only on advertising expenditure but also upon more illusive criteria such as brand penetration, that is, the ability to catch and hold the consumer's attention.

Inter- and Intra-Brand Competition

Inter-brand competition is rivalry between different brands of a product, and therefore reflects competition between different companies. Thus, the competition between Coke and Pepsi is inter-brand competition. Intra-brand competition describes the competitive situation between different sellers of the same brand of product, for example, all retailers of Sony video-cassettes or all wholesalers of a particular brand of chocolate. Competition authorities use measurements of inter- and intra-brand competition as indices of the health of competition in a market. For example, in a monopolistic, duopolistic, or oligopolistic market (see above), inter-brand competition may be weak. However, intra-brand competition may be strong in these markets; a monopolist may organize its distribution-networks so that all its dealers have to compete vigorously with each other for sales. Economists suggest, however, that where inter-brand competition is weak there is little incentive for a supplier or manufacturer to operate a lean and efficient distribution-network, and intra-brand competition may likewise suffer, to the detriment of the end-user. Conversely, economists suggest that where inter-brand competition is strong, suppliers will focus upon providing customers with a high-quality service; prices will be low; after-sales services will be more extensive; advertising and promotion will be more effective; better trained staff will be employed in better fitted-out shops, and so on.

[13] See *United Brands*, ibid., paras. 91–4.

In considering inter- and intra-brand competition one comes naturally to the distinction between commercial and trading practices which are 'horizontal' and 'vertical'. Put bluntly, a horizontal agreement is one between companies at the same level of trade, competitors in the ordinary sense of the word. Thus, a price-fixing agreement between rival manufacturers is a horizontal arrangement. A vertical agreement is one between companies at different levels of trade. For instance, an agreement between a manufacturer and a wholesaler or a dealer is a vertical agreement. In the context of inter- and intra-brand competition, horizontal agreements primarily involve restrictions on inter-brand competiton, whilst vertical agreements involve restrictions upon intra-brand competition.

Translating the above into legal policy is not easy. Our hypothetical economist would contend that the competition authorities need not intervene in the distribution-networks of suppliers unless the supplier in question has significant market power, that is, in cases where inter-brand competition is low. In EEC competition law this approach to regulation has found little favour. Traditionally, the European Commission and the Court of Justice have looked with some suspicion upon certain types of contractual clauses in distribution arrangements for goods, irrespective of the market power held by the supplier. Over the years this attitude has changed, though EEC competition law has not yet reached the position current in the USA. In *US* v. *Arnold Schwin & Co*,[14] the Supreme Court held, in a case brought by the government in respect of a distribution agreement which contained territorial and customer restrictions,[15] that such restriction were *per se* violations of the US anti-trust legislation. These were restrictions on intra-brand competition and were not to be tolerated. Ten years later, the Supreme Court overturned *Schwinn* in *Continental TV Inc* v. *GTE Sylvania Inc*,[16] and held that non-price vertical restraints could be legal; all depended upon the surrounding circumstances. Following *Sylvania*, vertical agreements are, as a general rule, only frowned upon where the supplier enjoys market power.

The liberal attitude prevailing in the US has found no counterpart in the EEC, where the contractual clauses which may be included in typical vertical agreements, such as exclusive dealing and purchasing agreements, and franchise agreements, are highly controlled by the Commission, to the extent that specific regulations have been adopted with regard to these forms of contract. These legislative measures are discussed in later chapters.

[14] 388 US 365 (1967).
[15] That is, a restriction on the supplier appointing more dealers in a territory; and a clause controlling who the dealer could sell to.
[16] 433 US 36 (1977).

Before leaving the topic of vertical arrangements, one final issue should be introduced. This is the problem of the so-called 'free-rider'. Under the standard case-law of both the Court and the Commission, it is a serious infringement of Article 85 for a supplier to grant a dealer a water-tight exclusive territory. Thus, what are termed 'export bans' are almost invariably strictly prohibited. A dealer may not be given a contract which provides that he may only sell to end-users situated in the exclusive territory, and therefore may not sell to buyers located outside the territory, buyers who come into the territory to purchase and then export the goods, and buyers located inside the territory who intend to take them outside the territory for resale. Under traditional EEC thinking, distribution-systems of this ilk are often set up by suppliers along national lines, that is, one dealer per Member State. To the Eurocrat this is the re-erection of barriers to trade between Member States that provisions such as Articles 30 (free movement of goods), 52 (freedom of establishment), and 59 (freedom to provide services) of the Treaty of Rome have sought to prohibit when introduced by national governments.

In this context sits the free-rider problem. The authorized dealer of a particular supplier views the problem thus: the dealer, in compliance with obligations in his contract, incurs the cost of opening a high-quality retail outlet, hiring qualified staff, undertaking advertising, and so on. The costs are relatively high, and this is reflected in the ultimate selling price. Given that the supplier imposes similar obligations on his dealers across the EEC, overall selling prices may necessarily be fairly high. However, because costs vary across the Community, the price at which the goods are sold is not uniform. A buyer goes to the retailer in a lower-priced country, say Greece or Portugal, and buys very large quantities of the goods. He transports them to a high-priced country, say Germany or France, and sells the products there in his low-quality, under-staffed, no frills shop at a price which is 20 per cent below that of the authorized dealer. Customers of the product visit the authorized dealer to try out the product in the showrooms and exploit the expertise and knowledge of sales staff; they then go to the no-frills retailer to purchase the product at the discounted price. To the authorized dealer, the parallel importer is 'free-riding' on the high level of sales services he provides. In the event that this parallel line of imports from Portugal or Greece persists, the authorized dealer may be unable to maintain the level of customer services required by the contract. The European Commission views this scenario through a different optic. They contend that the parallel importer provides a valuable service to the consumer by creating an additional and effective source of intra-brand competition which tends to keep prices down.

Actual and Potential Competition

The final general concept that requires some consideration is that of actual and potential competition. Actual competition is a measurement of the degree of competition that *de facto* prevails in the market-place. It may be gauged by, for instance, an appraisal of market shares. Potential competition focuses, not upon existing competitors, but, upon the effect that the threat of new entry to the market exerts upon existing companies. If entry barriers are low then there may exist a high level of potential competition; conversely, high entry barriers connote low or non-existent potential competition. The relevance of potential competition to a competition lawyer is that it materially affects the argument as to whether a particular agreement is restrictive of competition. For example, the European Commission has stated[17] that only joint ventures between actual or potential competitors fall within Article 85(1) of the Treaty of Rome. If X and Y are not potential competitors, then a joint venture between them will not be subject to the competition rules *per se*. Potential competition is also used to determine whether a company is dominant for the purposes of Article 86 of the Treaty. For illustration, a company may supply 75 per cent of the market, but given that entry barriers are very low, that company may be very conscious that it must keep prices down and the quality of its services high in order to retain its market position. That company may not be dominant, within the meaning of Article 86, because it cannot act independently of the threat of new entry. Potential competition acts as a effective disciplining force.

[17] See *Thirteenth Commission Competition Report* (1983), para. 55.

16

AGREEMENTS RESTRICTIVE OF COMPETITION

Article 85

Article 85 of the Treaty of Rome reads as follows:

'1. The following shall be prohibited as incompatible with the common market: all agreements between undertakings, decisions by associations of undertakings and concerted practices which may affect trade between Member States and which have as their object or effect the prevention, restriction or distortion of competition within the common market, and in particular those which:

(a) directly or indirectly fix purchase or selling prices or any other trading conditions;

(b) limit or control production, markets, technical development, or investment;

(c) share markets or sources of supply;

(d) apply dissimilar conditions to equivalent transactions with other trading parties, thereby placing them at a competitive disadvantage;

(e) make the conclusion of contracts subject to acceptance by the other parties of supplementary obligations which, by their nature or according to commercial usage, have no connection with the subject of such contracts.

2. Any agreements or decisions prohibited pursuant to this Article shall be automatically void.

3. The provisions of paragraph 1 may, however, be declared inapplicable in the case of:

—any agreement or category of agreements between undertakings;

—any decision or category of decision by associations of undertakings;

—any concerted practice or category of concerted practices;

which contributes to improving the production or distribution of goods or to promoting technical or economic progress, while allowing consumers a fair share of the resulting benefit, and which does not:

(a) impose on the undertakings concerned restrictions which are not indispensable to the attainment of these objectives;

(b) afford such undertakings the possibility of eliminating competition in respect of a substantial part of the products in question.'

In order to demonstrate the scope of Article 85 it is necessary to consider the constituent parts in detail. This chapter is of necessity devoted to a formalist analysis of the statutory language. Ensuing chapters which consider actual commercial practices and transactions revert to a more policy-based assessment of the currents and policies underlying competition policy.

Article 85(1)

In the text below the following elements of Article 85(1) are examined:-
1. 'agreement';
2. 'decisions by associations of undertakings';
3. 'concerted practices';
4. 'between undertakings';
5. 'may affect trade between Member States';
6. 'object or effect';
7. 'prevention, restriction or distortion of competition';
8. 'within the common market'.

1. 'AGREEMENT'

Article 85(1) does not apply unless there is an 'agreement', 'decision by an association of undertakings' or a 'concerted practice'. 'Agreement' is to be widely construed as including not only formally concluded, legally binding documents but also oral contracts and so-called 'gentlemen's agreements' or those which are binding in honour only.[1] Agreements whereby only one of the parties voluntarily agrees to restrict its freedom of conduct are likewise caught,[2] as are agreements where the restriction of conduct is not voluntary. An agreement may be inferred from the facts and circumstances of a case and notwithstanding the denials and protestations of the parties.[3]

2. 'DECISIONS BY ASSOCIATIONS OF UNDERTAKINGS'

These primarily cover the activities of trade associations and other collective or representative bodies.[4] It is immaterial whether the body enjoys legal personality[5] or, even, whether it is entrusted with the performance of a public function or task.[6] An association of associations

---

[1] See e.g. *ACF Chemiefarma* v. *Commission*, Case 41/69, [1970] ECR 661.
[2] See e.g. *Franco-Japanese Ballbearings*, OJ 1974, L 343/19, [1975] 1 CMLR D8.
[3] See e.g. *National Panasonic*, OJ 1982, L 354/28, [1983] 1 CMLR 497; *Tepea* v. *Commission*, Case 28/77, [1978] ECR 1391, 1412 *et seq.*
[4] See e.g. *Fedetab*, Joined Cases 209–15, 218/78, [1980] ECR 3125.
[5] See e.g. *Cecimo*, OJ 1969 L 69/13.
[6] See e.g. *Pabst & Richarz/BNIA*, OJ 1976 L 231/24.

(for example, a Pan-European Federation comprising all the national trade associations) is equally an 'association'.[7] The concept of a decision is also to be construed widely so as to include not only decisions binding on members but also recommendations to members, since these may influence members to act in a certain way regardless of their non-coercive nature.[8]

3. 'CONCERTED PRACTICES'

This concept brings within the prohibition in Article 85(1) informal arrangements which do not fall within the meaning of 'agreement' or 'decision of association of undertakings'. To this extent a 'concerted practice' is something of a sweeping-up provision. The classic definition of a concerted practice is that given by the Court in *ICI* v. *Commission*[9] (the dyestuffs case), where it stated that the phrase was used in the Treaty so as to bring within Article 85: 'a form of co-ordination between undertakings which, without having reached the stage where an agreement properly so called has been concluded, knowingly substitutes practical co-operation between them for the risks of competition.' A critical question for competition policy has been whether oligopolistic interdependence constitutes a concerted practice. The Court in the *ICI* case denied that it does. This important issue is dealt with in greater depth elsewhere so it need not be pursued here further. In terms of what is required in order to establish a concerted practice, decisions of the Commission suggest that evidence will be sought of contact or communication between the parties, together with evidence that these contacts or communications had the object or effect of influencing commercial conduct on the market. In determining whether a concerted practice exists or not, the Commission is required to take account of the characteristics of the market.[10] By this is meant that the Commission must consider whether the parallel behaviour being investigated is explicable as an independently derived natural response to the market by the undertakings concerned as opposed to a consensus between the undertakings as to the way to behave. Only if the parallel behaviour derives from the latter is there a concerted practice.

---

[7] See e.g. *Cecimo*, n. 5 above.

[8] See e.g. *Verband der Sachversicherer e.V* v. *Commission*, Case 45/85, [1987] ECR 405; [1988] 4 CMLR 264.

[9] Case 48/69, [1972] ECR 619, 655, para. 64. See also *Suiker Unie* v. *Commission*, Case 40/73, [1975] ECR 1663; *Musique Diffusion Française* v. *Commission*, Cases 100/80 *et seq.*, [1983] ECR 1825.

[10] *Suiker Unie* (n. 9 above), paras. 26–8.

4. 'BETWEEN UNDERTAKINGS'

For Article 85(1) to apply there must be an agreement etc 'between undertakings'. The use of the word 'between' indicates, of course, that there must be at least two undertakings concerned. Whilst this statement sounds fatuous, it is an important one when an agreement between a parent company and a subsidiary is in question. Is the parent/subsidiary one or two undertakings? Before answering this question it is convenient to consider in broad terms what is understood by 'undertaking'. The concept is to be construed broadly to embrace all natural and legal persons performing economic activity. The term includes public companies, limited companies, partnerships, trade associations, co-operatives, sole traders, public trading corporations, non-profit making bodies, and so on. Individuals (natural persons) may be undertakings provided they perform economic activities on their own account. Thus barristers, opera singers,[11] consultants,[12] inventors,[13] may all constitute 'undertakings'. Conversely, employees are not undertakings.[14] Some doubt exists as to the position of trade unions, particularly in so far as their actual union activities are concerned. Although industrial action has a profound impact upon competition in the market, it has traditionally been assumed by competition authorities in western economies that such activities should fall outside the rules for obvious political reasons.[15] The Commission, however, has accepted that the TGWU has *locus standi* to submit a formal complaint to it, though simply because a union has *locus standi* to complain does not necessarily imply that it can itself be the subject of a complaint.[16] An association of self-employed persons is an 'undertaking'.[17]

Turning now to the unanswered question: is a parent/subsidiary agreement concluded between one or two undertakings? Such an agreement does not fall within Article 85(1) provided the parent and subsidiary constitute, as a matter of fact, a single economic unit. For this to be the case an examination of the facts must indicate that the subsidiary has no independence from the parent, that is, may not

---

[11] See e.g. *RAI/Unitel*, OJ 1978 L 157/39, [1978] 3 CMLR, 306; see also *Twelfth Commission Competition Report* (1983), para. 90.

[12] See e.g. Dr Reuter in *Reuter/BASF*, OJ 1976, L 254/40, [1976] 2 CMLR D44.

[13] See e.g. Mr Beyrard in *AOIP/Beyrard*, OJ 1976, L 6/8, [1976] 1 CMLR D14; Mr Moris in *Vaessen/Morris*, OJ 1979, L 19/32, [1979] 1 CMLR 511; and Mr Watts and his 'Dust Bug' in *Tepea* v. *Commission*, Case 28/77, [1978] ECR 1391.

[14] *Suiker Unie* (see n. 9 above), p. 2007, para. 539.

[15] But cf. Section 79, Fair Trading Act 1973. See in particular the investigation by the Monopolies and Mergers Commission (MCC) into 'Labour Practices in TV and Film-making', Cmnd 666 (1989).

[16] See BP/TGWU *Llandarcy Refinery*, Fifteenth Commission Competition Report (1985), para. 44.

[17] See e.g. *EATE Levy* OJ 1985, L 219/35.

determine its own course of action.[18] In practice, it is very rare indeed for members of the same corporate group not to be considered as one, and exceptional facts would be required to dislodge what is a strong presumption.

5. 'MAY AFFECT TRADE BETWEEN MEMBER STATES'[19]

For Article 85 to apply, an agreement or concerted practice must 'affect trade between Member States'.[20] If no such effect exists, then EEC rules do not apply to an agreement and it is therefore only where national competition rules exist that the agreement is subject to any competition-law control at all. Thus, the words constitute a rule for determining the jurisdiction of the Community.[21]

It is necessary to consider separately the meaning of 'affect' and 'trade', dealing with the latter first.

'Trade' is to be interpreted broadly, and embraces all forms of economic activity.

In *Société Technique Minière* v. *Maschinenbau Ulm*,[22] the Court of Justice held that for Article 85 to apply: 'it must be possible on the basis of a set of objective factors of law or of fact that the agreement in question may have an influence, direct or indirect, actual or potential, on the pattern of trade between Member States.' In *Windsurfing International* v. *Commission*,[23] the Court of Justice held that in determining whether there is an effect upon trade one examines the agreement as a whole, so that if the agreement as a whole affects trade then it is irrelevant that individual restrictions might not do. In other cases, the Court has extended the scope of the words such that many agreements now clearly fall within the jurisdiction of the Commission. Thus, an agreement affecting a single Member State alone affects inter-State trade,[24] as does an agreement which relates to a raw material which, although not affecting inter-State trade itself, is incorporated into another product

[18] *Centraform* v. *Sterling Drug*, Case 15/74, [1974] ECR 1147; *Hydrothern* v. *Compact*, Case 170/83, [1984] ECR 2999.

[19] See the detailed treatment of this subject in Whish, *Competition Law* (1989), pp. 242–50.

[20] Given that, by virtue of Article 227, the Treaty of Rome applies to the Member States and to the French overseas departments and the European territories whose external relations is the responsibility of a Member State, Articles 85 and 86 probably apply also to those additional territories covered by Article 227.

[21] See e.g. *Consten and Grundig* v. *Commission*, Cases 56 and 58/64, [1966] ECR 299, 341; *Hugin* v. *Commission*, Case 22/78, [1979] ECR 1869, 1899.

[22] Case 56/65, [1966] ECR 235.

[23] Case 193/83, [1986] ECR 611.

[24] See e.g. *Vereeniging van Cementhandelaren* v. *Commission*, Case 8/72, [1972] ECR 977. See also *Cutsforth* v. *Mansfield Inns*, [1986] 1 CMLR 1; and *Holleran & Evans* v. *Thwaites*, [1989] [2] CMLR [917].

which is the subject of inter-State trade.[25] Agreements, the subject matter of which sits in close proximity to an EEC border, are especially prone to affect inter-State trade.[26] A *de minimis* rule applies such that not every effect upon trade is sufficient to trigger Article 85; the effect must be appreciable.[27] Thus, in *Megaphone* v. *British Telecom*[28] it was held, in interlocutory proceedings on affidavit evidence only, that a decision by British Telecommunications Plc to disconnect from the telephone network companies which provided so-called 'chatline' and 'message' services over the phone was not liable to affect inter-state trade sufficiently to activate Article 86.

In order to afford practical guidance to undertakings, the Commission has issued a non-binding Notice on Agreements of Minor Importance.[29] Under this Notice the Commission provides, as a rule of thumb, that an agreement does not fall within Article 85(1) where: (i) the goods and services the subject of the agreement do not represent more than 5 per cent of the total market for such goods or services in the area of the Common Market affected by such goods; *and* (ii) the aggregate turnover of the participating undertakings does not exceed 200 million ECU. It is to be noted that the tests are cumulative in that *both* must be satisfied if Article 85 is to be escaped. Thus, an agreement between two giants concerning a product in respect of which their combined market share was 0.1 per cent would not benefit from the Notice. Likewise, an agreement between two corporate minnows in respect of a product (perhaps in a very specialised, niche market) for which they had a 10 per cent market share would be outside the safe harbour of the Notice. Given that this element of Article 85 is jurisdictional, it will not surprise the reader to learn that the Commission frequently seeks to minimize the importance of the words and argue that many ostensibly local agreements may have indirect economic effects on inter-State trade. Clearly this approach expands the Commission's political remit. Conversely, national courts tend to be more stringent in their requirement that hard evidence be adduced to prove the actual effect on trade.

6. 'OBJECT OR EFFECT'

The inclusion of both 'object' *and* 'effect' makes it clear that Article 85 applies to both an agreement whereby the parties intended to restrict competition but failed to achieve their objective and one in which the parties sought a legitimate aim but in so doing innocently restricted

---

[25] *BNIC* v. *Clair*, Case 123/83, [1985] ECR 391.

[26] See e.g. *AEG Telefunken* v. *Commission*, Case 107/82, [1983] ECR 3151.

[27] See e.g. *Erauw Jacquery* v. *La Hesbignonne Société Co-operative*, Case 27/87, [1988] ECR 1969 [1988] 4 CMLR 576.

[28] (1988) QBD, unreported judgment of Drake J.

[29] For the latest version, see OJ 1986, C 231/2.

competition. The Treaty thus allows the Commission, as the relevant authority, to intervene at an early stage to pre-empt harm to the market-place.[30] The analysis of the effect of an agreement requires a consideration of all the economic and legal circumstances.[31]

7. 'Prevention, Restriction or Distortion of Competition'

The three words are disjunctive. In reality there is little difference between conduct that prevents or restricts or distorts competition. It has been held by the Court that competition of both a horizontal and vertical nature is caught.[32] Thus, Article 85 embraces a price-fixing or market-sharing agreement between competitors (that is, a horizontal agreement) and an exclusive dealing agreement between a manufacturer and a dealer or an intellectual property licence between a licensor and licensee (that is, a vertical agreement).

The main debate over these words has centred upon what (as a result of transatlantic phrase borrowing) is termed the 'rule-of-reason' approach to the words.[33] Put briefly, the rule-of-reason approach eschews an approach which condemns a particular type of clause as automatically restrictive of competition. Instead, to apply the rule-of-reason approach one examines the overall aim of the agreement in question and asks whether that aim is restrictive of competition. If it is not (that is, it is either pro-competitive or neutral of competition) then one considers whether the clauses in the agreement are necessary to achieve that aim. Again, if they are, then they cannot be restrictive, preventive, or distortive of competition; they are the necessary building-blocks for the construction of a project which is not harmful to competitive forces.

The Court has, without using the phrase 'rule of reason', adopted this approach on a number of occasions. For example, in *Remia* v. *Nutricia*[34] the Court was requested to rule on the application of Article 85 to restrictive covenants in an agreement for the sale of assets. Such clauses are, of course, extremely common throughout business. When a vendor of a company sells a business he will invariably agree to a clause being inserted in the sale agreement whereby he (the vendor) undertakes not to compete with the business being sold for a set period of years and within a fixed geographical area. The Court of Justice accepted the

---

[30] See e.g. *VdS* v. *Commission*, Case 45/85, [1988] 4 CMLR 264, para. 39—object alone sufficient; see also *Société Technique Minière* v. *Maschinenbau Ulm*, Case 56/65, [1966] ECR 235, 249.

[31] *Brasserie de Haecht* v. *Wilkin*, Case 23/67, [1967] ECR 407.

[32] *Consten and Grundig* v. *Commission*, Cases 56, 58/64, [1966] ECR 299.

[33] See Green, 'Article 85 in Perspective: Stretching Jurisdiction, Narrowing the Concept of a Restriction and Plugging a Few Gaps' (1988), 9 ECLR 10; Whish & Sufrin, 'Article 85 and the Rule of Reason' (1987), 7 YEL 1; Korah, 'EEC Competition Policy—Legal Form or Economic Efficiency' (1986), 39 CLP 85.

[34] Case 42/84, [1985] ECR 2545.

orthodox wisdom regarding such clauses, that is, that they were necessary to enable the goodwill in the business to be fully transferred to the buyer (in the absence of such a clause the vendor could set up in rivalry with the business and retain much of his old goodwill), and therefore held that a reasonable restrictive covenant was not subject to Article 85(1). In *Pronuptia de Paris* v. *Schillgallis*,[35] the Court held that franchise agreements were, generally speaking, pro-competitive (or at worst neutral of competition), and therefore that all the clauses (whether ostensibly restrictive or not) necessary to enable the franchise to operate fell outside Article 85(1).[36]

At the time of writing it is difficult to assess the status of the rule-of-reason doctrine. Undoubtedly it assumes a growing importance but, equally undoubtedly, there remain areas of Commission policy where a more rigid attitude prevails; the law relating to exclusive distribution is one such example.

8. 'WITHIN THE COMMON MARKET'

There is no doubt that agreements between undertakings located within the Common Market fall under Article 85, but what of agreements between undertakings within or outside the EEC which have as their focal point trade outside the Community? What if such agreements have residual effects upon the market in the Community?

It has been evident from numerous Commission decisions in the past that the existence of a non-Community ingredient in an agreement does not automatically result in jurisdiction being excluded. Thus, an agreement to export goods to a third (non-EEC) state coupled to a ban on re-export to the EEC may infringe Article 85 if there exists a realistic possibility of re-export. Usually no such prospect exists, since carriage and customs duties would eradicate any price differential which could have made re-export attractive.[37] Agreements between Community and third-country parties to restrict imports will infringe Article 85(1)[38] and

---

[35] Case 161/84, [1986] ECR 353.

[36] See also *Nungesser* v. *Commission*, Case 258/78, [1982] ECR 2015 (certain restrictive clauses in licences of plant breeders' rights necessary to encourage licensee to take the economic and commercial risk of adopting a new and therefore untried technology); *Coditel* v. *Cine Vog Films No. 2*, Case 262/81, [1982] ECR 3381 (certain ostensibly restrictive clauses in a copyright licence of a film fell outside Article 85 since they enabled the licensor to calculate the royalties he could expect from a film-showing and thereby went to an essential of copyright, viz., the right to a fair reward for creative effort).

[37] See e.g. *BBC Brown Boveri—NGK*, OJ 1988, [*], where an export ban on a Japanese company selling high-technology sodium batteries to the EEC was held to infringe Article 85(1) because a line of trade did exist for this product despite the distance and customs barriers.

[38] See e.g. *Re Franco-Japanese Ballbearings*, [1975] 1 CMLR D8; *Taiwanese Mushrooms*, [1975] 1 CMLR D83; *Aluminium Imports from Eastern Europe*, [1987] 3 CMLR 813.

will, if the products in question are considered to be of importance, be considered serious violations justifying fines.[39]

Attempts to impose the jurisdiction of the Community upon non-residents inevitably gives rise to prickly questions of diplomacy.[40] The question of the extraterritorial application of Community law has been considered judicially on very few occasions. In the *Dyestuffs* case[41] the Commission had imposed fines upon EEC and non-EEC producers of dyestuffs for alleged price-fixing. Three of the companies penalized—Geigy, Sandoz, and ICI—were (at that time) non-EEC companies. The question of jurisdiction over such companies was raised in the appeal before the Court, where it was held that jurisdiction was founded. The Court ruled that the parents and subsidiaries in question constituted a single economic undertaking. Thus, the fact that a non-EEC parent has a subsidiary within the EEC was sufficient to justify applying Article 85. Jurisdiction therefore depends on the parent's ability to control the subsidiary, which ability must be established by the surrounding facts.[42]

The *Dyestuffs* case did not address four-square the so-called 'effects doctrine', which preaches that jurisdiction is founded upon simple proof of a non-*de minimis* effect upon competition within the EEC.[43] In the most recent case on extraterritoriality—*Wood Pulp*[44]—the Court was confronted with appeals by forty-three producers of wood-pulp, none of whom was incorporated within the EEC, against a Commission decision prohibiting a price-fixing agreement and imposing fines. The Commission, in its decision, ruled that jurisdiction existed because the agreement exerted effects within the EEC. The Court held, by reference to the accepted tenets of international law, that, since the agreement had been 'implemented' in the EEC, Article 85 applied. Implementation could take effect as a result of the existence and operation of subsidiaries, branches, agencies, sub-agencies, and so on. Thus, the operation upon the territory of the EEC of the companies concerned in the form of agents and branches, and so on, gave the Community the territorial nexus that, under ordinary private international law, founded jurisdiction. On this basis there was no need for the Court to rule upon the effects doctrine.[45]

[39] See e.g. *Siemens—Fanuc*, [1988] 4 CMLR 948 (numerical tools).

[40] See generally Neale and Stephens, *International Business and National Jurisdiction* (1988).

[41] Cases 48/69 etc., [1972] ECR 619.

[42] See, for another case where this test has been applied, *Continental Can*, [1972] CMLR D11 (Commission decision, subsequently appealed to Court). See generally, Barack, *The Application of the Competition Rules of the EEC to Enterprises and Arrangements External to the Common Market* (1981).

[43] The Court hinted its approval in *Bequelin* v. *GL Import-Export*, Case 22/71, [1971] ECR 949.

[44] *A. Ahlström Oy* v. *Commission*, Cases 89, 104, 114, 116–17, 125–9/85, [1988] ECR (not yet reported).

[45] For commentary upon the case, see Mann, 'The Public International Law of

The real test will come when the Court is faced with an entirely external agreement with no physical nexus with the Community which none the less exerts restrictive effects within the EEC.

Article 85(2)

Pursuant to Article 85(2) all agreements prohibited by Article 85(1) are automatically void. Despite the wording of the provision the Court of Justice has held that it is only the offending clauses in the agreement which are avoided and further that it is for national courts to determine the legal significance of the fact that certain clauses are void.[46]

In practice, although parties can be fined by the Commission for entering illegal agreements, the real problem is the unenforceability of the agreement from a commercial point of view. Many legal advisers, when asked by their clients whether they should notify their agreements, evaluate the agreement to determine whether the invalidity of a particular (suspect) clause would benefit their client or the other side. If, upon consideration, it appears that invalidity would benefit the client, then the consequence of nullity may not be so problematic.

The question thus arises of the consequences in English law of the application of Article 85(2) to an agreement. The first point to note is that Articles 85 and 86 are directly effective and may, therefore, be pleaded as either sword or shield in national courts.[47] In English law, the contractual rules of severance govern the effectiveness of illegal agreements. In broad terms, if the offending clauses are severable, the agreement stands; conversely, if the offending clauses are not severable, the agreement falls in its entirety. How does one determine whether a clause is severable? In *Chemidus Wavin* v. *TERI*,[48] the Court of Appeal held that the 'blue pencil' test applies such that:

'In applying Article 85 to an English contract, one may well have to consider whether, after the excisions required by the Article of the Treaty have been made from the contract, the contract could be said to fail for lack of consideration or on

Restrictive Trade Practices in the European Court of Justice' (1989), 38 ICLQ 375; Lowe, 'International Law and the Effects Doctrine in the European Court of Justice' (1989), 48 CLJ 9; Whish, *Competition Law*, Chap. 11.

[46] *Consten and Grundig* v. *Commission*, Case 58/64, [1966] ECR 299, 392; *Sociéte de Vente de Ciments et Betons de l'Est S.A.* v. *Kerpen and Kerpen*, Case 319/82, [1983] ECR 4173.

[47] See generally, Green, *Commercial Agreements and Competition Law: Practice and Procedure in the UK and EEC* (1986), pp. 299 *et seq.*; Whish, *Competition Law*, pp. 268 *et seq.* Article 85 is enforceable in actions where all the usual remedies may be sought: declarations, injunctions, damages. It is of coure also relevant to actions for judicial review.

[48] [1978] 3 CMLR 514 (CA); [1976] 2 CMLR 387 (Walton J.); see also *Alec Lobb Ltd* v. *Total Oil GB*, [1985] 1 All ER 503.

any other ground, or whether the contract would be so changed in its character as not to be the sort of contract that the parties intended to enter into at all.'[49]

Article 85(2) has been used on a number of occasions, and indeed is being used to an ever-increasing degree in national courts.[50] Numerous complex legal questions arise. For example, if an entire agreement is declared invalid, what are the rights of the parties to claim restitution? The classic position[51] is that parties may *not* recover money paid or goods delivered under an illegal contract void for public policy; the courts will not assist wrongdoers, that is, the participants in an illegal contract,[52] to rely upon their illegality before the courts.

Article 85(3)

Not every restrictive agreement necessarily warrants outright proscription. Thus, Article 85(3) provides a formula whereby restrictive agreements may be granted exemption from the prohibition in Article 85(1). In order to obtain exemption, undertakings who have entered into restrictive agreements must either make a formal application to the European Commission or must draft their agreements to comply with regulations which have been specifically drawn up by the Commission such that an agreement in compliance with the regulation automatically obtains exemption without the necessity for a formal application.[53]

In order to obtain exemption a number of conditions must be satisfied. According to Article 85(3) there are two positive and two negative conditions. The 'positive' conditions are:

1. that the agreement must contribute to improving the production or distribution of goods or to promoting technical or economic progress; and
2. that the agreement allows consumers a fair share of the resulting benefit.

The 'negative' conditions are:

1. that the agreement does not impose upon the undertakings concerned restrictions which are not indispensable to the attainment of these objectives; and
2. that the agreement does not afford the undertakings the possibility

---

[49] Ibid., at 519, 520 *per* Buckley LJ.

[50] The European Commission actively encourages resort to national courts as a method of enforcing competition law in circumstances where the Commission has inadequate administrative resources to deal with every case referred to it: see *Fifteenth Commission Competition Report* (1986), paras. 38 *et seq.*; *Sixteenth Report*, paras. 41, 42.

[51] See Goff and Jones, *Law of Restitution* (1986), Chap. 21.

[52] See e.g. the classic exposition in *Holman* v. *Johnson* (1775) 1 Cowp 341, 343 *per* Lord Mansfield.

[53] See Green, *Commercial Agreements*, p. 290; Whish, *Competition Law*, p. 253.

of eliminating competition in respect of a substantial part of the products in question.

To obtain exemption, both the positive and negative conditions must be satisfied, that is, the conditions are conjunctive, not disjunctive.

FIRST POSITIVE CONDITION

A glance at the wording of the first condition reveals alternative benefits which must be proven. Improvements in production[54] may derive from the combining of different technologies to create an improved technology, or lower production costs or a method of production less harmful to the environment. Improvements in distribution[55] include a more-efficient sales-and-marketing structure, improved pre- and post-sales service, a more secure line of supply, and so on. Technical progress[56] may entail higher-quality products, better or more effective technology, greater consumer safety. Economic progress[57] may involve the more rational use of productive capacity and intellectual property rights, a more structured or cost-effective approach to investment or research and development. It will be appreciated that the first condition permits parties to raise many arguments in support of their agreements.

SECOND POSITIVE CONDITION[58]

'Consumers' means not just 'customers' or end-users but anyone who acquires the goods or services. A motor-manufacturer may be the consumer of a component-parts producer; a chemical company may be the consumer of a producer of raw chemicals or feedstuff.

The Commission expects the benefits of an agreement (as per the first condition) to be passed on down the line. The parties to an agreement have the burden of proving that there is a reasonable probability of such benefits being passed on. If there is strong inter-brand competition upon the supplier, the Commission generally accepts that competitive pressures will ensure the passing-on of benefits.

It is not necessary to prove that all the benefit of an agreement will be passed on: only a 'fair' share need be transmitted to consumers.

[54] See e.g. *Vacuum Interrupters*, [1977] 1 CMLR D67; *Rolled Zinc*, [1983] 2 CMLR 285; *WANO Schwarzpulver*, (1979) 1 CMLR 403 (exemption refused); *Sopelem/Vickers*, (1978) 2 CMLR 146 (development of new technology, interchangeability of parts, improved quality of production).

[55] See e.g. *Campari*, (1978] 2 CMLR 397; *Gin and Whisky Distribution*, [1986] 2 CMLR 664.

[56] See e.g. *Henkel Colgate*, OJ 1972, L 14/14; *BP/Kellog*, [1986] 2 CMLR 619; *X-Open Group*, OJ 1987, L 35/36.

[57] See e.g. *United Reprocessors*, [1976] 2 CMLR D1; *International Energy Agency*, [1984] 2 CMLR 186, noted by Green (1984), E.L.Rev. 449.

[58] See e.g. *Re KEWA*, [1976] 2 CMLR D15; *United Reprocessors*, ibid. In the latter case the Commission referred to the phrase 'equitable participation in the resulting profit'.

FIRST NEGATIVE CONDITION[59]

The agreement must contain no superfluous restrictions; such restrictions as exist must be indispensable to the attainment of the benefits identified under the first positive condition. In practice, the parties to agreements may negotiate with the Commission over the utility of a specific clause in a contract and the view of the Commission will be coloured by the views of the parties, the views of any party who has complained, and the approach adopted to clauses of the type in question by the Commission and the Court of Justice in the past.

SECOND NEGATIVE CONDITION[60]

The agreement must not eliminate too much competition. If two undertakings, each with 30 per cent of the market, combine in an agreement, then competition has been eliminated by 30 per cent, that is, the percentage by which the two parties combined have reduced competition *inter se*. Thus, to the Commission, the greater the combined market-share of the parties, the greater the threat to competition. The question of market power has been considered at some length in Chapter 15 and that discussion need not be repeated here. It will be evident from that chapter that, in assessing whether competition has been unacceptably eliminated, the degree of residual competition (that is, competition elsewhere in the market) and the extent of barriers to entry (that is, as a barometer of potential competition) must be taken into account.

HOW TO OBTAIN EXEMPTION: AN OVERVIEW OF PROCEDURE

How do the parties to an agreement go about obtaining exemption? In practice there are two methods: (i) notify the agreement to the Commission; (ii) draft the agreement so that it complies with the terms of a block exemption. Both these methods will be examined in turn.

(i) Notification[61]

Parties to agreements to which Article 85 applies may[62] make a formal application—using Form A/B—to the Commission for either negative clearance or an exemption. Negative clearance is a formal decision of the Commission stating that Article 85(1) is inapplicable (and thereby is to

---

[59] See e.g. *Consten and Grundig*, [1964] CMLR 489, (Commission decision).

[60] See examples given in Green, *Commercial Agreements*, pp. 289–330.

[61] See Kerse, *Antitrust Procedure* (1989), for by far and away the best analysis of competition-law procedure.

[62] There is no legal requirement on the parties to notify: compare the position under the UK Restrictive Trade Practices Act 1976.

be distinguished formally from exemption). This might, for example, be because there is an insufficient effect upon trade between the Member States, or because the agreements and the clauses therein do not restrict, distort, or prevent competition, or the parties constitute a single undertaking and therefore there is no agreement 'between' undertakings. In Form A/B, the parties may also apply for an exemption and in submitting Form A/B the parties are required, *inter alia*, to make submissions of fact showing how the agreement satisfies the requirements of Article 85(3).

Whilst it is not the function of this text to focus upon the nuts and bolts of practice, it is none the less useful to consider, very briefly, the procedure that applies in such cases. The basic procedure[63] is set out in Regulation 17/62/EEC and this governs:

—notification;

—the power of the Commission to grant negative clearance or exemption, or to prohibit the continuance of infringements;

—the power of the Commission to undertake investigations into suspected violations, including the power to require the disclosure of information, to commence inquiries into sectors of industry, to undertake on-the-spot investigation ('dawn raids') at the premises of suspected infringers;

—the power to impose fines; and

—the procedure governing the hearing of parties before decisions are taken.

The procedure under Regulation 17/62/EEC has been fleshed out over the years as a result of general improvements in Commission procedures, often engendered by exhortations from the European Court that basic rights of the defence (such as *audi alteram partem*) must be respected.

From amongst the extensive powers held by the Commission, the power to fine is an effective weapon. The Commission has the power[64] to impose fines, by formal decision, of up to either 1 million ECU or 10 per cent of the turnover in the preceding business year of each of the undertakings participating in the infringement, whichever is the greater. An undertaking may be fined for a violation of the law which is either intentional or negligent. The 10 per cent attaches to the worldwide turnover of the entire group (that is, the 'undertaking') to which the infringer belongs, and is in relation to *all* goods and services produced or provided by the undertaking. Thus, it will be appreciated that the Commission has power to impose enormous fines. In practice, of course, fines are proportional to the gravity of the offence and,

---

[63] See Kerse, *Antitrust Procedure*, *passim*.
[64] See Article 15 of Regulation 17/62/EEC.

indeed, the European Court has an unfettered power to reduce fines upon appeal.

To return to notification: once the Commission has received a notification, it will examine the documents and arrive at an informal decision as to how to proceed. The Commission does not have sufficient resources to issue formal decisions in respect of the many hundreds of notifications received each year. Accordingly, it endeavours to issue formal decisions in priority cases only, such as those where fines are to be imposed, cases involving new principles or markets, or cases involving a point of public interest. In the vast majority of cases, however, no formal decision is adopted. Rather, the Commission sends to the parties an administrative letter—the so-called 'comfort letter'— which provides that the Commission intends to close the file on the case but, had it proceeded with the formal procedure, it would have been minded to grant exemption or negative clearance. The Commission may issue between 100 and 350 comfort letters a year but only between ten to thirty formal decisions.[65]

(ii) Block Exemptions

The second means of obtaining exemption is to ensure that the agreement in question complies with the terms of an applicable block exemption. These are regulations issued by the Commission pursuant to which automatic exemption under Article 85(3) is conferred upon agreements which, in their form, comply with the terms of the regulation. If the agreement conforms to the regulation it need not be notified, nor does it require a formal Commission decision, yet it is automatically valid and enforceable despite the fact that it contains restrictive clauses. The Commission issues block exemptions in order to ease the regulatory burden upon industry and to enable it to focus its attention upon agreements and practices which give rise to more unusual or serious problems. To date, block exemptions have been issued in respect of:

(a) exclusive distribution agreements;[66]
(b) exclusive purchase agreements;[67]
(c) selective distribution in the motor-vehicle sector;[68]
(d) research-and-development agreements;[69]

---

[65] The number of comfort letters depends, *inter alia*, upon the number of block-exemption regulations in existence. If a new exemption is adopted, this can almost 'overnight' reduce the number of notifications made to the Commission and, *a fortiori*, the number of comfort letters needed to be issued.

[66] Reg. 83/83/EEC, OJ 1983, L

[67] Reg. 84/83/EEC, OJ 1983, L 173/5, as amended by OJ 1983, L 281/24.

[68] Reg. 123/85/EEC, OJ 1985, L 15/5.

[69] Reg. 418/85/EEC, OJ 1985, L 53/5.

(e) specialization agreements;[70]

(f) patent licences;[71]

(g) know-how licences;[72]

(h) franchise agreements;[73]

(i) Shipping Conference agreements (so-called Liner Conferences);[74]

(j) computer reservation systems in the airline sector;[75]

(k) joint planning and co-ordination of capacity-sharing of revenue and consultation on tariffs for scheduled air services and slot allocations at airports;[76]

(l) ground handling services at airports.[77]

At the time of writing, other block exemptions are either in the pipeline (insurance) or in the minds of Commission officials for future consideration (for example, computer software licensing and distribution). There is no obligation upon parties to fit their agreements within the scope of a block exemption. It has been held, by the Court of First Instance, that an agreement that is block-exempt may *still* be subject to Article 86.[78]

[70] Reg. 417/85/EEC, OJ 1985, L 53/1.

[71] Reg. 2349/84/EEC, OJ 1984, L 219/15, as amended by OJ 1985, L 113/34.

[72] Reg. 556/89/EEC, OJ 1989, L 61/1.

[73] Reg. 4087/88/EEC, OJ 1988, L 359/46.

[74] Reg. 4056/86, OJ 1986, L 378/14.

[75] Reg. 2672/88/EEC, OJ 1988, L 239/13.

[76] Reg. 2671/88/EEC, OJ 1988, L 239/9.

[77] Reg. 2673/88/EEC, OJ 1988, L 239/17.

[78] Case T–51/89, *Tetrapak* v. *Commission*, (judgment of 10 July 1990).

17

Different Types of Restrictive Agreement: Article 85

In this chapter discussion turns to the different types of agreement and concerted practice which may fall foul of Article 85(1). In practice this is a vast and rapidly increasing subject, and accordingly it is necessay in a text of this nature to be selective and to concentrate upon the main principles. This chapter hence concentrates upon agreements relating to price, distribution, and, intellectual property. The application of Article 85 to joint ventures and mergers is considered in Chapter 20. None the less, despite being selective it is still possible to identify important policy questions and, by examining such issues in the round, provide (hopefully) a critical perspective. In considering different types of agreement, reference is made to analytical tools and theories which have been discussed in greater depth elsewhere in this book and in particular in Chapters 14 and 15 on the objectives of competition law and the underlying economic assumptions.

Price Agreements

Agreements between competitors which directly impact upon either the method of determining price or the actual selling or purchasing price are almost always prohibited and unsuited to exemption under Article 85(3). Whilst there is no doctrine of *per se* illegality in Community law, such agreements may, with some confidence, be described as 'habitually' unlawful. Prices are at the heart of competition and represent the factor most likely to determine the customer's choice of supplier. This is not to downgrade other aspects of competitive choice, such as product or service quality, but, rather, to emphasize the essential role played by price in the dynamics of competition and to explain why any agreement which tampers with the price mechanism will attract the most extreme opprobrium.

In a textbook concerned more with the policy underlying the substantive law than with the nuts and bolts of the law itself, it is unnecessary to dwell in great detail upon the myriad forms of price-related cartel that have been unearthed and proscribed by the Commission, the participants being visited with heavy fines for their sins. In this section it is proposed to outline the major policy considerations which guide the Commission and the Court.[1]

First, price agreements are equally unmeritorious whether concluded between buyers *inter se*, or sellers *inter se*. They are prohibited whether concluded between suppliers or between dealers selling the same or a competing brand of a product. Indeed, price-fixing is prohibited regardless of whether it is effected at a horizontal or a vertical level. Horizontal price-fixing, between parties at the same level of trade, is generally perceived as the most invidious form of cartel. However, vertical price-fixing ('resale price maintenance'), which entails a supplier fixing the prices at which a dealer sells, is also a serious breach of competition rules.[2] The same prohibition applies to price maintenance in technology-transfer arrangements, whereby a licensor (of a patent or technical know-how, for example) seeks to determine or influence the prices applied by the licensee who manufactures the goods in question in accordance with the licensor's technology.[3]

Secondly, the strict application of Article 85 applies to all stages of the price-setting mechanism. Accordingly, an agreement between competitors to agree only upon the method by which they will set prices (so-called 'cost-calculation formulae') has the effect of harmonizing rivals' price systems, and ultimately has an effect upon prices. Thus, the Commission stated critically in *Bundesverband Deutscher Stahlhander*:[4] 'Model calculations of this type have the effect of recommendations. They encourage the user companies to work from the figures contained in the models, or at least to keep close to them, when calculating their costs and thus indirectly their selling prices.'[5] Price models are frequently prepared and disseminated to users by trade associations. Sometimes the model includes 'average' data relating, for example, to the price paid for an input raw material which members of the association utilize in production. The Commission, in the above case,

---

[1] For a detailed analysis of the different types of agreement which are prohibited by Article 85 see Green, *Commercial Agreements and Competition Law: Practice and Procedure in the UK and EEC* (1986), Chap. 8.

[2] See e.g. *VBVB & VBBB* v. *Commission*, Cases 43 and 63/82, [1984] ECR 19. Though, in the case Advocate General Verloren Van Themaat indicated that in exceptional cases resale-price maintenance could be exemptible under Article 85(3). In *Pronuptia de Paris* v. *Schillgallis*, Case 161/84, [1986] 1 CMLR 414, the Court held that a *recommended* resale-price-maintenance provision in a franchise agreement was not necessarily caught by Article 85(1).

[3] See e.g. Reg. 2349/84/EEC, OJ 1984, L 219/15, Art. 3(6), on patent licensing; see also Reg. 556/89/EEC, OJ 1989, L 61/1, Art. 3, on know-how licensing.

[4] [1980] 3 CMLR 193. See also *European Glass Manufacturers*, [1974] 2 CMLR D50; *IFTRA Rules for Producers of Virgin Aluminium*, [1975] 2 CMLR D20.

[5] *Bundesverband Deutscher Stahlhander* (n. 4 above), p. 204, para. 53.

stated: 'The inclusion of such data in model calculations leads many users to rely on fictitious quantities when calculating their operating costs rather than working from their actual costs and thereby to arrive at misleading figures.'[6] Not every cost-calculation model is illegal, but the divide between the permissible and impermissible is set such that only the anodyne is left within the realm of acceptability.[7] The prohibition on price agreements thus starts early and extends right until the final moment of the price-setting exercise. It follows inexorably that price agreements become increasingly unacceptable the nearer they move towards affecting the final selling price. It need hardly be reiterated that where producers combine to fix ultimate selling prices the condemnation of the Commission and Courts is almost automatic.[8]

Thirdly, there is no rule of *per se* illegality. As with all cases under Articles 85 and 86, legality is determined by an appraisal of all the relevant circumstances. Indeed, there are certain exceptional situations in which price-fixing is permissible. The most notable of these examples is the case of the liner conferences. A conference is a group of shipping lines which ply between two geographical areas. Thus, for example, a number of conferences ply between specified ports in Europe and West Africa; the United Kingdom West Africa Line (UKWAL) carries goods, both north-and south-bound, between West Africa and the United Kingdom. The 'conference' is the central organization which administers the operation of the conference agreement. In essence, the conference devises schedules of sailing and freight rates which it publishes. Pursuant to schedules, a shipping line will ply the route regardless of whether it is full, half-full, or near empty. By common scheduling and freight rates a service is provided to importers and exporters at either end of the route, thus facilitating the efficiency of international trade. However, because of the fact that a shipping line must, in accordance with the conference rules, sail irrespective of the freight it earns on the voyage, it is often a necessary concomitant of the system that price fixing and revenue-sharing be incorporated into the system. In practice, conferences involve price-fixing, route-scheduling and revenue-sharing, all matters ordinarily condemned by competition authorities. However, in recognition of the historical role played by liner conferences and their overriding advantages, they are, subject to certain conditions, granted block exemption pursuant to Regulation 4056/86/EEC.[9]

Another, this time more specific, instance of permitted price-fixing is

---

[6] *Bundesverband Deutscher Stahlhander*, p. 205, para. 65.

[7] Ibid., p. 05, para. 55 and p. 209, para. 69. See Green, *Commercial Agreements*, pp. 389–93; Korah, *Introductory Guide to EEC Competition Law and Practice* (1990) Ch. 7.

[8] From the numerous examples on price-fixing see: *Polypropylene*, OJ 1986, L 230/1; [1984] 4 CMLR 347; *Belgian Roofing Felt*, OJ 1986, L 232/15.

[9] OJ 1986, L 378/4.

to be found in the Commission decision in *Uniform Eurocheques*,[10] wherein the Commission granted exemption under Article 85(3) to the part of the Eurocheque system whereby the commission charged on each cheque transaction by each of the huge number of competing European banks and financial institutions which were party to the agreement was identical. One of the key factors involved was the truly vast number of individual transactions conducted daily by users (mainly travellers) of the Eurocheque card and cheque. Centralized computers control and determine the net credit and debit positions of the participating banks, and it was therefore argued by the banks (and accepted by the Commission) that, were every participating bank to negotiate individual commission rates with every other bank, then chaos would ensue given the number of daily transactions involved. Accordingly, a common commission fee is applied to ensure that the system operates efficiently and smoothly.[11]

Fourthly, it is necessary to appreciate the width ascribed to the word 'price'. It is clear that the Commission and the Court view with some considerable scepticism and hostility all agreements which concern either price in all its guises (buying, selling, offer etc) or elements or components of price (for example, discounts), or which diminish the effectiveness of price as the key ingredient in competition. Thus, for example, in addition to the classic type of price-fixing cartel whereby rivals agree to fix buying or selling prices, Article 85 prohibits such agreements as joint discount schemes, aggregated rebate systems, and profit-pooling. In a joint discount scheme sellers agree on the level of discount they will accord buyers.[12] Such an arrangement has the effect of stabilizing the *status quo*, since if the parties are selling at different list-prices the agreement will not affect the differential which is maintained. Thus, for instance, X, Y, and Z could agree to sell at list-price minus 5 per cent for customer purchasing over an agreed quantity. Alternatively, they could agree on the criteria to be used to determine the discounts. For example, they may conclude that buyers taking from 10 to 20 units receive 5 per cent off list-price, those taking from 20 to 50 units receive a 10 per cent discount, and those taking above 50 units receive 15 per cent. Howsoever the scheme is arranged, it is clear that neither the Commission nor the Court will countenance agreements affecting discounts.

In an aggregated rebate scheme, the level of the discount granted varies according to the total value or the total quantity of the individual

[10] OJ 1985, L 35/43; [1985] 3 CMLR 434.

[11] In *Insurance Intermediaries*, OJ 1987, C 120/5, the Commission expressed an intention to exempt an agreement between non-life insurers to fix maximum discounts. No formal decision was ever adopted, and it is understood that the Commission altered its position following opposition to the proposal.

[12] See e.g. *Gisa*, [1973] CMLR D125; *Community* v. *Fabbrica Pisana*, [1982] 3 CMLR 366.

customer's purchases from members of a defined group (that is, the parties to the agreement). The Commission objects for a variety of reasons. In *German Ceramic Tiles*,[13] the Commission complained that the scheme operated independently 'of the economic relations in fact operating between a given producer and a given purchase'. In other cases the Commission has objected on the basis that the scheme deprives undertakings 'of the possibility of determining all their conditions of sale in accordance with their own judgment and according to the services which the buyers do in fact give, quite apart from the category in which they are classed by the agreement'.[14] Additionally, the Commission has objected to the fact that such schemes tend to encourage buyers to concentrate their purchases on the group to the detriment of outsiders, since the more the buyer spends with the group the greater his discount.[15]

Distribution

Another area of commercial life much affected by Article 85 is distribution. Distribution is, broadly speaking, the process whereby a manufacturer of goods procures, by a series of sales for resale, that the goods in question reach the end-user. Thus, a manufacturer might: sell to end-users ex-factory; sell to a wholesaler for resale to retailers for resale to end-users; or sell directly to retailers for resale to end-users. In reality, there are many varieties and methods of distributing goods, and the contracts which underpin these methods represent the very core of international (and of course domestic) trade in goods. Generally speaking, it is possible to identify six broad types of distribution agreement: non-exclusive supply, exclusive dealing, exclusive purchasing, selective distribution, franchising, and agency. It is the purpose of this section to describe and compare the competition issues arising out of the different forms of distribution agreement; it is *not* the purpose of this section to provide a detailed account of the rules and regulations which govern specific types of contract clause. For this, recourse to detailed practitioner texts is advised.[16]

Non-Exclusive Distribution

This is the simplest form of distribution, entailing an outright sale of the goods in question by the manufacturer to the wholesaler or retailer. The

---

[13] [1974] CMLR D6.

[14] *Re Gas Water Heaters*, [1973] CMLR D231.

[15] *Groupe des Fabricants de Papier Peints de Belgique* v. *Commission*, Case 73/74, [1975] ECR 1491.

[16] See e.g. Green *Commercial Agreements*, Chap. 10; Korah, 'Exclusive Dealing Agreements in the EEC', Reg. 67/67 Replaced (1984); Whish, *Competition Law* (1989) Ch. 17, 18.

contract will reflect an ordinary sale-of-goods transaction. Typically, there will be terms governing: quantity, price to be paid, discount terms, delivery and carriage, retention and passage of title, etc. There will be *no* provision whereby the buyer may resell *only* in a specified territory, must purchase only from the supplier or must not sell competing goods. In practice, it is well understood by many businessmen and their advisers that the incorporation of such clauses restricting freedom of conduct is likely to give rise to questions of compatibility with EEC competition rules where trade between Member States may be materially affected. What appears to be less well comprehended is the fact that suppliers may not, under EEC law, restrict the customers to whom the buyer may resell. It is well established in case-law that, once the manufacturer/supplier has passed legal title in the goods to the buyer, then he loses the ability to determine to whom such goods are resold. Thus, a dealer may not be limited in his choice of customer. This, it is suggested, is a very formalistic analysis to adopt since there are frequently excellent commercial reasons for a supplier to exercise 'resale customer control' over a dealer. For instance, a manufacturer might, over a period of years, have directly supplied a large customer with special requirements (for example a health authority or nationalized industry etc.) and in respect of whom the supplier has a fund of knowledge and experience and with whom good relations have been carefully nurtured. Clearly such a supplier may not for good reason wish his wholesalers and dealers to commence marketing the goods to that buyer. It may very well be that the supplier has invested heavily in order to attract and retain the customer, and it would be unacceptable to the supplier for a buyer to exploit the investment of that supplier by selling to its favoured customer. In strict terms however should the supplier include in the sale agreement with the wholesaler/dealer a clause restricting the latter from selling to that customer, then such a clause would be automatically void pursuant to Article 85(2).[17] The illogicality of this rule—against customer restrictions—is that it stresses considerations of title over business efficiency. The author predicts that over time the Court and Commission will adopt a rule-of-reason/ancillary restraints doctrine towards the restriction, such that where the clause is necessary to facilitate or enable an agreement that is either pro-competitive or neutral of competition then it will be held not to infringe Article 85.

EXCLUSIVE DISTRIBUTION

An exclusive-distribution agreement exists where a supplier appoints a dealer to sell his goods within a defined geographical area and

[17] See e.g. *Kerpen & Kerpen*, Case 319/82, [1985] ECR 511.

covenants not to appoint any other dealer for that territory. There are varieties of this arrangement, for example typically the supplier may agree not to compete himself with the dealer (sometimes called the 'sole and exclusive' dealership agreement) and the dealer may agree to purchase the goods *only* from the supplier and not to sell goods which compete with those of the supplier. These arrangements are extremely common throughout European trade. Undoubtedly, many thousands of such agreements are concluded annually. Indeed, they are so common that the Commission adopted a block-exemption Regulation as early as 1967[18] in order to stem the flood of such agreements which were being notified to the Commission and which threatened to bring the administrative facilities of the Commission to a grinding halt. The 1967 Regulation was updated in 1983,[19] and in that latter Regulation is repeated an inconsistency in the legal analysis of exclusive dealing agreements which warrants mention. The fifth and sixth recitals to the preamble to the Regulation evidence the favourable light in which such agreements are appraised:

'Whereas exclusive distribution agreements lead in general to an improvement in distribution because the undertaking is able to concentrate its sales activities, does not need to maintain numerous business relations with a larger number of dealers and is able, by dealing with only one dealer, to overcome easily distribution difficulties in international trade resulting from linguistic, legal and other difficulties;

Whereas exclusive distribution agreements facilitate the promotion of sales of a product and lead to intensive marketing and to continuity of supplies while at the same time rationalising distribution; whereas they stimulate competition between the products of different manufacturers; whereas the appointment of an exclusive distributor who will take over sales promotion, customer services and carrying of stocks is often the most effective way, and sometimes indeed the only way, for the manufacturer to enter a market and compete with other manufacturers already present; whereas this is particularly so in the case of small and medium sized undertakings; whereas it must be left to the contracting parties to decide whether and to what extent they consider it desirable to incorporate in the agreements terms providing for the promotion of sales.'

In essence, exclusive-dealing agreements are accepted as facilitating market entry, enhancing inter-brand competition and stimulating competition. In these circumstances an obvious question emerges: if exclusive-dealership agreements are generally pro-competitive why is a block exemption needed to exempt them? The existence of such a regulation presupposes that the agreement is subject to Article 85(1). If it is pro-competitive, how can it be so subject?

[18] Reg. 67/67/EEC 1967, OJ Spec. edn. 10.
[19] See Reg. 83/83/EEC, OJ 1983, L 173/1 as amended by *corrigendum*, OJ 1983, L 281/24. See the Notice of the Commission on the Regulation at OJ 1983, C 355/7

There is no easy answer to the question posed above. The tension between the preamble and the substance of the Regulation which indicates that the restrictions described above fall within Article 85(1) is not easy to reconcile. In *Société Technique Minière* v. *Maschinenbau Ulm*,[20] the Court stated that: 'it may be doubted whether there is an interference with competition if the said [exclusive dealing] agreement seems really necessary for the penetration of a new area by an undertaking.' Thus, even the Court has accepted that certain exclusive dealing arrangements the reasons for the Commission's reticence in concluding that, as a rule, exclusive-dealing agreements escape Article 85(1) are not entirely clear but are predicated upon a variety of reasons. First, the Commission considers itself bound in law by the seminal judgment of the Court of Justice in *Consten & Grundig* v. *Commission*,[21] where it was held that agreements whereby a supplier sought to grant to a dealer a watertight territory from which the goods could not be re-exported (that is, so-called export bans) were 'of their nature' restrictive of competition. Thus, given that many exclusive-dealing agreements involved some degree of territorial isolation, the Commission has never considered itself to have jurisdiction to clear exclusive-dealing agreements in their entirety. Export bans in distribution agreements tend towards the erection of artificial barriers to the free movement of goods within the Common Market and were (as is explained in Chapter 14) anathema to the objective of European integration. The second reason why such agreements have never been fully cleared lies in the traditional view of the Commission that a restriction of competition entailed a restriction of *conduct*, (for example, supplier not to compete with dealer, dealer not to sell outside designated area, etc). Thus, if the dealer's conduct were constrained by a contractual covenant, then there must be a restriction of competition and Article 85 must apply. As has been explained throughout this text, more recent rulings of the Court of Justice have favoured the more pragmatic rule-of-reason analysis i.e. are the individual restrictions necessary to facilitate the pro-competitive objective of the agreement taken as a whole?), and had this doctrine been applied at an earlier stage in the evolution of the law on exclusive-dealing agreements a different rule might have emerged.

As has been noted, Regulation 83/83/EEC grants block exemption to certain categories of agreement. It is possible to summarize the Regulation as follows. Pursuant to Article 1, agreements between a reseller and a supplier whereby the supplier agrees to supply certain goods for resale only to the reseller within the whole or a defined area of the Common Market, are exempted automatically under Article 85(3) from the prohibition in Article 85(1). In addition, the supplier may agree

[20] Case 56/65, [1966] ECR 235.
[21] *Consten & Grundig* v. *Commission*, Cases 56 and 58/64, [1966] ECR 299.

not to compete with the reseller in the territory. The dealer may agree not to manufacture or distribute competing goods, to purchase those goods exclusively from the supplier, and to refrain from actively seeking customers outside the territory. It is very important to appreciate that, whilst it is possible to prohibit 'active' sales outside the territory it is not permissible to prevent 'passive' sales. A passive sale would occur where the dealer receives unsolicited orders to supply which originate from outside his territory, or where a buyer places an order within the territory for resale by that buyer outside the territory.[22]

The Regulation does not apply to mutual exclusive dealing whereby the competing suppliers appoint each other as their exclusive dealers for a territory. For example, X (in the south) appoints Y (in the north) as his exclusive dealer and *vice versa*. Where X and Y are competitors there will be a tendency for X to promote his own goods over Y's in the south and for Y to do the same with his goods in the north. The agreement may operate as a species of market-sharing agreement in the final outcome, and although there may be sound commercial reasons to justify mutual exclusive dealing, the Commission consider that parties to such agreements should seek exemption upon an individual basis..[23]

EXCLUSIVE PURCHASING

Exclusive purchasing exists where a dealer agrees to purchase exclusively from a particular supplier and may agree further to confine active selling to a defined territory. However, the agreement differs from exclusive dealing in that the supplier grants no exclusive territorial rights. Hence, the dealer has no expectation that the supplier will not appoint further dealers in the territory nor compete with the dealer himself. Regulation 84/83/EEC[24] is, in many respects, similar to Regulation 83/83/EEC, with the distinction described above. Moreover, Regulation 84/83/EEC contains specific provisions governing exclusive-supply arrangements in the beer- and oil-supply sectors, where the peculiarities of tied-house and filling-station arrangements necessitated special treatment.

SELECTIVE DISTRIBUTION

As has been explained, customer restrictions are prima-facie illegal pursuant to Article 85(1). However, in some circumstances such

---

[22] See Art. 2.

[23] See Art. 3. There is an exception to the rule that the Regulation does not apply to agreements between competitors where the agreement is non-reciprocal *and* where one party has a turnover of less than 100 million ECU. See, for a case where, upon individual notification, the Commission granted exemption, *Whiskey and Gin*, OJ 1985, L 369/19.

[24] OJ 1983, L 173/5 amended by corrigendum OJ 1983, L 281/24.

restrictions may be necessary in order to ensure proper handling for the goods and thereby to protect the reputation of the supplier and the brand, which would be prejudiced by low-quality handling of the product in question. For these reasons, suppliers of certain luxury or high-technology products may decide to supply only those dealers who meet criteria related to the suitability of premises and the qualifications of staff. In such a system it is clearly imperative that authorized dealers should be prevented from reselling the products to other dealers who fail to meet the requisite standard; accordingly, approved dealers will be contractually prohibited from selling other than to authorized dealers (so-called 'cross-supplies') and to end-users. As suggested above, the imposition of such a customer restriction should breach Article 85. However, the Court of Justice has held that 'selective-distribution' systems do not infringe Article 85 at all where they remain within certain parameters:

'Selective distribution systems [constitute], together with others, an aspect of competition which accords with Article 85(1), provided that re-sellers are chosen on the basis of objective criteria of a qualitative nature relating to the technical qualification of the re-seller and his staff and the suitability of his premises and that such conditions are laid uniformly for all potential re-sellers and are not applied in a discriminatory fashion.'[25]

Provided a supplier operates his distribution system according to objective qualitative criteria, Article 85 is excluded. However, the consistent case-law of the Court of Justice makes it clear that the adoption of quantitative criteria will result in Article 85 being applied. Examples of quantitative criteria include: a decision by the supplier to refrain from supplying a dealer meeting the qualitative criteria on the basis that there were sufficient dealers in the locality, and an obligation on the dealer to hold a substantial stock of the product.

Not every product justifies selective distribution, only those products which require specialized handling may benefit from this relaxation of the normal rules.[26] The additional costs involved in a selective-distribution system (that is, those borne by the dealer) inevitably have an inflationary effect upon retail prices, thus raising the question of why competition law encourages a system which tends to result in higher consumer prices. The Court has answered this question as follows:

'For specialist wholesalers and retailers the desire to maintain a certain price level, which corresponds to the desire to preserve, in the interests of consumers,

---

[25] See *Metro* v. *Commission (No. 1)*, Case 26/76, [1977] ECR 1875, 1904, para. 20.
[26] See e.g. *Ideal Standard*, OJ 1985, L 20/38 and *Grohe*, OJ 1985, L 19/17 concerning plumbing fittings. In *IBM Personal Computer* [1984] 2 CMLR 347, para. 15, there is a hint that, as the consuming public become more sophisticated technologically, even products such as personal computers may no longer justify special treatment.

the possibility of the continued existence of this channel of distribution in conjunction with new methods of distribution based on a different type of competition policy, forms one of the objectives which may be pursued without necessarily falling under the prohibition contained in Article 85(1), and, if it does fall thereunder, either wholly or in part, coming within the framework of Article 85(3).'[27]

Thus, price is not necessarily of the essence to every competition-law issue.

FRANCHING

Franchising has, in Europe, been a story of phenomenal growth since the early 1980s. A typical franchised operation starts with an individual entrepreneur developing a winning formula for a particular type of small business. The formula will comprise a combination of shop design, logo or trademark, selling style, and product type. Having established this winning method, the entrepreneur comes to a realization that by selling, in consideration for a lump sum and/or royalties, the 'formula', the revenues from the initial idea can be maximized. Thus, the idea is franchised. The franchisor (the entrepreneur) seeks out or advertises for franchisees to learn the method. The prospective franchisee finds the proposition attractive (and is therefore prepared to pay for the system) because it has a proven track record and, should he decide to join the franchise network, he will be given expert assistance in the running of the business venture. Thus, in an overall sense, franchising eases new entry to the market and is thereby pro-competitive.

The European Court adopted a rule-of-reason analytical approach towards franchising in *Pronuptia de Paris* v. *Schillgallis*,[28] and laid down a legal framework for franchising which, if adopted, would result in a franchise agreement escaping Article 85. In particular, the Court held that certain clauses were necessary constituents of a franchise agreement. These were clauses which went to the protection of the franchisor's reputation and to the preservation of the secrecy of the know-how transmitted by franchisor to franchisee. The Court cited many examples of clauses which would satisfy these dictates and hence escape Article 85(1). Conversely, the Court concluded that any clause which had the effect, directly or indirectly, of sharing markets or limiting the franchisee's right to determine freely prices, would fall within Article 85(1).

On the basis of this ruling the Commission adopted Regulation 4087/

---

[27] *Metro* (n. 25 above), para. 21.
[28] Case 161/84 [1986] 1 CMLR 414.

88,[29] which provides block exemption for distribution and services franchises. The Regulation does not cover production franchises or wholesale franchises.

AGENCY

Agency is a concept well understood in English law. Competition law has adapted to agency agreements by taking the view that most such agreements do not fall within Article 85(1) at all. Indeed, by a Notice[30] of December 1962 (the so-called 'Christmas Message'), the Commission stated that certain types of exclusive agency agreement whereby the agent accepted no financial risk (other than the normal *del credere* guarantee), and whereby the principal fixed the agent's prices and terms and conditions of trade, did not fall within Article 85(1). For Article 85(1) to be avoided the agent must be a true auxiliary to the principal; the label 'quasi-employee' is sometimes used to describe the requisite degree of proximity between principal and agent. The Court of Justice has made it clear that representatives who act as agents for some parties but as dealers for others cannot escape Article 85. In *Suiker Unie*,[31] the Court arrived at this conclusion in respect of large trading houses which acted as agents for the sale of sugar in some territories but as independent dealers in respect of exports from the EEC and sales within the EEC for denaturing.

More recently, the Court has further limited the scope of the agency exception. In *Vlaamse Reisbureau*,[32] the Court was confronted, *inter alia*, with a situation whereby tour operators were collectively fixing certain discounts offered by travel agents. The Court pointed out that travel agents sold holidays on behalf of many different tour operators, and concluded that despite the fact that the travel agent concluded holiday agreements on behalf of tour operators this was insufficient to preclude the operation of Article 85. This ruling has encouraged the Commission to review the 1962 Notice and, at the time of writing, the Commission was nearing completion of a new Notice.

---

[29] OJ 1988, L 359/49—see Korah, 'Franching and the EEC Competition Rules, Reg. 4087/88' (1989).

[30] OJ 1962, 2921, Notice of 24 Dec. 1962.

[31] Case 40/73, [1975] ECR 1663, 2008–10; see especially at para. 547.

[32] *Vereniging van Vlaamse Reisbureaus* v. *Sociale Dienst van de Plaatselijk en Gewestelijke Overheidsdiensten*, Case 311/85, [1989] 4 CMLR 213.

Intellectual-Property Licensing

INTRODUCTION

The licensing of intellectual-property rights is an extremely common form of transaction throughout industry. There are many reasons why a company may seek to license another person to use the technology it has developed and which is subject to intellectual property protection. For example, the licensor may be a small company which can only optimize the revenue from the technology through having a third party pay a royalty for the right of exploitation. Alternatively the licensor may be a large undertaking with a large research-and-development capability, the fruits of which labour include many inventions that the corporate group would not view as sufficiently 'core business' to warrant exploitation itself. Thus, the only way to obtain a return on the research-and-development investment is to license the technology. EEC competition law has long sought to regulate the contracts entered into for the licensing of technology, and two block exemptions relating to the licensing of patents and technical know-how have been adopted by the Commission. These are considered below. A basic question that deserves some discussion is why the Commission is interested in regulating technology licences at all. The traditional answer lies in the Community's obsessional anxiety over the need to protect the forces of economic integration. Clauses in, say, a patent licence whereby the patentee (i.e., the owner) licenses the patented technology, and whereby the patentee accepts restriction upon his licensing third parties in a territory reserved for the licensee, raise the same spectres as do exclusive territories in exclusive-dealing arrangements. These concerns are, it is submitted, highly formalistic and tend to ignore two other economic considerations which should be, but which are not, major components of Article 85 analysis.

First, the appraisal of intellectual-property licences has never focused upon the competitive relationship between licensor and licensee. If for instance a licensor grants rights in his combined patent and technical know-how to a licensee who was perfectly capable of entering the relevant market without the licensor's technology (for example, because the licensee could easily have developed a competing technology itself), then the effect of the agreement will be to deter the creative and inventive efforts of a potential competitor, the licensee. Conversely, where the licensee could not enter the market without the licensor's technology (or at least some third party's technology), then the agreement does not per se have any anti-competitive effects. In practice, most technology licences are between non-competitors (i.e. where the licensee is incapable of independent market entry). In this latter case many of the clauses in the agreement which curtail the commercial liberty or freedom of the licensee have no material impact upon competition between licensor and licensee. Indeed, many ostensibly restrictive clauses may be predicated upon a sound commercial rationale under which the limitations operate to focus the attentions of the licensee on markets that are best suited to its abilities or to operations for which there is a demand. However, the normal analysis under Article 85(1) adopted by the Commission has proven highly formalistic and has not (to date) relied upon the analysis described above.

Secondly, the amount of market power held by the licensor has not played a central role in analysis. A similar comment may be made about the analysis of distribution arrangements. Where a licensor holds considerable market power, then the impact upon competition of each restrictive clause in the agreement is the greater; conversely, where the licensor has minimal market power (a not insignificant number of important patents are invented by individuals), then restrictive clauses may have a minimal impact upon competition. The analysis of the Commission under Article 85(1) has not focused upon the licensor's market power as a critical factor of analysis, though it has been relevant under Article 85(3) under the heading of 'elimination of competition'.

THE MEANING OF RESTRICTION

In the context of intellectual property, what is meant by a 'restriction'? Of critical importance to this question is the distinction between the so-called 'existence' and 'exercise' of an intellectual-property right. In competition-law terms, if a particular contract clause may be analysed as going to the very 'existence' of the intellectual-property right then it escapes Article 85; conversely, if the clause goes to the 'exercise' of that right, then it may fall within Article 85. For example, in a patent licence a clause prohibiting the licensee from manufacturing a product with the technology that falls within the patent specification (usually called a field of use restriction) goes to the very essence of the patent itself, and such a clause escapes Article 85(1). However, if the clause states that the licensee shall not sell the product manufactured using the patented technology for less than £x, then this goes to the exercise of the right and may fall within Article 85.[33] In the absence of Community-wide harmonized rules on different types of intellectual property, it is up to national law to determine the scope of the existence of an intellectual

---

[33] For examples of European Court cases setting out this distinction between the existence and the exercise of a right (which applies under Art. 30 as well), see: *Merck* v. *Stephar*, Case 187/80, [1989] ECR 2063; *Coditel* v. *Cine Vog Films (No. 2)*, Case 262/81, [1982] ECR 3381; *Hydrotherm* v. *Compact*, Case 170/83, [1984] ECR 2999; *B.A.T.* v. *Commission*, Case 35/83, [1985] ECR 363; *Consten & Grundig* v. *Commission*, Cases 56 and 58/64, [1966] ECR 299; *Sirena* v. *Eda*, Case 40/70, [1971] ECR 69.

property right. At least, this is the rule established in Article 30 cases. However, it is also true to say that in competition cases the Court of Justice has not relied upon national law as the determinant of the existence of a right but has, conversely, expressed its own view as to the essential existence of the right. Thus, the analysis of Article 85 in this area has largely been determined by judicial thinking. As is explained below, the Court (as opposed to the Commission) has been quite pragmatic in its approach to intellectual-property licensing.

A second issue concerning the scope of a 'restriction' focuses upon the notion of a limited and defined right. Up until 1984, the Commission was of the view that when a right-holder licensed a third party to use his right and subjected that use to certain delimiting conditions (i.e. restrictions), then the licensee was not restricted but, on the contrary, was granted defined rights. As such, a restrictive clause simply defined the scope of the rights granted rather than curtailing the liberty of the licensee. Indeed, the licensee, not having the right prior to the licence to use the right, had given up no pre-existing freedom in accepting the restrictive clauses in the licence. This idea of limited rights was first espoused by the Commission in a 1962 Notice, but was formally withdrawn in 1984.[34] It is clear now that this somewhat theoretical analysis of the concept of a restriction has been replaced by a more economic analysis tempered by a desire to establish firm rules and principles which will confer greater legal certainty on the area.

TYPES OF LICENCE

Intellectual-property licences may take various forms. The traditional distinctions are between patents, copyright, trademarks, and secret know-how. The latter is not, classically speaking, a form of intellectual property, since it is not generally recognized at law as conferring any exclusive rights upon the owner (though the laws of secrecy and breach of confidence may assist); none the less, in practice know-how is often viewed as a near relative of the patent. In many respects a patent is the same as technical secret know-how, except that it is not secret, i.e. they are both constituted of valuable technical knowledge. Many technology-transfer arrangements include the licence of a bundle of the above. For example, a licence for the production of a certain chemical may entail a patent for the actual chemical and know-how describing the best procedures to adopt in order to obtain the optimal result from the patent. Copyright could also be involved if the licensee is to construct or procure the construction of certain equipment and requires drawings or

---

[34] Patent Notice of 24 Dec. 1962, withdrawn by OJ 1984, C 220/14. The doctrine is, however, fully accepted in English law. See *Ravenself* v. *Director-General of Fair Trading*, [1977] 1 All ER (QBD), *Annual Report of the Director General of Fair Trading* (1976), p. 36.

computer software. Finally, if the final product is to be sold, then the licensee may take a trademark licence in order to benefit from the licensor's established reputation in promoting the product.

PATENT LICENCES

Pursuant to Regulation 2349/84/EEC,[35] certain types of exclusive patent licence are granted block exemption. Article 1 of the Regulation sets out a series of clauses relating to non-competition between licensor and licensee and with regard to territory which may be incorporated within a licence, and which are automatically exempted under Article 85(3). Article 3 lays down clauses which are within Article 85(1) but not worthy of exemption, and Article 2 lays down clauses which are not within Article 85(1) at all. The Regulation has, generally speaking, been successful, and it is notable that very large numbers of patent licences currently operating in the Community have been carefully drafted so as to fit within the Regulation. The block exemption does, however, pose the problem that characterizes all block-exemption regulations, and (ironically) particularly those which have proven successful. Block exemptions offer a very attractive safe harbour to industry and their legal advisers, and invariably agreements are drafted so as to benefit from the regulation. However, this inevitably means that patent licences throughout Europe present a similar form, and this raises the question whether the agreement reflects more the desires of the drafting lawyer for legal certainty than that of the businessman for commercial advantage. There are, no doubt, many good ideas that are presented by the businessman to the adviser for incorporation in the agreement which are rejected because inclusion would result in loss of exemption. The overall impact of a successful block exemption can be the strait-jacketing of agreements into specified contractual forms. The alternative to squeezing the agreement into a block exemption is to undertake an individual notification, with all the attendant delays, uncertainties, and costs involved.

KNOW-HOW LICENCES

Regulation 556/89/EEC[36] was adopted so as to plug the gaping hole left by the patent-licensing regulation. As explained above, know-how licences are frequently on a commercial par with a patent licence; both, in essence, concern the transfer of valuable technical knowledge. In many instances an inventor will refrain from applying for a patent for his invention because the process of applying can be drawn out and

---

[35] OJ 1984, L 219/15, as amended by *corrigendum* OJ 1985, L 113/34.
[36] OJ 1989, L 61/1.

expensive, and the inventor might consider that the useful life of the invention may only be a few years and certainly not the twenty-year period of protection granted an invention under a patent. Under Regulation 556/89/EEC, licences of secret, substantial technical know-how are granted block exemption upon terms that (not surprisingly) are very similar to those under Regulation 2349/84/EEC. Where know-how and patents are licensed together in a package then the know-how block exemption applies where the know-how is the most important compon-ent in the package and the patent block exemption applies where the patent component is predominant.

Copyright Licences

There is no block exemption for copyright licences, despite their importance, particularly in the field of licences of computer software. This lacuna is due largely to the relatively small number of agreements which have been notified to the Commission with the consequence that the Commission are unable to call upon sufficient experience of the problems raised to be able to draft a suitable block exemption regulation. Frequently, licences of copyright are a subsidiary part of some other licence. For example, a copyright licence will often be granted in respect of drawings accompanying a patent and/or know-how licence. The rules governing copyright are generally similar to those governing patents. However, as is described below in the context of the *Coditel* litigation, the Court of Justice has, to some degree, concluded that copyright licences exhibit certain special features which may warrant their being treated in a more sympathetic manner.

Trademark Licences

Trademark licences are common, though only as part of other licences. Indeed, both Regulations 2349/84/EEC (patents) and 559/89/EEC (know-how) expressly provide for the grant of accompanying trademarks provided they are subsidiary to the main rights granted. The require-ment that such trademarks be ancillary or subsidiary may be criticized. In many cases where the licensor is a well-established undertaking with a developed public image, the grant of a trademark licence to the licensee can be critical to the success of the licence, since it enables the licensee to exploit the goodwill attaching to the licensor. As such, the trademark may be as pivotal to the marketing side of the licence as the patent or know-how is to the actual production side of the licence. Where the licensor is a small inventor who licenses a large undertaking as licensee, then the latter will not need the trademark in order to establish itself. Though, in such circumstances, if the licensee uses the small licensor's mark this can provide an excellent opportunity for the licensor to enter the market and develop its name by, in effect, 'piggy-backing' upon the existing reputation and goodwill of the licensee. Thus, in summary, it has always seemed to the author that the role of the trademark licence has been somewhat undervalued.

The Role of the Court of Justice in the Analysis of Intellectual Property Licensing

Whereas the work of the Commission has concentrated upon the day-to-day assessment of agreements according to established principles, the Court of Justice has, in recent years, shown a degree of activism and commercial sensitivity that has served to foster a dynamic analysis of different types of issue. In particular, it will be seen that the Court has been concerned with a number of economic objectives such as the penetration of new markets, the dissemination of new technology, the protection of the inventor's economic reward, and the encouragement of risk-taking.

In one of the earlier cases, *Nungesser* v. *Commission*,[37] the Court was required to consider an exclusive manufacturing-and-sales licence for plant breeders' rights. The Court stated:

'In the case of a licence of breeder's rights over hybrid maize seed newly developed in one Member State, an undertaking established in another Member State which was not certain that it would not encounter competition from other licensees for the territory granted to it, or from the owner of the right himself, might be deterred from accepting the risk of cultivating and marketing that product; such a result would be damaging to the dissemination of a new technology and would prejudice competition in the Community between the new product and similar existing products.'[38]

This exposition of principle has become known as the 'new technology' doctrine and provides that 'open exclusive licences' (i.e., where the licensee is protected from the licensor and from licensees with regard to manufacturing rights) may escape Article 85(1) where they concern 'new technology'. For current purposes the rationale behind this concession is important. It is clear from this dictum that the Court was concerned to protect (and encourage) a commercial environment where the taking of technological risk by a licensee was possible, and inherent in the ruling are a number of economic assumptions:

1. That the dissemination of new technology is a desirable economic objective for competition policy to pursue since it enhances competition by promoting new products;

---

[37] Case 258/78, [1982] ECR 2015. See also *Erauw Jacquery* v. *Hesbignonne Société Co-Operative*, Case 27/87, [1988] 4 CMLR 576.
[38] Ibid., p. 2069, paras. 57–8.

2. That dissemination will only occur where inventors can encourage third parties to take a licence of the technology;
3. That potential licensees need an incentive to take on new, untested technology;
4. That a greater degree of commercial security from competitors is an incentive which will encourage prospective licensees to enter a licence for new technology;
5. That a more minimalist application of EEC competition rules is therefore justified to achieve the objective of enabling licensees to take the risk of manufacturing new technology.

Thus, the Court focused upon the importance of incentives in the evolution of a market. Here it asked the question: if the dissemination of new technology is desirable, what does it take to incentivize a potential licensee to take the risk of manufacturing the new technology? The Court is therefore examining the market-place from the perspective of the licensee *prior* to his entering the licence agreement. The process of shaping the rules according to an assessment of incentives is sometimes described as the *ex ante* approach.

An integral component of an incentive is financial: what return will I get for taking this risk? Given the connection between risk and projected return, the Court has, in other cases, sought to fashion the application of the competition rules to ensure that an inventor obtains a fair reward for his effort. Thus, in *Coditel No 1*[39] (a case on Article 59 on the freedom to provide services), the Court held that the right to obtain a royalty from a copyright was part of the existence of the right. In *Coditel No 2*[40] (applying Article 85 to the facts of *Coditel No 1*), the Court stated of an allegation that an exclusive territory in a copyright licence for films fell within Article 85(1):

'The mere fact that the owner of the copyright in a film has granted to a sole licensee the exclusive right to exhibit that film in the territory of a Member State and, consequently, to prohibit, during a specified period its showing by others, is not sufficient to justify the finding that such a contract must be regarded as the purpose, the means or the result of an agreement decision or concerted practice prohibited by the Treaty. The characteristics of the cinematographic industry and of its market in the Community, especially those relating to dubbing and subtitling for the benefit of different language groups, to the possibilities of television broadcasts, and to the system of financing cinematographic production in Europe serve to show that an exclusive exhibition licence is not, in itself, such as to prevent, restrict or distort competition. For example X and Y may incorporate XY Ltd in which they both hold a 501 shareholding.'[41]

It is clear from the facts of the case that the Court was fully aware of the

---

[39] Case 62/79, [1980] ECR 881, pp. 902–4.
[40] *Coditel* v. *Cine Vog Films (No. 2)*, Case 262/1, [1982] ECR 3381.
[41] Ibid., p, 3401.

financial risks associated with film production (where commercially successful films outnumber and cross-subsidize less commercially successful films) and the dictum indicates that it was further aware that a strict application of competition rules would undermine the willingness of film producers to invest in film production.

18

Abuse of Dominant Position

Article 86

Article 86 provides as follows:

'Any abuse by one or more undertakings of a dominant position within the common market or in a substantial part of it shall be prohibited as incompatible with the common market in so far as it may affect trade between Member States. Such abuse may, in particular, consist in:

   (a) directly or indirectly imposing unfair purchase or selling prices or other unfair trading conditions;

   (b) limiting production, markets or technical development to the prejudice of consumers;

   (c) applying dissimilar conditions to equivalent transactions with other trading parties, thereby placing them at a competitive disadvantage;

   (d) making the conclusion of contracts subject to acceptance by the other parties of supplementary obligations which, by their nature or according to commercial usage, have no connection with the subject of such contracts.'

Article 86 is concerned with the conduct of undertakings with dominant market power to the extent that the undertaking misuses its power. It follows that in any Article 86 case there are always two elements. First, proof that the undertaking is dominant. Secondly, proof that there has been an abuse of that dominance. It should be fully understood from the outset that the mere possession of dominance is not, prima facie, illegal. Article 86 proscribes the misuse of market power, not its existence *simpliciter*.

In broad terms, dominance sits near the extreme of the concentration spectrum discussed in Chapter 15. It describes the situation of a company which is liberated from the fetters of competition. Many reasons may account for this pre-eminent commercial position. The company may have invented a critical technology which, having been patented, affords an unassailable market position. Alternatively, the quality of its commercial performance (in terms of price, quality, range of product and service) may have resulted in the failure of its rivals who, having fallen by the wayside, leave the field to the sole occupancy of the (now) dominant company. Not every dominant position is the result of merit; dominance may be acquired as a consequence of a protected domestic market where rivals encounter entry and expansion barriers erected by governments or indeed by the incumbent firm itself.

Once dominance is acquired, the possessor of that privileged status may determine its corporate behaviour in the light of a new set of lodestars. No longer must managers monitor the conduct and demands of rivals, suppliers, or customers and adapt their commercial behaviour accordingly. When the disciplining effect of competition is chilled, the spur to innovation may diminish, the pressure to keep costs and prices down may decline, and the incentive to improve quality and service may recede. In essence, the dominant company can reap where it has not sown. Moreover, the conduct of a dominant company can exert an often disproportionate impact upon the market. Conduct that may be relatively costless to the dominant company in the short term can lead to the ruination of new entrants; the occasional act of aggression can deter potential entrants; profits made from one sector can be diverted to subsidize the efforts of another sector in which it is not dominant, thereby providing a source of 'easy money' to which other participants have no access.

Dominance is, by its very nature, a rare condition and raises legal questions of great complexity. The remainder of this chapter is devoted to unravelling these questions and to explaining the policy issues underlying the questions. The text centres upon the twin problems of abuse and dominance.

The Mischief of Article 86: the Scope of Abuse

Originally it was assumed that Article 86 was concerned with the misuse of market power but not with conduct that sought to establish or maintain dominance. A glance at the illustrative list of abuses in Article 86 reveals that concepts of fairness (Article 86(a)), prejudice (Article 86(b)), and discrimination (Article 86(c)) were perceived as the mischiefs sought to be protected against.[1] This narrow perception was rejected by the Court of Justice in the first case on dominance. In *Continental Can*,[2] the Court of Justice, in a case concerning the compatibility of a merger with Article 86, held that Article 86 had to be construed in the light not only of its spirit, general scheme, and wording but also in the light of the 'system and objectives of the Treaty'. The Court pointed out that Article 3(f) of the Treaty provides for a system ensuring that competition in the Common Market is not distorted.

---

[1] See e.g. Joliet, *Monopolization and Abuse of Dominant Position* (1970), pp. 10–12; Temple Lang, *Abuse of dominant positions in European law, Present and Future: Some Aspects*, 1978 Fordham Corporate Law Institute 25.

[2] *Europemballage and Continental Can* v. *Commission*, Case 6/72, [1973] ECR 215.

Accordingly, the Court stated: 'the provision is not only aimed at practices which may cause damage to consumers directly, but also at those which are detrimental to them through their impact on an effective competition structure, such as is mentioned in Article 3(f) of the Treaty.'

Following *Continental Can*, it became clear that Article 86 covered conduct which was not only abusive in the sense of its being unfair or prejudicial or discriminatory but *also* conduct which harmed the structure of a market regardless of its impact upon consumers. In *Hoffman La Roche* v. *Commission*,[3] the Court went one additional step further away from an analysis of Article 86 as a curb on exploitation when it held that:

'The concept of abuse is an objective concept relating to the behaviour of an undertaking in a dominant position where, as a result of the very presence of the undertaking in question, the degree of competition is weakened and which, through recourse to *methods different from those which condition normal competition* in products or services on the basis of the transactions of commercial operators, has the effect of hindering the maintenance of the degree of competition still existing in the market or the growth of that competition.'

Thus, the mischief targeted by Article 86 is multi-faceted. It is exploitative or unfair behaviour; it is conduct which is detrimental to an effective market structure; and it is business methods different from those prevailing under normal competitive conditions. If these are the mischiefs sought to be curtailed it follows that they will also be definitional terms for different categories of actual abuse.

Dominance: Product and Geographical Markets

So much for the consequences of dominance that Article 86 seeks to curb. How does the Court of Justice define the actual station of dominance? In *Michelin* v. *Commission*,[4] the Court reiterated its long-held view of dominance as:

'A position of economic strength enjoyed by an undertaking which enables it to hinder the maintenance of effective competition on the relevant market by allowing it to behave to an appreciable extent independently of its competitors and customers and ultimately of consumers.'

At the heart of this definition lies the notion of the 'relevant market'. The Commission has pointed out that the product market as a tool in competition law has its limitations:

'When a relevant market is referred to, it is primarily the dominance linked to

---

[3] Case 85/76, [1979] ECR 461, para. 6.
[4] Case 322/81, [1983] ECR 3461, 3561, 3503, para. 50.

horizontal expansion that it highlighted. A company which relies mainly on vertical integration or diversification strategies will not necessarily experience an increase in its horizontally defined market shares.

When considering dominant positions of a vertical or conglomerate nature, a somewhat artificial definition of relevant market is sometimes required. Recourse to the concept of obligatory trading partner, which concerns the relationship of dependence which may exist between two economic operators owing to their commercial dealings, may prove to be useful.'[5]

1. The Relevant Product Market

It is of the essence that the product market over which the allegedly dominant undertaking holds sway is defined. The central role of the product market in competition law is exemplified by imagining an undertaking involved in production and sale of fruit, and in particular bananas. If the market is 'all food', the market share of the company concerned is infinitesimal; if it is all fruit, it will still be *de minimis*; if it is soft fruit, the market share may be small but significant; if it is bananas, then the market share may be substantial. To determine the scope of the product market one examines substitutes. The analysis of substitutes entails a two-pronged examination. First, of demand-side substitutability; secondly, of supply-side substitutability.

Demand-side Substitutability

This determines which products compete with each other from the perspective of the consumer who may be the end-user or simply a purchaser for resale. Whilst there is no precise definition of demand-side substitutability, the European Commission has traditionally referred to the criteria of price, quality, and intended use as the primary tools of assessment. Thus, with regard to price, caviar and fish paste, whilst of the same constituents, are almost inevitably non-substitutable. Respecting quality, a gold fountain pen is not (in normal terms) a substitute for a pencil, albeit that both are writing implements. With regard to intended use, an antique Roman vase is not a substitute for a modern vase, despite both being potential receptacles for daffodils.[6] In each and every case, demand-side substitutability is a question of fact.

---

[5] See *Sixteenth Commission Competition Report* (1986), p. 234, para. 340. The Commission adds that it is: 'studying the possibility of employing this concept as a supplementary tool in cases of abuse of dominant position.'

[6] In *Hoffman La Roche* (see n. above), pp. 514–17, the Court held that vitamins for industrial and bio-nutritive uses formed different product markets because of intended use. In *Mitchelin* v. *Commission* (see n. 4 above) p. 3507, the Court held that the market for replacement tyres for buses and trucks was different to the market for the supply of tyres for original vehicles. The latter was a market for a vehicle comprising four or more wheels; the former was a market comprising single wheels. In *Hugin* v. *Commission*, Case 22/78,

None the less, over the years pointers have been given in case-law. One test apparently favoured by the Court is to measure the cross-elasticity of demand. By this is inferred that a percentage rise or fall in price will have an effect upon the levels of consumptions of a range of ostensibly substitute products. If a rise in the price of salmon paste does not stimulate an increase in demand for caviar, one may reasonably assume no or no significant cross-elasticity of demand between the two products. Conversely, if the same price-rise leads to a switch in consumer preference to pilchard paste, then a degree of elasticity exists which may indicate that salmon paste is part of a wider market for fish paste. In *United Brands* v. *Commission*,[7] the issue before the Court of Justice was whether bananas were in the same product market as fresh fruit. In arriving at the conclusion that bananas constituted a separate market, the Court was confronted with facts suggesting that bananas had 'special features' or attributes, that is, all-year-round availability, limited ability of other fruits to compete at seasonal peak periods, and the capacity of the humble banana to meet the particular needs of the young, the old, and the infirm (that is, those without teeth!) The Court also noted that there *was* an impact upon banana prices at particular times of the year when other fruits were in season; however, that this imposed only a limited price constraint which was insufficient to overturn the conclusion that bananas constituted their own market.

Supply-side Substitutability

This is concerned with the ability of a manufacturer to switch his production technology from product X to product Y, and therefore constitutes a test of whether the manufacturer of X is a rival to the manufacturer of Y. Take for instance, two chemicals performing disparate functions but with similar constituents, manufactured by two separate producers, A and B. To the consumer, the chemicals are entirely different products and are not in the same product market. However, given that A may, with but moderate cost, switch production from one chemical to the other, then A may be seen as a competitor of B in the market for B's chemical (and vice versa). In *Continental Can*, the Court criticized the Commission for failing to take sufficient account of supply-side conditions in the market for the production of tin cans:

'In order to be regarded as constituting a distinct market, the products must be individualised, not only by the mere fact that they are used for packing certain products, but by particular characteristics of production which make them specifically suitable for this purpose. Consequently, a dominant position on the

[1979] ECR 1869, the Court held that a spare part for a cash-till was in a different product market to the till itself, such that a manufacturer could dominate the spare-parts market whilst being subject to strict competition in the main-product market.

[7] Case 27/76, [1978] ECR 207.

market for light metal containers for fish and meat cannot be decisive, as long as it has not been proved that competitors from other sectors of the market for light metal containers are not in a position to enter this market, by a simple adaptation, with sufficient strength to create a serious counterweight.'[8]

In order to determine whether, and if so to what degree, supply-side substitutability exists, it is hence necessary to examine actual costs and methods of production. In *Michelin*,[9] upon examination, the Court concluded that significant differences in the plant and equipment required in the manufacture of tyres for heavy vehicles and cars meant that producers of tyres for the two vehicle-types were not in the same market.[10]

2. The Relevant Geographical Market

Once the product market is defined it becomes necessary to delineate the geographical market. A producer meeting 90 per cent of the demand from the United Kingdom might meet only 15 per cent of demand from the Community as a whole. Whereas 90 per cent of the market connotes dominance, 15 per cent does not.

It will be recalled that Article 86 speaks of dominance 'within the common market or in a substantial part of it'. Thus, it is not necessary for a company to predominate in the entire Community, provided dominance is held over a substantial part thereof. In *Suiker Unie* the Court stated:

'For the purpose of determining whether a specific territory is large enough to amount to 'a substantial part of the Common Market' within the meaning of Article 86 of the Treaty the pattern and volume of the production and consumption of the said product as well as the habits and economic opportunities of vendors and purchasers must be considered.'[11]

In applying this test to the facts of a given case, an answer is usually attainable fairly easily. Thus, the selling-area of the allegedly dominant company is often a strong indication of the size of the market. Thus, in *Suiker Unie* the geographical area was held to be Southern Germany since that was where the undertaking actually concentrated its sales.

Joint Dominance

Article 86 refers to abuse 'by one or more undertakings' of a dominant position, thus suggesting that a dominant position may be shared by

---

[8] See n. 2 above, pp. 247, 248.
[10] See also *Hugin* (n. 6 above).

[9] See n. 4 above, p. 3506.
[11] [1975] ECR 1663, 1977.

different undertakings. The meaning of these words has caused much debate. Thus, on the one hand, it is argued that joint dominance is no more than the aggregate power of a number of companies within the same corporate group.[12] Conversely, it is argued that the words have wider import, and that given that the word 'undertaking' has been construed by the Court to connote the entire corporate group, the reference to 'one or more undertakings' must, *a fortiori*, imply dominance held by a multiplicity of independent corporate groups. In *Hoffman La Roche* v. *Commission*[13] the Court implicitly limited the scope of the doctrine when it held that Article 86 could not apply to the conscious parallelism that flowed out of an oligopoly:

'A dominant position must also be distinguished from parallel courses of conduct which are peculiar to oligopolies in that in an oligopoly the courses of conduct interact, while in the case of an undertaking occupying a dominant position the conduct of the undertaking which dervies profits from that position is to a great extent determined unilaterally.'[14]

The curtailing of Article 86 has always disappointed the Commission, which has long harboured ambitions to use Article 86 as a device to prise open oligopolies (it will be recalled that Article 85 does not apply to conscious parallelism). In its *Sixteenth Competition Report* the Commission thus recorded that it had commissioned a study on the concept of 'shared dominance'. It identified two essential features of shared dominance:

'(i) the fact that a small number of enterprises account for most of the turnover in the market in question without any single enterprise having a dominant position;

(ii) the high degree of interdependence among the decisions of the enterprises.'[15]

Having enumerated these features, the Commission identified 'tacit collusion' as the mischief to be proscribed:

'In the case of a tight oligopoly, the reduction in the intensity of competition does not necessarily lead to the appearance of tacit collusion. Tacit collusion may, however, arise from the fact that members of the oligopoly become aware of their interdependence and of the probably unfavourable consequences of adopting a competitive attitude.'

---

[12] See e.g. Commission decision in *Continental Can OJ* 1972, L 7/25; *CMLR* D11, where *the* Commission focused upon the conduct of the US parent, its German subsidiary and Europemballage (also a subsidiary); see also Cases 6/73 et seq., *Commercial Solvents* v. *Commission* [1974] ECR 223, concerning the US parent and its Italian subsidiary.

[13] See n. 3 above; see also *Züchner* v. *Bayerische Vereinsbank* Case 172/80 [1981] ECR 2021, para. 10.

[14] *Hoffman La Roche*, para. 39.

[15] *Sixteenth Commission Competition Report* (1986), p. 230, para. 331.

Later,[16] the Commission stated: 'Abuse of shared dominant positions may have many unfavourable consequences for the economy as a whole, including the final consumer (e.g., higher prices, a slowdown of technological progress, imposition of unfair terms of trade).'[17]

What warrants comment about this statement is that the Commission appears to believe that there must be a degree of tacit collusion before Article 86 is triggered. If this is so, then there exists a legal symmetry between shared dominance under Article 86 and a concerted practice under Article 85 which invites the question: If Article 85 applies, why bother to extend Article 86? One answer is that the Commission seeks to use Article 86 as a means of overcoming evidential deficiencies. If the evidence does not exist to prove a concerted practice, so that Article 85 is excluded, can the surrounding economic evidence be used to infer shared dominance under Article 86 which does not rely upon proof of collusion? As noted above, the Commission believes that 'tacit collusion' arises from awareness of two facts: (i) interdependence; (ii) the probably unfavourable consequences of adopting a competitive attitude. This awareness may not be provable by documentary or other 'hard' evidence; it may, however, be deducible from the commercial conduct of the undertakings concerned over a period of time.

Perhaps spurred by the study, the Commission decided, in *Flat Glass*,[18] that three producers of flat glass in Italy enjoyed a position of collective dominance which they had abused. The market was characterized in terms redolent of their comments in the *Sixteenth Competition Report*: 'FP, SIV and VP, as participants in a tight oligopoly, enjoy a degree of independence from competitive pressures that enable them to impede the maintenance of effective competition, notably by not having to take account of the behaviour of the other market participants.'[19] In arriving at the concluson that collective dominance existed, the Commission identified a number of factors: (i) a joint market share of between 79 and 95 per cent for different types of glass; (ii) an insularity from competition to a significant degree; (iii) high barriers to entry in terms of the scale of investment required to enter relative to the forecast small increase in demand over the next decade. In addition, the Commission noted a high level of co-ordination between the parties as to marketing. The Commission decision in *Flat Glass* concentrates as much on Article 85 as 86, thus showing that, in the view of the Commission, the provisions are not mutually exclusive.

The view of the non-mutual exclusivity of Articles 85 and 86 was largely confirmed in the first substantive ruling on competition law by

---

[16] *Sixteenth Commission Competition Report* (1986), p. 231.
[17] Ibid., p. 232, para. 333.
[18] OJ 1989, L 33/44, on appeal, *SIV* v. *Commission*, Case 75/89.
[19] Para. 78.

the Court of First Instance in *BTG-Tetrapak*,[20] where the Court, in a fully reasoned judgment, held that the fact that an agreement was exempt pursuant to a block exemption under Article 85(3) did *not* preclude the operation of Article 86.

[20] (July 1990).

19

Different Types of Abuse

In this chapter attention is focused upon different types of abuse. It is not the purpose of this chapter either to provide nuts-and-bolts detail or to be exhaustive in its coverage of different types of conduct that may be abusive. However, it is hoped that the commentary and analysis will provide an understanding of the themes (economic and legal) which underpin decisions of the Commission and judgments of the Court, and will enable the reader to adopt a more questioning approach to the issues raised. To this end, the chapter concentrates upon a number of areas, principally: excessive pricing; predatory pricing; abusive discounts; tying and delivered pricing; the acquisition of exclusive access to critical technology; and refusals to supply goods or information, or to license technology.

Excessive Prices

The classic example of abusive behaviour is the monopolist charging excessively high prices for its goods and services. Article 86(a) prohibits the imposition of 'unfair' prices. In *Sirena* v. *Eda*,[1] the Court stated: 'As regards the abuse of a dominant position, although the price level of the product may not of itself necessarily suffice to disclose such an abuse, it may, however, if unjustified by any objective criteria, and if it is particularly high, be a determining factor.' In *General Motors Continental*,[2] the Court went one step further and held that a price was abusive if it: 'is excessive in relation to the economic value of the service provided.'

Whilst it is relatively easy to define an excessive price, as in the terms above, it is a task of some complexity to devise a workable method for determining when a price is unfair. In *United Brands*,[3] the Court repeated the General Motors test ('charging a price which is excessive because it has no reasonable relation to the economic value of the produce supplied is . . . an abuse').[4] However, the Court went on to lay down the following test of excess or unfairness:

---

[1] Case 40/70, (1971) ECR 69, 85. See also *Parke, Davis* v. *Probel*, Case 24/67, [1968] ECR 55, 72.

[2] Case 26/75, [1975] ECR 1367, 1378, 1379.

[3] Case 27/76, [1978] ECR 207.

[4] Ibid, p. 301.

'The questions therefore to be determined are whether the difference between the costs actually incurred and the price actually charged is excessive, and, if the answer to this question is in the affirmative, whether a price has been imposed which is either unfair in itself or when compared to competing products.'

Prima facie, therefore, the Court has stipulated that a dominant company's prices should be measured against their costs. This test is one applied regularly by the United Kingdom Monopolies and Mergers Commission, so is evidently not beyond the capabilities of an anti-trust agency.[5] None the less, it is a methodology which the Commission appears to find singularly unattractive. First, the assessment of production costs entails the regulator in a 'hands-on' accountancy analysis of the undertaking being investigated. This is a complex task, consuming a considerable portion of the resources of the regulator if the task is to be performed effectively. Naturally, the Commission can demand the costings of the dominant undertaking (it has extensive powers of investigation). However, when in possession of such data how can the Commission test its veracity? Unlike the United Kingdom MMC, the Commission is not armed with a back-up staff of economists and accountants who specialize in these sorts of investigations. Secondly, even if the Commission were able to undertake full-scale cost/price analyses, what criteria should be used to determine when a price is excessive? A very high price may (arguably) be justified by a number of factors, for instance: (a) the need to recoup very high past research-and-development costs incurred over an extended period in developing new products, many of which failed to prove viable; (b) the need to make provision for future or continued research and development into the product in question in circumstances where the life-cycle of the product in its current form is short; or (c) the need to overcome high levels of initial marketing-and distribution-costs.[6]

In *United Brands*, the Court recognized that cost/price analysis was, in some instances, a difficult task:

'While appreciating the considerable and at times very great difficulties in working out production costs which may sometimes include a discretionary apportionment of indirect costs and general expenditure and which may vary significantly according to the size of the undertaking, its object, the complex nature of its set up, its territorial area of operations, whether it manufactures one or several products, the number of its subsidiaries and their relationship with each other, the production costs of the banana do not seem to present any insuperable problems.'

Notwithstanding such problems, it seems that prima facie the Commission

---

[5] See e.g. MMC Report into Chlordiazepoxide and Diazepam (1973) HC 197.
[6] See e.g. MMC Report into Supply of Credit Car Franchising Services (1982) Cmnd 8034. The justification for high prices may disappear after the initial period: see Report on Chlordiazepoxide and Diazepam (1973) HC 197.

has a duty to undertake cost/price analysis. Only if this proves impossible to perform owing to insuperable complexity may the Commission turn to alternative tests for determining whether a price is unfairly excessive. In recent times the Commission has, as noted above, turned from cost/price analysis to what one may loosely define as a test of deduced logic. Under this test, the Commission decides whether an abuse has occurred by comparing the dominant undertaking's prices, not with its own *costs*, but with the *prices* charged both by the dominant undertaking in the past and with prices charged by other undertakings selling the same product in the same or another geographical market. The logical test, therefore, relies upon a deduction made upon a comparative assessment of prices, not costs. For example, a graph of the dominant company's prices over an extended period of time may reveal substantial jumps in price to levels which cannot be attributed to inflation. This graph leads to the conclusion that, by steadily increasing prices above the level of inflation, the dominant undertaking must (logically) be charging an excessive price. Alternatively, a comparison of prices between the dominant undertaking and other undertakings selling the same product in other markets may reveal significant price differences leading to the conclusion that the dominant company's prices are excessive.

The Commission considers that excessive pricing can occur also in other circumstances. In *British Telecommunications* (BT),[7] it decided that the statutory monopoly of BT had been abused by, *inter alia*, making:

'The use of telephone and telex installations subject to the acceptance by message-forwarding agencies of an obligation to charge prices that had no connection with the type and quality of the telecommunications services provided by them, but rather arose out of [the monopolist's] desire to protect the revenue of other national telecommunication authorities.'

Thus, excessive prices to protect a third party's revenues are an abuse equal to excessive pricing to protect the dominant undertaking's revenues. In *C.I.C.C.E.*,[8] the Commission accepted that a dominant purchaser could, in principle, abuse its position by offering excessively low purchase-prices to suppliers.

The approach of the European Commission and Court may be placed in context by adverting to the approaches adopted by the US authorities. In the US, excessive pricing by a monopolist has never played a significant role in anti-trust analysis. Thus, in *Berkey Photo*[9] it was held:

---

[7] OJ 1982, L 360/36, affirmed on appeal, *Italy* v. *Commission*, Case 41/83, [1985] ECR 873.

[8] *C.I.C.C.E.* V. *Commission*, Case 298/83, [1985] ECR 1105; complaint of abusive purchasing rejected, however, on the facts.

[9] *Berkey Photo* v. *Eastman Kodak* 603 F.2d 263 (2d Cir 1979), *certiorari* denied 444 US 1093 (1980).

'Excessive prices, maintained through exercise of a monopolist's control of the market, constituted one of the primary evils that the Sherman Act was intended to correct . . . But unless the monopoly has bolstered its power by wrongful actions, it will not be required to pay damages merely because its prices may later be found excessive. Setting a high price may be a use of monopoly power, but is not in itself anti-competitive. Indeed, although a monopolist may be expected to charge a somewhat higher price than would prevail in a competitive market, there is probably no better way for it to guarantee that its dominance will be challenged than by extracting the highest price it can . . . Judicial oversight of pricing policies would place the courts in a role akin to that of a public regulatory commission . . . We would be wise to decline that function unless Congress clearly bestows it upon us.'

In summary, a number of points are worthy of mention. First, the Commission and Court support intervention into the excessive-pricing strategies of dominant companies. There is some apparent confusion in the precise test to be adopted to determine whether a price is excessive or not. Secondly, it should be appreciated that the value of intervention is not universally recognized and that a number of (somewhat controversial) objections or caveats can be posited: (i) high prices are not anti-competitive where they serve to stimulate market entry; (ii) monopoly profits stimulate innovation; (iii) the task of assessing the fairness or otherwise of a dominant undertaking's prices is an imprecise art form which is unsatisfactory where a finding of infringement can result in penalties being imposed; (iv) there is no accepted wisdom as to when high prices are justified, for example, to support future research-and-development efforts; (v) excessive prices do not impair actual or potential rivals' opportunities, rather, as noted above, they can stimulate such opportunities; (vi) price regulation is at base at odds with the concept of the free market-place underlying competition law. Thirdly, whilst the Commission and the Court would eschew much of the above it is notable that, almost without exception, the only cases in which excessive prices have been challenged have been cases of dominant undertakings cushioned by very high or insuperable entry barriers (such as statutory monopolists). In such circumstances, potential competition is at best improbable and, most likely, impossible. Accordingly, the excessive price will not operate as a green light stimulating new entry. Moreover, even a cursory examination of the case-law reveals that intervention has occurred in non-high-tech areas, thus circumventing difficult questions such as whether excessive prices are justified to amortize or justify past and future development costs.

Predatory Prices

The converse of the excessive price is the predatory price, being a price set at a low level with an anti-competitive consequence. To take a very simple example: a Dominant Undertaking, D, receives intelligence of the entry of Hopeful Company, H. Accordingly, D drops its prices to the market to a level that it knows H cannot compete with. H's entry to the market is, therefore, forced to be at a level at which an inadequate return is made and which cannot be sustained. By its conduct D has precluded H as a rival and protected its dominant position. Predatory-pricing cases have played a minor role in EEC competition law, with one notable exception. In *ECS–AKZO*,[10] the Commission fined the Dutch chemicals giant, AKZO, 10 million ECU as a penalty for predatory pricing in relation to a small, Gloucester-based, company called ECS. The latter had until 1979 produced benzoyl-peroxide which it had sold as a bleaching agent to customers who used it to treat flour. Subsequently, ECS decided to sell the chemical to customers in the polymer industry. AKZO notified ECS that this expansion would be responded to by AKZO with a reduction in its prices to customers in the flour-additives sector. ECS's refusal to bow to such threats resulted in AKZO implementing price-reductions in quotes to ECS's customers. The Commission considered this conduct to amount to an abuse of dominance. It found that the prices quoted were, in some instances, very substantially below the cost of production. However, it concluded that abuse can occur at price levels which cover the aggressor's costs:

'The dominant firm has an interest in achieving its aim at the lowest cost to itself (thus in the present case AKZO concentrated its price cuts on the flour additives market which was extremely important to ECS but of relatively minor significance to AKZO in the context of its overall organic peroxides business). The important element is the rival's assessment of the aggressor's determination to frustrate its expectations, for example as to rate of growth or attainable profit margins, rather than whether or not the dominant firm covers its own costs. There can thus be an anti-competitive object in price-cutting, whether or not the aggressor sets its prices above or below its own costs (in one or other meaning of the term).'[11]

For dominant undertakings, the Commission's decision that an above-cost price may be abusive creates significant problems of classification. If, to revert to the original hypothetical example, H had entered the market with an aggressive marketing campaign which

---

[10] OJ 1985, L 374/1. See Green, *Commercial Agreements and Competition Law: Practice and Procedure in the UK and EEC* (1986), pp. 351–9, for a more detailed analysis of the issues involved, together with an explanation of the different definitions of 'cost' in question.

[11] *ECS–AKZO*, para. 79 of decision. See also *Napier Brown–British Sugar*, OJ 1988, L 284–41.

entailed very-low-price offers, would D be abusing its dominance if it responded in kind so as to avoid losing market share? Is there any difference, in effect, if D pre-empts H's entry by dropping prices in anticipation of a determined price war engendered by H?

Abusive Discounts

Not only must dominant companies refrain from over- and under-pricing their goods and services, they must also ensure that any discounts they confer upon their customers do not have any anti-competitive consequences. This they can ensure by avoiding the grant of any discount that is not objectively justified. The principal objection to non-justified discounts is that it creates both a barrier to entry to potential suppliers and distortions of competition between different customers. Invariably, illegal discounts occur at the level of sales between supplier and dealer. Thus, in *Michelin*[12] the Commission challenged a discount system operated in the Netherlands by the Michelin tyre company which the Commission alleged abused the supplier's dominance in that territory in both of the ways identified. In addition, the Commission considered, as an independent abuse, the lack of transparency inherent in the Michelin pricing system. The company gave target bonuses to its dealers according to their marketing efforts; dealers were only kept vaguely informed of the level of bonus to which they would be entitled. The level of bonus varied significantly between dealers *inter se*, and were often negotiated on an individual basis. The Commission stated that the system had the effect of ensuring that dealers remained tied into the Michelin system by the invisible pull of these uncertain, yet anticipated, bonuses. To this extent dealers were reluctant to obtain supplies from suppliers competitive with Michelin. The Court of Justice confirmed the Commission decision on appeal, and reiterated that, to be legal, discounts had to be justified by a benefit conferred upon the supplier by the dealer which reduced the supplier's burden and enabled the supplier to pass on that benefit in terms of reduced prices. In practice, it is nigh impossible to compute with precision the scope of a discount warranted by a buyer, and indeed the Commission expects only to see a reasonable relationship between the level of discount granted and the benefit obtained by the supplier. The typical justifiable discount is the volume discount, whereby the size of the purchase enables the supplier to make cost-savings in carriage and

---

[12] OJ 1981, L 353/33; [1982] 1 CMLR 643, on appeal Case 322/81 [1983] ECR 3461. See also *Hoffman La Roche* v. *Commission*, Case 85/76, [1979] ECR 461—discounts because of loyalty of customer are abusive.

administration which cost-savings may be passed on to the buyer in terms of a lower price.

The Court has condemned across-the-board discounts offered to buyers if they will take a range of products from the supplier, since this operates to tie the buyers to the supplier and heightens the entry barrier to rival suppliers who perhaps offer only one of the products supplied by the dominant company.

In summary, discounts may cause 'abusive' consequences at two levels of the market. First, they may operate to tie (in a loose, non-formal, sense) buyers to the dominant supplier such that rival suppliers are foreclosed from the market; secondly, in so far as the discount is not granted in a uniform manner, it distorts competition at the level of the buyer where competing buyers (for example, competing wholesalers or dealers) are offered the same goods at different prices. The real complaint against lack of transparency of price is not that it has an independent anti-competitive effect, but rather that it exacerbates the harm flowing from the discount. By creating a degree of mystique or secrecy over prices and the levels of discounts that will be offered, dealers will be reluctant to acquire products from a supplier other than the dominant supplier since they may believe (correctly or falsely) that they will prejudice their chances of an increased discount. Where prices and discounts are transparent, the buyer may plan to maximize his discount from the dominant supplier whilst simultaneously buying from a third party.

Tying and Delivered Pricing

Article 86(d) prohibits: 'making the conclusion of contracts subject to acceptance by the other parties of supplementary obligations which, by their nature or according to commercial usage, have no connection with the subject of such contracts.' This describes a 'tie' whereby the supplier requires that the purchaser must purchase its requirements of a second product (the tied product) as a condition of being able to purchase a first product (the tying product). Typically, the seller has market power over the tying product such that buyers who wish to acquire the tying product have no option but to take the two products combined, there being no effective alternative source of the tying product other than from the dominant supplier. Tying can occur in many different circumstances. For example: Supplier S refuses to sell widgets over which he is dominant unless Purchaser P also takes gidgets; alternatively, S sells widgets together with a service contract therefore, and if P wishes to obtain maintenance services from an independent third party S refuses to drop the price.

Tying is objected to for many reasons. First, it enables a dominant company unfairly to extend its dominance into markets in which it does not enjoy dominance; secondly, it forecloses legitimate sales opportunities in the tied product market to rival suppliers; thirdly, it distorts consumer choice, in that consumers are denied choice of sources for the tied product. Conversely, commentators have pointed out that not every instance of tying is necessarily objectionable. For example, the tied and tying products may be related in some way which means that one product will not operate effectively without the other. Thus, a piece of novel, highly complex equipment may be tied in with a maintenance contract entered with the supplier in circumstances where only the manufacturer has the necessary 'hands-on' technical skills to service and maintain the equipment properly. In the absence of the tie the reputation of the supplier may be jeopardised since if servicing is performed by unqualified third parties the equipment may not work properly to the obvious dissatisfaction of the purchaser. Alternatively, tying may be a means of facilitating market entry of a new product or technology. The US Department of Justice thus stated in 1985:

'Another pro-competitive use of tying is to redistribute risk. For example, a manufacturer may induce distributors to carry a new product by selling it to them at a low price, while relying on expected sales of some item used in conjunction with the new product to generate his profits. The manufacturer, thus, assumes a greater share of the risk that the new product will be rejected by consumers. If the new product proves very popular, the distributors will require many of the related items, and the manufacturer will receive a large reward. If the new product does not succeed, however, the distributors will require very few of the related items and will have to pay very little. The 'risk sharing' efficiency may apply to a wide range of licensing, franchising, and similar distributional arrangements that involve tying.'[13]

The European Commission has been largely unsympathetic to attempts to justify tying. In *Hilti*,[14] the Commission, with minimal analysis, decided that the requirement imposed by Hilti upon users of its patented nail cartridges that they should also purchase nails from them abused the undertaking's dominance over the cartridges. The Commission rejected the argument raised by Hilti that the tie was necessary to preserve safety standards and to prevent operators from being injured by nail guns. In *British Sugar*,[15] the Commission condemned so-called delivered pricing by British Sugar whereby prices quoted were for sugar as delivered to the customer. This constituted a tie as between the product and the carriage function. The Commission

[13] US Department of Justice, *Vertical Restraint Guidelines* (25 Jan. 1985), para. 5.1.
[14] *Eurofix-Banco* v. *Hilti*, OJ 1988, L 65/19; [1969] 4 CMLR 677, on appeal, *Hilti AG* v. *Commission*, Case 98/88.
[15] OJ 1988, L 284/41.

made British Sugar offer an option between a delivered price and an ex-factory price, such that buyers could opt for the ex-factory price and arrange their own transport. In *Sabena*,[16] the Commission prohibited the attempt by SABENA—the Belgian airline—to require that access to its computer reservation system by London European (another airline) be conditional upon London European using its ground handling services. In *IBM Settlement*,[17] the Commission challenged the tie, imposed by IBM the computer manufacturer, of memory capacity to that of central processing units. Certain manufacturers of memory capacity had complained to the Commission that they were foreclosed from the memory market as a result of IBM's tie. IBM contested this assertion on the basis that memory was an integral part of the central processing unit but, to avoid a protracted legal battle, gave without prejudice undertakings to the Commission to the effect that they would, in future, offer customers the option of units with and without surplus memory. Customer preferences over subsequent years tended to suggest that IBM were correct in their analysis, since on very few occasions was the company requested to provide units without memory.

Acquisition of Exclusive Access to Critical Technology

In *BTG-Tetrapak*,[18] the Commission investigated the acquisition by Tetrapak, the dominant company in the market for aseptic cartons and equipment used for their manufacture, of a smaller rival company which was the exclusive licensee of a new and important patent from the licensor, the British Technology Group (BTG). As a result of the acquisition therefore Tetrapak became the effective licensee of this new technology licensed by BTG. On the basis of the analysis of the market by the Commission, Tetrapak was found to have 91.8 per cent of the EEC market for machines capable of filling cartons by an aseptic process with UHT-treated liquids. It is important to appreciate that as a result of the acquisition the technology in question was accessible only to Tetrapak and one other company in the EEC which had a technology with an equivalent technology, although the Commission noted that this rival technology was probably not as advanced as that acquired by Tetrapak. The Commission clearly objected to the notion of a dominant company obtaining access to a critical technology. Its concern lay in the barrier to entry that this scenario provided:

'Furthermore, acquisition by Tetra of the exclusive licence from BTG for a

---

[16] OJ 1988, L 317/47; [1989] 4 CMLR 662.
[17] [1984] 3 CMLR 147.
[18] OJ 1988, L 272/27 upheld on appeal. See Case T–51/89 judgment of 10 July 1989.

competitive technology eliminates totally any new potential competitors from using this technology to enter an already very highly concentrated market.[19]

This acquisition not only strengthened Tetra's very considerable dominance but also had the effect of preventing, or at least considerably delaying, the entry of a new competitor into a market where very little if any competition is found. The abuse therefore lasted until Tetra renounced the exclusivity.'[20]

The case raises a number of important questions. In particular, was it critical to the decision that the technology was of great technical importance? Would there have been an abuse had Tetrapak acquired an exclusive licence to a technology that was of considerably less significance? These questions are of some relevance, since they focus upon whether a dominant company can enter exclusive arrangements *at all*. It is submitted that the abuse identified by the Commission requires a critical technology or at least a technology that affords the right holder a material advantage over non-users. Had Tetrapak acquired exclusive rights to a non-critical technology, then no entry barrier of materiality would have been erected and Tetrapak's dominance would have been strengthened, if at all, to a marginal degree only. The difficulty with this approach is that, by definition, a patent has novelty and inventiveness and should confer a commercial advantage upon its holder and the holders licensees.

The approach of the Commission in *Tetrapak* was not wholly unheralded. In *Eurofirma*,[21] in 1973, the Commission considered that a purchaser of railway rolling-stock (Eurofirma) had imposed restrictive conditions on its suppliers. In particular, Eurofirma was to enjoy rights to all patents resulting from development contracts, including the right to sub-licence third parties without additional consideration. Following objections by the Commission, the contract terms were modified so as to allow Eurofirma to claim only such patent rights as were justified by its own requirement, and, further, to grant sub-licences of such patents where necessary to promote product-standardization and only then with consent of the supplier/licensor and with payment of royalties.

Refusal to Supply Goods or Information, or License Technology

Competition law is a law at odds with many traditional tenets of contract law. An example highlighting this tension is freedom of contract with its attendant doctrines of laissez faire, and, pacta sunt servanda. Contrary to these vintage contract principles, a dominant company may not choose freely with whom it wishes to contract.

---

[19] Ibid., p. 39, para. 44(1).
[20] Ibid., p. 39, para. 45.
[21] [1973] CMLR D217.

Prima facie a dominant company may not refuse to supply the goods or services over which it is dominant. The party refused supplies has no, or no adequate, alternative source of supply, and is thereby threatened with exclusion from the market-place. Refusal to supply is abusive because it is exclusionary. However, the rule is not an absolute one, and over the years exceptions and provisos have evolved. In particular, three categories of refusal require consideration: (i) refusal to supply goods and services; (ii) refusal to disclose information; (iii) refusal to license intellectual property rights.

With regard to refusals to supply goods and/or services, a dominant undertaking may refuse supplies only where it can raise an objective justification. In *Commercial Solvents* v. *Commission*,[22] the fact that the party refused supplies had been an intermittent purchaser was not an objective justification, especially given that the refusal coincided with the decision by the dominant supplier of the raw material in question to enter the downstream market in competition with the victim of the abuse. Conversely, in *BP* v. *Commission*,[23] BP refused to supply an intermittent purchaser of oil during the oil embargo of Western Europe by the OPEC states in the early 1970s. BP had drawn up a list of supply priorities which ranged from full supplies to regular customers to partial supplies (if any) to infrequent customers. The European Court held that, in the circumstances of a supply crisis, a refusal to supply could be justified. In *United Brands*,[24] the Court held that it was not an objective justification for a refusal that the purchaser was advertising a competitor's brand, since the same was normal commercial practice.

Is there a difference between blowing hot and cold (supplying then terminating supplies) and refusing ever to blow hot at all (never having supplied)? The answer, apparently, is that there is no distinction to be drawn. In *BL* v. *Commission*,[25] the Court thus condemned the refusal by British Leyland to supply type approval certificates for Metro cars imported from other Member States in circumstances where there had been no prior trading relationship.

It is clear that, for the Commission at least, a refusal to supply may be express or constructive. In *British Sugar*,[26] the Commission imposed fines for, *inter alia*, the quotation of prices that, the supplier knew, the purchaser could not possibly accept.

With regard to refusals to supply information, the Commission, in *IBM Settlement Case*,[27] challenged the refusal by IBM to disclose the interface data between its mainframe 370 computers and plug-compat-

[22] Cases 6 and 7/73, [1974] ECR 223.
[23] Case 77/77, [1978] ECR 1513.
[24] Case 26/76, [1978] ECR 207. See also *BBI/Boosey and Hawkes*, OJ 1987, L 286/36.
[25] Case 226/84, [1987] 1 CMLR 185. See also *London European–Sabena*, OJ 1988, L 317/47; [1989] 4 CMLR 662.
[26] OJ 1988, L 284/41.   [27] [1984] 3 CMLR 147.

ible equipment. The refusal to supply this technical data meant that competitors of IBM manufacturing peripheral equipment to be attached to the IBM mainframe did not have the technical information so as to ensure that their equipment could connect effectively to the IBM mainframe and 'talk' to it in an identical language. IBM denied that it was dominant over the mainframe market or that its refusal to supply the data constituted an abuse. However, in a without-prejudice settlement in 1984, IBM agreed to disclose the interface data. In *Magill TV Guide/ITP, BBC and RTE*,[28] the Commission challenged the refusal by the publishing arms of TV companies to disseminate advance listings of programmes. The Magill TV Guide wished to publish listings for each company in a single publication. The Commission required the companies, which, it decided, were dominant over their own pro-gramme data, to supply the information. So far as the Commission is concerned, information is equivalent to goods. However, with regard to this conclusion, it is necessary to consider how the Commission's position is compatible with the fact that compilations of data may be protected by copyright, and the sympathetic rulings of the Court of Justice discussed below in *Veng* v. *Volvo*[29] and *Maxicar* v. *Renault*.[30]

Turning finally to the question of the refusal to license copyright (or indeed other intellectual property rights), one is drawn ineluctably to consider the position of spare parts. It has long been established that whilst a company may have little market power over its principal product range, it may none the less be dominant over the spare parts or components used in the principal product.[31] In *Veng* v. *Volvo*,[32] the Court of Justice was asked to rule on whether a motor-vehicle manufacturer, who was alleged to be dominant over its spare parts, could refuse to license the design rights to an independent spare-parts manufacturer who wished to produce parts. The Court ruled that the specific subject matter of the intellectual property right included the right to decide whether or not to license third parties, and therefore it was not an abuse under Article 86 for the car manufacturer to refuse to license its design rights. However, the Court did add three caveats. It stated that it would be an abuse for the manufacturer to over-price its products; to refuse to supply the finished product; and to under-produce the product such that demand was under-satisfied. The Court did not go one step further, however, to clarify whether the remedy for any of these abuses was a compulsory licence or was merely a fine and/or an order to terminate the abuse.

[28] OJ 1988, L 78/43, on appeal *RTV* v. *Commission*, Case 76/89 *et al.*
[29] Case 238/87, [1989] 4 CMLR 122, noted Korah (1988), 12 EIPR 381.
[30] Case 53/87, judgment of 5 Oct. 1988.
[31] See e.g. *Hugin* v. *Commission*, Case 22/78, [1979] ECR 1869; Commission decision OJ 1978, L 22/23; [1978] 1 CMLR D19.
[32] See n. 29 above.

20
Mergers, Take-overs, and Joint Ventures

In this chapter the analysis focuses upon the application of both Articles 85 and 86. In focus are take-overs, mergers, and joint ventures. Take-overs and mergers entail a change in corporate structure: X acquires Y which is brought under the legal control of X, perhaps as a subsidiary. Alternatively, Y may disappear as a discrete legal entity and its assets simply be absorbed into the organization of X. A joint venture results in two (or more) companies setting up a joint company to perform a function on behalf of the parents. For example, the joint venture may conduct pure research and development into a product or process; alternatively it may manufacture a product. It may even sell products manufactured by the parents separately. The common feature of a merger and a joint venture which makes them suitable for common analysis is the degree of permanent integration that is brought about in the organization of the parties. Obviously, mergers represent a form of total integration whereas joint ventures constitute partial integration. In considering the text below, it must be borne in mind that, as with all forms of commercial transaction, the market-place engenders an infinite variety of different commercial and corporate vehicles for co-operation. Accordingly, this text deals in generalization only and does not take account of the peculiarities of different transactions.

Mergers and Take-overs

Mergers and take-overs have been one of the most vexed areas of European competition law. As a result of the complexity of the issues raised, the European Commission has, until recently, intervened rarely in such transactions. Indeed, until 1989 the only merger case under Article 86 to come before the Court of Justice was *Continental Can*,[1] and this case forms a logical starting-point. In this case the Commission held

---

[1] Commission decision OJ 1972, L 7/25; [1972] CMLR D11; judgment of the Court, *Europemballage Corporation and Continental Can Co. Inc.* v. *Commission*, Case 6/72, [1973] ECR 215; [1973] CMLR 199.

that the take-over by Continental Can (an American company) of Thomassen and Drijver-Verblif (a Dutch company) abused a dominant position. On appeal the Court upheld the legal analysis of the Commission to the effect that Article 86 could apply to mergers: 'Abuse may . . . occur if an undertaking in a dominant position strengthens such position in such a way that the degree of dominance reached substantially fetters competition, i.e. that only undertakings remain in the market whose behaviour depends on the dominant one.'[2] The Court, however, reversed the Commission decision on the factual basis that the Commission had failed adequately to define the product market. In concluding that Article 86 applied to mergers, the Court rejected a number of arguments that were put forward and which had attracted the support of commentators. First, it was contended that since Article 66 ECSC contained detailed provisions governing mergers in the coal and steel sector the absence of an equivalent provision in the EEC Treaty meant that no such provision or power could be implied. Secondly, it was argued that Article 86 and the examples of abuse recited in the text of the Article applied only to practices harming consumers or trading partners, but not the market structure. In rejecting these points the Court placed reliance upon the broader aims and objectives of the Treaty, in particular as set out in Articles 3(f) and 85. The former provision, of course, states boldly that competition is not to be distorted in the Common Market.

The ruling in *Continental Can* sat uneasily with the traditional approach of the Commission towards take-overs and mergers under Article 85. In 1966 the Commission explained, in a 'Memorandum on the problems of concentration within the Common Market',[3] that Article 85 did not apply to 'agreements whose purpose is the acquisition of total or partial ownership of enterprises or the reorganisation of the ownership of enterprises'.[4] The logic behind the Memorandum was more pragmatic than juridical. The Commission claimed:

1. The application of Article 85 would ensnare too many transactions;
2. The criteria for exemption in Article 85(3) was unsuited to mergers and, in particular, the revocability of exemption would result in the undermining of vested property rights (would the acquiring company have to divest itself after the expiration of, for instance, a ten-year exemption under Article 85(3)?);
3. The sanction of automatic voidness under Article 85(2) was less suitable than the mechanism in Article 66 ECSC for de-concentration;

[2] Commission decision para. 26.
[3] 'Le problème de la concentration dans le marché commun', Études CEE, Série Concurrence No. 3 (1966).
[4] Ibid., p. 24.

4. Article 85 would not, in any event, catch take-overs such as the open-market hostile take-over occurring across a stock exchange. This would leave open the possibility of evasion.[5]

Much of this traditional wisdom was cast into doubt by the judgment of the European Court in *BAT* v. *Commission*.[6] In that case the Commission applied Article 85 to an agreement between Philip Morris (PM) and Rembrandt (R) (rival tobacco-products manufacturers). R owned Rothmans Tobacco (Holdings) Ltd (RT), which itself owned Rothmans International plc (RI), a rival of PM. The effect of the PM/R agreement was to give the parties joint control over the business affairs of RI. British American Tobacco (BAT) and RJ Reynolds (RJR) complained to the Commission that the agreement between PM and R was anti-competitive. Following negotiations between the Commission and PM and R, the latter modified the agreement such that PM reduced its shareholding to 30.8 per cent in RI, which shareholding equated to 24.9 per cent of the voting rights (that is, just below that required to block a special resolution (75 per cent of votes) of the target company). R retained control over the target. Each party gave the other rights of first refusal should either intend to sell the shares. The Commission, following these changes, addressed formal letter decisions to the complainants rejecting their complaints. These decisions were appealed, under Article 173 EEC, to the Court which, in a seminal judgment, held, *inter alia*:

'37. Although the acquisition by one company of an equity interest in a competitor does not in itself constitute conduct restricting competition, such an acquisition may nevertheless serve as an instrument for influencing the commercial conduct of the companies in question so as to restrict or distort competition on the market on which they carry on business.

38. That will be true in particular where, by agreement, the investing company obtains legal or *de facto* control of the commercial conduct of the other company or where the agreement provides for commercial cooperation between the companies or creates a structure likely to be used for such cooperation.

39. That may also be the case where the agreement gives the investing company the possibility of reinforcing its position at a later stage and taking effective control of the other company. Account must be taken not only of the immediate effects of the agreement but also of its potential effects and of the possibility that the agreement may be a part of a long-term plan.

40. Finally, every agreement must be assessed in its economic context and in particular in the light of the situation pertaining on the relevant market . . .'.

---

[5] See also *Mecaniver/PPG*, OJ 1985, L 35/54.
[6] Joined Cases 142 and 158/84, [1988] 4 CMLR 24.

It should be borne in mind when considering this dictum that the case concerned the acquisition of a minority shareholding in a competitor (PM's 24.9 per cent share of voting rights in RI; see above) and not the acquisition of a controlling interest. A number of points warrant mention. First, it is clear that the mere holding of a passive share of a competitor is not anti-competitive. Thus, X can hold 20 per cent of the shares in its arch-rival Y as an investment without Y coming thereby under the sway of X. Secondly, it is the agreement that offends under Article 85 and not the vesting of property rights (that is, the shares) in the purchaser; were it to be otherwise, chaos would ensue as the authorities sought to unravel share transactions occurring over stock exchanges between anonymous sellers and buyers. Thirdly, it is tolerably clear that the percentage holding in the rival is not the key to the application of Article 85. Rather, it is the ability of the purchaser to influence the commercial conduct of the target, and this is a very broad and difficult-to-define trigger for Article 85. Fourthly, paragraph 39 appears to catch so-called 'springboard clauses' whereby the purchaser obtains the 'possibility' of acquiring the capacity for influence. Thus, for example, a clause which states that the purchaser may (at a price) call for (say) 1½ per cent of the shares of the purchaser in circumstances where the purchaser's existing holding falls just short of affording the capacity to influence, could infringe Article 85. Fifthly, paragraph 40 makes it clear that the economic context is important. On the facts of the case, the tobacco market was oligopolistic and protected by high barriers to entry thus encouraging the view that an agreement whereby shares were acquired in a rival could, in such a market, restrict competition.

Following the BAT judgment, the law on take-overs and mergers was in disarray. Article 86 applied as per *Continental Can*; Article 85 applied to influence-bearing minority shareholding as per *BAT*; uncertainty applied to acquisitions of majority shareholdings. Did *BAT* apply by implication or did the 1966 Memorandum remain valid as to the minimalist intentions it conveyed?

The solution to the problem arrived in 1989 in the wake of innumerable years of political wrangling. In that year the Council of Ministers finally adopted a regulation on the control of concentrations.[7] Pursuant to this Regulation, 'concentrations' as defined in Article 3 must be pre-notified to the Commission. From Article 1 it is clear that only concentrations whereby the aggregate world-wide turnover of all the undertakings concerned is more than 5,000 million ECU, and the aggregate Community-wide turnover of at least two of the undertakings concerned is more than 250 million ECU, fall within the Regulation. These thresholds are to be reviewed before the end of the fourth year

[7] Reg. 4064/89/EEC, OJ 1989, L 395/1 (30 Dec. 89), coming into force 21 Sept. 1990.

following that of the adoption of the Regulation by the Council. Under Article 2 of the Regulation a long list of economic criteria are set out and are to be used as the criteria of appraisal. It is notable that the criteria are loosely based on Article 85(3). However, under Article 2(3) a concentration is unacceptable where it creates or strengthens a dominant position. Thus, the Regulation combines features of both Articles 85 and 86.[8] The Regulation disapplies Regulation 17/62/EEC (the normal competition-procedure regulation), with the legal consequence that for concentrations not within the Regulation, in effect, only national competition authorities may intervene. In policy terms the Regulation will allow the Commission to control concentrations pursuant to a special statutory regime and thereby avoid many of the legal problems posed by the application of Articles 85 and 86 in their unmodified form.

Joint Ventures

As explained in the introduction to this chapter, a great variety of joint venture exists in the market-place. Variety occurs not only with respect to the structure of the joint venture in corporate terms but also with regard to the functions ascribed to the joint-venture vehicle. In a typical joint venture, X and Y will set up a new company—Newco—which X and Y will own in equal part. The parents will subscribe to the share capital of Newco, appoint its directors, and determine the shape of its constituent documents (such as the articles and memorandum of association). Invariably, X and Y will conclude a joint-venture or shareholders agreement which will specify the commercial purpose and function of Newco and will make provision for the grant (by way of licence, assignment, or otherwise) to the joint venture of intellectual property and any other rights necessary to enable Newco to operate effectively.

Where does EEC competition law apply? Article 85 can apply in two principal ways: first, it can apply to the very existence of the joint venture; secondly, it can apply additionally or alternatively to the individual clauses contained in the joint-venture agreement. It is necessary to consider both of these issues separately.

First, when will Article 85 apply to the very existence of the joint venture? The Commission has taken the view that Article 85(1) applies to the entire agreement when the parent companies are *actual* or *potential* competitors. It is generally relatively easy to determine whether X and Y are *actual* competitors; they will be producing substitutable products and selling to the same categories of customer. Considerable difficulty,

---

[8] See the statements of the Council and the Commission on the application of the Regulation, [1990] 4 CMLR 314, 315, para. (d).

however, arises in determining whether X and Y are *potential* competitors. In the *Thirteenth Annual Competition Report*,[9] the Commission laid down the tests it applies to determine the question:

'Input: Does the investment expenditure involved substantially exceed the financing capacity of each partner? Does each partner have the necessary technical know-how and sources of supply of input products?

Production: Is each partner familiar with the process technology? Does each partner itself produce inputs for or products derived from the JV's product and does it have access to the necessary production facilities?

Sales: Is the actual or potential demand such that it would make it feasible for each of the partners to manufacture the product on its own? Does each have access to the necessary distribution channels for the JV's product?

Risk: Could each partner bear the technical and financial risks associated with the production operations of the JV alone?'

In essence, the Commission is asking whether the parties had the necessary financial, technical, and operational ability and willingness to enable them to enter the market without a joint-venture partner. If the answer to the questions is that the parties had the necessary ability, then an agreement between them restricts competition between undertakings which could have been in the market as independents competing with each other. Conversely, if the answer to the questions is that either one[10] or both of the joint-venture parties could not have 'gone it alone', then the joint venture will not eliminate a prospective entrant from the market and there is no competition between the parties to be restricted.[11]

Whilst the above analysis is fine in theory, in practice the Commission has a tendency to conclude on equivocal evidence that many large parties are potential competitors. There is an unwritten presumption that large, international companies may enter almost any market that they are seriously interested in, given their huge financial resources or ready access to venture capital and the ready availability of technology in the form of either licensed-in patents or technical know-how. Notwithstanding, the 1983 guidelines do present a step towards a more realistic and less interventionist regulatory approach. The guidelines contrast markedly with the approach prior thereto, such as was evidenced in *Rockwell-Iveco*,[12] when the Commission concluded that Article 85(1) applied to a production joint venture between a manufacturer of axles and a manufacturer of commercial vehicles.

[9] Para. 55.
[10] See e.g. *Mitchell Cotts-Sofiltra*, OJ 1987, L 41/31.
[11] See *Optical Fibres*, OJ 1986, L 236/30.
[12] OJ 1983, L 224/19.

Individual Clauses in Agreements

If a joint venture *per se* falls within Article 85 because its parents are actual or potential competitors, this affects the analysis of the individual clauses in the agreement to a substantial degree. Clearly, a clause may exert a different economic impact depending upon whether it limits the behaviour of rivals or not. Before considering, briefly, certain different types of clause, it is convenient to describe what may be termed an 'economic rule of thumb', that is, the nearer the agreement is to the actual market-place, the greater its vulnerability to competition law. In very broad terms it is possible to identify three operational stages for the typical joint venture: first, joint research and development (R&D); secondly, joint production; and thirdly, joint sales and marketing. The latter stage entails the joint venture being an active participant in the heart of the market; the first two stages are pre-market. Clearly, joint R&D is furthest from the market.

In 1990 the Commission issued a non-binding Notice on the application of Article 85 to joint ventures. In that Notice the Commission acknowledges the applicability of the ancillary restraints doctrine. Thus, clauses in joint-venture agreements which are directly related to the joint venture and necessary for its proper functioning may escape Article 85(1). Those not meeting such criteria fall to be considered under Article 85(3).

The Commission has adopted two block-exemption regulations on joint ventures. These concern R&D agreements and specialization agreements. In addition, there exists a long-standing Notice of 1968 on Co-operation Agreements, which remains of some value as a guide to Commission policy.

In Regulation 418/85/EEC, the Commission provided a block exemption for certain types of R&D agreement. In many respects the Regulation reveals a high degree of intellectual sophistication, it lays down rules for a wide range of issues that arise in R&D arrangements. However, notwithstanding such sophistication, in practice it has largely failed to achieve its purpose. The Regulation is a victim of its own cleverness and in practice it has proven rare for an actual R&D agreement to fulfil all the conditions and complex rules of the Regulation. One example shows the problem. For an R&D agreement to obtain exemption it must satisfy certain 'conditions' set out in Article 2. Article 2(c) reads: 'The exemption provided for in Article 1 shall apply on condition that . . . (c) where the agreement provides only for joint research and development each party is free to exploit the results of the joint research and development *and any pre-existing technical knowledge necessary therefore* (emphasis added).' For many companies this condition is unacceptable. In many R&D agreements the parties contribute to the venture certain basic pre-existing technology (sometimes described as the 'background' technology) which is essential if the venture is to create a new or advanced technology (sometimes described as the 'foreground' technology). The *raison d'être* of the venture will be to realize the new or advanced technology, and it will be understood by the parties that they will all have unlimited access to the fruits of the labour. However, it will rarely be part of the expectations of the parties that the background technology they contribute to the venture will be available to the other parties for them to exploit freely as they see fit, yet this is the implication to be drawn from the language of the Regulation. As such, the condition in Article 2(c) operates to deter many parties from seeking to use the block exemption.

Perhaps the most useful legal point to arise from the Regulation is to be found in paragraph 2 of the preamble, which states:

'As stated in the Commission's 1968 Notice concerning agreements, decisions and concerted practices in the field of cooperation between enterprises, agreements on the joint execution of research work or the joint development of the results of the research, up to but not including the stage of industrial application, generally do not fall within Article 85(1) of the Treaty.'

Many parts of industry have viewed this statement as a green light to enter pre-industrial stage joint ventures but not to notify the same to the Commission.

Regulation 417/85/EEC provides block exemption for specialization agreements. These exist where, say, X and Y agree to concentrate their production efforts on a single product and then, in order that both parties may supply a full range of product, cross-supply each other. The block exemption exempts such agreements where certain thresholds are met. These are: (1) that the products in question do not amount to more than 20 per cent of the market; and (2) that the aggregate annual turnover of all parties does not exceed 500 million ECU.

The 1968 co-operation-agreements Notice sets down Commission policy on certain types of co-operation agreement. A co-operation agreement may be distinguished from a joint venture in that the parties do not incorporate or employ a separate company or corporate vehicle for the performance of the task agreed upon. The Notice recognizes the commercial value of certain co-operative activities as enhancing efficiency. In particular, the Commission views the Notice as beneficial to small and medium-sized undertakings seeking to combine in order to compete more effectively with larger competitors. The Notice covers, in summary: (i) exchanges of information relating to non-price matters such as opinion or experience, the execution of joint market studies, and the joint preparation of statistical and calculation models; (ii) joint accounting or financial management; (iii) joint research and development;

(iv) joint use of transport, production, storage, and transportation equipment; (v) joint execution of orders where the parties are not competitors; (vi) joint selling or after-sales and repairs where the parties are not competitors; (vii) joint advertising; and (viii) joint use of common labels to designate a certain quality.

21
State Aid

Articles 92 and 93 of the Treaty of Rome read as follows:

'Article 92

1. Save as otherwise provided in this Treaty, any aid granted by a Member State or through State resources in any form whatsoever which distorts or threatens to distort competition by favouring certain undertakings or the production of certain goods shall, in so far as it affects trade between Member States, be incompatible with the common market.

2. The following shall be compatible with the common market:

(a) aid having a social character, granted to individual consumers, provided that such aid is granted without discrimination related to the origin of the products concerned;

(b) aid to make good the damage caused by natural disasters or exceptional occurrences;

(c) aid granted to the economy of certain areas of the Federal Republic of Germany affected by the division of Germany, in so far as such aid is required in order to compensate for the economic disadvantages caused by that division.

3. The following may be considered to be compatible with the common market:

(a) aid to promote the economic development of areas where the standard of living is abnormally low or where there is serious underemployment;

(b) aid to promote the execution of an important piece of common European interest or to remedy a serious disturbance in the economy of a Member State;

(c) aid to facilitate the development of certain economic activities or of certain economic areas, where such aid does not adversely affect trading conditions to an extent contrary to the common interest. However, the aids granted to shipbuilding as of 1 January 1957 shall, in so far as they serve only to compensate for the absence of customs protection, be progressively reduced under the same conditions as apply to the elimination of customs duties, subject to the provisions of this Treaty concerning common commercial policy towards third countries;

(d) such other categories of aid as may be specified by decision of the Council acting by a qualified majority on a proposal from the Commission.

Article 93

1. The Commission shall, in cooperation with Member States, keep under constant review all systems of aid existing in those States. It shall propose to the latter any appropriate measures required by the progressive development or by the functioning of the common market.

2. If, after giving notice to the parties concerned to submit their comments, the Commission finds that aid granted by a State or through State resources is not compatible with the common market having regard to Article 92, or that such aid is being misused, it shall decide that the State concerned shall abolish or alter such aid within a period of time to be determined by the Commission.

If the State concerned does not comply with this decision within the prescribed time, the Commission or any other interested State may, in derogation from the provisions of Articles 169 and 170, refer the matter to the Court of Justice direct.

On application by a Member State, the Council, may, acting unanimously, decide that aid which that State is granting or intends to grant shall be considered to be compatible with the common market, in derogation from the provisions of Article 92 or from the regulations provided for in Article 94, if such a decision is justified by exceptional circumstances. If, as regards the aid in question, the Commission has already initiated the procedure provided for in the first subparagraph of this paragraph, the fact that the State concerned has made its application to the Council shall have the effect of suspending that procedure until the Council has made its attitude known.

If, however, the Council has not made its attitude known within three months of the said application being made, the Commission shall give its decision on the case.

3. The Commission shall be informed, in sufficient time to enable it to submit its comments, of any plans to grant or alter aid. If it considers that any such plan is not compatible with the common market having regard to Article 92, it shall without delay initiate the procedure provided for in paragraph 2. The Member State concerned shall not put its proposed measures into effect until this procedure has resulted in a final decision.'

Introduction

The purpose of Articles 92 and 93 is to prevent government behaviour creating distortions of competition in the market place and between Member States. Consequently, the state-aid rules are directed at the same objectives as are the rules on competition, and form part of the Title of the Treaty on competition. Article 92 is therefore unconcerned with the form of the state intervention but appraises it according to its effects.[1] The Commission has thus criticized state aid because of its propensity to favour national producers and 'transfer difficulties on to competitors in other States'.[2] State aid is tempting to Member States for a variety of reasons: to ward off the short-term effects of recession; to plant seed capital where financial institutions are reluctant to invest; to

[1] See *Duefil*, Case 310/85, [1988] 1 CMLR 553, 556.
[2] See *Twelfth Commission Competition Report* (1983), para. 158.

facilitate the restructuring of industry; to smooth the path to the privatization of industry; and so on.

As is evident from the language of Article 92, state aid is 'incompatible' with the Community. The Article does not thus prohibit state aid outright in the manner of the prohibitions contained in Articles 85 and 86. The ostensible rationale for this choice of diluted sanction is that state aid is (arguably) less of a black-and-white issue than pure competition rules. The Commission has accordingly stressed that subvention may be an acceptable component of governmental policies to adapt local economies to evolving European and world circumstances and to fight or mitigate unemployment and regional deprivation; clearly, not every form of state aid can therefore be proscribed. Article 92 therefore recognizes that aid may be legitimate in certain circumstances and sets out fairly flexible definitions of categories of aid that are either valid *ipso facto* (Article 92(2)) or potentially valid (Article 92(3)).

The Definition of State Aid: Article 92(1)

From the language of Article 92(1) it is clear that the definition of aid comprises a number of discrete ingredients or characteristics which may be summarized as follows:

1. The aid must be granted by a Member State or through State resources;
2. The aid can take any form whatsoever;
3. The aid must distort or threaten to distort competition by favouring certain undertakings or the production of certain goods; and
4. The aid must affect trade between Member States.

Before examining each of the above, it is necessary to consider what constitutes an 'aid'. The Court of Justice has held that 'aid' is wider than a mere subsidy, which is

'Normally defined as a payment in cash or in kind made in support of an undertaking other than the payment by the purchaser or consumer for the goods or services which it produces. An aid is a very similar concept, which, however, places emphasis on its purpose and seems especially devised for a particular objective which cannot normally be achieved without outside help. The concept of an aid is nevertheless wider than that of a subsidy because it embraces not only positive benefits, such as subsidies themselves, but also interventions which, in various forms, mitigate the charges which are normally included in the budget of an undertaking and which would without, therefore, being subsidies in the strict sense of the word, be similar in character and have the same effect'.[3]

In very broad terms, therefore, the concept of aid embraces an

---

[3] *Steenkolenmijnen* v. *H.A.*, Case 30/59, [1971] ECR 1, 19.

advantage or benefit quantifiable economically which is granted to particular undertakings. Aid may hence adopt many guises: low interest-rate loans; direct cash hand-outs; sales to undertakings at an under-value; investment by the state in the equity or capital of a company in circumstances where the market-place would not have supported the undertaking; mitigation of social or fiscal charges; export credit guarantees at less than market-driven rates; payment of bonuses to attract foreign investors; and so on.[4]

It seems tolerably clear that an aid must contain an element of gratuity. In *Denkavit*,[5] Advocate General Reischl considered that an aid must be conferred for no consideration or countervailing benefit. Thus, if a site for a factory were sold by the state for a price 60 per cent of its market value, then aid worth 40 per cent of the market value would have been granted. The gratuitous element of aid is not, however, the external defining feature of aid. In *Germany* v. *Commission*,[6] the Court went further and held that assistance, whether fully paid for or otherwise, which would not under normal circumstances have been granted, could constitute aid. Thus, for instance, if the state granted a loan at commercial rates to a company who would not have been so favoured by the banks or financial markets, then the company will have received assistance it would not otherwise have obtained. Taking this to its logical extreme, an aid may constitute any assistance from the state that would be unavailable were normal market forces to operate.

The aid must be granted by a Member State or through State resources. The source of the aid may be central or local government or indeed any other public or private agency subject to the control of the State.[7] Further, bodies (whether public or private) appointed to administer an aid constitute the State or State resources for the purposes of Article 92.[8] The 'grant' of the aid may be the result of unilateral or autonomous governmental decisions. In *Denkavit*,[9] the Court stated that Article 92(1): 'refers to the decisions of Member States by which the latter, in pursuit of their own economic and social objectives, give by unilateral and autonomous decisions, undertakings or other persons

---

[4] For dozens of examples of state aid, see the Commission's annual compeition Reports.

[5] *Amministrazione delle Finanze dello Stato* v. *Denkavit Italiano*, Case 61/79, [1980] ECR 1205.

[6] *Germany* v. *Commission*, Case 84/82, [1984] ECR 1451; see per Advocate General Slynn, p. 1501.

[7] In *Dutch Natural Gas*, OJ 1982, L 37/29, OJ 1985, L 97/49, the Commission considered that an organization 50 per cent owned by the State and 50 per cent owned by private industry constituted the State for Article 92 purposes.

[8] See e.g. *Steinike und Weinlig* v. *Germany*, Case 78/76, [1977] ECR 595. Financial benefit which derives from the application of Community funds by Member States is not caught by Article 92: *Norddeutsches Vieh- und Fleischkontor* v. *BALM*, Cases 213–15/81, [1982] ECR 3583.

[9] See n. 5 above, para. 31.

resources or procure for them advantages intended to encourage the attainment of the economic and social objectives sought.'

It appears that for Article 92 to apply, the financial benefit accorded the recipient need only have been *brought about* by the State. It is not necessary that the benefit resulted in a debit to the governmental purse. The point is illustrated by the judgment of the Court in *Commission* v. *France*,[10] where a payment made by the Caisse Nationale de Crédit Agricole (a public body) out of the surplus proceeds of *private* funds was condemned as state aid because the payment was initiated by, and subject to the approval of, the State. Advocate General Verloren Van Themaat, in *Norddeutsches Vieh- und Fleischkontor* v. *BALM*,[11] considered Article 92 to be extendable even further:

'It is quite possible to argue that the independent grant by Member States of pecuniary advantages which are not paid for by the Member States is caught by Article 92. Advantages which come to mind here are, on the one hand, reduced rates which Member States might require private electricity companies or haulage contractors, for example, to grant (without reimbursement) to certain undertakings or in respect of certain products.'

The aid can take 'any form whatsoever'. Since, as has been explained, aid is defined by effect not form, it is somewhat difficult to lay down rules of form. Guidance as to the different types of measure which can constitute 'aid' thus derives from decisions of the Commission and rulings of the Court of Justice in respect of such decisions. An analysis of the cases, however, is of little assistance in distilling the essence of the meaning of aid. In one of the earliest cases,[12] the Commission issued a decision requiring the withdrawal of an Italian law granting textile undertakings a reduction in the rate of contributions payable in respect of family allowance from 15 per cent to 10 per cent; the concession was to last for three years. The Italian government appealed the decision to the Court of Justice, which rejected the appeal and upheld the decision. For the Court, in determining whether an aid existed, the point of departure was the competitive position existing within the Common Market prior to the grant of the alleged aid. Should the pre-existing competitive position be altered or modified in a manner resulting in the reduction of production costs, an aid may have been granted.[13] Clearly, were this test to be applied in undiluted form, then Article 92 would have an astonishingly wide ambit. For instance, if central government reduces corporation tax or national security charges then the competitive position of the domestic industry is favoured *vis-à-vis* their Community rivals. However, such a broad measure of economic policy

---

[10] *Commission* v. *France*, Case 290/83, [1985] ECR 439.
[11] Cases 213–15/81 [1982] ECR 3583, 3617.
[12] *Italy* v. *Commission*, Case 173/73, [1974] ECR 709.
[13] See Quigley, 'The Notion of a State Aid in the EEC' (1988), E.L.Rev. 242.

could not, common sense dictates, constitute an aid else Government could raise but never lower taxes. Accordingly, a distinction must be made between general and specific measures. In the textiles case (above), the distinguishing factor appears to have been that the concession was granted to a specific sector and was limited in temporal terms. The measure was not an instrument of general macroeconomic policy, but a focused fiscal advantage conferred upon a sector of industry to alleviate its burden of costs.[14]

The aid must distort or threaten to distort competition by favouring certain undertakings or the production of certain goods. It is not necessary in this chapter to discuss further the meaning of distortion of competition. Since this has been considered at some length in Chapter 16 on Article 85 it may be assumed that similar principles apply here. The important point deriving from these words concerns the implications to be drawn from 'favouring certain undertakings', which words underpin the distinction that must be drawn between general and specific measures. As has already been explained, general financial measures escape Article 92 whereas specific measures are caught. Thus, benefit accorded an individual company, or a discrete group of companies, or a sector of industry, is a specific measure; benefit conferred across the board by way, for instance, of a reduction in corporation tax, is a general measure. In this context it is critical to analyse not the breadth of the class of recipients of the aid but rather the breadth of the class of those denied it. Thus, aid to exporters is an aid, albeit that the measure may exhibit all the features of a general measure, because producers for the domestic market are excluded.[15]

The aid must affect trade between Member States. The requirement that the aid affect inter-State trade is, of course, found also in Articles 85 and 86 and there is no reason to believe that the two sets of provisions (competition and state aid) should receive different interpretations in this regard.

Aid that is Automatically Compatible with the Treaty: Article 92(2)

Article 92(2) describes categories of aid which, *ipso facto*, are compatible with the Common Market. Such automatically compatible aid is subject to Commission control since the Commission remains under the duty (see Article 93, discussed below) to keep under review 'all systems of

---

[14] See *Eighteenth Commission Competition Report* (1988), p. 144; 'It is not always to delimit state aids from general measures for certain forms of intervention given by way of tax expenditure or through the social security systems.'
[15] *Commission* v. *France*, Cases 6 and 11/69, [1969] ECR 523, 540, and also p. 552 per Advocate General Roemer.

aid' and, it follows, to ensure that aid alleged to fall within Article 92(2) does in fact do so. The first category of automatically compatible aid is aid to individual consumers of a non-discriminatory nature in so far as the origin of goods is concerned. 'Christmas butter' gifts or discounts to pensioners may be an example. Advocate General Reischl opined that the acquisition of wheat at the intervention price by the state and its subsequent resale at a discount, which had the effect of reducing bread prices, might be another example.[16] The second example concerns aid to ameliorate the consequences of natural disasters or exceptional circumstances. The third example, which was (ironically) always assumed to be an anachronism, concerns aid to compensate for the consequences of the post-war division of Germany. Whether aid to assist in reunification is to be counted as aid granted as a result of the division of Germany (the latter being the necessary precursor of the former) remains to be seen.

Aid that May be Compatible with the Common Market: Article 92(3)

Article 92(3) covers aid that *may* be compatible with the Common Market but requires formal Commission clearance to determine that status.

Article 92(2) itemizes four categories of aid for which power to permit exists. It is notable that three types of aid in these categories are subject to control by the Commission whereas, pursuant to Article 92(3)(d), the Council has a power of decision which may be exercised positively in favour of other categories of aid (upon a proposal from the Commission). Further, under Article 94, the Council may, upon a Commission proposal, make regulations for the application of Articles 92 and 93.

The three categories of aid subject to Commission permission may be summarized as: regional aid (Article 92(3)(a) and (c)); aid to promote projects of common European interest or to remedy a serious disturbance in the economy of a Member State (Article 92(3)(b)); and sectoral (and regional) aid which does not adversely affect trading conditions to an unacceptable degree (Article 92(3)(c)). It will be seen that there is some degree of overlap between Article 92(3)(a) and (c). In the *Philip Morris*[17] case, the Commission set out the criteria it employs in its decision whether or not to exercise its power to approve aid, which criteria were approved by the Court of Justice. In essence, the criteria are:

1. The aid must promote or further a project that is in the Community interest as a whole; *a fortiori*, aid which promotes national interest is unacceptable;
2. The aid must be necessary for the achievement of the result in 1;

[16] *Benedetti* v. *Munari*, Case 52/76, [1977] ECR 163, p. 190.
[17] *Philip Morris* v. *Commission*, Case 730/79, [1980] ECR 2671.

3. The modalities of the aid must be proportional to the importance of the sought-after result. By modalities is to be understood inter alia: the duration, intensity, and ambit of the aid, the anti-competitive risks associated with the aid.

The Court, in endorsing these criteria, stated that aid was only compatible with Article 92(3) if the beneficiaries could not have attained the objective in question in its absence, that is, there must be established an element of indispensability.

It should be said that, whilst it is possible to bring proceedings under Article 173 EEC to obtain judicial review of Commission decisions under Article 92(3), the prospects for a successful challenge are limited. As with cases under Articles 85 and 86, the Court will rarely overturn substantive decisions of the Commission arising out of the exercise of its discretion. In this respect the Court is slow to contradict decisions of the Commission which entail detailed analysis of facts and economic evidence unless certain circumstances can be shown. In outline these are:

1. Where the Commission has drawn incorrect findings of fact from the evidence before the Commission;
2. Where the Commission is guilty of an abuse of power;
3. Where the Commission is guilty of a manifest error of law, which includes a case where it is clear that the Commission has exercised its discretion in a manner which is outside the purpose of the Treaty.[18]

In *Deufil*, Advocate General Darmon reiterated that the Commission enjoyed a relatively wide margin of discretion in cases under Article 92(3): 'In the application of each of the derogations laid down in Article 92(3), the Commission must be entitled to exercise a particularly wide discretion.'[19]

In the context of a text such as the present there is scope for only a limited review of Commission policy under Article 92(3). Any discussion of policy must be prefaced with the caveat that policy changes according to the prevailing political and economic climate. For instance, in 1987 the Commission affirmed the application of the state-aid rules in the framework of the single market:

'The progressive moves towards the creation of a single unified internal market by 1992 will place new emphasis and importance upon the application of the State aid rules. The maximization of the benefits of the single market will depend upon firms acting on the premise of the existence of this market, allowing efficient resource allocation, and upon creating the confidence that their enterprise will not be affected by competition distorting government

---

[18] *Commission* v. *Germany*, Case 84/82, [1984] ECR 1451, 1499, 1500 per Advocate General Slynn.
[19] See n. 1 above, 1 CMLR 553, 560; see also p. 567, para. 18 per the Court.

intervention in favour of their competitors. The creation of the single market and the need for convergence and cohesion between and within the economies of the Community, require that aid measures aimed at overcoming regional disequilibrium be examined favourably.'[20]

More recently, the Commissioner responsible for competition policy and state aid has singled out a number of areas for especial scrutiny and challenge from a policy perspective: export aid to third countries; general investment aid whereby Member States intervene in sectors of the economy; nationalized industries whereby states protect such undertakings at the expense of private industry; and the protection of 'national champions'.[21]

We now turn to the specific areas covered by Article 92(3).

First, aid to areas of economic depression (Article 92(3)(a)). In *Philip Morris*, the Court, in construing the meaning of 'aid to promote economic development of areas where the standard of living is abnormally low or where there is serious under-employment', stated that standards of living and employment were to be measured not against national norms but against a Community-wide standard.[22] Examples of aid decided under this heading are to be found in every Commission Competition Report. For example, in the *Eighteenth Report* (1988) are to be found notes of Commission decisions permitting regional aid: in the depressed Belgian province of Limbourg; granted under a Greek law concerning investment in the Mediterranean; in the Spanish province of Ternel to assist coalfields.[23] Regional aid under Article 93(2)(a) is also often viewed as part and parcel of a wider regional-aid policy under the rubric of aid to 'certain economic areas' under Article 92(3)(c), hence the overlap between the two provisions referred to earlier.

In the light of political and legal developments, and in particular the entering into force of the Single European Act and the enlargement of the Community to embrace the Iberian peninsula, the Commission decided in 1987 to adopt a systematic approach to the evaluation of aid in less-developed regions, and in August 1988 published a Communication[24] describing in detail the method for the application of Article 92(3)(a) and (c) to regional aid. Regions covered by Article 92(3)(a) are according to the notice, those suffering from abnormally low living standards or serious underemployment where the per capita gross domestic product does not exceed 75 per cent of the Community average

---

[20] *Seventeenth Commission Competition Report* (1987), p. 137, para. 169.
[21] Speech by Sir Leon Brittan, 'A bonfire of subsidies', Mar. 1989.
[22] See n. 17 above.
[23] See *Eighteenth Commission Competition Report* (1988), pp. 187–96, *passim*.
[24] OJ, C 212 (12 Aug. 1988). See *Eighteenth Commission Competition Report* (1988), para. 167.

in purchasing-power parities. These regions lie mainly on the southern and western periphery of the Community.[25]

Regions falling under Article 92(3)(c) are those with more general development problems in relation to the national as well as the Community situation. Frequently, they suffer from the decline of traditional industries and are not uncommonly located in the more central and more prosperous parts of the Community. In this context, the Commission measures underdevelopment by two alternative primary indicators which enable regional problems to be placed in the context of the Community. The two alternative indicators—income (as measured by gross domestic product or gross value added) and structural unemployment—are assessed in a national context. The better the position of the Member State in which the region is located, relative to the Community as a whole, the wider must be the disparity between the region and the State in order to justify the aid. Put in very crude terms, regions in wealthy Member States must in relative terms be worse off than regions in poorer Member States before regional aid will be permitted under this provision. In cases under Article 92(3)(c) the aid must be linked to initial (start-up or seed) investment and/or job creation.

Secondly, aid to promote the execution of an important project of common European interest (Article 92(3)(b)). In the past the Commission has permitted aid to encourage energy-saving projects and environmental schemes. Aid to remedy a serious disturbance in a Member State will not be condoned if it results in investment being located in a Member State if, but for the aid, it would have been located in another Member State with an even less favourable situation.[26]

Thirdly, sectoral and regional aid (Article 92(3)(c)). Aid may be granted to facilitate the development of 'certain economic activities' (sectoral aid) or to 'certain economic areas' (regional aid). The latter aid is clearly related to aid under Article 93(2)(a), and discussion of regional aid is therefore to be found above. With regard to sectoral aid, the current Commission's policy was laid down in a long-standing communication to the Council of May 1978. This laid down policy guidelines in respect of aid for investment, or for crisis or rescue measures, both being typical situations for which aid is granted. In that Communication the Commission stressed that sectoral aid was to be considered as the exception, not the rule, and was only justified where: (i) there was real need; (ii) the aid would lead to the restoration of long-term viability; (iii) the aid would make a positive contribution to the economic, social, and regional policies of the Community; (iv) the aid was intended to bring

---

[25] These regions account for approximately 20 per cent of the Community population; see *Seventeenth Commission Competition Report* (1987), para. 236.
[26] See e.g. *Philip Morris* (n. 17 above), pp. 2691, 2672.

about adjustments to changing economic structures and *not* to preserving industrial sectors unchanged despite economic developments; and (v) the aid would be proportional to the object sought to be achieved. In 1987 the Commission reaffirmed the above policies and added:

'As far as possible aids should be degressive, if granted over time, and should not deviate more than absolutely necessary from the basic principle of undistorted competition in the Community. The granting of State aids by one Member State must not lead to the transfer of industrial difficulties and unemployment to other Member States nor should inefficient companies be artificially kept in existence through State aids to the detriment of their efficient competitors in other Member States. This aspect must be re-emphasised in the perspectives of 1992 as undertakings will only adjust their activities, optimise their resource allocation and bring to the Community the benefits of the single market if they can be reasonably certain of gaining the just benefits from such action and do not face unfair competition from rivals receiving state aid.'[27]

It will be seen that sectoral aid is potentially the most diverse category of aid, being applicable to all sectors of industry without limitation and, accordingly, the category of aid requiring the strictest control. Over the years the Commission has scrutinized aid given to a wide variety of industrial sectors. Particular sectors which have given rise to complex issues of compatibility have included: synthetic fibres; steel; shipbuilding; automobiles.

The Procedure for Governing State Aid under the Treaty

Responsibility for the supervision of state aid lies with the Commission in collaboration with Member States, pursuant to Article 93 of the Treaty. That article differentiates two types of aid—existing and new aid.

Existing aid embraces aid in operation when the Treaty came into being or when new Member States acceded to the Treaty of Rome. More importantly, it also includes aid granted by Member States which is legally implemented in accordance with the Treaty, that is, with the consent of the Commission, the due procedures having been observed. New aid, according to Article 93(3), covers aid which is proposed to be granted and existing aid which is to be altered. It is convenient to deal with the procedure for existing and new aid separately.

---

[27] *Seventeenth Commission Competition Report* (1987), para. 206. In the *Eighteenth Commission Competition Report* (1988), para. 164, the Commission made the additional objection that, 'over-reliance on state aid to solve problems of industrial adjustment *vis-à-vis* third country producers undermines the competitiveness of EC car manufacturing by hindering the economically healthy influence of market forces'.

[28] See Article 190 Treaty of Rome, *Commission* v. *Belgium*, Case 52/84, [1986] ECR 89, 103, para. 9.

EXISTING AID AND THE ARTICLE 93(2) PROCEDURE

Under Article 93(1) the Commission, in co-operation with Member States, is required to keep under constant review all systems of aid existing in Member States. The Commission must propose to Member States any appropriate measures required by the progressive development or functioning of the common market. The proposal issued by the Commission is not binding on the Member State, yet retains legal relevance as a result of its being a mandatory step in the process pursuant to which the Commission may initiate the contentious procedure laid down in Article 93(2). This procedure is concerned with aid the Commission considers as prima-facie incompatible with the Community. The procedure operates as follows:

1. The Commission gives notice to the parties concerned (i.e. Member State and recipient) to submit their comments.
2. The Commission, in the light of comments received, makes a finding of incompatibility (or, if appropriate, compatibility), or that the aid is being misused.
3. The Commission takes a formal decision requiring the Member State to abolish the aid or alter the aid within a set period of time.
4. If the Member State fails to comply within the prescribed time, the Commission or any other 'interested' State may refer the matter directly to the European Court of Justice.

Article 93(2) also provides a back-door route whereby Member States may undertake some 'special pleading'. A Member State may apply to the Council of Ministers for a decision permitting aid, on the ground of its being justified by 'exceptional circumstances', notwithstanding its incompatibility with Article 92. Where the Commission has already initiated the contentious procedure, the simple fact of application operates to suspend the Commission proceedings, pending such time as the Council 'has made its attitude known'. If the Council fails to so act within three months, the Commission may proceed to give its decision.

A negative decision of the Commission must be properly reasoned,[28] has prospective effect only,[29] and must indicate to the Member State concerned the aspects of the aid which are regarded as incompatible with the Treaty and therefore subject to abolition or alteration.[30] Failure by the addressee Member State to comply within the time-period prescribed in the decision empowers the Commission to commence proceedings before the Court of Justice under either Article 169 or Article 93(2) of the Treaty for a declaration that the Member State has failed in its legal duty under the Treaty. The advantage for the

---

[29] See per Advocate General Warner in *Pigs and Bacon Commission* v. *McCarren*, Case 177/78, [1979] ECR 2161, 2206.

[30] *Commission* v. *Germany*, Case 70/72, [1973] ECR 813, 831; and *Commission* v. *Belgium* (n. 28 above).

Commission in proceeding under Article 93(2) lies in the absence of any requirement for further dialogue with the defaulting Member State (compare this procedure with that under Article 169). Conversely, Member States have two months to commence judicial review proceedings under Article 173. If they fail to take this option they are denied the right to challenge the legality of the Commission decision when the latter takes them to Court under Article 93(2) (or Article 169).

A graphic example of how the procedure operates is *Commission* v. *Belgium*.[31] The case concerned the investment of capital, in the form of a decision to purchase shares in a ceramics company which for some years had been sustaining heavy losses. The investment was intended to enable the beneficiary company to reconstitute its capital and reserves, and to enable it to continue trading while a reconstruction plan for the sector as a whole was being formulated. The Belgian government did not notify the aid to the Commission which, upon learning of the aid, initiated the aid-review procedure under Article 93(2), which resulted in a negative decision dated 16 February 1983, stating that the aid was incompatible with the Treaty and must be withdrawn. The decision further required the Member State to inform the Commission within three months of the measures taken to comply with the decision. The Belgian government did not commence proceedings under Article 173 within the prescribed two-month limitation period. On 3 June 1983 the Member State, by letter to the Commission, challenged the decision as incorrect in law and substance. Further correspondence followed to no ultimate conclusive end and the Commission, without further notice to the Member State, commenced proceedings before the Court under Article 93(2). In their defence the Belgian government argued: first, that despite repeated requests, the Commission failed in its duty under Article 93(2) to supply the necessary particulars enabling them to establish what was entailed by their obligation to abolish the alleged aid, and that they could not, therefore, be criticized for failing to discharge that obligation; secondly, that stated Commission policy[32] on the holding by states in the capital of certain undertakings could only be appraised *ex post facto*, and thereby the Commission itself prevented the withdrawal of capital holdings 'because to demand that the holdings should be redeemed would seriously harm the rights of innocent third parties whenever the profits of an undertaking were insufficient to permit such redemption'.[33] The Member State pointed out in particular that redemption of the shareholding would entail the winding-up of the recipient company. In response to these submissions the Court, in a judgment of considerable rigour, held: first, that upon the expiry of the

---

[31] Ibid.

[32] Contained in the *Second* (1972) and *Seventh* (1977) Commission Competition Reports.

[33] Judgment, *Commission* v. *Belgium* (see n. 28 above), para. 11.

two-month limitation period in Article 173 the validity of a decision may not be called in question in proceedings under Article 93(2);[34] secondly, in such circumstances the sole remaining defence is to plead the 'absolute impossibility' of proper implementation of the decision;[35] thirdly, that the defence was inapplicable where the attainment of the requirement set out in the Commission decision (i.e. withdrawal of the aid) could be achieved through the State commencing proceedings in national law *qua* shareholder or creditor to wind up the recipient, the impecuniosity of the recipient being no defence;[36] fourthly, in a case where a Member State encounters unforeseen or unforeseeable difficulties or perceives consequences overlooked by the Commission, that State should submit these problems to the Commission together with proposals and, pursuant to the duty of genuine co-operation inherent in Article 5 of the Treaty, the two parties should work together in good faith with a view to overcoming the problem.[37]

New Aid under Article 93(3)

Under this provision Member States must inform the Commission of plans to grant new aid or alter existing aid. The notification must be timed so as to give the Commission 'sufficient time' to enable it to submit its comments to the State concerned. If the Commission considers the aid to be incompatible with the Treaty, then it must initiate the Article 93(2) procedure. The Member State may not put its proposed measure into effect until this procedure has resulted in a final decision.

The obligation to notify aid is absolute and operates regardless of whether the Member State considers that the measure may fall outside Article 92(1) or is compatible with either Article 92(2) or Article 92(3). The payment of aid in breach of this procedure is illegal and may be the subject of a negative Commission decision notwithstanding that the aid *per se* might be compatible with the Treaty.[38]

In *Germany* v. *Commission*[39] the Court took the opportunity to review the procedure for the appraisal of aid schemes, and in so doing laid down a number of important procedural rules. The case concerned a Belgian government plan for restructuring the Belgian textile and clothing industry, which was notified to the Commission by letters dated 22 July and 11 August 1980. The Commission, by a letter dated 15 September 1980 but which was received at the beginning of 1981,

---

[34] Judgment, *Commission* v. *Belgium*, para. 13. See also *Commission* v. *France*, Case 52/83, [1983] ECR 3707.

[35] Ibid., para. 14. [36] Ibid. [37] Ibid., para. 16.

[38] See n. 30 above; see also Commission Communication of 24 Nov. 1983 OJ, C318/3; and Commission policy statement of 30 Mar. 1987 OJ 1987, C 82/2.

[39] See n. 6 above.

requested further data from the Belgian government. Following substantial correspondence between the State and the Commission, the former proposed a modified plan which was accepted by the Commission on a twelve-month basis. It will be appreciated that the Commission had granted the permission following a preliminary review, and had *not* initiated the Article 93(2) procedure. The German government objected to the authorization on the ground that the sole effect of the Belgian plan would be to unload the problems of the Belgian industry on to the corresponding industry in Germany and other Member States. Accordingly, Germany sought judicial review under Article 173 of the Commission decision and, in the alternative, a declaration under Article 175 that by failing to initiate the main review procedure under Article 93(2) and by not adopting a negative decision, the Commission had infringed the state-aid rules. In giving judgment, the Court summarized previous case-law[40] and set out a series of procedural rules for the governance of Article 93(3). In summary these are as follows.

1. The preliminary stage of the procedure for reviewing aid under Article 93(3) is intended merely to enable the Commission to form a prima-facie opinion on the partial or complete conformity of an aid scheme with the Treaty. Given that Member States may not (pursuant to Article 93(3), last sentence) implement an aid scheme pending a Commission decision, it behoves the Commission to act with due expedition in undertaking this prima-facie assessment.[41]
2. The Commission therefore has two months in which to undertake this assessment, at the expiry of which the Member State may implement the aid after having given the Commission prior notice thereof.[42]
3. If at the end of the prima-facie investigation, the Commission's view of the aid is positive, it must communicate that decision to the Member State. At this point the aid becomes an 'existing' aid and hence subject to the supervision rules of Article 93(1).[43]
4. If the Commission's view is negative it must immediately initiate the full review procedure under Article 93(2), which involves the duty to give the parties concerned notice to submit their comments.[44]
5. Given that the preliminary procedure (unlike the Article 93(2) procedure) does *not* entail giving notice to interested parties to submit their views, and that in undertaking its appraisal the

---

[40] See *Lorenz* v. *Germany*, Case 120/73, [1973] ECR 1471; *Markmann* v. *Germany*, Case 121/73, [1973] ECR 1495; *Nordsee* v. *Germany*, Case 122/73, [1973] ECR 1511 *Lohrey* v. *Germany*, Case 141/73, [1973] ECR 1527—all judgments of 11 Dec. 1973.

[41] *Germany* v. *Commission* (n. 6 above), para. 11.

[42] Ibid., para. 11. [43] Ibid., para. 12. [44] Ibid., para. 12.

Commission does not, therefore, have such extensive data available to it as it would under the Article 93(2) procedure, the Commission may take a positive decision in favour of a notified aid scheme *only* 'if it is convinced after the preliminary examination that the plan is compatible with the Treaty'.[45]

6. If the Commission is not convinced as per (e) above, then it must initiate the Article 93(2) procedure in order to obtain all the requisite opinions and data.[46]

Applying these rules to the facts, the Court held that the Commission had exceeded the two-month preliminary review period; had permitted the aid to proceed for twelve months despite having expressed reservations about the aid; and had failed to initiate the Article 93(2) procedure. Therefore the Commission had infringed an essential procedural requirement, and judicial review under Article 173 was granted to the plaintiff Member State. The decision was declared void.

The Direct Effect of Article 93(3), Last Sentence: The Position of the Recipient of Aid and the Role of Competitor

DIRECT EFFECT

The last sentence of Article 93(3) is directly effective.[47] It provides that: 'The Member State concerned shall not put its proposed measures into effect until this procedure has resulted in a final decision.' The procedure referred to is that provided for under Article 93(2). In *R.* v. *Atty-Gen. ex p. ICI plc*,[48] Lord Justice Oliver (as he then was) held with regard to the direct effect of Article 92:

'It is not in dispute that, as a result of section 2 of the European Communities Act 1972, directly effective provisions confer upon an individual affected a cause of action in the English Court . . . and the Court has been referred to a number of cases in the European Court which it is unnecessary to cite in any detail here and from which the following propositions emerge, viz.:

(1) In the case of a directly effective provision of the Treaty, enforcement is properly a matter for the national court.

(2) The national court must make available for the enforcement of the directly effective provision the same remedies as are available for the enforcement of an equivalent right in domestic law.

(3) In applying these remedies, the national court may apply the same procedural or substantive limitations (e.g. as to limitation, evidence and

---

[45] *Germany* v. *Commission*, para. 13.
[46] Ibid., para. 13.
[47] See e.g. *Costa* v. *ENEL*, Case 6/64, [1964] ECR 585.
[48] [1987] 1 CMLR 72 (CA); see also [1985] 1 CMLR 588 per Woolf J (as he then was).

limits on recoverable damage) as are applicable in a domestic case, but subject to one important qualification, namely,
(4) Such procedural or substantive limitations must not be such as to render the enforcement of the right practically impossible.'[49]

In most cases it will be rivals of the recipient of the aid who will seek to invoke Article 93(3) in an attempt to deny the latter a competitive advantage. However, the action will be against the grantor Member State as defendant. To date at least, the Court of Justice has not imposed a positive duty upon recipients of aid not to receive the aid or, alternatively, to hold it in trust, pending a final decision under the Article 93(2) procedure.

In the United Kingdom most actions against the state will be commenced by way of judicial review for a declaration that the measure in question constitutes an aid. However, it appears also to be the case that actions premissed upon the direct effect of a Community law provision may be proceeded with in an action commenced by way of writ.[50]

It is to be noted that the rights of the plaintiff are unaffected by the reasonableness, or otherwise, of the aid in question. Article 93(3), last sentence, imposes an unequivocal prohibition on the Member State's introducing measures of aid prior to expiry of the decision-making process. Thus, the grantor of a perfectly reasonable aid can be made a defendant in national proceedings in the case of premature implementation of an aid that the Commission would have approved, had the state delayed implementation until the Commission decision had been issued.

Private Party as Complainant

Private parties can complain to the Commission of aid granted to their competitors. In *COFAZ* v. *Commission*,[51] the Court held that, as complainants to the Commission during the Article 93(2) procedure, a producer's trade association which had objected to the Commission's closing its file on a matter had *locus standi* under Article 173 of the Treaty to challenge the Commission decision before the Court. The association was directly and individually concerned by the Commission decision and the Commission could not challenge admissibility upon the basis that the members of the association were not the only persons affected by the decision in question. In arriving at this result the Court referred to cases involving the competition and dumping provisions of Community

[49] Ibid., p. 102.
[50] See *An Bord Bainne* v. *Milk Marketing Board*, [1984] 2 CMLR 589 (CA); *CATO* v. *MAFF*, [1989] 3 CMLR 513 (CA).
[51] Case 169/84, [1986] ECR 391.

law.[52] In particular, the Court stated that a complainant was individually concerned by a Commission decision where it had acted as the original complainant whose complaint led to the initiation of proceedings, where it had been heard during the procedure and where the conduct of the procedure was largely determined by its observations.[53] In the *COFAZ* case the Court also held that the Commission's decision to terminate the procedure was of direct concern to the applicants since it necessarily left intact the effects of the aid system in question.[54]

Thus, the *COFAZ* ruling established the role of complainant as an important and central one. The formal complaint is hence an alternative or dual remedy for the aggrieved competitor to follow. The student of Article 173 judicial review will not require reminding of the critical importance of the two-month limitation period, which runs from notification of the decision. In *Irish Cement* v. *Commission*,[55] the complainant received a polite letter from the Commission which, closer examination would have revealed, rejected the complaint. Delay in commencing the procedure beyond the limitation period subsequently proved fatal to the applicant in judicial review proceedings before the Court.

THE POSITION OF THE RECIPIENT OF AID

The recipient of an aid that has been properly notified to the Commission and in respect of which the proper procedures have been completed is safe from any legal threat. Where the grantor Member State has failed in its duty under Article 93(3) to delay implementing the aid pending the Commission decision, the position of the recipient is precarious. Aid may become illegal in a number of ways:

1. Aid may be granted without notification under Article 93(3);
2. Aid may be notified, but implemented prior to the two-month stand-still time limit (see above);
3. Aid may be notified, but not approved by the Commission within two months; the Article 93(2) contentious procedure is initiated yet, despite this, the Member State implements the aid scheme.

The Court has long held that the Commission is empowered to require the repayment (to the grantor state) of aid illegally granted, such recovery to be in accordance with applicable national law.[56] In *Commission* v. *Belgium*,[57] the Court held further that the financial impecuniosity of the recipient does not absolve the grantor state from its

---

[52] Case 169/84, [1986] ECR 391, paras. 23, 24, pp. 414, 415.
[53] Ibid., para. 24.
[54] Ibid., para. 30, p. 416.
[55] Cases 166/86 and 220/86, judgment of 15 Dec. 1988.
[56] *Commission* v. *Germany* (n. 30 above).
[57] See n. 28 above.

duty to obtain repayment of the aid. If necessary, it should take steps, in its capacity as creditor or shareholder, to have the recipient wound up. In cases where repayment has been ordered, the *only* defence left to a Member State is to plead that it was *absolutely impossible* for it to implement the decision properly.

Whilst the Court has stated that actions for recovery are subject to the applicable national law, it has also foreseen, and pre-empted, the possibility that national law could operate to bar recovery. In *Commission* v. *Germany*[58] the Court stated:

'In so far as the procedure laid down by national law is applicable to the recovery of an illegal aid, the relevant provisions of national law must be applied in such a way that the recovery required by Community law is not rendered practically impossible and the interests of the Community are taken fully into consideration in the application of a provision which, like that relied upon by the German Government, requires the various interests involved to be weighed up before a defective administrative measure is withdrawn . . .'[59]

In that case the Commission had issued a repayment decision to the Federal Republic of Germany in respect of aid granted to Alcan. In proceedings commenced by the Commission against Germany for failing to comply with the decision, Germany argued that the aid could not be recovered from the recipient without involving the State in a breach of the administrative-law principle of protection of legitimate expectations. It contended therefore that the Commission decision 'should be interpreted merely as a reference to the principle that unlawful aid must be recovered, subject to the principles of domestic law, that being the law applicable to the recovery of the aid'.[60] The judicial response quoted above was, in these circumstances, hardly surprising: any other would have entailed the tail (national law) wagging the dog (Community law). It is an interesting, and open, question whether the Court was, in the dictum above, leaving open the possibility that in exceptional circumstances national law could preclude recovery. Indeed, the Court has, for instance, identified one scenario where recovery may be impossible, that is, where recovery is 'absolutely impossible'. In *Commission* v. *Belgium* it was argued that recovery was impossible where the aid had been dissipated by the recipient. The Court rejected this argument, but at least accepted the possibility of a defence based on impossibility in principle.

In English law a series of fascinating and unresolved issues arise. For instance, if the grant is illegal as a result of a breach of the Treaty, then courts of equity will not assist the wrongdoer (the recipient) to obtain

---

[58] Case 94/87, judgment of 2 Feb. 1989.
[59] Ibid., para. 12.
[60] Ibid., para. 6.

restitution of monies illegally paid. The plaintiff (that is, the state) seeking recovery may be denied relief on the ground that *ex turpi causa non erìtur actio.*[61] In reality, peculiarities of English law should not, following *Commission* v. *Germany*, protect the recipient. With specific regard to the defence of legitimate expectations (if such exists in English administrative law), the Commission nowadays publishes a summary of aid proceedings in the Official Journal and expressly warns all concerned of the legal possibility of repayment decisions. Publication to the world at large in this manner is intended to thwart any 'expectation' and, *a fortiori*, any defence of legitimate expectations. In the United Kingdom it is normal practice for grantor government departments, when granting aid, to condition the money or assistance upon Commission approval.

The recipient of aid who suffers severe financial damage as a result of a repayment decision may be able to obtain compensation in damages. In *Garden Cottage Food* v. *Milk Marketing Board*,[62] the House of Lords held that breaches of Articles 85 and 86 were actionable upon the basis of breach of statutory duty. In *Bourgoin* v. *MAFF*,[63] the Court of Appeal held that Article 30 was actionable upon the basis of misfeasance in public office if the plaintiff sought damages in an action commenced by way of writ, though the ordinary remedies available upon judicial review were also available. Can the hapless recipient of aid sue the government for damages in its capacity as the victim of a tort? First, although Articles 92 and 93 are found in the title of the Treaty concerning competition, the action is one against the state and hence may be closer in nature to *Bourgoin* than *Garden Cottage Foods*. If that is so, then the recipient must prove misfeasance as a precondition for obtaining damages and, as will be appreciated, the burden upon the plaintiff is therefore an onerous one. Secondly, what is the plaintiff's loss? Presumably, the recipient of aid cannot claim as damages the same sum as he repaid. If this were available, it might be argued that the plaintiff was receiving aid through the back door, though, to date, the Court has not gone to this length.

Though, in *Asteris* v. *Greece and Commission*,[64] fifteen Greek companies sued the Greek government in the domestic courts for damages in respect of aid which had not been paid to Greek tomato-concentrate producers as a result of a technical error contained in Community legislation (which error had been confirmed by the Court in earlier proceedings). In the national court the producers claimed the difference between the aid actually received and that to which they would have

---

[61] See Goff and Jones, *Law of Restitution* (1986), Chap. 21.
[62] [1984] AC 130 (HL).
[63] [1985] 3 All ER 585 (CA).
[64] Joined cases 106–120/87, judgment of 27 Sept. 1988.

been entitled but for the illegality established by the Court's earlier ruling. One of the questions referred under Article 177 asked whether any damages the Greek state might be ordered to pay in compensation should be regarded as 'aid' within the meaning of Articles 92 and 93. The Court replied:

. . . state aid, that is to say measures of the public authorities favouring certain undertakings or certain products, is fundamentally different in its legal nature from damages which the competent national authorities may be ordered to pay to individuals in compensation for the damage they have caused to those individuals.

. . . damages which the national authorities may be ordered to pay to individuals in compensation for damage they have caused to those individuals do not constitute aid within the meaning of Articles 92 and 93 of the EEC Treaty.[65]

Conversely, if the recipient of aid has suffered loss and damage over and above repayment, this incremental amount should be claimable. For example, upon the expectation that the aid was his, the recipient might have commissioned construction work which had to be cancelled resulting in the payment of penalties to the contractor. Thirdly, the issue of causation must not be overlooked. The plaintiff's damage must flow from the failure to notify (not the repayment order), since it is that which constitutes the breach of Article 93(3) though it might be said that the failure to notify and the repayment order were inextricably connected so that there was sufficient causation between the two.

[65] Ibid., paras. 23, 24.

Index

Index